Dialogical Self Theory

Dialogical Self Theory provides a comprehensive social-scientific theory
that incorporates the deep implications of the process of globalization, and its impact on individual development. Hubert Hermans and
Agnieszka Hermans-Konopka present a new and compelling view of
the historical changes in perceptions of social realities, and how these
changes affected motivation, emotion, leadership, and conflict resolution. They detail the improvement of dialogical relationships both
within the self and between individuals, groups, and cultures, providing evidence from everyday life. The book addresses a variety of
problem areas that are analysed in new and unexpected ways: the pros
and cons of traditional, modern, and post-modern models of self, the
role of emotions, power and dominance, motivation, leadership, and
conflict resolution. This book will be of interest to scholars in a wide
range of fields including psychology and sociology.

HUBERT HERMANS is Emeritus Professor at the Radboud University of Nijmegen. His previous publications include *The Dialogical
Self: Meaning in Movement* (1993), *Self-Narratives: The Construction of
Meaning in Psychotherapy* (1995) and he was the co-editor of *The Dialogical Self in Psychotherapy* (2004).

AGNIESZKA HERMANS-KONOPKA is a scientist and practitioner in an independent practice near Nijmegen. Along with Hubert Hermans, she
coaches individual clients and provides workshops and training on
emotional coaching.

D1260769

Dialogical Self Theory

Positioning and Counter-Positioning in a Globalizing Society

Hubert J. M. Hermans and
Agnieszka Hermans-Konopka

CAMBRIDGE
UNIVERSITY PRESS

CAMBRIDGE UNIVERSITY PRESS
Cambridge, New York, Melbourne, Madrid, Cape Town,
Singapore, São Paulo, Delhi, Mexico City

Cambridge University Press
The Edinburgh Building, Cambridge CB2 8RU, UK

Published in the United States of America by Cambridge University Press, New York

www.cambridge.org
Information on this title: www.cambridge.org/9781107411746

First published 2010
First paperback edition 2012

A catalogue record for this publication is available from the British Library

Library of Congress Cataloguing in Publication Data
Hermans, H. J. M.
    Dialogical self theory : positioning and counter-positioning in a globalizing
    society / Hubert J.M. Hermans, Agnieszka Hermans-Konopka.
        p.   cm.
    Includes bibliographical references and index.
    ISBN 978-0-521-76526-8
    1. Self.   2. Identity (Psychology)   3. Globalization.
    I. Hermans-Konopka, Agnieszka, 1978-   II. Title.
    BF697.H438 2010
    302.5-dc22   2010000058

ISBN 978-0-521-76526-8 Hardback
ISBN 978-1-107-41174-6 Paperback

To our parents and grandparents
who meet each other in us

Education is a kind of continuing dialogue, and a dialogue
assumes different points of view

Robert M. Hutchins

Contents

Illustrations

Acknowledgments

We want to thank several people who supported us in preparing this book.

Sunil Bhatia inspected Chapter 1 and made various suggestions that clarified the cultural implications of the presented view. Frank Richardson read Chapter 2 and his comments helped us to gain more insight in the historical dimensions of self and identity. Marie-Cécile Bertau contributed to Chapter 4 and her detailed remarks led to a more thorough investigation of the linguistic elements in dialogical self theory. Jaan Valsiner has given us valuable advice during the whole project. We thank Elisabeth Thijssen for her editorial remarks and improvement of the language.

Introduction

In a world society that is increasingly interconnected and intensely involved in historical changes, dialogical relationships are required not only *between* individuals, groups and cultures, but also *within* the self of one and the same individual. This central message of the present book is based on the observation that many of the social processes, like dialogue and fights for dominance, that can be observed in society at large also take place within the self as a "society of mind." The self is not considered as an entity in itself, as pre-given, with society as a facilitating or impeding environment, but rather as emerging from social, historical, and societal processes that transcend any individual–society dichotomy or separation.

The central notion of this book, the dialogical self, weaves two concepts, self and dialogue, together in such a way that a more profound understanding of the interconnection of self and society becomes possible. Usually, the concept of self refers to something "internal," something that happens within the mind of the individual person, while "dialogue" is typically associated with something "external," processes that take place between people who are involved in communication. The composite concept "dialogical self" goes beyond this dichotomy by bringing the external to the internal and, in reverse, to infuse the internal into the external. We will describe the self along these lines, in terms of a diversity of relationship between different "self-positions" and consider society as populated, stimulated, and renewed by individuals in development. We believe that the self–society interconnection allows one to abandon a conception in which the self is regarded as essentialized and encapsulated in itself. Moreover, it avoids the limitations of a "self-less society" that lacks the opportunity to profit from the richness and creativity that the individual human mind has to offer to the innovation of existing social practices.

Dialogical self theory is not an isolated development in the social sciences. It emerged at the interface of two traditions: American Pragmatism and Russian Dialogism. As a self theory it finds a source of inspiration

1

in James's (1890) and Mead's (1934) classic formulations on the work-ings of the self. As a dialogical theory, it elaborates on the fertile insights in dialogical processes proposed by Bakhtin (1929/1973). Although some of the basic views of these authors have significantly contributed to the development of dialogical self theory, we want to go beyond these authors by developing a theory that receives challenging impulses from the explicit awareness that we are part of significant historical changes on a global scale.

Self as extended in space: globalization and localization

A central assumption of the presented theory is that the self is extended in space and time (see also James, 1890; Rosenberg, 1979; and Aron *et al.*, 2005). From a *spatial* perspective, the self is increasingly part of a process of (cultural) globalization that has the potential to extend the self to a larger degree than ever in the history of humankind. Individuals are no longer living within the stabilized traditions of a demarcated local culture. Rather, different cultures, including their different traditions, values, and practices, are meeting each other in the life of one and the same individual. On the interface of different cultures, a self emerges with a complexity that reflects the contradictions, oppositions, encoun-ters, and integrations that are part of the society at large and, at the same time, *answers* to these influences from its own agentic point of view.

Globalization is not to be considered as a "sea" that floods all areas of our planet with the same water. There is a powerful counter-force, local-ization, which can be seen as the other side of the same coin. Confronted with the process of globalization that transcends the borders of cities, regions, countries, and continents, people no longer experience their own culture as purely self-evident and "natural." Instead, they become explicitly aware of its specific values, the particularity of its history, and experience it as the "soil" in which they feel rooted and at home. They are willing to defend this home and even use violence in order to protect it. In this sense, globalization and localization are not mutually exclu-sive but complement each other. Moreover, when involved in the pro-cess of globalization, people get in touch, via international contacts and cooperation, travel and trans-locality, tourism, and mass media, with localities at the other end of the world. They are able to open and enrich their selves as part of these encounters or are involved in attempts to close themselves off from any intruding environment. In any case, glo-balization evokes and even includes localization as its counter-force. In order to articulate the deep interconnectedness of the global and the local, Robertson (1995) proposed the composite term "glocalization" to emphasize that the global manifests itself in local forms. As we will argue, the processes of globalization and localization are reflected in the mini-society of the self in terms of global and local positions that can lead to identity confusion or lift the self up to a higher level of integration (for discussion, see Arnett, 2002 and Chapters 1 and 4 below).

In the context of the processes of globalization and localization, special attention is devoted to the experience of uncertainty. We will argue that this experience can be a gift as it opens a broad range of unexpected possibilities, but, particularly at high levels of intensity, it also leads to anxiety and insecurity. Given the central role of the experience of "uncertainty" in the present book and the different connotations with which the concept is often associated, a more detailed description is required. We see the experience of uncertainty as composed of four aspects: (i) *complexity*, referring to a great number of parts (of self and society) that have a variety of interconnections; (ii) *ambiguity*, referring to a suspension of clarity, as the meaning of one part is determined by the flux and variation of the other parts; (iii) *deficit knowledge*, referring to the absence of a super-ordinate knowledge structure that is able to resolve the contradictions between the parts; and (iv) *unpredictability*, implying a lack of control of future developments. We assume that the experience of uncertainty reflects a global situation of multi-voicedness (complexity) that does not allow a fixation of meaning (ambiguity), that has no super-ordinate voice for resolving contradictions and conflicting information (deficit knowledge), and that is to a large extent unpredictable.

The question is how the self copes with increasing levels of uncertainty in a globalizing situation. We describe five reactions: (i) uncertainty can be reduced by diminishing the number and heterogeneity of positions or voices in the self (e.g., retreating from the cacophony of contemporary life); (ii) it can be reduced by giving the lead to one powerful or important position or voice that is allowed to dominate the self as a whole (e.g., adhering to a political or spiritual leader); (iii) it can be minimized by sharpening the boundaries between oneself and the other, considering the other as different, strange, or even as "abject" (e.g., xenophobia or supporting extreme right-wing political parties); (iv) in a paradoxical way, uncertainty can be reduced by increasing instead of diminishing the number of positions or voices in the self, particularly when new positions are expected to offer rewards that earlier positions were not able to provide (e.g., searching for new and additional jobs, tasks, and challenges resulting in a cacophonous self); and (v) a dialogical reaction that copes with uncertainty by going into and through this uncertainty rather than avoiding it, in such a way that initial positions are influenced or changed, marginally or essentially, by the encounter itself (e.g., meeting with another person, with a group, or with oneself in order to learn, develop, and create). Whereas the latter reaction aims at post-dialogical certainty, the former ones take refuge in pre-dialogical forms of certainty. Along these lines, we argue that uncertainty is not just a positive or negative feeling state, but rather an experiential feature of a self in action.

Self as extended in time: three models of the self in collective history

The self is not only extended in space but also in time. The self is seen as emerging not only from processes of globalization and localization but also from personal (Chapter 4) and collective history (Chapter 2). Spatial and temporal changes in society are reflected in the self as collective voices that are not simply outside the individual self but rather are constituting it. Three models of self and identity, associated with different historical phases, will be distinguished: traditional, modern, and post-modern. The *traditional self* is characterized by the following: a distinction between a lower and imperfect existence on earth and a higher and perfect existence in the after-world; the body and senses as a hindrance to spiritual life; the existence of a moral telos; social hierarchy; authority; dogmatic truths; and connection with the natural environment. The *modern self* is portrayed in terms of autonomy; individualism; the development of reason; the pretension to universal truth; and strict and sharp boundaries between an internally united self and an external other. Moreover, it is expressed in an attitude of control of the external environment, a separation of fact and value, science and faith, politics and religion, and theory from practice. The *post-modern self* is portrayed in terms of a profound scepticism of the universalistic pretensions of master-narratives with their emphasis on totality and unity. In opposition to the modern self, it highlights the importance of difference, otherness, local knowledge, and fragmentation. It tends towards dissolution of symbolic hierarchies with their fixed judgments of taste and value and prefers a blurring of the distinction between high and popular culture. It reflects a far-reaching decentralization of the subject and tendencies towards a consumer culture, and argues for the dependence of "truth" on language communities with an important role of social power behind definitions of what is true and not true, right and not right.

We will show in Chapter 2 that an analysis and comparison of the three models of the self will provide the building blocks for the conception of a dialogical self. In order to arrive at a dialogical view on the self, we start from the assumption that the different historical phases associated

with the different models are not purely successive but rather simultaneous, in the sense that the previous phase *continues* when the next phase is
starting. The simultaneity of traditional and modern elements is exemplified by the coexistence of reason and the belief in destiny and fate, as
typical of the contemporary self. The simultaneity of the modern and
post-modern models of the self will be illustrated by the upsurge of ego-
documents and the "democratization of history." The simultaneity of
the different models results in a *spatialization* of the temporally ordered
models creating interfaces in which more complex selves and identities
with dialogical potentials emerge. Such a conception of the self recognizes not only the workings of decentralizing movements that lead to an
increasing multiplicity of the self (see the post-modern model) but also
of centralizing movements that permit an integration of the different
parts of the self (see the modern model). The dialogical self is described
as being involved in both decentralizing and centralizing movements.
Along these lines a dialogical self is portrayed that functions as multi-
voiced, yet being coherent and open to contradictions, as well as substantial (see Abbey and Falmagne, 2008; Falmagne, 2004).

In the awareness that any evaluation of historical developments is risky
as it may be colored by a contemporary perspective, we give an overview
(Chapter 2) of what we see as assets and shadow sides of the different models of the self. For example, as assets of the pre-modern self we
consider the connection with nature, the existence of community-based
meaning and moral awareness, whereas the strong hierarchical order, the
overly moralistic attitude, and restrictive religious dogmas are marked as
shadow sides. As assets of the modern self, we refer to the emergence of
personal autonomy and self-development that has liberated many people from the oppressive forces of the hierarchical structures and dogmatic truth pretensions of the traditional period. On the other hand, we
see several shadow sides in the modern model: it has led to a self that
is encapsulated within itself and is at risk of loneliness; it has resulted
in a loss of the basic contact with the external environment and with
nature; its typical dualism between self and other and its exaggerated
attitude of control and exploitation has eroded the intimate ties of traditional community life and has threatened the ecological balance of the
entire planet. As assets of the post-modern model we refer to several
developments: the liberation of the self from its imprisonment within
the walls of an intrinsically centralized and stable structure; the recognition of historical and social circumstances and the impact of history,
language, social networks, globalization, and technology; the broadening of the role-repertoire of women beyond traditional constraints and
the improvement of their participation in society; freedom and variation

beyond the masculine ideals and patriarchal social structures of modernism; more sensitivity and openness to the multiplicity and flexibility of the human mind, the perception of daily life from an aesthetic perspective, and more room for humor and play. The post-modern model, however, also has its shadow sides: the relativistic stance leading to an "anything goes" attitude; the lack of an epistemological basis for a meaningful dialogue between groups or cultures; pessimism and lack of hope; persistent doubts about progress; a one-sided focus on change, flux, and discontinuity resulting in a lack of rootedness or feeling at home; and the flattening of experience resulting from an increasing consumerism, as the "easiest road to happiness." On the basis of a comparison of the three models of the self – traditional, modern, and post-modern – we sketch a fourth model, a dialogical one, that is the result of a *learning process* that takes into account both the assets and shadow sides of the other models.

The extension of the self in space and time forms the basis of dialogical self theory. It would be a misunderstanding to conceive the self as an essence in itself and its extensions as secondary or "added" characteristics. In contrast, the dialogical self is formed and constituted by its extensions.

Dialogue refers not only to productive exchanges between the voices of individuals but also between collective voices of the groups, communities, and cultures to which the individual person belongs. Collective voices speak through the mouth of the individual person (e.g., "I as a psychologist," "I as a member of a political party," or "I as a representative of an ecological movement"). Dialogues not only take place between different people but, closely intertwined with them, they also take place between different positions or voices in the self (e.g., "I'm a smoker but I'm also concerned about my health, therefore I make the agreement with myself to ..."). Dialogue, moreover, assumes the emergence or creation of a "dialogical space" in which existing positions are further developed and new and commonly constructed positions have a chance to emerge. Dialogue implies addressivity and responsiveness in human interchanges, but it is more than that. It implies a learning process that confirms, innovates, or further develops existing positions on the basis of the preceding exchange. As a learning process it has the capacity to move the self to higher levels of awareness and integration. As such, it is more specific than the broader concept of "communication." Dialogue is one of the most precious instruments of the human mind and is valuable enough to be stimulated and developed, particularly in situations where learning is hampered by monological communication. At the same time, we believe that a profound insight into dialogue and knowledge about its potentials can only be achieved when we recognize its constraints. There are situations where there is no dialogue or where it is not possible (e.g. in situations with large power differences between the participants) or even not required (e.g., a general who has to take a quick decision in wartime). The crucial question is not: Is the person dialogical or not? But rather: When and under which conditions is dialogue possible and can it be fostered.[1]

The dialogical self has to be distinguished from "inner speech," usually described as the activity of "silently talking to oneself" and emerging in the literature in the form of equivalent concepts such as "self-talk" or "self-verbalizations" and related concepts such as "private speech" or "egocentric speech" (for review, see Morin, 2005). The dialogical self is different from inner speech in at least four respects: (i) it is explicitly multi-voiced rather than mono-voiced and is engaged in interchanges between voices from different social or cultural origins; (ii) voices are not only "private" but also "collective," and as such they talk through the mouth of the individual speaker; (iii) the dialogical self is not based on any dualism between self and other: the other (individual or group) is not outside the self but conceptually included in the self; the other is an intrinsic part of a self that is extended to its social environment; (iv) the self is not only verbal but also non-verbal: there are embodied precursors of dialogue before the child is able to verbalize or use any language.[2]

The process of positioning as basic to dialogical self theory

One of the basic tenets of dialogical self theory is that people are continuously involved in a process of positioning and repositioning, not only in relation to other people but also in relation to themselves. This tenet is elaborated in Chapter 3, which leads us to the heart of dialogical self theory. Inspired by the three models of the self, traditional, modern, and post-modern, we focus on some of the main concepts of the theory. Referring to the notion of "difference," central in the post-modern model, we deal with multiplicity and differences in the self, showing that actions that take place between people (e.g., conflicts, criticisms, making agreements, and consultations) occur also within the self (e.g., self-conflicts, self-criticism, self-agreements, and self-consultations), illustrating how the self works as a society of mind.

Given the basic assumption of the extended self, we argue that the other is not outside the self but rather an intrinsic part of it. There is not only the actual other outside the self, but also the imagined other who is entrenched as the other-in-the-self. This implies that basic processes, such as self-conflicts, self-criticism, self-agreements, and self-consultancy, are taking place in different domains in the self: within the *internal* domain (e.g., "As an enjoyer of life I disagree with myself as an ambitious worker"); between the *internal and external* (extended) domain (e.g., "I want to do this but the voice of my mother in myself criticizes me"); and within the *external* domain (e.g., "The way my parents were interacting with each other has shaped the way I deal with problems in my contact with my husband"). As these examples show, there is not a sharp separation between the internal life of the self and the "outside" world, but rather a gradual transition. This, however, contrasts clearly with the phenomenon known in the literature as "othering" that is characterized by a sharp demarcation between self and other. Surprisingly, the transition between self and other is gradual in some situations, but sharp in other ones. This leads to the conclusion that the dimension open–closed is crucial for permitting dialogical relationships.

On the basis of the philosophical literature, we argue that the mind does not simply coincide with itself, but rather *needs itself* in order to arrive at some clarity about itself and the world. In order to find meaningful answers in uncertain situations the person has to interrogate himself in order to find the proper direction. The mind is involved in a series of proposals and disposals to itself that reflects the basic "imperfection of the mind," that is, the mind is a question to itself that cannot immediately be answered or a problem to itself that cannot immediately be resolved. This imperfection, which leaves room for the darker realms of the self (populated by "shadow" or "disowned" positions), strongly contrasts with the clarity and transparent unity of the modern Cartesian conception of the self. The metaphorical movements from one position to another in the landscape of the self are ways of gaining understanding about the self in relation to the world.

The verb "positioning" is a spatial term. It refers to the process in which the self is necessarily involved when part of a world in which people *place* each other and themselves in terms of "here" and "there." When a person positions herself "somewhere," there are always, explicitly or implicitly, other positions involved that are located in the outer space around us or in the inner metaphorical space of the self. In this sense, I position myself as agreeing or disagreeing, as loving or hating, or as being close or opposed to another or to myself. An important theoretical advantage of the term positioning is that it can be used not only as an active but also as a passive verb. From birth onward we are *positioned* by our social environment (e.g., as boy or girl, as black or white, as belonging to a majority or minority) and much of our active positioning can be seen as a monological or dialogical answer to these influences. We get engaged in dialogues or monologues when such positions become voiced positions that are heard or not heard, answered or not answered, and receiving space for expression or not.

In the dialogical self both multiplicity, (in the line of the post-modern model of the self) and unity (in the line of the modern model) are central concepts. Therefore, it is our concern to make the notion of unity and continuity fit with a conception of a self that acknowledges the existence of difference, multiplicity, contradiction, and discontinuity. With this purpose in mind, we introduce several concepts that are discussed with reference to the considerations of unity and multiplicity: *I-position*, *meta-position*, *coalition of positions*, *third position*, *composition*, and the process of *depositioning*. Together, these concepts elaborate on the tenet that the process of positioning is basic to understanding the workings of the dialogical self as a spatio-temporal process. Moreover, they give access to the study of a rich diversity of phenomena that can be explored in their interconnection.

In the notion of *I-position*, multiplicity and unity are combined in one and the same composite term. Unity and continuity are expressed by attributing an "I," "me," or "mine" imprint to different and even contradictory positions in the self, indicating that these positions are felt as belonging to the self in the extended sense of the term (e.g., "I as ambitious," "I as anxious," "my father as an optimist," "my beloved children," and even "my irritating colleagues"). As differentially positioned in time and space, the self functions as a multiplicity. However, as "appropriated" to one and the same *I*, *me* or *mine*, unity and continuity are created in the midst of multiplicity.

Another concept that leaves room both for multiplicity and unity is the *meta-position*: the *I* is able to leave a specific position and even a variety of positions and observe them from the outside, as an act of self-reflection. The advantage of taking a meta-position, alone or together with others, is that the self attains an overview from which different, more specialized positions can be considered in their interconnections so that "bridges of meaning" can emerge and well-thought-out plans can be executed. We will discuss the main features of meta-positioning as an observing or meta-cognitive activity.

Unity and multiplicity are also combined in a *coalition of positions*: positions do not work in isolation, but, as in a society, they can cooperate and support each other, leading to "conglomerations" in the self that may dominate other positions. For example, a conflict between "I as ambitious" and "I as enjoyer" can influence the self for some time in negative ways. However, when "I as ambitious" learns to cooperate with "I as exploring something new," a reorganization of the self can be achieved with more coherence between the original positions of "ambitious" and "enjoyer" as a result.

Finally, when there is a conflict between two positions in the self, this can be reconciled by the creation of a *third position* that has the potential of unifying the two original ones without denying or removing their differences (unity-in-multiplicity). In order to examine the societal importance of the development of third positions, we will discuss several examples: the case of a lesbian woman in Catholic Brazil, Roman Polanski's film *The Pianist*, and the case of Griffin, a white man who lived for some time with a black identity.

In the context of artistic considerations, we will discuss the concept of *composition*, where the emphasis is on positions in the self as part of a pattern. This concept will be illustrated by an analysis of the mescaline experience depicted in Aldous Huxley's book *The doors of perception*, and the prominence of patterns in Cézanne's paintings. In this context, we also explore the similarity between Rollo May's treatise of creativity and Martin Buber's exploration of *I–You* relationships.

Inspired by the experience of a "meaningfully ordered cosmos," central in the traditional model of the self, we will deal with the possibility of the *I* as becoming involved in a process of *depositioning*. This notion emerges from the insight that the farther-reaching experiences of the human mind are not so much *in* the self-positions but rather *between* them, giving the self access to a wider field of awareness. We will discuss three forms of experience in which the *I* becomes depositioned: (i) a unifying form of awareness where the *I* is able to identify itself with a great variety of positions, at the same time being detached from them; (ii) a "dualistic" form of awareness where the *I* is strongly detached from specific positions, while remaining conscious of their existence (however, not identifying with them as in the unifying awareness); and (iii) a form of awareness that is characterized by an absence of any sensory experience, yet offering an experience of "union." In all these forms of awareness, silence, not in the sense of absence of words but rather as a "speaking silence" and "being fully present," is a constitutive part of the experience. They illustrate that there are experiences in which dialogue evolves not as successive turn-taking but as simultaneous presence.

Inspired by the moral nature of the traditional self, we will examine the main features of "good dialogue," as a desirable societal and developmental enterprise. Nine features were outlined: good dialogue, as a learning experience, *innovates* the self; it has a certain *bandwidth* referring to the range of positions allowed to enter the dialogue; it acknowledges the unavoidable role of *misunderstandings*; it develops in a *dialogical space*; it recognizes and incorporates the *alterity* not only of the other person but also of other positions in the self; it recognizes the importance of societal *power* differences as reflected in the relative dominance of positions in the self; it recognizes the existence of different "*speech genres*" and their role in misunderstanding and deception; it can be deepened by the participation in a broader *field of awareness*; and it profits from "*speaking silence.*" We consider these features of good dialogue as relevant to learning processes in a society in which individuals and groups are confronted with differences, not only between each other but also increasingly within themselves.

Altogether, the concept of positioning, and its variations such as "repositioning," "*I*-position," "meta-position," "third position," "coalition of positions," "composition," and "depositioning" allow us to stretch the theory into different directions so that phenomena that are usually treated in their separate qualities can be brought together in a more comprehensive theoretical framework. The advantage of such a bridging framework is that it brings insights, meanings, and experiences, back and forth, so that the description or analysis of one phenomenon can profit from the other ones.

What is known in the literature as "positioning theory" has some significant similarities with the present dialogical theory. Positioning theory is often contrasted with the older framework of role theory. Whereas roles are relatively fixed, long-lasting and formally defined, positioning theory is interested in conventions of speech and action that are unstable, contestable, and ephemeral (Harré, 2004; Harré and van Langenhove, 1991). Dialogical self theory is also sensitive to the dynamic qualities of the process of positioning and repositioning.[3] There is, however, an important difference. More than conventional positioning theory, dialogical self theory is focused on the self as an agentic and original source of meaning production (see also Raggatt, 2007). Like positioning theory, dialogical self theory is interested in the role of language, social conventions, collective history, and linguistic communities. However, while positioning theory is focused on the processes that take place between people, dialogical self theory aims at a profound exploration of the experiential richness and emotional qualities of the self in close connection with inter-subjective processes. Therefore, we present a special analysis of emotions as expressions of an embodied self (Chapter 5) and elaborate on a developmental view (Chapter 4) that explains how dialogues *between* parents and children develop into dialogues *within* the self and how these within-dialogues then contribute to the between-dialogues from an original point of view. Moreover, the developmental approach enables us to investigate the embodied nature of the process of positioning as preceding the use of language by the child.

The developmental origins of the dialogical self

In order to understand the workings of the dialogical self, it is necessary to gain insight into its developmental origin. We will describe in Chapter 4 some phenomena that can be considered as precursors or early manifestations of the dialogical self, such as tongue protrusion, imitation and provocation, imagination, memory, pseudo-dialogues in early mother–infant relationships and the acts of giving and taking in the first year of life as non-verbal or pre-verbal manifestations of dialogue. A decisive moment in development is when joint attention, at the end of the first year of life, allows the child to perceive objects from the perspective of another person. The development of joint attention makes it possible for parents or caretakers to point to the child herself as a common focus of attention, so that the child learns to regard herself from a common reference point. We will show that self-reflection and self-knowledge take place, from the beginning, in indirect ways (via the other) rather than in direct ways. Role-playing further expands the capacity of the child to introduce new positions in the self.

Building on Mead's well-known distinction between play and game, we will discuss the notion of the generalized other. We argue that this notion is based on a homogeneous society metaphor but that it is less relevant to understand the uncertainties typical of a globalizing world where different social rules meet on the interface of different (sub)cultures. The differences and contrasts between social rules can rather be understood as associated with collective voices that meet and confront each other as parts of a complex and interconnected world society.

Relevant to the spatial aspects of the dialogical self is the emergence of a personal space as an invisible, dynamic, and transportable space in the first year of life. Typical of a personal space are semi-permeable self–other boundaries indicating the relevance of the dimension open–closed to the notion of dialogue from a developmental point of view. In the line of the discussion of a larger "field of awareness" as discussed in Chapter 3, we describe some transcendental experiences in childhood, which are characterized not so much by a disappearance of self–other boundaries but rather by their increased openness and permeability.

Given the assumption that the dialogical self is basically embodied, we describe the development of the body and its corresponding movements (e.g. rolling over, crawling, standing, and walking) as leading to important turning points in the way the world is perceived. This leads to a discussion of the metaphorical implications of the body and its movements for the emergence of self-positions. Special emphasis is given to two main dimensions of the body, each with their polar opposites: the vertical dimension (up versus down, or top-dog versus underdog) and the horizontal dimension (here versus there, or close versus distant). In this line, we explore the connection between the body and the social and, moreover, between the social and the personal.

For the development of the dialogical self, both in childhood and adulthood, the concept of "promoter position" is crucial. Such a position is distinctive by its relevance to the future development of the self, by its potential to produce a diverse range of more specialized positions and by its power to integrate and synthesize positions. In order to illustrate the influence of promoter positions in the development of the self, we discuss two very different examples: the emergence of the position "I as acceptant" in the course of a psychotherapeutic process and, from a cultural-anthropological point of view, the phenomenon of "shape-shifting," which refers to the process of identification with a totem animal. We will analyze the similarities between these two seemingly divergent examples from the perspective of dialogical self theory.

Given the field of tension between multiplicity and unity of the self, a model will be presented in which different developmental movements are detailed: "progressive movements" that stimulate the self to a higher level of integration, and "regressive movements" that bring the self to a lower level of integration. In this context, the concept of "positive disintegration" will be introduced, referring to the existence of crisis as a possibility of progressive or regressive movements of the self. For making progressive movements, the integrative power of promoter positions will be emphasized because they have the potential to compensate for the disorganizing influence resulting from the change or even loss of core positions in the self.

The presented developmental view gives room for the distinction between two kinds of *conflict*, labeled as "uni-level" and "multi-level" conflict. The former kind of conflict is most familiar both in everyday life and in the social sciences. It is a conflict between two positions at the *same* level of integration. For example, an employer has to take a decision that affects the life of a friend in a negative way, leading to a conflict between the positions "I as employer" and "I as friend." In a multi-level conflict, a position located on one level is in conflict with a position on *another* level. This occurs when a particular position is more developed than another one, while the less-developed "lower" position is interfering with the more developed "higher" one. For example, a position such as "ambitious" or "competitive" that was helpful when a person was young and building up a career, loses its relevance when the person becomes older and is developing his more cooperative side. However, his ambitious position is still active, although it has lost its function in his new developmental period.

We see "multi-level conflicts" as particularly relevant to the process of globalization. When the developmental trajectories of self-positions emerging from different cultural backgrounds are different in their speed, direction, or flexibility, one cultural position can be experienced as progressive while another one is felt as regressive, resulting in a multi-level conflict. Promoter positions are then needed to transform a multi-level conflict into a form of integration so that the self is able to cope with serious conflicts.

A dialogical view of emotions

Emotions are of direct relevance to the functioning of the dialogical self because some emotions (e.g. persistent anger) work as obstacles to dialogical relationships, whereas other emotions (e.g. love) are able to facilitate such relationships. In reverse, dialogue has the potential to change emotions (e.g. a good dialogue can create a dialogical space in which anxiety or anger is reduced). Given the rather complex interconnection between self and emotions, we start in Chapter 5 from the assumption that the relationship between self and emotion is bi-directional: emotions have an impact on the self and the self, for its part, is able to influence and change emotions. This bi-directional influence is confirmed by neurological evidence that deals with the relationship between self and emotion. As LeDoux (2002) has argued, there are two paths for producing an emotion in the brain, a lower and a higher one. The low circuit is involved when the amygdala, a part of the limbic system involved in the processing of emotions, senses danger and produces an emergency signal to the brain and the body. The high circuit, which is considerably slower than the low road, becomes involved when the danger signal is carried from the lower parts of the brain to the neocortex. Because the lower path transmits signals more than twice as fast as the higher circuit, the self-conscious brain is not well able to intervene and stop the emotional response in time. One is jumping back from a figure suddenly appearing in the dark before one has a chance to correct oneself. In some situations it is most adaptive to respond rapidly (e.g., in situations of danger), while in other situations it is more adaptive to reflect on one's emotions and dialogue with oneself before acting (e.g., taking the intentions of the other into account). As representatives of psychotherapeutic approaches have argued, it is important to make use of the higher but slower road in the brain as an attempt to transform particular maladaptive responses into adaptive ones (Greenberg, 2002).

As phenomena that have immediate implications for the functioning of the self, we conceptualize emotions as temporary self-positions. This has the apparent advantage that emotions can be studied as interactional and dialogical phenomena that are influenced by counter-emotions. Two developments in the literature of emotions are particularly important from a dialogical point of view. One is a distinction proposed by Lambie and Marcel (2002), between "first-order phenomenology" in which emotional experiences have a "truth pretension" (e.g. "He *is* a bastard"), and "second-order awareness" that involves a reflexive awareness of the emotion ("I'm aware that I'm angry"). We will argue that second-order awareness is a necessity for the dialogical processing of emotions. Another distinction relevant to the accessibility of emotions is between "primary" and "secondary" emotions (Greenberg, 2002). Primary emotions are first responses to a stimulus situation (e.g. anger at violation or fear at threat). Secondary emotions are responses to or defenses against primary emotions (e.g. anger as a reaction to sadness or anxiety) and they obscure what people experience on a deeper affective level. For developing dialogical relationships it is required that primary emotions are accessible to the self so that they are liberated from covering or obscuring secondary emotions.

The existence of a multiplicity of transient emotions in the self evokes the question of what is emotional authenticity from a dialogical point of view. We acknowledge the general consideration that authenticity implies access to one's self and emotions and the ability to act on that, but propose a wider conception of this phenomenon. From a dialogical point of view, authenticity is achieved when the person takes into account not only their own emotions but also the emotions of the other-in-the-self and the actual other, with attention to the learning processes that are connected with them.

In Chapter 5 we address, moreover, three emotions that we consider as particularly significant to different models of the self: (i) self-esteem emotions as typical of the modern model; (ii) enjoyment as relevant to the post-modern model; and (iii) gratitude as one of the emotions characteristic of the traditional model. In our discussion of self-esteem emotions, we consider the costs of a persistent pursuit of self-esteem, as typical of the modern model with its bias of self-sovereignty and independence. By way of contrast to the strong emphasis of esteem in the Western literature, we discuss the less familiar Korean phenomenon of *Shimcheong* that celebrates we-ness in human relationships. The difference between *Shimcheong* and the Western concept of emotional intelligence will be highlighted.

In line with the post-modern model of the self, we will discuss the experience of enjoyment against the background of increasing consumerism and its implications in contemporary society. This discussion leads to the distinction between short-term enjoyment as typical of consumerism, and enjoyment with long-term implications as typical of experiences that reach the deeper regions of the self.

With the traditional model of the self in mind, we consider the emotion of gratitude and summarize the results of an investigation that shows that words relevant to individualism and consumerism (e.g., "purchase" or "want more") have increased in recent decades, while words referring to solidarity or gratitude decreased in the same period.

A dialogical view of emotions requires a treatment of love. We discuss this emotion in the sense of "deep love" or "dialogical love" and argue that it can properly be understood only when one realizes that love is not only oriented to the other as a separate person but also to the extensions of the self of the other. In other words, deep love is an "extension of an extension." In spatial terms, love is described as a movement in two directions at the same time: to the inner parts of the self and to the actual, imagined, or remembered other. As a dialogical emotion in the life of a person, love can be qualified as a *relationship* of the self with the self of the other in its extensions. In this context we consider the difference between self-love and love of the other.

In order to explore the methodological implications of the presented view of emotions, we propose a stage model devised for the articulation, clarification and change of emotions. The model consists of seven phases: (i) identifying and entering an emotion; (ii) leaving the emotion; (iii) identifying and entering a counter-emotion; (iv) leaving the counter-emotion; (v) developing dialogical relations between emotions; (vi) creating a composition of emotions; and (vii) developing a promoter position in the context of the emotions. The stage model will be illustrated by an actual case. In order to place the model in the broader context of the present book, the interpersonal and cultural implications of the model will be highlighted in the context of the process of globalization.

On the interface of theory and practice

Inspired by American pragmatism we are interested in the practical implications of the presented theory. As clarifying examples, we explore in Chapter 6 three topics: the culture of organizations with proper attention to leadership, the issue of motivation, and the problem of social conflict resolution.

Contemporary organizations are becoming increasingly international, intercultural, and inter-local and, as a result, they become increasingly populated by people with multi-voiced selves and identities. Like container views of self and identity, container views of the culture of organizations are becoming increasingly obsolete in an interconnected world society. Organizations are becoming more complex and *extended*, as exemplified by the widely used notion of "stakeholder." This term refers to individuals and groups that have direct interest in what is going on in the organization, such as its employees, vendors, customers, and shareholders. Even members of the broader community affected by the local economy or environment of the organization, such as the labor unions, professional associations, ecological movements, universities, and even the global community, are implied. We will analyze contemporary organizations as located in a field of tension between centralizing movements necessary for the coordination and integration of activities, and decentralizing movements in the form of rapidly changing circumstances and the presence of contradictory voices in the environment. These changes require the participants to develop a multi-voiced self that is able to move flexibly from one position to another with attention to the coherence of these positions.

For the culture of an organization we see dialogical leadership as indispensable. A dialogical leader has developed the capacity to make flexible movements between a variety of *I*-positions, such as entrepreneur, manager, coach, and professional. Such positions are part of the repertoire of a leader who knows when and where these positions should be actualized. Involved in mutual dialogical relationships, the different *I*-positions learn from each other in the service of their further development. A dialogical leader is, moreover, authentic in the sense that she acts on the basis of emotions and positions that take the positions and emotions of the other into account, that is, these emotions and positions profit from the communicative feedback from colleagues and stakeholders. A dialogical leader has the capacity to create coalitions between people in the service of the realization of the mission of the organization. We will argue that dialogical leadership develops in an optimal way when the leader is included as a promoter position in the selves of her colleagues.

Because organizations have become increasingly complex in their tasks, missions, and environments, a broadening of the range of positions in the self of the participants and, in addition, flexible and dialogical movements from the one to the other position are required. We will illustrate this thesis by analyzing changes in two types of organizations: the expansion of the repertoire of teachers in school organizations and the expansion of the repertoire of members of police organizations. On the basis of discussions with key people from the two types of organization, we found that they both made a plea for a more open organizational culture in which different contradictory positions should be developed. Moreover, they found it undesirable that conventional roles would be abandoned in favour of new ones, but rather preferred to combine them.

Apparently, there was a need to include the old positions as parts of a coalition with the new ones in order to give an adequate answer to the needs of contemporary society challenged by the growing multiplicity and diversity of components in the cultures of organizations.

On the border-zone between theory and practice, we will enter a discussion of the process of motivation as relevant both to individual selves and to the development of organizations. First, we will stress the importance of "creating space" in one's own self and the selves of other people as indispensable for stimulating motivation to reach particular goals. The basic idea is that motivation flourishes if it is based on a larger variety of positions in the self and if the repertoires of different people fit with one another. Starting with an insight from James (1890) a *basic self-conflict* is described that emerges from the tension between the development of a specific position and the development of the self as a whole, that is, of a large variety of possible positions. We will argue that, although it is difficult or even impossible to fully resolve the basic self-conflict, it leaves room for the reconciliation of conflicts and for bringing together opposites that seem to be mutually exclusive. Our main tenet is that coalitions of conflicting or opposing positions have the potential of creating strong motivation that takes the interests of specific positions into account and combines them as parts of a more encompassing structure (e.g., bringing social, artistic, and cultural interests together in one and the same activity). Such coalitions lead to forms of "integrative motivation" emerging in a field of tension between centralizing and decentralizing movements in the self. Such motivation is relevant to the development not only of individuals but also of teams and organizations.

Finally, we consider the process of social conflict resolution on the assumption that conflict and dialogue are not mutually exclusive categories, but that conflict is a challenge to dialogue and can function as its starting point. Involved in strong negative emotions, the conflicting parties typically restrict their repertoire to one or a few positions and find it difficult to take a meta-position from which a larger variety of possibilities can be taken into account. An apparent obstacle to conflict resolution is the phenomenon of a "claim to exclusive truth" that tends to reduce the multi-positionality of the self so that only one view of the conflict and its solution is allowed. In order to solve social conflicts, or at least deal with them, it is necessary that both parties arrive at the awareness that their view is not "truth" but "perspective" and that more perspectives are possible. Furthermore, we emphasize the relevance of narratives and space to conflict resolution. For example, visiting places that are significant to the lives of the adversary and becoming engaged in common activities to which the participants contribute each, from their own point of view, may contribute to mutual understanding and conflict resolution. A special discussion will be devoted to the Israeli–Palestinian conflict with attention to some of the main psychological obstacles that hamper dialogue between these groups (Chaitin, 2008).

For the understanding of social conflicts and the way contestants deal with them, awareness of the so-called "dialogical paradox" is required: *there where dialogue is most needed, it does not take place.* This paradox becomes visible in all those cases where people avoid, ignore, or withdraw from conflicts or fight with each other in ways dominated by monological power. Elaborating on the preceding analysis, we will present some specific guidelines for social conflict resolution.

Some specific features of this book

As the preceding introduction has suggested, it is not the main purpose of the theory we put forward to formulate testable hypotheses, but to generate new ideas. It is certainly possible to perform theory-guided research on the basis of the present theory, as exemplified by the research mentioned at the end of Chapter 1, and also by the special issue on dialogical self research in *Journal of Constructivist Psychology* (2008) and in other publications that will be discussed in this book. Yet the primary purpose is the generation of new ideas that lead to continued theory, research, and practice on the basis of links between the central concepts of the theory.

The writing of this book was stimulated by discussions that take place in the *International Journal for Dialogical Science* and at the biennial *International Conferences on the Dialogical Self* as they are held in cities in different countries: Nijmegen (2000), Ghent (2002), Warsaw (2004), Braga (2006), Cambridge, UK (2008) and Athens (2010). The discussion in the *Journal* and at the conferences have not only generated many ideas, but have also aroused questions about the present state of the art and about the directions of the theory in the future. This book is an attempt to point to some of the main directions and to stimulate further activity around the theory. Our aim is to transcend the boundaries of (sub)disciplines, countries, and continents and create fertile interfaces where theorists, researchers, and practitioners meet in order to become involved in innovative dialogue.

After the first psychological publication on the dialogical self (Hermans, Kempen, and Van Loon, 1992), the theory has been applied in a diversity of fields: cultural psychology (e.g. Bhatia, 2007; Chaudhary, 2008; Choi and Han, 2008; Aveling and Gillespie, 2008; Hermans, 2001a); educational psychology (e.g., Akkerman *et al.*, 2006, Ligorio and Pugliese, 2004); psychotherapy (e.g. Dimaggio *et al.*, 2003; Goncalves, Matos, and

Santos, 2009; Hermans and Dimaggio, 2004, Rowan, 2010); personality psychology (e.g. Puchalska-Wasyl, Chmielnicka-Kuter, and Oles, 2008); psychopathology (e.g. Lysaker and J. Lysaker, 2002, 2008; Semerari *et al.*, 2004); developmental psychology (e.g. Bertau, 2004; 2008; Fogel *et al.*, 2002; Lyra, 1999; Valsiner, 2002); experimental social psychology (e.g. Stemplewska-Żakowicz, Walecka, and Gabińska, 2006); career counseling (McIlveen and Patton, 2007), social work (Van Nijnatten, 2007); brain sciences (e.g. Lewis, 2002; Schore, 1994); psychoanalysis (e.g. Beebe, 2002; Bromberg, 2004); psychodrama (Verhofstadt-Deneve *et al.*, 2006); cultural anthropology (e.g. Gieser, 2006; Van Meijl, 2006, 2009); religion (Belzen, 2006); literary analysis (Rojek, 2009); constructivism (e.g. Neimeijer and Buchanan, 2004); the philosophy of Martin Buber (e.g. Cooper and Hermans, 2007); the psychology of the internet (e.g., Hevern, 2004; Rowiński, 2008; Van Halen and Janssen, 2004) and media (e.g. Annese, 2004; Cortini, Mininni, and Manuti, 2004); the psychology of globalization (Hermans and Dimaggio, 2007) and methodology (e.g. Hermans, 2001b; Kluger, Nir, and Kluger, 2008; Leiman, 2004; Osatuke *et al.*, 2004; Raggatt, 2000). In incorporating developments in many of these fields, the present book aims to take a step further and to place these developments in a broader theoretical framework. In working on this framework we became more than before, aware of being part of an increasingly interconnected world society and we are convinced that these changes have far-reaching implications for conceptions of self and identity.

NOTES

1 This statement was made by Giancarlo Dimaggio at the Fifth International Conference on the Dialogical Self in Cambridge, UK, August 26–29, 2008.

2 See also J. Lysaker (2006) who critically discusses Wiley's (2006) view in which the dialogical self and inner speech are seen as equivalent concepts.

3 The present theory acknowledges not only unstable, changing, and ephemeral positions, but also stable and trait-like ones (see Chapter 5).

1 The impact of globalization and localization on self and identity[1]

We are all framed of flappes and patches, and of so shapelesse and diverse a contexture, that everie piece, and everie moment playeth his part. And there is as much difference found betweene us and our selves, as there is betweene our selves and others.

Montaigne (1580/1603)

Understanding globalization and its impact on self and identity is a crucial task for social scientists and practitioners today. As a result of increasing demographic, economic, ecological, political, and military interconnections on a global scale, cosmopolitanism is becoming an aspect of the everyday life of people in many parts of the world. Educational contacts crossing the borders of nationalities; tourism as the biggest industry in the world; the daily use of the internet by adults, adolescents, and children; business contacts with people on the other side of the world; and intensive communication between diasporas and homelands illustrate that never in the history of humankind have global connections had such a broad reach and deep impact on the selves and identities of an increasing number of people.

Although globalization broadens the scope and opens new horizons for an increasing number of people from diverse origins, it has its evident shadow sides. Tragic events such as the 9/11 terrorist attacks in New York City and Washington, DC, and the bombings in Bali, Madrid, and London are fixed forever in our memories. They happened in a globalizing world filled with tensions, oppositions, clashes, prejudices, and misunderstandings between people from different cultural backgrounds, who never in history have been so interconnected with each other as in the present era.

Without doubt, the process of globalization opens new vistas and broadens our horizons. It offers increasing possibilities of international contacts and fosters economical, ecological, educational, informational, and military forms of cooperation across the borders of regions, countries, and cultures. However, it also restricts and closes the selves of many people as a counter-reaction to what they experience as a threat, as evidenced by

21

the resistance to the world-wide immigration flows, to the religious practices and rituals of other cultural groups that are experienced as "strange" or "alien," to the economic gap between "haves" and "have-nots," and to the power of multi-nationals. In this chapter, we argue that to understand both the positive and the negative implications of the process of globalization on the individual level, a dialogical conception of self and identity is required, one that can account for the different and even opposing demands resulting from the processes of globalization and localization.

Globalization, localization, and uncertainty: a socio-cultural analysis

Before we present a dialogical analysis of self and identity, we discuss the intimate interconnection between the global and the local. As we will show, the experience of uncertainty is a significant psychological factor in this interconnection. Such uncertainty is typical of a globalizing word in which selves and identities are shifting between global and local positions. We will argue that this shifting between positions requires a dialogical approach that takes into account not only the relationships *between* individuals, groups, and cultures, but also the relationships between positions *within* a multi-voiced self.

Globalization and localization as its counter-force

Conceptions that treat globalization and homogenization (e.g., Americanization) as equivalent processes have become increasingly obsolete (e.g., Castells, 1997, Featherstone, 1995). Whether homogenization is seen positively in terms of the utopia of the global village or negatively in terms of cultural imperialism, such notions are based on the questionable assumption that we are moving toward an increasing global uniformity. However, as Meyer and Geschiere (1999) and others have observed, one of the ambiguities of the notion of globalization is that the homogenizing tendencies inherent in globalization imply a continued or even intensified heterogeneity that stresses cultural differences and even oppositions. Rather, the process of globalization, with its implied technological advances, leads to a sharpening of cultural contrasts or even engenders new oppositions.

Indications of such paradoxical articulations are numerous. A few examples (see Meyer and Geschiere, 1999) may suffice. Modern technical devices, such as tape recorders, facilitated the spread of Muslim fundamentalism in North Africa and the Middle East, creating a giant market for cassettes of the latest star imam. The desire of many Westerners for an encounter with the "exotic" world of particular cultural groups requires these groups to produce local "authenticity" as a commodity for global tourism. The recent economic boom of industrializing countries in East Asia was accompanied by an equally vibrant boom of popular religions and spirit cults in local situations (see Weller, 1994). In some parts of Africa, witchcraft is used as a levelling force, undermining inequalities in wealth and power. Paradoxically, the same force is regarded as indispensable for the accumulation of such wealth and power. Witchcraft is used both to express envy and to accumulate Western goods as an indication of success. Obeysekere (1977) has already observed that, from a historical point of view, spirit cults and sorcery assumed a heightened status in the more modern sectors of Sri Lanka and concluded that this finding contradicts the well-known Weberian equation of "modernization" and "disenchantment" (see also Adams, 2004, who presented similar data from contemporary England). Such observations suggest that globalization and localization imply each other and can be regarded as two sides of the same coin. On the level of the self, this interconnection is expressed as a movement between positioning (as participant in a global discourse) and counter-positioning (as representative of a local community).[2]

"Glocalization," civilization, and the problem of global optimism

One of the problems in understanding the nature of globalization is the widespread tendency to regard the global–local opposition as a polarity consisting of mutually excluding components. This polarity is manifested in the claim that we live in a world of local assertions *against* globalizing trends. As a consequence, localization is cast as a form of opposition or resistance to the global, which is seen as hegemonic. An example of such exclusive opposition can be found in the idea that people retreat into their smaller communities as a defense against the overruling process of globalization. Although there are clear examples of defensive localization (e.g., aversion to immigrant populations), globalization is not necessarily a process which overrides locality. In an attempt to articulate the deep interconnectedness of the global and the local, Robertson (1995) proposed the composite term "glocalization" in order to emphasize that the global manifests itself in local forms.

Globalization in its broadest sense increasingly involves the creation and incorporation of locality, as reflected, for example, in the emergence of TV enterprises such as MTV, CNN, and, more recently Al Jazeera, seeking global markets and focusing on a great diversity of local developments. Therefore, it makes sense to conjure up a process of glocalization as it combines two seemingly opposing trends: homogenization and heterogenization. These trends can be described as not only simultaneous but also complementary and interpenetrative. The past century, in particular, has seen a remarkable proliferation with respect to the international organization and promotion of locality. One can refer to the current attempts to organize globally the promotion of the rights and identities of native, or indigenous, peoples (e.g., the Global Forum in Brazil in 1992 or the Global Forum on Migration and Development in Belgium in 2007). This trend is also reflected in the attempts by the World Health Organization to promote "world health" by the reactivation or even the invention of "indigenous" local medicine. The global–local interpenetration is not only visible at the level of international organizations, but it can be experienced as part of daily life. As a result of international transport and travel facilities, local traditions at the other end of the world become accessible and, as surfers on the internet, we are introduced to the lives and values of people that were largely unknown to previous generations. (For the interpenetration of the global and the local, see Chen, 2006; Featherstone, 1995; Kahn, 1995; and Robertson, 1995.)

The coexistence of the global and the local is also visible in discussions of the process of civilization. Wilkinson (1995) proposed the thesis that on earth only one civilization exists: a single, global civilization. This civilization is the direct descendant of a civilization that emerged about 1500 BC in the Near East when Mesopotamian and Egyptian civilizations collided and fused. Since then this fused entity has expanded over the entire planet and absorbed all other previously independent civilizations (e.g., Japanese, Chinese, and the West).

For the coexistence of globalization and localization Wilkinson's criterion for defining a civilization is relevant. He proposes a transactional definition and a criterion of connectedness rather than uniformity for locating the spatio-temporal boundaries of society. When people interact intensely, significantly, and continuously, they belong to the same civilization, "even if their cultures are very dissimilar and their interactions mostly hostile" (1995: 47). Why does he propose this criterion? Because conflict, hostility, and even warfare, when durable (i.e., habitual or inescapable) create a social system comprising contestants and antagonists who do not or cannot live in isolation.

Varieties of antagonistic bonding can be observed in religious and social life, as well as in language itself. Words like "contradiction," "argument," "disagreement," "dissonance," "drama," "collision," "war," etc., refer to the existence of entities which consist of oppositions between ideas, sounds, persons, characters, bodies, and groups: "Israel and Judah, the Homeric pantheon, Congress, counterraiding tribes, the two-party system, the Seven Against Thebes, a Punch and Judy show, and the

Hitler–Stalin pact are all antagonistic couples and collections of separate entities commonly recognized as internally antagonistic unities" (Wilkinson, 1995: 48–9). Disagreements, conflicts, and wars are part of a continuous process of positioning and counter-positioning.

However, the existence of opposites may conceal deeper processes that are inherent in the perception and evaluation of differences between the poles of any pair of opposites. Such evaluative differences may precede or coexist with relations of disagreement, collision, and war. As Sampson (1993) has argued, pairs of opposites have a master-term which is dominant and an opposite term that is not-dominant (male–female; young–old, West–East, white–black). The minor pole of a dichotomy is typically defined in a negative way, that is, lacking the (positive) features of the master-term. Female is not-male, old is not-young, blacks are not-white, out-groups lack the favourable features of the in-group from which the members of this group derive their cherished identities. The result is that the perceiver is focused on the absence of the features of the master-term more than on the specific and original features of the opposite term. This psychological organization creates a basis for devaluation of the opposite pole and for the treatment of the "other" as inferior or alien. The inclusion of the other at the minor side of a polarity of opposites establishes a basis for treating the other as inferior or can be used as a justification of the exploitation of the other in the service of one's own (economic) profit.

Conceiving globalization in terms of one growing civilization or in terms of "glocalization" significantly contributes to the understanding of the apparent interpenetration of the global and the local which is so typical of our era. At the same time, these conceptions carry the risk of seeing the implied differences or opposites as representing equally strong forces that disagree or are involved in a conflict. The effect of seeing differences or opposites as stemming from equal or as equivalent parties may conceal the pervasive influence of power differences and, moreover, blind us from seeing and valuing the opposite pole (the other individual, group, culture) in its own merit, history and aims.

The perception of civilization in terms of antagonistic unities, with explicit attention to the implied power differences, has two advantages. First, it strengthens the awareness that interconnectedness of groups, societies, and cultures, although different and even opposed, belong to each other as part of an interconnected world civilization. As part of one civilization, *different* groups and cultures – intensely interconnected by international contacts, modern technology, media, and transportation as never before – can no longer avoid the necessity of dialogue. The fact that different individuals, groups, and cultures belong, more than ever, to an intensely interconnected world system, requires the recognition and exploration of dialogical relationships. Such relationships offer the possibility of adequate answers to unavoidable differences that emerge at the interfaces of communities and cultures, differences that work otherwise as unworkable misunderstandings. Second, the conception of civilization in terms of antagonistic unities recognizes the important role of power in intercultural and inter-group relationships. Capitalistic and cultural imperialism, economic exploitation of the natural resources of local communities, and discrimination of immigrant groups create situations of strong inequality (see also Stiglitz, 2002, who referred to globalization as creating dual economies and technological or digital divides in societies). In such situations the less powerful groups are seen as less significant, inferior, or serviceable and, as a result, their voices are neglected or even silenced. Inequality and injustice of this kind underscores the significance of the exploration of the concept of monologue.

The awareness of large-scale poverty, imperialism, exploitation, and discrimination may caution against uncritical global optimism. Both globalization and localization have their shadow sides. The dark faces of globalization are economic exploitation, excessive consumption, lack of roots, and loneliness. Localization can easily lead to a nostalgic longing for a remote past where everything was "better," to an experience of illusory safety, and to a defensive closure for the values, practices, and traditions of other people that are experienced as alien.

In summary, two socio-cultural trends can be observed that are closely intertwined: (a) globalization as boundary crossing and leading to international and intercultural connectedness, spread and exchange of goods, capital, practices, values, and information and (b) localization as sets of goods, customs, values, practices, and information emerging from particular places, regions, or countries. Globalization and localization are not to be seen as mutually exclusive opposites but rather as involved in a dialectical process. Differences, disagreements, and conflicts among groups that are strongly affiliated to their local communities, homelands, histories, and traditions form "antagonistic unities" within a condensed and diversified world civilization. Although globalization offers new possibilities for innovation, development, and growth of individuals, groups, and civilization as a whole, there are reasons to avoid forms of "global optimism" as it can be observed that both globalization and localization have their shadow sides.

Globalization and uncertainty

Globalization is not a new phenomenon, because it is preceded by urbanization, development of transport, growth of capitalism, and the spread of industrialization over the centuries. Typical of our era is that its scale, speed, and import have changed (Kinnvall, 2004). In terms of scale, the number of economic, ecological, demographical, political, and social linkages is greater than in any previous time in history. In terms of speed, we are witnessing a compression of space and time as never before experienced. In terms of import, the globe is perceived as an ever smaller place: events elsewhere have important implications for our everyday lives in our local situation.

Global and local identities Focusing on the psychology of adolescence, Arnett (2002) discussed the uncertainty resulting from globalization. He noted that in a globalizing world, people have to face the challenge of adapting not only to their local culture but also to the global society. He argued that, as a consequence of globalization, most people in the world, and adolescents in particular, now develop a bicultural identity: part of their identity is rooted in their local culture, and another part is attuned to the global situation. Or they may develop a hybrid identity, successfully combining elements of global and local situations in a mix (see also Hermans and Kempen, 1998). However, Arnett referred also to the increase of "identity confusion" among young people in non-Western cultures. As local cultures are challenged and changed as a result of globalization, some young people feel themselves at home in neither the local situation nor the global situation.

Indeed, increasing uncertainty about social and economic developments is a central feature of globalization in the more advanced economies. Empirical support was provided by a study by Blossfeld (2007; see also Mills and Blossfeld, 2003), who summarized the results from the first phase of the international research project GLOBALIFE. As these results suggest, youth in all thirteen countries under investigation are clearly exposed to uncertainty in the course of globalization. Yet uncertainty is clearly unequal, with risk accumulating in certain groups, particularly those at the bottom of society. It was found that uncertainty impacts family formation, with those in more precarious situations more likely to postpone or even forgo partnership and parenthood.

Aspects of uncertainty Given the central role we attach to the experience of "uncertainty" – a term to which different authors ascribe alternative meanings – a more detailed description is required. We see the experience of uncertainty as composed of four aspects: (i) *complexity*, referring to a great number of parts that have a large variety of relations; (ii) *ambiguity*, referring to a suspension of clarity, as the meaning of one part is determined by the flux and variation of the other parts; (iii) *deficit knowledge*, referring to the absence of a superordinate knowledge structure that can resolve the contradictions between the parts; and (iv) *unpredictability*, implying a lack of control of future developments. We assume that the experience of uncertainty characterizes a global situation of multi-voicedness (complexity) that does not allow a fixation of meaning (ambiguity), that has no superordinate voice for resolving contradictions and conflicting information (deficit knowledge), and that is to a large extent unpredictable.

As this description of globalization suggests, it is not necessarily a negative experience; for many people, the experience of uncertainty may open and broaden the space for possible actions, adventures, and explorations of the unknown (e.g., traveling, international contacts, forms of international and intercultural cooperation). Moreover, uncertainty can be seen as a definitive farewell to the dogmas and ideologies of institutions that restricted and confined the self in earlier times. However, when uncertainty reigns in many life areas or when one's survival is at stake, as international terrorism demonstrates, the experience of uncertainty may be intensified to a degree that it changes into an experience of insecurity or anxiety. As we have suggested, the latter experience motivates people to find local niches in which they try to find security, safety, and certainty (Adams, 2004; Giddens, 1991). So, the experience of uncertainty can be a gift as it opens a broad range of unexpected possibilities, but a burden in so far as it leads to confusion and anxiety.[3]

The experience of uncertainty should not be equated with the experience of risk taking, although they are similar in some respects. Like uncertainty, risks can be experienced as rewarding, as expressed in the commonplace observation that successful entrepreneurs, salesmen, and managers feel comfortable in taking risks. However, like in uncertainty, most people eschew its possible outcomes when risks become very high. There are, however, some apparent differences. You may take a risk by consciously engaging in a particular situation, whereas you may be subjected to an experience of uncertainty that you never chose, yet that requires you to give an answer. Moreover, uncertainty implies some degree of complexity and ambiguity and is characterized by the absence of a superordinate knowledge structure, whereas in risk these aspects may be lacking. One can engage in a dangerous sport activity or risky sex, or become a heavy smoker, but there is not much complexity or ambiguity as the nature of the danger is well known.

From a dialogical perspective, we see the experience of uncertainty (in the neutral sense of the term) as an intrinsic feature of a dialogical self that opens a process of interchange with an outcome that is, to a larger or lesser degree, unknown. As a result of this process, certainty does not result from avoiding uncertainty but from *entering* it. It emerges from the dialogical interchange itself that leads to the relative dominance of one position over the others or to a new combination of existing positions. Inspired by the views of figures such as Bakhtin (1973, 1981), James (1890), and Mead (1934), we envision the existence of a multi-voiced dialogical self that is involved in internal and external interchanges and that, although socially and biologically constrained, never reaches a final destination. This self is conceived of as potentially open to an ambiguous other and is in flux toward a future that is largely unknown. As we show in the next section, this uncertainty challenges our potential for innovation and creativity to the utmost, and at the same time, it entails the risks of a defensive and monological closure of the self and the unjustified dominance of some voices over others.

A multi-voiced and dialogical self

Three reasons for a dialogical approach

Our central thesis is that global–local connections require a dialogical conception of self and identity for several reasons. Three reasons, in particular, warrant such a conception: the increasing multiplicity of self and identity, the need for developing a dialogical capacity, and the necessity of acknowledging the alterity of the other person with whom one enters in dialogical contact.

Multiplicity of voices in the self   In a globalizing world society, individuals and groups are no longer located in one particular culture, homogeneous in itself and contrastingly set against other cultures, but are increasingly living on the interfaces of cultures (e.g., Appadurai, 1990; Hermans and Kempen, 1998; Raggatt, 2000; Spiro, 1993; Wolf, 1982). The increasing interconnectedness of nations and cultures leads not only to an increasing contact between different cultural groups but also to an increasing contact between cultures within the individual person.[4] Different cultures come together and meet each other within the self of one and the same individual. This process may result in such novel and multiple identities as a business representative educated in a French school system but working for a Chinese company; Algerian women participating in an international football competition but afterward praying in a mosque; English-speaking employees living in India but giving technical training courses via the internet to adolescents in the United States; and a scientist with university training in Zimbabwe desperately looking, as an immigrant, for a job in Britain. The focus here is on intercultural processes that lead to the formation of a multiplicity of cultural positions or voices coming together in the self of a single individual (Pieterse, 1995). Such positions or voices, as parts of a heterogeneous self, may become engaged in mutual negotiations, agreements, disagreements, tensions, and conflicts (e.g., "As a German I'm used to giving my honest opinion in case of disagreement with my colleagues but in the Iranian company where I work now, I found out that it is better to be deferential"). These examples have in common that different cultural voices are involved in various kinds of dialogical relationships and produce positive or negative meanings in fields of uncertainty. In other words, the global–local nexus is not just a reality outside the individual but is rather incorporated as a constituent of a dialogical self in action.

Dialogical capacity In contrast to earlier closed and homogeneous societies, the globalizing society is characterized by strong cultural differences, contrasts, and oppositions. As Marsella (1998) observed, cultures and nations are competing for survival as life in contemporary society pits secular, religious, humanist, and scientific cultural traditions against one another in seemingly irreconcilable struggles because of fundamental differences in cultural practices, worldviews, and ideologies. It is our conviction that fundamental differences in an intensely interconnected world society not only require dialogical relationships between people to create a world that is liveable in but also a self that has developed the capacity to deal with its own differences, contrasts, tensions, and uncertainties (Cooper and Hermans, 2007). When the world becomes more heterogeneous and multiple, the self, as part of this world, also becomes more heterogeneous and multiple. As a consequence, increasing differences in the social milieu result in increasing differences in the self in which some parts of the self become more dominant than other parts (Callero, 2003). Cultural and historical differences require a well-developed dialogical capacity (Watkins, 2003) in order to perceive, recognize, and deal with differences, conflicts, and oppositions and to arrive at workable solutions to the problems and challenges that result from an accelerating process of globalization. This requires a conception of the self in which processes of question and answer, agreement and disagreement, and negotiations between different self-positions are recognized as intrinsic features of problem solving (Bertau, 2004; Hermans, 1996a).

Alterity The potential of dialogue goes beyond the familiar situation of two people in conversation.[5] Participants involved in conversation may express and repeat their own view without recognizing and incorporating the view of the other in their exchange. Innovative dialogue exists when the participants are able and willing to recognize the perspective of the other party in its own right and, further, are able and willing to revise and change their initial standpoints by taking the preceding messages and utterances of the other into account (Marková, 1987). In his *Nichomachean Ethics*, Aristotle (1954) described, at the higher levels of communication, the experience of the other as "alter ego." The other is like myself (ego), but at the same time, he or she is not like myself (alter). Dealing with differences in a globalizing world requires the capacity to recognize and respond to the other person or group in its alterity. Alterity, as a central feature of well-developed dialogue, is a necessity in a world in which individuals and cultures are confronted with differences that they may not understand initially but that may become comprehensible and meaningful as the result of a dialogical process.

In the elaboration of a dialogical view of the self, three propositions are indispensable: (i) other persons, groups, or cultures are parts of an extended self in terms of a multiplicity of contradictory voices or positions; (ii) relations of social dominance are not alien to dialogue but belong to its intrinsic dynamics; and (iii) emotions play a crucial role in closing or opening the self to global and local influences. As we demonstrate, these three propositions require linkages between the level of the global, the local, and the individual.

The other-in-the-self: a multiplicity of voices

In a historical analysis of the concept of identity, Hall (1992) contrasted an "Enlightenment subject" and a "decentered or postmodern subject." The Enlightenment subject "was based on a conception of the human person as a fully centered, unified individual, endowed with the capacities of reason, consciousness and action, whose 'center' consisted of an inner core" (p. 275). The decentered subject is composed of different parts that are highly contingent on the changes in the environment: "Within us are contradictory identities, pulling in different directions, so that our identifications are continually being shifted about. If we feel that we have a unified identity from birth to death, it is only because we construct a comforting story or 'narrative of the self' about ourselves." (p. 277)

From the perspective of psychology, Hermans (1996a, 2001a) and Hermans, Kempen, and Van Loon (1992) proposed a (partly) decentralized conception of the self as multi-voiced and dialogical.[6] More specifically, they described the dialogical self in terms of a dynamic multiplicity of *I*-positions or voices in the landscape of the mind, intertwined as this mind is with the minds of other people. Positions are not only "internal" (e.g., I as a man, white, husband) but also "external," belonging to the extended domain of the self (e.g., my wife, my children, my colleagues, my country, my opponent). They can also take the form of combinations of internal and external positions (e.g., I as a father of three children, I as friend of an Iranian refugee, I as an opponent to demagogic political leaders). (For the extension of the self, see also Aron *et al.*, 2005; James, 1890; and Rosenberg, 1979).

Dialogues may take place among internal positions in the self (e.g., "As an answer to the conflict between my position as a father and my position as a hardworking scientist I found a workable solution"), between internal and external positions in the self (e.g., "As the son of my father I'm used to talking with him about my successes and disappointments and, although he is physically absent, he gives me advice") and between external positions of the self (e.g., "Two colleagues in my department solved their serious conflict and I learned a lot from that"). The dialogical self is not only part of the broader society but functions, moreover, itself as a "society of mind" with tensions, conflicts, and contradictions as intrinsic features of a (healthy functioning) self (Hermans, 2002).[7]

Such a multi-voiced dialogical conception acknowledges the extension of the self to the local and global environment. The personal voices of other individuals or the collective voices of groups enter the self-space and form positions that agree or disagree with or unite or oppose each other. Along these lines, real, remembered, or imagined voices of friends, allies, strangers, or enemies can become transient or more stabilized positions in the self-space that can open or close itself to the globalizing environment (Hermans, 2001a).

Features of a globalizing position repertoire   As far as the dialogical self is open to the globalizing society, the position repertoire of the self has some specific features: (a) It is populated by an unprecedented density of positions (internal and external ones) that requires the self to organize and reorganize itself and implies the risk of a "cacophony of voices" (Lysaker and Lysaker, 2002); (b) when the individual is increasingly faced with a great diversity of groups and cultures on a global scale, the position repertoire becomes more heterogeneous and laden with differences, oppositions, and contradictions (see also Falmagne, 2004); (c) as a result of the speed and unpredictability of global changes, the repertoire is subjected to increasing changes and receives more "visits" by unexpected positions; and finally (d) as a consequence of the increasing range of possible positions, there are larger "position leaps" (e.g., immigration to another country, cosmetic surgery, instant fame as the result of TV performance; Hermans, 2001a).

"I as a lover of music:" the *Portuguese fado*   Our contention
is that, as a result of globalization, positions increase in density and
heterogeneity but so do their sub-positions. Let's illustrate that by the
example of the fado, the national music genre of Portugal. The fado
(translated as "destiny" or "fate") is characterized by mournful tunes
and lyrics, although it can also be cheerful at times. It can be traced
from the 1820s in Portugal, but probably has a much earlier origin. The
music is usually linked to the Portuguese word "saudade," describing
a sentiment that has no accurate translation in any other language,
but comes close to the verb "to pine for" although often mixed with
an element of pride or strength. Originally, the fado could be heard in
local pubs in Alfama and Mouraria in Lisbon and also flourished, in a
somewhat different style, at the inner core of Coimbra, long before it
was accepted by the upper societal levels in Portugal. The fado became
widely known as the result of the admired performances of famous
singers, particularly Amalia Rodrigues, the "Queen of the Fado," who
became a truly international star and a national symbol at the same
time. She was a source of inspiration for later singers, like Madredeus,
Dulce Pontes, Mariza and Cristina Branco, who, in alliance with the
expansive CD industry, brought the fado to all corners of the world.
In this way the more introverted fado was globally distributed in ways
similar to those of the more extroverted Spanish flamenco, which
spread its wings to fly over the globe in an earlier period.

The fado, like flamenco, jazz, and many varieties of folk music, exemplifies two phenomena that are central in the present chapter. First, it
shows how a music genre of local origin becomes globally distributed
over the world community, in such a way that people at other locations can expand and enrich their musical preferences. Second, one
can imagine that the local people of Lisbon and Coimbra in the beginning of the nineteenth century were strongly attached to the fado as
a collective expression of their feelings. When, 200 years later, people
from Portugal and other places in the world talk about themselves as
"lovers of music," they typically refer to a relatively great mix of music
genres, varying from the broad variety of composers of classical music
to present-day pop and folk music from all parts of the world. In other
words, when a person involved in a conversation presents himself as
a "music lover," a great variety of music genres and styles forming a
complexity of sub-positions (I as a lover of fado, flamenco, dixieland,
Mozart operas, the Doors, etc.) is implied. Global–local dynamics
produce not only a greater density and heterogeneity of positions but
also of sub-positions.

Contradiction of cultural positions   The process of globalization and its counter-force localization engender contradictions between cultural positions in self and identity. Drawing on participant observation and in-depth interviews, Bhatia (2007) studied the experiences of a group of Indian Americans who belong to one of the fastest growing immigrant communities in the United States. Unlike previous generations, the members of these communities are marked by a high degree of training as engineeers, medical doctors, scientists, and university professors. On the one hand, these professionals function as respected members of American society, but on the other hand they feel that they are seen as racially different and as not "real Americans." Bhatia found that his participants used particular forms of dialogicality to understand their racial assignations: They emphasized that they were not only different from but *also the same* as members of the American majority, pointing to their individual merits as professionals who are well-integrated in American society. They all have experiences with racism (and their children notice it at school), yet they say that racism has not had an adverse effect on their work life. They seem to simultaneously accept and reject their differences from the majority, being engaged in a "double-voiced" discourse between their individual voices and the majority's dominant voice.

In contrast to universal models of acculturation in cross-cultural psychology, Bhatia argues that a dialogical view does not insist that conflicting positions or voices need to be replaced by harmonious voices. Moreover, he explicitly refers to the notion of power in American-Indian identities. This notion is largely neglected in well-known psychological terms, such as "bicultural competence" and "integration strategies" that are based on the assumption that both host and immigrant cultures share equal status and power. Instead of presenting a model based on equal cultural positions that move toward integration or arrive at a bicultural identity, Bhatia agrees with Arnett (2002) and Hermans and Kempen (1998) in taking a "hybridity" perspective on the acculturation process. This perspective helps us to understand "how immigrants living in post-colonial and diasporic locations are negotiating and reconciling conflicting histories and incompatible subject positions" (Bhatia, 2007: p. 233).[8]

Collective voices and audiences   The dialogical self is inspired both by the tradition of American pragmatism, as represented by authors such as James (1890) and Mead, and by dialogism in the tradition of Bakhtin (1973; 1981). While the notion of self arises out of the fertile work of James, the notion of dialogue is inspired by Bakhtin. James's distinction between *I*, or self-as-knower, and *Me*, or self-as-known, is classic in the psychology of the self (Rosenberg, 1979). The *I*-as-knower continuously organizes and interprets experience in a purely subjective manner. Three features characterize the *I*: continuity, distinctness, and volition. The *continuity* of the self-as-knower is manifested in a "sense of personal identity" and a "sense of sameness" through time (p. 332). A feeling of *distinctness*, that is, having an existence separate from others, is also intrinsic to the *I*. In order to emphasize the active nature of the *I*, James refers to a sense of personal *volition* as expressed by the continuous appropriation and rejection of thoughts, by which the *I* manifests itself as an active processor of experience. Together these features (continuity, distinction, volition) imply the awareness of self-reflectivity that is essential for the self-as-knower (Damon and Hart, 1982).

In defining the *Me*, or self-as-known, James (1890) was aware that there is a gradual transition between *Me* and *Mine*. Therefore, he identified the *Me* as the empirical self that in its broadest sense is defined as all that the person can call his or her own, "not only his body and his psychic powers, but his clothes and his house, his wife and children, his ancestors and friends, his reputation and works, his lands and horses, and yacht and bank-account" (p. 291). These primary elements or constituents reflect for James a basic feature of the self, its extension. The incorporation of these constituents suggests that the self is not an entity, closed off from the world and having an existence in itself, but, rather, extended toward specific aspects of the environment (Rosenberg, 1979).

Elaborating on the Jamesian distinctions, Mancuso and Sarbin (1983) and Sarbin (1986) have proposed a translation of the *I–Me* distinction into a narrative framework. In their view, James, Mead, Freud, and others emphasized the distinction between the *I* and the *Me* and their equivalents in other European languages in order to emphasize the narrative nature of the self. In this narrative view, the uttered pronoun *I* stands for the author, the *Me* for the actor or narrative figure. As an author, the *I* is able to imaginatively construct a story in which the *Me* is the protagonist. The *I* as author imagines the future and reconstructs the past and tells a spatially and temporally organized story about the *Me* as protagonist. Moreover, this narrative construction functions as an instrument for organizing episodes, actions, and accounts of actions (Sarbin, 1986).

Elaborating on Sarbin's narrative conception of the self, Hermans, Kempen, and Van Loon (1992), proposed a dialogical translation of the *I–Me* distinction. They did so on the basis of the consideration that a central feature of a narrative is that it is *told* to another person or to oneself. This consideration led the authors to focus on the relationship between self and dialogue and to explore their links with some of the insights proposed by Russian dialogism. In Bakhtin's view, all utterances are multi-voiced and dialogical at the same time (Skinner, Valsiner, and

Holland, 2001). They are multi-voiced because in the act of speaking there are at least two voices: the voice of the speaking person and the voice of a social language (e.g., one's dialect, one's professional group, one's generation). In a sense, Bakhtin argued, the word in language is "half-foreign" because the collective voice of the social group speaks through the mouth of the individual speaker. The collective voice becomes one's own when the speaker populates it with his or her own intentions and expressive tendencies (e.g., "I speak as a psychologist, but at the same time I'm expressing my personal opinion or conviction"). The speaker adapts the social languages to his or her meaningful and expressive personal tendencies.

Although Bakhtin did not say much about cultural groups, they can easily become incorporated in a dialogical view of the self. Both the cultural groups to which one belongs and those to which one is emotionally opposed can be part of an extended, multi-voiced, tension-laden dialogical self. In order to clarify this, two kinds of addressees should be distinguished – visible and invisible ones. One can talk to a visible party with an invisible party as the object of speech. However, as part of the conversation, the invisible party can be addressed in an indirect way. For example, a representative of one cultural group can talk about representatives of another cultural group in an ironic or even deprecatory way, imitating or ridiculing their words, accents, or facial expressions and using characteristic intonations and gestures to express their own evaluation of the other person or group in verbal and non-verbal ways. When people communicate with each other in dialogical ways, there is not only a speaker and an addressee, but also one or more implicit or hidden audiences (Marková, 2006; Salgado and Hermans, 2005) that are, as third parties, the objects of speech (the ridiculed group in the example). The process of globalization implies not only an increase in the number and heterogeneity of addressees and their various cultural backgrounds but also the number and heterogeneity of audiences that are implicitly present in the speech of everyday life.

Psychopathology The increasing density and heterogeneity of positions of the self in a globalizing era are also reflected in the literature on psychopathology. Some dysfunctions that were once of peripheral importance in psychiatric diagnostic systems have assumed almost epidemic proportions at the present time. Borderline personality disorder and eating disorders, for example, have "identity disturbances" among their core features (American Psychiatric Association, 2000), suggesting that an increasing number of patients are faced with a disorganizing instability of the self and the impossibility of choosing a limited number of favorite and stable positions to help them find a meaningful direction in their lives. Moreover, psychiatrists maintain that we are facing an epidemic of multiple personality disorder (or, to use its more recent name, dissociative identity disorder). Whereas up until 1980 no more than a hundred of these cases had been diagnosed (Boor, 1982), the number of multiple personality disorder diagnoses has increased dramatically since then (Hacking, 1995). Of particular interest for the multi-voiced nature of the self is the increase in the number of "alters" in this disorder. In the beginning of the twentieth century, the few patients with these kinds of troubles were simply "double personalities." At the end of the same century, patients diagnosed with multiple personality disorder were frequently found to have a great variety of alters, at some extremes numbering in the hundreds (Putnam, 1989). Not only the number but also the nature of the alters have changed over time. In earlier diagnoses, typical symptoms included alters that were ascribed to the etiology of the dysfunction: childlike positions and persecutors, in cases of a diagnosed history of child abuse. Today, however, alters show increasing variation: Frequently, they have the names of characters in soap operas, TV movies, and comedies, some of them being of the opposite sex and differing in race, religion, and age (Hacking, 1995). It is very hard to imagine a patient of Pierre Janet in France at the end of the nineteenth century displaying an alter with black skin and devoted to Islam. The changing pattern of diagnostic symptoms, implying differences in the number and nature of the alters, suggests the workings of cultural factors. For other pathologies such as schizophrenia, whose cause may be of a more genetic nature, such an increase of incidence is not reported (American Psychiatric Association, 2000). Therefore, we propose that some cultural changes in the realm of psychopathology reflect the increasing density and heterogeneity of positions in a globalizing era.

At the same time, we should make a sharp distinction between functional multi-voicedness and dysfunctional multi-voicedness, such as "multiple personality," "dissociative disorders," and the more recent notion of "dissociative identity disorder" (e.g., Carson, Butcher, and Mineka, 1996; Putnam, 1993). In healthy multi-voicedness there is a simultaneity of positions among which the *I* is capable of moving back and forth in flexible ways, so that question and answer, agreement and disagreement between the several positions are in line with the demands of the situation at hand. In the dysfunctional case, the interaction between the several positions is severely constrained, although in some cases one personality may be co-conscious with another and different personalities may even communicate with each other (Barresi, 1994; Radden, 1999). Generally speaking, however, there is little cooperation among the several positions and the accessibility of significant positions may be seriously reduced. In one position the person is doing or saying things that are often beyond the control of the person in the other position. As Watkins (1986) has argued, a main difference between (normal) imaginary dialogues and (abnormal) dissociative disorders is that in the abnormal case there is a sequential monologue, rather than a simultaneous dialogue.

Dialogue and social dominance

Often the notion of dialogue is regarded as essentially different or even as opposed to the notion of social dominance. Usually, *dialogue* evokes an image of people sitting at a round table discussing their views and problems as perfectly equal partners. As far as there is any dominance, it is the strength of arguments that counts. Such a conception of dialogue, however, can be regarded as an ideal speech situation or even a romantic ideal. In apparent opposition to this image, Linell (1990) has argued that asymmetry exists in each individual act–response sequence. As participants in a well-organized turn-taking process, the actors continually alternate the roles of speaker and listener in the course of their dialogue. As long as one party speaks, the other party is required to be silent. As long as the dominant party talks, the subordinate party allows, or must allow, his or her contributions to be directed, controlled, or inhibited by the interlocutor's moves (interactional dominance). Moreover, one party can predominantly introduce and maintain topics and perspectives on topics (topic dominance). The amount of talk also reflects dominance relationships: The party who talks a lot prevents the other party from taking a turn. Finally, the speaker who makes the most strategic moves may have a strong impact on a conversation without needing to talk a lot. In other words, although the topic of a meaningful conversation is under mutual control, relative dominance is not extrinsic but rather intrinsic to the dialogical process (see also Guilfoyle, 2003, for a discussion of social dominance as an intrinsic feature of dialogical relationships between psychotherapist and client).

Social dominance as reflection of power differences

Social dominance plays a more structural role when institutional power differences are taken into account. This can be illustrated by starting from two basic forms of dialogue in the sense of Bakhtin (1973): (i) the play of question and answer and (ii) relationships of agreement and disagreement. When differences in social power between parties are minimal (as in a talk between two good friends), the dialogical process is reciprocal, that is, the parties involved are relatively free to ask questions of each other at any time in the exchange. In the situation of a legal inter-rogation, in which differences in power are strongly increased, questions and answers are highly uneven, with one party posing the questions and the other party forced to answer within the frame determined by the questioner as a representative of the institution. In similar ways, rela-tionships of agreement and disagreement are organized on the basis of institutional positions. In modern schools that aim to stimulate the per-sonal responsibility and creativity of the learners, pupils are permitted to disagree not only with their classmates but even with their teachers, pro-vided that these teachers regard such disagreements as signs of a creative, independent mind. In traditional, hierarchically organized educational settings, however, pupils are not permitted to disagree with teachers on any subject at all, as any disagreement is regarded as questioning the self-evident authority of teachers as the exclusive power-holders within the educational setting. As these examples suggest, societal institutions entail social positions that deeply influence or even inhibit the dialogical process in structural ways. When one of the parties is not allowed to play a role as an active and reciprocal contributor of the interchange, dialogue is reduced to monologue because one voice is in control of the situation at the expense of the active contribution of the other to a commonly produced result.

Social dominance and hierarchical organization of self

Monological processes can be observed when localizing forces reduce the multiplicity of voices of globalization in protective or defensive ways, as can be seen in the case of fundamentalist movements or orthodox reli-gions. In a study of Jewish orthodoxy, Kaufman (1991) was interested in women who grew up in secular Jewish homes in the United States and felt that the secular values of their education did not give them an adequate foundation for their lives. Despite the limitations that traditional beliefs place on women, they converted, in their teens or twenties, to orthodox Judaism. They did so in the conviction that an orthodox religious sys-tem offered them a meaningful place in the world and the experience of being rooted in a long, durable tradition. Placing Kaufman's study in the broader context of globalization, Arnett (2002) discussed the emer-gence of fundamentalist movements in both Western and non-Western societies and argued that many of these movements arose in the late 20th century as a reaction to the changes caused by globalization. Apparently, the upsurge of these movements can be regarded, for a considerable part, as localizing reactions to the process of globalization. They provide the self with a stabilized religious position that is based on a belief in a sacred past, a social hierarchy of authority of men over women, adults over children, and God over all (Arnett, 2002; Marty and Appleby, 1993).

In a similar vein, Kinnvall (2004) argues that the emergence of Bin Laden and al-Qaeda cannot be grasped without taking into account the extent to which many Arab countries pursued paths of modernization that were inspired by Western developments in the period soon after the Second World War. Initiated by the state, not by the people, such reforms were often rationalized by the conviction that the "modern" few were planning the future for the more "traditional" and less-educated segments of society. The uncertainty created by the problems and failures of such experiments motivated young people to revolt against these reforms and to seek refuge in older and more familiar concepts. In the case of Egypt, this led to identity constructions based on patriotism and religion, whereas Saudi Arabians tried to find certainty in ethnicism and Islamic guardianship (see also Ayubi, 1999; Haddad and Esposito, 1998). Also, Nandy (1997) has pointed to the destabilizing effects of the process of globalization and the tendency to withdraw into local niches. He observed that in recent years many expatriate South Asians in the West have become "more aggressively traditional, and more culturally exclusive and chauvinistic" and "more protective about what they think are their faiths and cultures" (p. 158). From a dialogical point of view, religious orthodoxy, the rise of fundamental movements, and the phenomenon of patriotism find their expression in collective voices that encourage a hierarchical organization of the position repertoire of the self and a reduction of the heterogeneity of positions with a simultaneous avoidance of internal disagreement, conflict, and uncertainty. The monological dominance of one voice or a few voices over the others leads to a reduction of the experience of uncertainty, but at the same time it has the questionable effect that other voices, as possible contributors or innovators of the self, are silenced or split off.

Recognition of social power in theories of self

For a deeper understanding of the process of globalization and its implications for self and identity, the notion of social power is indispensable. Contemporary theories of the self, with their strong emphasis on unity, often lack insight about the intense interplay between power relations in the society at large on the one hand and relations of dominance in the "minisociety" of the self on the other hand. In a review of the literature on the self, Callero (2003) listed a number of concepts representing the focus of mainstream psychology: self-enhancement, self-consistency, self-monitoring, self-efficacy, self-regulation, self-presentation, self-verification, self-knowledge, self-control, self-handicapping, and self-deception. In one of his critical comments on these concepts, he raised the issue of social power:

The self that is socially constructed is never a bounded quality of the individual or a simple expression of psychological characteristics; it is a fundamentally social phenomenon, where concepts, images, and understandings are deeply determined by relations of power. Where these principles are ignored or rejected, the self is often conceptualized as a vessel for storing all the particulars of the person. (Callero, 2003: 127; see also Sampson, 1985, who, from a social constructionist point of view, criticized the self-contained individualism as typical of many psychological theories of the self in the West.)

Because power differences and dominance fights are usually controversial issues, they require a more explicit psychology of emotion. Therefore, we discuss in the following section the role of emotions in relation to globalization, localization, and identity formation (for a more thorough analysis of emotions, see Chapter 5).

Emotional voices

Dialogical voices can be reasoned or emotional. They can argue, negotiate, and convince, but they can also shout, accuse, beg, regret, laugh, and cry, and express anger, joy, sympathy, love, fear, anxiety, hate, or disgust, to mention just a few ways in which people relate to their environment or to themselves. As Kemper (1978) suggested, a large class of human emotions results from real, imagined, anticipated, or recollected outcomes of social relationships (see also Averill, 1997; Parkinson, 1996; Sarbin, 1989; Shaver, Wu, and Schwartz, 1992). In the field of psychotherapy, Stiles (1999) has expressed the view that voices in the self are emotionally laden, have agent-like qualities, and are more or less integrated in the larger community of voices in the self. As these literatures suggest, a social psychological perspective of emotions can be helpful in understanding the ways in which people respond to the processes of globalization, localization, and identity formation.

Home and homesteading From a social psychological perspective, the emotional implications of globalization were presented by Kinnvall (2004), who argued that global changes have intensified "ontological insecurity" and "existential uncertainty." A primary way of responding to these experiences is to seek reaffirmation by drawing closer to any localized group that is seen as capable of reducing uncertainty and insecurity. In particular (institutionalized) religion and nationalism are identity markers in times of rapid change and uncertain futures. In more general terms, Kinnvall pointed to the significance of the notion of "home" as a bearer of certainty and security and as constituting a spatial context in which daily routines can be performed in rather stabilized circumstances. Whereas for many individuals feeling at home in a family, neighborhood, workplace, or religious group may be a self-evident part of their life situation, for other people, particularly immigrants, refugees, and those living in diaspora, homes have to be actively created. In this context, Kinnvall referred to the phenomenon of "homesteading" (see also Sylvester, 1994, and Kronsell, 2002) as a strategy for coping with homelessness. In new and uncertain circumstances, people shape a political space for themselves in order to cope with the uneasiness and anxieties of homelessness. This may motivate people to become members of an exile community (e.g., the Sikhs in Canada, the Pakistanis in Britain, or the Kurds in Sweden) and to create common places of assembly (e.g., gurdwaras, mosques, or Kurdish community halls). Certainly, the tendency to create homes when separated from one's homeland has been part of the (voluntary as well as forced) immigrant experience throughout history. However, the increasing global immigration gulfs have stimulated a process of homesteading on a larger scale than ever before.

To understand the process of globalization and its impact on identity, Kinnvall (2004) posed a significant question concerning the emotional aspects of the opposition between in-group and out-group. How can we comprehend why feelings of fear, loathing, and even hatred creep into "our" perceptions of "them," and how can we understand these emotions in times of uncertainty? To find an answer to these crucial questions, Kinnvall built on psychoanalytic accounts of identity and identity conflicts. Kristeva's (1982, 1991) psychoanalytic work is particularly relevant from a dialogical point of view.

Subject, object, and abject   A basic tenet in Kristeva's (1982, 1991) and Kinnvall's (2004) analyses is that the psychological roots of xenophobia, anti-immigrant discourses, racism, and the marginalization of others are to be found in "the enemy in ourselves," as the "hidden face of identity." It is an unconscious part of the self that has become internalized as an "enemy" in the past, fuelling our imagination in times of opposition or conflict. The important role of imagination can be illustrated by situations in which the enemy is perceived as threatening without actually being present. Anti-Semitism in Poland exists despite its relative lack of Jews, and sometimes stronger anti-immigrant feelings can be found in places with few or no immigrants than in places with a large number of immigrants. This combination of interiorization and imagination produces "another" that is perceived not as a subject, not as an object, but as an "abject." The other is rejected on emotional grounds and not considered an integrative part of the conscious self. This is done in the service of maintaining a secure identity: "The construction of an abject-other becomes a means to securitize subjectivity as it reduces anxiety and increases ontological security" (Kinnvall, 2004: 753; see also Appadurai, 1999, for a treatment of extreme violence as a response to the experience of uncertainty, and Moghaddam, 2005, who describes the circumstances in which young people living in economically deprived circumstances and frustrated by feelings of injustice, find a "home" by affiliating themselves with terrorist organizations where they learn to perceive non-believers as abject-others.)

In an attempt to study the abject-other in a psychotherapeutic context, Hermans and Hermans-Jansen (1995) examined a dream from a client in which two characters played central roles: an abjected murderer who was depicted as a threat to a village community and another character, the pursuer, who had the responsibility of defending the community against the murderer. As part of a dialogical procedure, the client, Paul, was invited to separately produce some utterances from the perspective of the two positions. Whereas the pursuer phrased socially acceptable statements (e.g., "I chase him to the pinnacles of the tower"), the murderer expressed his intention in the form of extremely crude statements (e.g., "I hate them, I kill them all"). In the discussion of the dream, Paul recognized himself clearly in the position of the pursuer and accepted this figure and his emotions as very close to the internal domain of his self. In contrast, Paul perceived the murderer as an enemy-other, and the murderer's aggression was regarded as totally external. After a closer inspection of the dream content, however, Paul found out that the pursuer possessed information that he earlier perceived only in the mind of the murderer. From that moment on, he had to admit to himself that the murderer and the associated emotions of hate and anger were also closely related to his internal self. This was reason for the therapist to invite the client to give, from his own position as Paul, an answer to the extreme statements and emotions of the murderer. He then produced some statements that suggested that he opened himself, to some degree, to the unwanted position: "The feelings that are associated with my experiences – I'm not very well aware of them"; and "There are a lot of situations in which I have harmed myself by not defending myself" (p. 135). The results of this investigation were interpreted in terms of the identity-in-difference phenomenon (Gregg, 1991). Whereas initially the unwanted position was clearly outside the internal domain of the self, at some later point in time this position stood somewhere in a transitional field where it was at the same time experienced as "belonging to myself" and "not belonging to myself." As this study suggests, the boundaries between the internal and external domains of the self are not necessarily sharp. Rather, it argues for the existence of a field of transition between internal and external, where an individual knows at some level of consciousness that the "bad guy" is part of the internal domain and at another level that this position is part of the external domain. Moreover, these results suggest the existence of a dynamic self that allows, under special conditions, the movement of an enemy-other from the external to the internal domains of the self. If this happens, there is a chance that the abject-other, rather than being silenced or excluded, becomes an accountable voice in the polyphony of the self (Hermans and Hermans-Jansen, 1995).

As this case study suggests, the inclusion of the enemy-other or the stranger-other is part of a self-construction that is built on the contrasting distinction between "superior" and "inferior." Positions that correspond with one's own national, religious, or ethnic group represent purity, order, truth, beauty, good, and right, whereas those on the outside are affected by pollution, falsity, ugliness, the bad, and the wrong (Kinnvall, 2004; Moghaddam, 2005). The problem of defensive forms of localization is that the permeability of the boundaries between internal and external domains of the self is closely linked to the exclusive opposition between the superior and the inferior. Permeability decreases when particular positions in the external domain are perceived as inferior.

Five strategies to cope with a heightened level of uncertainty   Given the central role of uncertainty in the present chapter, the question is how people respond to a heightened level of uncertainty so characteristic of a period of accelerated globalization. It seems "unliveable" to find oneself always and everywhere in situations of high uncertainty. Five ways of reducing uncertainty can be distinguished:

1. Uncertainty can be diminished by a *reduction of the number and heterogeneity of positions* in the repertoire. This reaction can be observed when people, who are fully engaged in societal life and even seem to enjoy it, retreat to a simple form of life or a quiet place to find peace of mind or recover an inner calm that they had long lost. Such a decision is often the result of a gradually increasing feeling of discomfort that may emerge in a period of doubts about the meaning of all the distracting activities in which one is usually involved. Sometimes this change comes quite suddenly and even unexpectedly. A background position comes to the foreground when the

self is in a state of, what James (1902/2004) would call, "unstable equilibrium": a particular position is "pressing" to become dominant but is not yet strong enough to take the lead. After some time the unstable equilibrium is suddenly resolved, often without strong external causation, by the breakthrough of the position that caused tension and discomfort during a period of inner turmoil. The change comes as a surprise to the environment and even to the person him- or herself. Life was filled with dissatisfaction but it did not reach a level of sharp awareness, suppressed as it was by an overdose of concerns, activities, and duties. Suddenly, as if an invisible hand is touching one's shoulder, a sudden "conversion" takes place, whereby hitherto neglected or suppressed positions come to the surface and lead to dramatic changes in one's life-style or circumstances.

2. Uncertainty can be reduced by *giving the lead to one powerful position* that is permitted to dominate the repertoire as a whole. When people are located in a field of divergent and contradictory positions where they have to give answers to a variety of complex situations, the transfer of responsibility to some authority, guru, strong leader, or "godfather" may be a way to reduce the burden of uncertainty when it has reached the level of negative feelings. This reaction can be seen in cases of religious orthodoxy or political fundamentalism as they thrive on simplification. It can also be noticed in the supporters of political parties that take an extreme and radical stance on issues of immigration and want to close national boundaries for newcomers. This reaction typically expresses a strong hierarchical organization of the repertoire, with one or a few positions at the top dominating all other positions.

However, it should be noted that many people may organize their lives around one or a limited amount of positions that are of great personal value to them. A person may find much satisfaction in an inspiring job situation that provides enough certainty to permit the development of long-term goals; he/she may be involved in a stable relationship that provides the deep certainty of mutual trust and commitment. In an essential respect, these situations are different from the examples in which people give the exclusive power to only one dominant position in their lives (e.g., religious fundamentalism). Whereas the latter case represents monological dominance, the former case refers to dialogical dominance. That is, in a stable and deep (dialogical) commitment to a person or task, there is space not only for agreement, but also for disagreement; not only for a supporting voice but also for a critical one. At the same time, there is space for input that corrects, complements, or further develops the position that has such a central place in the repertoire.

3. Uncertainty can be minimized by *sharpening the boundaries* between oneself and the other and between in-group and out-group, as we have already seen in the preceding discussion on the distinction between subject, object, and abject. Hall (1991) noticed that identity is a construction, which achieves its positive by the narrow eye of the negative and results in the production of a very Manichean set of opposites (e.g., "we" versus "they"). By sharpening the boundaries between in-group and out-group and by placing one's own group above the other group, an identity is constructed that augments positive positions and diminishes negative positions in an identity that is involved in the increase of self-esteem and pride ("We are not like them").

4. Paradoxically, some people try to reduce uncertainty by *adding instead of diminishing* the number of positions in the self. At first sight it seems odd to assume that uncertainty can be reduced by the increase of the number of positions that led to an increase of the individual's experience of uncertainty in the past! However, the reaction becomes comprehensible when one recognizes that the additional position is expected to give the solace, rest, structure, pleasure, or prospect that other positions lack. So, after a series of jobs, a person may have the expectation that a new job could give the "real" satisfaction that earlier jobs did not provide; the relationship with a new partner may give the stability and warmth that earlier contacts were in need of, and moving to another city, country, or even culture is expected to solve the uncertainties that pervaded daily life heretofore. In these cases new positions are expected to give a temporary hold in the otherwise fleeting and transitory position repertoire, open as it is to the over-stimulation of the globalizing environment. However, adding new positions to an already crowded repertoire entails the risk of a cacophony of voices.

5. The reaction to uncertainty that is central in the present book is a dialogical one. The special nature of dialogue is that it copes with uncertainty by *going into this uncertainty* rather than avoiding it. Entering a dialogue, with other individuals or with oneself, opens a range of possibilities that are not fixed at the beginning but remain flexible and susceptible to change during the process itself. During this open-ended and broadly ranged interchange, the initial positions of the participants are influenced or changed, marginally or radically, by the encounter itself. This process implies a

certain degree of complexity because every position, subjected to dialogue, is exposed to an ambiguous other (actual or imagined) with the simultaneous absence of a pre-existing and superordinate knowledge system that comprises a final answer. It is more or less unknown which positions will be developed or changed and which ones not. During the process of interchange, the positions that are relevant to a particular problem, including their needs, aims, and expectations, can be organized, reduced, and simplified; they also can be evaluated on their merit as contributing to problem solving. During the interchange some positions become more dominant than others, or different positions become combined and integrated in a new coalition that is experienced as common to the participants and functions as a centrepiece in creative decision making. This is what happens when one is relieved after a good meeting in which participants were able to listen to themselves and to the other and to provide a creative and workable problem solution. It is typical of a good talk between friends, colleagues, and acquaintances or of engaging meetings with new people, particularly when institutionalized power differences are not too large and participants are able to construct a common dialogical space in which they permit themselves to be influenced by the parties involved. It can also happen when your own mind gives you an answer to a problem after you were walking around with a question that you were not able to answer in a period of fruitless exploration. In other words, dialogue can be seen as a "travel into uncertainty" with the possibility of uncertainty-reducing outcomes. Whereas the dialogical reaction aims at post-dialogical certainty, the former ones strive for pre-dialogical forms of certainty. Learning to cope with uncertainty in dialogical ways is not something that is simply given, but it can be learned as part of developing a dialogical self (Chapter 4) that achieves an adequate way of dealing with emotions (Chapter 5).

The five reactions to uncertainty described above can take place in the life of one and the same individual. At times, we want to retreat from our daily business and become engaged in forms of meditation in order to empty our minds; or we come temporarily under the spell of a guru who promises us a life free from stress and the burden of uncertainties; or we feel opposed to all the information, advertisements, and people that are continuously intruding into our daily lives; or we feel attracted to a new job or relationship that seems to solve the problems of the past; or we find ourselves engaged in an interchange that is felt to be both confusing and inspiring at the same time.

On the mutual complementarity of the social and the biological

In the second part of this chapter, we want to argue that the dialogical self, open and unfinalizable as it may be in its potentials, is actually constrained from two sides. *Biological* factors put limits on the unlimited range of possible dialogical interactions in which the individual could become immersed. Biological and evolutionary needs for safety and security prevent individuals from engaging in an endless array of positions and from entirely "freeing" themselves from any attachment to their homes, homelands, and the traditions and rituals of their in-groups to which they feel a sense of belongingness. At the same time, the self is also constrained from a *social* point of view. Societies do not tolerate an unlimited expression of desires, wishes, dreams, and aspirations, which an individual as a representative of a particular age, race, class or religion may have. Social and societal rules and restrictions form and limit the position repertoire and its expression in behavior. There are two problem areas that are particularly central to our argument and, at the same time, challenge us to consider the relationship between the biological and social aspects of the self: (i) the issue of stability in a changing world and (ii) the social nature of emotions.

Biologically based need for stability in a changing world

In a thorough analysis, Falmagne (2004) argued for the necessity of establishing a "site" in the self that remains continuous and sufficiently stable through moments of dialogical and discursive meaning construction. Conceptually, the self remains the same through the different ways in which it is dialogically constructed and through the experiential and contextual ways in which it moves through time and space. It can be observed, from a conceptual point of view as well as from an empirical perspective, that the self is involved in rapid movement and change, as part of the globalizing process, but at the same time there is a deep need for local stability. Stability and change do not exclude each other but coexist as simultaneous processes in the self, as extensively discussed by Chandler *et al.* (2003).

The apparent need for stability raises the important question of whether a substantial self exists or not. As Falmagne (2004) explained, some social-constructionist conceptions of the self have led to the radical rejection of a substantial self and resulted in a shift toward a non-substantial, fluid notion of subjectivity. Because in these views the center of the self "does not hold," its different parts are decentralized to such a degree that the self becomes scattered and loses its coherence (see, e.g., Gergen's [1991] notion of "multiphrenia"). Apparently, for some social constructionist accounts, non-homogeneity and contingency in discursive positioning are taken as reasons to reject the self as a theoretical notion. In contrast to these views, we argue – in agreement with Falmagne – for a substantial embodied self that includes multiplicity, heterogeneity, contradiction, and tension. We see such phenomena not as an impasse for a theoretical notion of the self, but as intrinsic aspects that are "owned" by an embodied self. Like the experience of uncertainty, fluidity and contradictions are regarded as intrinsic features of a dialogical self in a globalizing world. A theory is needed that is able to explain the mechanisms by which individuals, as agentic subjects, do or do not identify with positions to which they are summoned through dialogical or discursive relationships. Part of this identification is how individuals fashion, stylize, and personalize the positions they occupy as participating in global and local situations (Falmagne, 2004; Hall, 1996). In this view, the self is not only a social but also a personal construction. Two or more voices in the self can construct a personal space as a productive field for inner dialogues and for the authentic construction of meaning. This field functions as an original source of meaning construction that contributes to the further development of social and societal processes. The self is not just a product of social and societal relationships but is substantial and agentic enough to contribute to these relationships from its own original point of view (Salgado and Hermans, 2005).

Apparently, people are in need of an environment stable enough to feel at home and to experience a feeling of security and safety in a quickly changing world. Moreover, people tend to respond with anxiety, anger, hate, loathing, or disgust when they feel threatened in their need for protection and local security. Such observations require that a psychology of emotions be included as part of the processes of globalization and localization. As Kinnvall (2004) has noted, reducing emotions to present social relations in society would neglect the deeply rooted need for safety and stability in one's life circumstances, strongly emphasized by object relations theorists (e.g., Winnicott, 1964).

Referring to the important role of emotions for survival, evolutionary psychologists (Buss, 1995), psychoanalysts (Lichtenberg, Lachman, and Fosshage, 1992), and cognitivists (Gilbert, 1989) have presented evidence that human behavior can be understood as driven by a set of evolutionary-based motives that grant survival and fitness both to the individual and to the group (in competition, cooperation, sexuality, and fight–flight). When these motives are at risk of not being fulfilled, emotions arise and are expressed in behavior that signals the corresponding states of mind (e.g., shouting and crying by children in situations of threat). In the course of life, a large percentage of self-narratives, populated by a number of characters representing a variety of internal and external self-positions, are built around these universal, transcultural, biological motives.[9] People are motivated to construct narratives centered on themes that help them deal with fundamental life issues while sharing these narratives with others (McAdams, 2006; Salvatore, Dimaggio, and Semerari, 2004). A significant implication of this view is that some positions or voices in the self become exclusively important and, particularly in situations of anxiety and threat, they receive priority above other voices on emotional grounds, moving the self in a monological direction. At the interface of the social and the biological, we witness a paradoxical situation: Whereas globalization has the potential to increase the density and heterogeneity of positions of the self in unprecedented ways, it evokes, under certain conditions, defensive forms of localization that are driven by deeply rooted biological needs that cause a considerable reduction and restriction of positions in the repertoire of the self.

A Pakistani family   In the field of tension between social-historical developments and biological urgency, the dialogical self is particularly challenged. Let's illustrate this with an example of a Pakistani family living in England. The family is traditionalist and deeply affected by the fact they are not accepted for what they are by the dominant communities in the host country. The collective voice of the out-group community is critical and urges them to change. From the other side, there is an inner voice, deeply rooted in the collective voices of their original culture, that presses them to stay faithful to their origins. This traditional voice is empowered by the myths, stories, and autobiographical memories associated with their attachment history. So they must find a way to negotiate between their wish to be accepted by the host culture, which stands in hard opposition to their original culture, and their adherence to their original culture, which, as an embodied reality of their selves, they cannot renounce. Located in this field of tension, they are forced to negotiate among the several contrasting voices to find a dialogical solution.

Tensions between voices representing original and host cultures are certainly not unique to the situation of globalization. What the example illustrates, however, is that the process of globalization creates new and intensified fields of tensions between global and local positions, with strong differences, conflicts, and oppositions between voices, which require dialogical interchanges both between and within different selves to arrive at workable solutions. Surely, the demands and opportunities of globalization are broadening the range of differing, opposing, and conflicting voices and may lead, along these lines, to an increasing discontinuity and incoherence of the self. However, biological survival needs work as a restricting and even opposing force on these demands and possibilities. Biological needs, particularly if frustrated, restrict the position repertoire, because they have a strong urgency, are associated with a high degree of tension, and have a tendency to dominate the repertoire as a whole.

The "dialogical brain"   Further arguments for the need of the mutual complementation of social and biological conceptions of self and identity can be derived from brain research relevant to the dialogical self. Lewis (2002), proposing the notion of a dialogical brain, questioned the idea of unlimited flexibility within the dialogical self and emphasized the apparent need of people to return to "ordinary positions" in their lives. Lewis based this insight on a study of the workings of the orbitofrontal cortex, a region at the base of the frontal lobe that is tuned to rewards and punishments in social relationships. By its dense connections with the amygdala, a structure primarily responsible for fear, anxiety, and some kinds of anger, the orbitofrontal cortex favors emotionally based monological responses rather than flexible dialogical movements. The tendency to seek, often in automatic ways, for routine or standardized positions raises the question of whether a dialogical self, which assumes the existence of a variegated and flexible position repertoire, is possible.

In an attempt to answer this question, Lewis (2002) analyzed automatic phrases such as "That was stupid" or "You are dumb" that the person (or an imagined other) is saying, in passing and almost not heard, to him- or herself during the performance of a task. In these examples, there is no clear-cut other voice and there is not much turn-taking or an explicit sequence of question and answer. Instead, internal activity is sublingual and inchoate, and there is not much elaboration and development of a dialogue with another voice. In this case, the person automatically operates from a familiar *I*-position and continuously returns to situations in which this position can be reached. On this sublingual and inchoate level, we are more conservative and monological than innovative and dialogical. In keeping with dialogical self theory, Lewis concluded that in our daily lives we are involved in a relation with an anticipated, almost-heard other from the perspective of a familiar and continuous *I*-position. As part of the external domain of the self, such a position produces statements like "good!" "too bad!" and "stupid!" or more complex utterances such as, "You see, this leads to nothing, as always!" or "You are not able to achieve anything, whatever you do!" Lewis supposed that these utterances come from voices of significant others in the remote past whose positions are incorporated as stabilized parts into the external domain of the self.

Similarly, in a discussion of the orbitofrontal area in the brain, Schore (1994) pointed to the existence of repetitive neural mechanisms in the development of the dialogical self. He described the emergent capacity of the growing brain to switch adaptively between psychobiological states that are colored by different affects. When children develop a dialogical self, they are increasingly able to transcend an immediate negative state (e.g., distress) and enhance "self-solace" capacities that help them to make a transition between the two states when the mother is not present ("Mommy is away, but she will come back"). As Schore explained, the child develops the capacity to make transitions from negative to positive affective states of mind and realizes, in recurring ways, an adaptation of the self to a problematic situation. This adaptation is seriously reduced in forms of insecure attachment. As this research suggests, the experience of insecurity reduces the self's capacity to make the transition from a negative to a positive position. This reduction impoverishes the variation of the position repertoire and flexible movements between different voices. As discussed earlier in this chapter, the lack of flexibility associated with strong negative emotions is a central problem in defensive forms of localization.

Both Lewis's (2002) and Schore's (1994) work is focused on the orbito-frontal cortex, which produces, in its linkage to the subcortical limbic system, an affectively charged, fuzzy sense of an interpersonal respond-ent, based on stabilized expectancies from many past interactions. Both models have the advantage in that they show how relatively stable, sub-lingual voices and recurrent routines put limits on the flexibility of dia-logical processes. These limits are not to be evaluated necessarily as a disadvantage because they may contribute, when adaptive enough, to our action readiness and behavioral efficiency.

Basic needs as reducing the openness of the dialogical self   In the tradition of Bakhtinian dialogism, it is commonplace to emphasize the openness and unfinalizability of the notion of dialogue (e.g., Holquist, 1990). The difference between logical and dialogical relationships may serve as an example of the open nature of dialogue.

Take two phrases that are identical: "life is good" and again "life is good" (Vasil'eva, 1988). From the perspective of Aristotelian logic, these two phrases are related in terms of identity; they are, in fact, one and the same statement. From a dialogical perspective, however, they may be seen as two remarks expressed by the voices of two *spatially* separated people in com-munication, who in this case entertain a relationship of agreement. Here we have two phrases that are identical from a logical point of view, but different as utterances: The first is a statement, the second a confirmation. In a similar way, the phrases "life is good" and "life is not good" can be compared. In terms of logic, one is a negation of the other. However, as utterances from two different speakers, a dialogical relation of disagreement exists.

In principle, dialogical relationships are open and move toward an unknown future. Every speech act opens a dialogical space (Hermans, 2001a) that allows a range of possible statements or opinions in the future, and at every step in the process the next step is largely unpredictable. Logical relationships, however, are closed, in so far as they do not permit any conclusion beyond the limits of the rules that govern the relationship. A syllogism, for example, starts from a set of premises and leads, through a number of logical steps, to a conclusion that is necessarily true, rejecting any other possibility. In apparent contrast to a dialogical relationship, nothing is left to be said, nor is an opening created to the domain of the unexpected.

However, the question can be raised as to whether dialogical relationships are as open as suggested by Bakhtinian dialogism. An everyday example may illustrate that dialogues are highly restricted by vested interests and emotional affinities. Two people, A and B, start a discussion, exchanging a variety of experiences in a casual way. At a certain point, A expresses an opinion with which B disagrees. For his part, B expresses a counter-opinion that is not compatible with A's point of view. In the case of an open dialogue, one would expect that the two discussion partners would exchange their opinions and develop them in such a way that they learn from each other and revise their initial position in light of the input they have received from the partner.

However, this is not what can be observed in many, perhaps even most, cases of disagreement. As soon as the discussion partners notice that the other party disagrees, they feel that their opinion, in which they have invested part of their identity ("This is *my* opinion"; "This is the way *I* see it"), is at stake, and from that moment they are motivated to "defend" their position against that of their opponent. Given this motivation, they repeat or paraphrase their initial point of view in an attempt to "protect" it against the "undermining" statements from the other. Gradually, the discussion assumes a competitive character, and both partners try to strengthen their own position to make it dominant over the position of the other party. Owing to this repetition and striving for dominance, the openness of the dialogue is seriously reduced and moves to the monological end of the continuum.

As the notion "continuum" suggests, we conceive of dialogue and monologue not in terms of a dichotomy but as a scale with different gradations. Although dialogue and monologue can be described – at the level of meaning – as qualitatively different (the meaning of creative interchange is different from the meaning of being closed up in fixed and inflexible positions), they can be considered, from an analytical point of view, as representing different degrees on a continuum. Suppose two people are involved in an interchange and both of them (a) try to dominate the discussion; (b) are not aware of possible misunderstandings that are slipping through; (c) do not allow themselves to learn from the preceding interchange. In doing so, one or both of them move the relationship to the monological end of the continuum. On the contrary, the relationship is on the dialogical end of the continuum when the participants (a) give each other the chance to bring in their own experiences and point of view; (b) are aware of misunderstandings and able and willing to correct them; and (c) learn from each other during the interchange (e.g., they arrive at a new, shared insight or experience or are able to articulate, recognize, and even respect their differences).[10] There are, however, situations when an interchange can be described as a *mixture* of both dialogical and monological elements. For example, person A listens very well to the other party and develops parts of his initial point of view on the basis of the preceding interchange and shares this with person B. However, in the same discussion, person A neglects or even negates other elements emerging from the interchange that are of significance to person B, who then feels understood at some points but misunderstood at others.

The fact that people exchange opinions in a discussion is no guarantee of an open and innovative dialogue. In case of disagreement they often defend their point of view against the opinion of the other, and in case of agreement they use the opinion of the other party as a means to further corroborate or even expand their initial viewpoint. In a globalizing environment, people are confronted with myriad opinions and ideologies that are different from those that they have learned in their local environments. When these views are experienced as threatening or undermining their local point of view, they are motivated to defend their local positions, often in emotional ways. In general terms, persistent defense, protection, and conservation of existing local practices and values restrict the range of possible positions in the self and the openness and innovative potential of dialogue.

Social nature of emotions

In the preceding section, we emphasized the apparent need for stability, safety, and self-maintenance and have argued that these basic motives restrict the range of the position repertoire and the openness of the dialogical self. We drew on some literatures from biology and the neurosciences to underline the emotionally tuned need for stability. Does this mean that we propose an essentializing view of emotion? Or are we advocating making physiological the emotional basis of the self? The answer is a clear no. From a dialogical point of view, emotions are not isolated things and not just internal physiological processes. A dialogical view of self and identity in a globalizing world is in need of theories of emotions that are intrinsically social and societal. To underscore this view, we present in the following sections three significant concepts: emotion work, emotion rules, and emotional positions.

Emotion work and the power of expectations   Our treatment of the role of neural connections (e.g., the dialogical brain) in the genesis and development of emotions, and our discussion of evolutionary-based needs (e.g., safety, self-defense, and self-enhancement), do not claim that emotions have no significant social and societal context. Our purpose is not to downplay the role of social factors in the field of emotion theory, but rather to bring biological and social factors together as interconnected elements of a dialogical approach (see also Blackman, 2005).

A concept that links emotions to social positions is the notion of "emotion work." Emotions are not things in themselves or purely internal processes, but parts of a highly dynamic social and societal process of positioning. Depending on the positions in which people find themselves, particular emotions are *expected* to emerge in a particular situation, whereas other emotions are expected to be absent or suppressed. Under the influence of position-bound expectations, some emotions are tolerated, accepted, emphasized, exaggerated, or denied, whereas others are not. In an extensive treatise on the management of emotions, Hochschild (1983) gave the following examples: A secretary creates a cheerful office that announces her company as friendly; the waiter fashions an atmosphere for pleasant dining; a tour guide makes us feel welcome; the social worker makes the client feel cared for; the funeral parlor director makes those who are bereaved feel understood; and the minister creates a sense of protective outreach. Such emotion work is typical not only of social positions that are organized on the basis of social or societal expectations but also of expectations or requirements of a more personal nature. People act on their emotions when they are trying to feel grateful, trying not to feel depressed, let themselves feel sad, permit themselves to enjoy something, imaginatively exalt their feelings of love, or put a damper on their love. In all those cases, emotions are conceived of not as purely internal impulses that have an existence on their own or as purely physiological reactions that take place within the skin, but as integral parts of an agentic process of social or personal positioning. Depending on the positions and the dialogical spaces in which they find themselves, people act on their emotions, under the influence of position-bound expectations and requirements (e.g., "As a rich guy who has everything he wants, I expect myself to be happy").

Sometimes emotion work becomes a struggle of the person with him- or herself. In a moving excerpt, Hochschild (1983: 44) described a woman who fell in love with the "wrong guy." Although in love, she discovered that he had regularly broken off relationships with his many former girlfriends after only a short time:

> I attempted to change my feelings. I talked myself into not caring about him … but I admit it didn't work for long. To sustain this feeling I had to invent bad things about him and concentrate on them or continue to tell myself he didn't care. It was a hardening of emotions, I'd say. It took a lot of work and was unpleasant because I had to concentrate on anything I could find that was irritating about him.

Apparently, this person found herself in two different positions in clear conflict, "I'm in love" and "I must protect myself." As part of this conflict, she became involved in internal struggles in which she tried to change her feelings of love in the service of self-protection. Fighting against herself, she aimed at a "dominance reversal" (Hermans, 1996b) in which the self-protecting forces would become stronger than her feelings of love.

Emotion rules and emotional positions   Emotion work takes place under the guidance of emotion rules. Such rules are standards used in internal and external dialogues to determine what it is right or wrong to feel. Emotion rules serve as standards that tell us what is "due" in a particular social or personal position. From a social constructionist view of emotions, Averill (1997) has argued that the rules of emotion help to establish a corresponding set of emotional roles or, in our terms, "emotional positions" (for elaboration see Chapter 5). An emotional position can be analyzed in terms of privileges, restrictions, obligations, and entrance requirements. There is a *privilege* when, for example, a person in love may engage in sexual behavior that otherwise may be viewed as socially inappropriate. *Restrictions* refer to limits on what a person can do when acting under emotion. For example, lovers are expected to be discrete and honorable in their affairs. Whereas restrictions forbid a person to feel and do particular things, *obligations* instruct the person what should be felt or done. For example, in many societies those who are bereaved are expected to perform particular mourning practices. An individual who fails to comply with these expectations is often subject to severe sanction. Finally, most social positions have *entry requirements*, that is, they can be occupied only by persons of a certain age, sex, training, or social status. This also applies to emotional positions. For example, persons higher in authority (e.g., parents) are afforded more right to become angry than persons lower in authority (e.g., children) (Averill, 1997).

Implications for globalization, localization, and self

In the preceding sections, we have discussed some neurologically and biologically based literatures that deal with the emotionally based tendency to return to ordinary, familiar, and self-protecting positions and to engage in repetitive routines. In addition, we presented research that refers to the social and societal nature of emotions. Both streams of literature have in common that they put constraints on the openness of dialogical relationship and the range of possible positions. Moreover, evolutionary-based motives that grant survival and fitness and the need for safety, protection, and stability lead to establishing a set of positions that create a split between in-group and out-group in the service of confirming the identities of individuals and groups. The neurologically based tendency to return to ordinary and familiar positions and the existence of repetitive routines have the advantage that people can use an economical set of stereotypical or abbreviated dialogues (Lyra, 1999) or "almost dialogues" (Lewis, 2002), but they do not permit the individual to move easily beyond the constraints of traditional or familiar interactions. The socially based emotion rules, on the other hand, help individuals and groups to interact in ways that are shared and appreciated by the community to which they belong, but they restrict the range of positions and limit the openness of dialogical relationships with people outside the community. What are the implications of these insights for the processes of globalization and localization?

Emotion rules and globalization   Contemporary social scientists are confronted with a situation in which privileges, obligations, restrictions, and entry requirements typical of emotion management in a particular society are basically challenged by the process of globalization. Emotion rules about love, anger, or grief are typically limited to a particular group, community, or culture, but they can be very different in different cultures. Such rules organize and regulate interactions between people within a particular community that are accepted as belonging to the culture to which one belongs, but that may be strange, unfamiliar, or even offensive to people from another community (e.g., the rage of many Muslims over the portrayal of Mohammed in Danish cartoons published in a Western liberal democracy with its strong preference for freedom of expression). In the contemporary world, each individual is increasingly confronted with the emotion rules from different communities in which the individual participates as a member of a globalizing society. The result is an increasing sense of uncertainty, particularly in situations where there are different sets of rules and where it is not clear which set has priority. An example may illustrate this.

American gay tourist Chris Crain was walking hand in hand with his male friend in Amsterdam at the festival of the birthday of the Queen of the Netherlands in 2005. Suddenly, he was spat on by a passing man, who was raised in a Moroccan culture but lived in the Netherlands. When the victim objected, he was knocked down. This event, reported and discussed in the Dutch newspapers (and in some American media), happened in a city that, for many decades, has been known as the most gay-friendly city in the world. However, in the past decades, the Netherlands has become populated by immigrants from an increasing variety of different cultures (e.g., Turks, Moroccans, and Surinamese) and has become a multi-cultural society. As a result of this process, the emotion rules concerning gay love that were accepted by large parts of the Dutch community in earlier times are now highly controversial in the eyes of some cultural groups of the "same" country.

The accelerating process of globalization requires increasing amounts of emotion work. When emotion work is required and organized by one position (e.g., the flight attendant being friendly, the minister being protective, the funeral director understanding those who are bereaved), it does not imply an excessive amount of emotion work as long as these social roles are felt as "ordinary positions" (Lewis, 2002) by the person in charge. Emotion work may even take place in automatic ways when performed in usual circumstances and when it is part of one's daily routines. However, in the case of different, conflicting, or opposing positions a significantly greater amount of work is required. A simple example may illustrate this.

On one of his travels, a German man falls in love with a woman from Cuba. She reciprocates his love, and they decide to marry and begin living in Germany. However, while he goes to work each day, she regularly phones her family members in Cuba to whom she feels strongly attached and tells them how much she misses them. She is in love with her German husband, but does not like the German setting (no work for her, cold climate, lack of music and street dancing). Although she is not happy in Germany, she is convinced of her love for her husband and is doing her best to be a good partner to him (happy, active, and caring). After some time, however, she gets depressed and has to admit that she can no longer stay in Germany. Her husband takes leave from his work and goes with her to Cuba. However, after some weeks he has to return because of work obligations in his own country. Finally, the couple decides to live separately, and eventually they divorce. In this example, the woman feels herself in a field of tension between at least two conflicting positions: "I as loving my husband" and "I as loving my own family and country." Torn between two strongly attractive positions, she vacillates and must convince herself that she loves her husband, particularly at those moments in which she most wants to return to her homeland. In general terms, the process of globalization locates individuals and groups in fields of tensions between different cultural positions. Each of these positions represents a different or even conflicting cultural voice that requires multi-voiced emotion work, with one voice speaking in ways that are different from and even opposed to how the other voice speaks. Such multi-voiced emotion work coexists with intensified internal and external dialogues that aim at the reduction of tensions.

In the preceding sections, we discussed two groups of factors that are considered highly relevant to the processes of globalization and localization: neural and biological factors and social and cultural factors. We have argued that both groups of factors restrict the openness of self and the range of the position repertoire. We discussed the tendency of the brain to return to ordinary and familiar positions; the pervasive influence of the need for safety, protection, and stability; and the role of biological survival needs as they organize the self and restrict its boundaries, particularly in times of globalization and increasing uncertainty. We also discussed social-cultural factors in terms of emotion work and emotion rules and explored how they are influenced by the process of globalization. On the basis of these insights, we propose a model for the organization of the dialogical self in the context of globalization and localization.

Globalization, localization and the organization of the extended self The implications of the preceding considerations for self and identity are summarized in Figure 1.1. In agreement with James (1890) and Jung (1959), the self can be depicted as a circle. In line with the conception of the self as extended, it can be represented by two (open) *circles*, the inner one symbolizing the internal domain and the outer one the external (extended) domain. At the same time the self is open to the deep influences of globalizing forces. These influences are represented by the *straight lines* demarcating a number of "global landscapes" that can be seen as variations on a proposal of Appadurai (1990), who considered the simultaneous processes of globalization and deterritorialization. This requires a brief explanation.

Appadurai (1990) distinguished between a variety of categories of global landscapes: ethnoscapes (immigrants, tourists, refugees, guest workers, exiles); mediascapes (newspapers, television stations, film production studios); technoscapes (global configuration of technology, both mechanical and informational); financescapes (currency markets, stock exchanges, commodity speculations); and ideoscapes (ideology of states and counter-ideologies of movements; ideas about freedom, rights, welfare). Whereas in traditional homogeneous societies, technology, ideology, and media communication are to some degree integrated, they are widely separated and disjunctive in contemporary societies. For example, a disjuncture between mediascapes and ideoscapes can be seen in many countries in the Middle East and Asia where the lifestyles presented on national and international TV and cinema undermine the rhetoric of national politics. In Appadurai's (1990) analyses the globalscapes create new contact zones across national groups and cultures leading to their deterritorialization, which he considers one of the central developments in contemporary society. The notion of deterritorialization applies to each of the scapes. For example, it brings laboring populations from abroad into the lower-class sectors of relatively wealthy societies. At the same time many of these groups are involved in intensive media communication with their homelands, often leading to criticisms or attachments to the politics of their country of origin. In this way the scapes create transnational contact zones of a global kind, running across a great diversity of cultures and transforming their locality into translocality. This translocality, together with increasing globalization and complexity, implies a far-reaching deterritorialization and diversification of culture.

In agreement with the global–local dialectics, as discussed earlier in the present chapter, self and identity are subjected not only to globalizing (deterritorializing) but also to localizing influences. Both types of influence establish positions in the self that are related to each other in dialogical or monological ways: global positions (non-italics in Figure 1.1) receive reactions from local positions (italics in Figure 1.1) and vice versa. They give meaning to each other and one can become more dominant and laden with more power than the other. The examples in Figure 1.1 can be read in the form of "but-sentences" representing relationship between contrasting *I*-positions. In the ecoscape (economic scape) a person might say: "I'm used to buying English-language books from Amazon.com, but I'm also interested in buying books written in the dialect of the region in which I was brought up." In this sentence "I as a buyer of Amazon books" represents the globalizing influence in the internal domain of the self, whereas Amazon.com refers to the external (extended) domain of

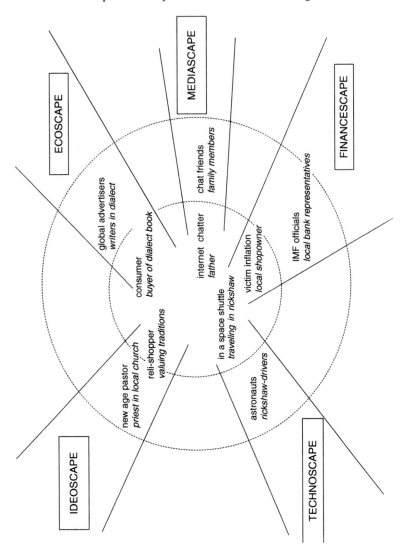

Figure 1.1 Scape model with global positions and their local
counter-positions

the self. Correspondingly, the position "I as a reader of books in dialect"
refers to the localizing influence in the internal domain, whereas writers
in dialect belong to the external domain.

In similar ways, the positions in other scapes can be read. For example,
as involved in the mediascape I can say: "As a user of the internet I'm a

member of a chat-room where I can talk to many people whom I have never met physically, but I also like to have good contact with my family members." Or, in the ideoscape: "I like to listen to that new-age pastor and I'm reading his book, but I'm also used to visiting my local church in order to participate in the rituals of my past."

The circles and straight lines indicate different movements in the self. The circles refer to *centering* movements in the self: as expressed by these movements the self aims at unity, coherence, and continuity. The straight lines refer to *decentering* movements in the self which reflect its multiplicity, discontinuity, and diversification. Both movements are indispensable for the understanding of the self in an interconnected world society and they can be seen as complementing each other. Together, they construct the self as unity-in-multiplicity or multiplicity-in-unity. The model in Figure 1.1 can be seen as a contemporary and transformed version of the classic notion of *unitas multiplex* as proposed by critical personalism (Stern, 1924; see also Hermans, 2000).

As already discussed, the self can be conceptualized in terms of a dynamic multiplicity of *I*-positions in the landscape of the mind (Hermans, Kempen, and Van Loon, 1992). In Figure 1.1 this landscape is expressed in terms of global landscapes, indicating that the landscape of the mind as a "society of mind" is never a self-contained unity, but is constantly subjected to the opposing forces of globalization and localization. The corresponding movements, centering and decentering, impel the self in opposite directions. When the decentering movements dominate over the centering ones, the self becomes discontinuous, fleeting, and fragmented; when the centering movements dominate over the decentering ones, the self becomes stabilized, with the risk of closing itself off from innovative impulses. In a sense, the dialogical self can be seen as a pendulum swinging between the decentering movements of globalization and the centering movements of localization. (What these basic movements imply for the deeper, personal levels of the self, will be discussed in Chapter 3.)

The fact that global landscapes are described as disjunct by global systems theorists might not suggest that they are entirely dissociated in the realms of the self. Given the centering movements of the self (the circles), positions and their associated practices, aims, and expectations, originating from different scapes (straight lines), can be brought together in the form of *coalitions*. For example, people living in diaspora in different parts of the world, can easily buy products from their homeland (ecoscape), distributed as they are over the world, and discuss their quality via the internet (mediascape). Or, under the influence of television programs (mediascape), people become interested in the possibilities of neurofeedback (technoscape), and use this as a way to deepen their spiritual experiences (ideoscape). As these examples suggest, elements of global landscapes that are disjunct and decentering by their nature can, at times, become linked and even brought together by the centering forces of self and identity.

In the following sections, we continue our exploration by resuming the three issues that were central to the first part of the article: the other as extension of the self, the role of social dominance and power, and the significance of emotions. We argue that the three concepts (the other, dominance, and emotion) require a linkage between three levels of analysis: global, local, and individual. By distinguishing these levels, we want to integrate the insights that emerged from the exploration of the biological and the social domains of inquiry.

A three-level proposal: global, local, individual   In the theoretical framework we present, we have analyzed self and identity at three levels: the global level, the local level, and the individual level. We have done so in the conviction that the process of globalization, which forms and changes the lives of an increasing number of people in the world, requires theoretical approaches that overcome any self-contained individualism. As we have argued, globalization is not to be equated with homogeneity, uniformity, or cultural imperialism, but can only properly be understood in its dialectical relation with localization, leading to the acknowledgment of heterogeneity, difference, and cultural diversity. To create a link between the level of the self and the levels of globalization and localization, we discussed the self as being extended to the social environment, a conception that has played a central role in both theoretical and empirical traditions in psychology (e.g., Aron *et al.*, 2005; James, 1890; Rosenberg, 1979). We argued that, in the present era, self and identity can only be properly understood as being extended to the global and local environment and as being formed and transformed by processes on these levels. An important implication of the self as globally extended is the experience of uncertainty that is pervasively present in the selves of people of our world today.

The self as dialogically extended

We propose to conceptualize the self not only as extended to the world, but also, and more specifically, as *dialogically* extended to the world, because we believe that a globalizing world can only be a liveable-in world when dialogical relationships play a central role in the relationships between individuals and between groups. One of the main tenets of this chapter is that our world can only become more dialogical when the self is becoming dialogical as well. The self as a society is not separate from society at large.

The other as self-extension serves as a first link between the three levels. Given the basic extension of the self to the world, we argued that the other is not simply outside the self but rather a constitutive part of the self, in terms of a multiplicity of voices emerging from global–local dialectics. In the field of psychoanalysis, object relations theorists (e.g., Guntrip, 1971; Winnicott, 1964) have made important contributions to understanding the role of the other as interiorized parts of the self. In an era of increased globalization, however, the number and nature of voices in the self have been expanded dramatically, and we are increasingly involved in mediated forms of dialogue: In contrast to earlier times, dialogical relationships make use of technological advances such as the internet, e-mail, mobile telephones, multi-user dimensions, and short-message systems that expand our dialogical possibilities beyond the boundaries of self and identity as described in traditional theories (Annese, 2004; Cortini, Minnini, and Manuti, 2004; Hermans, 2004; Hevern, 2004; Ligorio and Pugliese, 2004; Van Halen and Janssen, 2004). As we have discussed, globalization in particular increases the number of individual and collective voices and their mutual relationships dramatically, whereas localization aims more at the stabilization and even limitation of voices in the dialogical field. Particularly when localizing tendencies function as exclusive identity markers (e.g., one's own nation or religion as opposed to and above other nations or religions), the localizing voices move the self to the monological end of the continuum between dialogue and monologue. On the global–local interface, we see two risks: One is the monological domination by only one voice (e.g., nationalism, fundamentalism, sexism, or terrorism); another is the disorganized and chaotic cacophony of voices (e.g., identity confusion, or adding extra positions to an already crowded repertoire). Taking these risks into account, individuals and groups in our time are placed in fields of tension between globalizing and localizing forces. In these fields, they are challenged to make creative use of the experience of uncertainty and to open and close themselves according to their own needs and the possibilities offered by their situation.

Institutionalized power and dominance

The notions of power and dominance also point to the necessity of a linkage between the three levels. Because social power relations are intrinsic features of the society at large, they are also characteristic of the functioning of the self as a mini-society (Gillespie, 2005; Tappan, 2005). Therefore, power and dominance relationships suggest the existence of linkages between the levels of the individual, the local, and the global. It should be emphasized that social power and dominance are not to be regarded as necessarily positive or negative from an evaluative point of view. In the present theoretical context, relative dominance is considered an intrinsic aspect of a well-ordered dialogical relationship (turn-taking). Relations of power and dominance, however, become problematic when institutional and societal structures and ideologies prevent individuals and groups from expressing their voices from their own particular points of view and on the basis of their own specific sources of experience. As we suggested earlier, social power and dominance are important reactions to an experience of heightened uncertainty as it results in protective or defensive forms of localization. Such localizations tend to sharpen and essentialize the differences between in-group and out-group, and between self and other, with one's own group and self defined as superior and the other group and self defined as inferior. The consequence is that particular positions in society (e.g., jobs, responsibilities, privileges) remain inaccessible to particular individuals or groups and result in a forced restriction of their position repertoire (Hong and Chiu, 2001). (For the role of social power in relation to gender, race, and class, see Falmagne, 2004; for a discussion of the self in the context of racialization and diaspora from a dialogical point of view, see Bhatia, 2002; Bhatia and Ram, 2001.)

Emotion and defensive localization

The third linking concept, emotion, is a necessary element in the dialogical self because, particularly in the context of defensive localization, voices can express indignation, anger, and even hate, and such emotions often lead to uncontrollable escalation (Valsiner, 2002) of violence and destruction on a societal level (Appadurai, 1999). It should be noted that it is not our intention to restrict the psychological reactions to globalization to negatively experienced emotions only. On the contrary, the loosening of boundaries between cultures, groups, and traditions, and the global interchange of (local) goods, practices, and ideas may be a source of positive emotions. In this chapter, we have emphasized negative emotions as they are characteristic of protective or defensive forms of localization. We have elaborated on the role of such emotions by referring to the distinction between the other as object and the other as abject and described the reaction of excluding this other from one's own self-definition. Again, we want to emphasize the significant role of imagination in the depiction and construction of the abject other. In the context of globalization, Appadurai (1996) has proposed a distinction between individual and collective senses of imagination and has emphasized that the faculty of imagination is not restricted to the individual mind. Collective experiences of the mass media, especially film, video, and DVD, can create communities not only of worship and charisma, but also of animosity and abjection. Conditions of collective reading, pleasure, hate, rejection, and exclusion make groups imagine and feel things together and lead individuals to feel themselves part of a group that derives its identity not only from separation from other groups, but even from their rejection and demonization. Rejection and demonization of other groups, fueled by individual and collective imagination, can be regarded as emotional responses to situations of intolerable uncertainty. The significant role of emotion in relation to the abject other or group of others, the collective experience of animosity, and the dynamics of escalation between groups in the service of identity protection require an analysis in which emotions of individual people are linked to processes at the local and global levels. Finally, globalization may cause uncertainty about emotion rules as the individual person is exposed to different rules originating from different cultures. Moreover, globalization increases the number and heterogeneity of positions, often leading to tensions between conflicting or opposing positions. Such conflicts require large amounts of emotion work and, as a reaction, may motivate individuals to retreat to local groups, practices, and traditions.

In the preceding sections, we have dealt with three main concepts (other-in-the-self, dominance, and emotion) that function as bridges between the levels of the individual, the local, and the global. At the same time, these concepts can be used to demarcate settings and situations where there is no dialogue. Dialogue is not everywhere. It is restricted or even impossible when the self is populated by a high number of disconnected voices, resulting in a cacophony in which any meaningful exchange is impeded (Lysaker and Lysaker, 2002). Dialogue is even impossible when social power or dominance in interpersonal or institutional settings becomes so unbalanced that the voice of the subjugated party is silenced or suppressed so that it has no chance to express itself from its own particular point of view. Dialogue is also seriously restricted when the person is absorbed in a particular narrative and its corresponding emotional state to such an extent that the flexibility to move to another emotional state (or the capacity to understand the different emotional state of another person) is seriously reduced.

Some research implications

Although it is not our purpose to present a review of the literature that provides empirical evidence or contra-evidence for dialogical self theory, we want to sketch briefly some lines of empirical research that can be suggested by some of the insights described in this chapter. We do so in the expectation that the views presented have the potential of leading to new research and to the connection of existing lines of research, insti-gated by the challenges of globalization, localization, and uncertainty. We limit ourselves to three lines of research: (i) a dialogical approach to private audiences, (ii) friendship with out-group partners, and (iii) the innovative power of dialogues.

A dialogical approach to private audiences

Inspired by the work of symbolic interactionists, Baldwin and Holmes (1987) assumed that a sense of self is experienced in relation to some audiences: people who are present or imagined, specific or generalized, actual or fantasized. These authors referred to the common observation that people respond to a range of different significant others who repre-sent distinct ways of evaluating the self. They termed such an evaluating other as a "private audience" that could include such divergent figures as a spouse, best friend, religious leader, or business colleague. In one of their studies, a group of undergraduate women visualized the faces either of two friends from campus or of two older members of their own fam-ily. Later they were asked to read a sexually permissive piece of fiction. When they were afterward asked to rate the enjoyableness of the story, it appeared that participants who had thought of friends from campus reported liking the story more than those who thought of their (suppos-edly more moralistic) older family members. Apparently, they tended to respond in ways that were acceptable to their salient private audiences. The self-evaluative process was guided by cognitive structures that were primed by the preceding perception of significant others. (For a similar study, see Baldwin, Carrell, and Lopez, 1990.)

The concept of private audience is very well in agreement with one of the premises of dialogical self theory, that positions or voices are always addressing somebody (Salgado and Hermans, 2005). Voices convey mes-sages, knowledge, or information in sign-mediated ways to somebody who is assumed to listen to the message and may respond, in one way or another, to it. The existence of private audiences is quite compatible with the idea that a person or a group is imagined to respond to messages that have become part of the self. However, it should be noted that in

Baldwin and Holmes's experiment the audience is imagined but does not explicitly convey a message. The respondents see faces, but the faces do not speak or give any explicit sign-mediated response.

We suggest performing social psychological experiments in which private audiences are primed and explicitly talking with the participants so that the effect of messages can be studied on subsequent evaluative responses. Moreover, different kinds of audiences could be introduced, not only those who are familiar to the respondent but also those who are unfamiliar, strange, or belonging to other cultures, or even those perceived as direct opponents or enemies. The guiding idea is that the process of globalization implies the introduction of a heterogeneous set of audiences to the self to which the self can respond in various ways (e.g., approaching, avoiding, or opposing).

Friendship with out-group partners and friendship with oneself

As we have argued in this chapter, significant others are represented as intrinsic parts of the self. In close correspondence with this idea, Aron and colleagues (2005) have presented an inclusion-of-other-in-the-self model. The basic idea of this model is that when standing in a close relationship with another person, one includes in the self, to some degree, the other person's perspectives, resources, and identities. To give some idea of the kind of research that this model has stimulated, we restrict ourselves to two examples.

In psychological research, it is a well-known finding that people recall past successes as more recent, and past failures as more distant in time than they actually are. Building on this finding, Konrath and Ross (2003) examined whether people are subjected to the same effect when they take the perspective of their romantic partners. In agreement with the hypothesis, they found the same effect when their participants recalled past events for their romantic partners, but only in those cases in which the partners were felt as close, not when they were felt as distant.

In one of the applications of the inclusion-of-other-in-the-self model, Aron and colleagues (2005) investigated prejudices toward out-groups. They reasoned that inter-group contact is most likely to reduce prejudice when intimate contact with an out-group member is involved. Usually, people treat in-group members as parts of themselves and out-group members as not part of themselves. However, what happens when one develops a friendship with an out-group partner? Aron *et al.* hypothesized that not only the out-group member but also the out-group member's group identity become part of the self. In this way, they expected that it was possible to undermine negative out-group attitudes and prejudices. On the basis of several studies, Aron *et al.* concluded that there is support for the proposition that contact with a member of an out-group is more effective in reducing prejudice when one has a close relationship rather than a more distant relationship with that out-group member.

The research on friendship with out-group members opens a welcome avenue for studies on the effects of globalization and localization because it may contribute significantly to the understanding of how prejudices between social and cultural groups can be reduced, and closed boundaries between individual groups opened. However, the process of globalization poses a problem that goes beyond the pure opposition between in-group and out-group. As we argued earlier, globalization increasingly leads to the emergence of a multiplicity of cultural voices within one and the same individual (e.g., an American man married to a Japanese woman, a Polish scientist studying in the United Kingdom, an Iranian artist looking for asylum in France). The existence of multi-voiced individuals creates a more complex situation because there is typically more than one group to which an individual feels attached. Given the existence of cultural differences or oppositions, the different voices may criticize each other or may be involved in a mutual conflict, although they may come from groups who are all felt as in-groups. An example may illustrate this complexity.

From struggling cultural positions to internal friendship   From the perspective of dialogical self theory, Clarke (2003) studied the clinical phenomenon of burnout in people living at the interface of different cultures. One of her respondents, Hawa, had immigrated with her family from Turkey to the Netherlands when she was 5 years old. At the age of 30, she suffered from a burnout that was reason for her to contact a psychotherapist. The psychotherapist proposed that Hawa perform a self-investigation in which she told two self-narratives, one from the perspective of her Dutch position and another from the perspective of her Turkish position. The results showed a severe conflict between the two positions. She described her relationships with several boyfriends, which were acceptable from her Dutch position but a forbidden area from the perspective of her very moralistic Turkish position. Although her parents were very important in her life, she could only talk with them about matters of business, never about the things that were of emotional value to her. In the course of therapy, she found out that she was investing an enormous amount of energy in suppressing her Turkish identity as a result of her tenacious attempts to defend her Dutch way of life against the collective voices of her family and original culture. She wanted to be an independent and powerful woman but suffered from guilt feelings because she acted in conflict with the mores that she had learned as the daughter of Turkish parents. The result of the therapy affected her in two ways. She discovered that her Turkish position had more facets (sub-positions) than she had ever thought. It was not purely moralistic and expressive only of an aloof attitude. She realized that part of her emotions and her aesthetic preferences were the result of her Turkish education. Also, her Dutch position became more multi-faceted. She found out that this position did not purely coincide with her independence and freedom to choose her own friends, but also gave her the space to reflect about herself and to see things from many sides. Gradually she discovered and emotionally accepted that her Dutch and Turkish positions were not purely competitive, with one criticizing the other, but were complementary. At the final phase of therapy, she had enough courage to introduce her newest friend to her parents, who, somewhat to her surprise, accepted him as a welcome guest.

The example of the Dutch-Turkish woman illustrates two phenomena that are significant to understanding the influence of globalization on the self. Hawa was not living in one cultural group as in-group with the other group as out-group. Rather, both groups were parts of her. The problem was that the two cultures presented her with two very different emotion rules that she was not able to reconcile. Her attempts to be a decent woman who obeyed her parents and her striving to become a strong independent woman required so much emotion work that she ended up burnt out. From an empirical point of view, this case study suggests that it is important to distinguish three lines of future research in the context of the process of globalization and localization. The multiplicity of positions in which individuals find themselves as a result of immigration and intercultural contact requires: (i) the investigation of conflicting emotion rules, the experience of uncertainty, and the nature of emotion work that is required to cope with conflicts in the self; (ii) the investigation of the ways in which severe conflicting positions can be reconciled so that they are no longer experienced as competitive or mutually exclusive, but as cooperating and mutually complementing; and (iii) the study of the multi-faceted nature of each position separately. The idea behind this suggestion is that the chances of reconciling conflicting positions increases when their various facets and possibilities are taken into account (Cooper, 2003). When the multi-faceted nature of each position is acknowledged, there is a greater chance that the positions can cooperate on the basis of non-conflicting elements and form effective coalitions (Hermans and Hermans-Jansen, 2004).

Innovative power of dialogues

One of the central features of dialogical relationships is that they have the potential of innovating the self. The most straightforward way in which the self can be innovated is when new positions are introduced that lead to the reorganization of the repertoire in such a way that the self becomes more adaptive and flexible in a variety of circumstances (Hermans, 2003). From a developmental point of view, Fogel and colleagues (2002) have argued that children innovate their selves in role-playing situations in which they learn to reverse roles (first the mother is the lion and then the child) and build on them in their own play. From a clinical point of view, Dimaggio *et al.* (2003) showed how clients, using the Self-confrontation Method (Hermans and Hermans-Jansen, 1995), were able to "rewrite" their self-narratives in innovative ways. Neimeyer and Buchanan-Arvay (2004) described how clients can "relearn" the self by revising their self-narratives after traumatic loss. In a role-playing study, Puchalska-Wasyl, Chmielnicka-Kuter and Oles (2008) found that if players confront themselves with their heroes, this typically leads to new insights concerning the mutual connections between the player's usual self and the hero as part of the extended self of the player.

How can dialogical relationships and the introduction of new positions be used, in empirical ways, to innovate the self? Two ways are briefly described, one referring to the communication with real others, the other focusing on the contact of an imaginary other. In an experimental study Stemplewska-Zakowicz *et al.* (2005) asked students to discuss whether psychological knowledge could be helpful in passing exams. Some of the students were instructed in such a way that they believed themselves to be in the position of an expert, whereas others received an instruction that made them believe that they were in the position of a layperson. In some experimental conditions, moreover, students were placed in the position of expert or layman in a direct way (both participants received the instruction that they were expert or layperson), whereas in other conditions students were positioned in an indirect way (their interlocutor was instructed that they were an expert or layman, but they themselves did not receive this instruction). The experimenters' intention was that in the latter condition the participants not see themselves as expert or layman, but that they be perceived as such by their interlocutors. The experiment provided confirmation for one of the basic premises of dialogical self theory: that different positions produce different narratives (the students positioned as experts gave more advice than those positioned as laypersons). Moreover, it was found that even indirect ways of positioning showed this effect, although to a minor degree (students positioned as experts by their interlocutor but not by themselves gave more advice than those that were positioned, also in an indirect way, as laypersons). (For another experiment with similar outcomes see Stemplewska-Zakowicz, Walecka, and Gabinska, 2006).

Experimental research in which participants communicate on the basis of a variety of instructed positions may be relevant to innovation in the self. In the context of globalization, people who are in contact with an increasing diversity of significant others raised in other groups, communities, or cultures may become positioned in direct or indirect ways. Experiments like the one described above could be run with participants instructed to believe that they communicate with people from groups of diverse cultural origin. Such experiments could examine under which conditions participants positioned as members of a particular culture would learn from interlocutors positioned as members of another culture. A particularly relevant question would be whether participants are able or willing to modify their selves, taking the alterity or otherness of the interlocutor into account. (For the relevance of otherness in the self, see Simão and Valsiner, 2006.)

Imaginary dialogues and innovation   Whereas experiments like those performed by Stemplewska and colleagues (2006) are focused on dialogues with real others, other work has examined dialogues with imaginary others. Drawing on Marková's (1987) work, Hermans (1996a) invited clients in psychotherapy to enter into an imaginary dialogue with a person depicted in the 1930 painting *Mercedes de Barcelona*, by the Dutch artist Pyke Koch (1901–92). The painting depicts a middle-aged woman, facing forwards so that eye-contact with the viewer is possible. Clients were invited to select a personally meaningful part of their previously told self-narrative (a so-called "valuation") and imagine that they were telling it to the woman in the painting. They were asked to concentrate on the picture and imagine that the woman responded to their valuation. After the woman had given an imaginary reaction to their valuation, participants were invited to return to their original valuation with the possibility of revising this valuation in light of the woman's response. In fact, this procedure involved three steps:

Step 1: Participant presents a valuation to the woman.
Step 2: Woman gives an imaginary response.
Step 3: Participant responds to the woman.

Different clients responded in very different ways to the woman's imaginary response. One client, Bob, a 50-year-old man who participated in this investigation after a four-year period of depression, gave the following responses:

Step 1: Bob: "I always had to manage things on my own; didn't receive any attention, or affection; was superfluous at home; this has made me very uncertain."

Step 2: Woman: "This sounds very familiar to me: I've had the same experience."

Step 3: Bob: "I recognize the sadness in your eyes."

As this example shows, in Step 3 there is no clear development of the original formulation in Step 1. Rather, in Step 3 Bob expresses a feeling that was already present in Step 1 and confirmed by the woman in Step 2. In fact, the dialogical movement does not produce many innovative elements, although Bob perceives an experience of sharing.

A different process can be observed in the example of Frank, a 48-year-old man, who referred to his work as manager in a company:

Step 1: Frank: "I trust most people in advance; however, when this trust is violated, I start to think in a negative way; this can have harmful consequences."

Step 2: Woman: "You should keep your openness; however, your trust should become somewhat more reserved and take into account the topic involved."

Step 3: Frank: "You are right; I must pay attention to this; reservations in this will also help me to control my negative feelings."

In this case, the woman, in the role of a wise advisor, offers Frank a new perspective (Step 2) that is incorporated in his final reaction (Step 3), so that the original formulation (Step 1) has been further developed. The content of his final valuation in Step 3 involves not only a central element of the woman's response (reservation), but also a central theme in his original valuation (negative thinking). Frank brings together and integrates elements from Steps 1 and 2 in Step 3 and thus constructs a final valuation with a considerable innovative and synthesizing quality. Dialogical procedures are particularly relevant in light of Appadurai's (1996) discussion of the role of imagination in collective experiences in the mass media and especially in film, video, and DVD, a role that can create not only worship and charisma but also animosity and hate. Three-step procedures like the one proposed by Marková (1987) may be helpful in studying in detailed ways to what extent people involved in contact with remembered, anticipated, or imagined others innovate their selves in dialogical ways or confirm and defend it in a monological fashion. Such studies should pay attention to the ways in which emotions (associated with liked, disliked, and abject others) can be changed and innovated as a result of internal and external dialogues. (For the notion of emotional creativity, see Averill, 2004.)

For the future of dialogical self theory, it is necessary to expand its empirical evidence and implications in order to avoid a gap between theory and research. Further development of the theory might profit from research traditions and methodologies devised in mainstream psychology. We are in strong agreement with Sakellaropoulo and Baldwin (2006), who proposed interconnecting the recent field of dialogical science and the more established field of interpersonal cognition in this way:

> We believe that to further increase the understanding of both interpersonal cognition and dialogical science, researchers should strive to incorporate each area's fundamental principles into the other. Although research into interpersonal cognition has progressed significantly in the last decade, much work remains. Despite dialogue being a core component of self and identity, a dialogical component to interpersonal cognition is essentially lacking. Indeed, the majority of the dependent variables in the studies we reviewed in this article [Sakellaropoulo and Baldwin's review of developments in the field of interpersonal cognition] are fundamentally non-dialogical in nature (e.g., affect, self-esteem). On the other hand, dialogical science, still a relatively recent enterprise, could benefit greatly from the methods and findings already available in the interpersonal cognition literature. (p. 63)

Future research in the field of dialogical science may very well profit from the foundational work by classic theorists such as James, Mead, Cooley, Pierce, and Bakhtin (see Wiley, 2006, for a review of the literature; and Colapietro, 2006; Leary, 2006, and J. Lysaker, 2006, for commentaries). However, to be recognized as a respected science, it is necessary for dialogical science to develop the dialogical field in a theory-guided, empirical direction, taking advantage of both quantitative and qualitative methods and of both experimental and experiential approaches. Building on the work of the founding fathers, new and challenging theories should be created that may profit from equally developed assessment methods and research procedures that are essential to revise and improve existing theoretical notions.

Differences from other theories

There are other theories in psychology and the social sciences that deal with similar phenomena to those of dialogical self theory. What are the differences? In social identity theory, for example, there is not one personal self, but rather several selves or positions that correspond to widening circles of group membership. An individual has multiple social identities, dependent on perceived membership in social groups (Hogg and Vaughan, 2002). The existence of collective voices in dialogical self theory corresponds with the notion of internalized group membership in social identity theory. An important difference between the two theories is that social identity theory asserts that group membership creates self-categorization in ways that favor the in-group at the expense of the out-group. According to dialogical self theory, however, other individuals or groups are conceived of as voices that are able to entertain dialogical relationships with other individuals or groups in a multi-voiced self and they are able to dominate and silence each other as a result of struggles and conflicts. In other words, whereas social identity theory is based on the notion of categorization, dialogical self theory is based on the notion of addressivity.

A comparison can also be made with optimal distinctiveness theory (Brewer, 1991), which suggests that people, in their affiliations with groups, try to maintain a balance between the desire to fit in and the desire to stand out. Whereas feelings of belonging create a need to individuate oneself, feelings of uniqueness lead to attempts to re-embed oneself in the collective. There exists a dialectical opposition between these tendencies: Meeting one signals a deficit in the other and leads to increased efforts to reduce this deficit. Whereas optimal distinctiveness theory and dialogical theory both assume the existence of tension and conflict between opposing parts of the self, the latter theory acknowledges sign-mediated dialogical relationships between voices that may agree or disagree with each other and question each other in processes of negotiation, deliberation, and mutual criticism.

Dialogical self theory also shows some similarities to and differences from intersectionality theory (Collins, 2000). In contrast to theories that consider race, gender, and class as discrete or additive processes, intersectionality theory sees the effects of race, class, and gender as intersecting and interlocking. For example, a woman's gender status cannot be separated from her class or racial status. A black woman is confronted with other challenges and disadvantages from a black man. Gender, class, and race work together in creating an overarching structure of domination, creating different outcomes for individuals and for groups positioned at the point at which a particular race meets a particular gender and a particular class status. In agreement with intersectionality theory, dialogical self theory considers self or identity as located on the interface of social positions and as subjected to relations of social domination. An important difference, however, is that dialogical self theory is interested not only in processes on the interface of social positions (e.g., gender, class, race), but also in personal positions (e.g., I as imprisoned, I as an optimist, I as a clown).

The distinction between personal and social positions becomes particularly salient in the context of a discussion about the separation of self and society, so typical of the modern model that tends to define the self as an entity or essence in itself (see Chapter 2). Dialogical self theory explicitly considers personal positions and social positions (roles) as interconnected elements of the self as a society of mind. Whereas social positions reflect the way the self is subjected to social expectations and role-prescriptions, personal positions leave room for the many ways in which the individual responds to such expectations from his own point of view and for the various ways in which the individual fashions, stylizes, and personalizes them.

Summary

In this chapter we explored the relationship between globalization and localization with special attention to the experience of uncertainty. We analyzed globalization and localization on the level of self and identity where they are reflected as dynamic relationships between local and global positions. Globalization is supposed to have a deep impact on the organization of the self: its repertoire is populated by an unprecedented density of positions; the repertoire becomes more heterogeneous and laden with differences, oppositions and contradictions; it is confronted with a variety of changes in the environment and receives more "visits" by unexpected positions; and there are larger "position leaps" (jumping from one position to another).

Globalization is not to be equated with increasing homogeneity and uniformity but receives an answer from localization as its counter-force. Rather than a unidirectional impact of globalization on the self, a dialectical relationship between globalization and localization can be observed. This relationship implies that global and local influences interpenetrate each other and create hybrid combinations of global and local elements.

Special attention is devoted to the experience of uncertainty. We argued that the experience of uncertainty can be a gift in opening a broad range of unexpected possibilities, but a burden in so far as it leads to anxiety. When globalization is experienced as creating new possibilities and chances for the self, it is associated with lower or intermediate levels of uncertainty and with more positive than negative feelings. However, when globalization is experienced as a threat, uncertainty is raised to higher levels, resulting in defensive forms of localization and evoking more negative than positive feelings.

The question is how people cope with higher levels of uncertainty. We have described five reactions: (i) uncertainty can be diminished by a *reduction of the number and heterogeneity of positions* in the repertoire; (ii) it can be diminished by *giving the lead to one powerful or important position* that is allowed to dominate the repertoire as a whole; (iii) it can be minimized by *sharpening the boundaries* between oneself and the other, considering the other as different, strange, or even as "abject"; (iv) in a paradoxical way, uncertainty can be reduced by *increasing instead of diminishing* the number of positions in the self, particularly when a new position is expected to give what earlier positions were not able to; and (v) a dialogical reaction that copes with uncertainty by *going into this uncertainty* rather than avoiding it, in such a way that initial positions are influenced or changed, marginally or essentially, by the encounter itself. Whereas the latter reaction aims at post-dialogical certainty, the former ones strive for pre-dialogical forms of certainty.

We have described three arguments for a dialogical approach to the processes of globalization and localization. First, when society becomes more complex and heterogeneous, the self, as a *society of mind*, also becomes more complex and heterogeneous, resulting in a multiplicity of divergent or conflicting positions or voices in the self. These voices live well with each other only when their mutual relationships are sufficiently dialogical. Second, there is a need for developing a dialogical capacity in order to deal with differences, conflicts and oppositions. Third, there is the necessity of acknowledging the alterity of the other person, implying that the otherness of the other is recognized and valued. The other person as an "alter ego" is both similar to us and different from us at the same time, creating the challenge to acknowledge and respect the other person not only as "like me," but also as "different from me."

In order to understand the workings of dialogue in the context of society at large, it is necessary to explore not only its potentials but also its constraints. Referring to a variety of literatures, we discussed two constraints: biological and social. From a biological and evolutionary perspective, we referred to basic needs of safety and continuity as they are expressed in the continuous need to return to "ordinary positions," which works as a counter-force to the exploration of new environments and possibilities. Such basic needs motivate people to discover local niches where they find security, safety, and certainty and shield themselves against the increasing discontinuities of crossing borders, diasporas, immigration, and the power of multi-nationals. From a societal point of view, we discussed the workings of emotion rules as they organize and constrain the ways emotions are expressed in social situations. We argued that uncertainty is heightened when, in a situation of globalization, different cultures, each with their own emotion rules and devices for expression, come together in one local situation and in the self of one and the same individual, educated or trained as this individual can be in different cultural environments.

Taking the preceding considerations into account, we argued that for a comprehensive study of self and identity, it is necessary to study these

entities on three levels: individual, local, and global. Moreover, we proposed three concepts to function as linkages between these levels: (i) the
other-in-the-self, that is, the self as extended to the environment, as an alternative to the idea of self-contained individualism, so typical of mainstream
psychological theories of the self and, more generally, of the Western image
of the person; (ii) *relative dominance* between positions in the self, which
mirror and answer power differences between individuals, groups, and cultures in a world where people are different, yet intensely interconnected;
and (iii) *emotions* as emanating from the contact between people at the
interfaces of their communities. The opening of boundaries between local
communities and the global interchange of (local) goods, practices, and
ideas are sources of positive emotions for many people. However, when
localization becomes defensive, voices express indignation, anger, and
even hate, with the risk of uncontrollable escalation.[11]

NOTES

1 This chapter is a revision and further elaboration of an article titled "Self,
  identity, and globalization in times of uncertainty: A dialogical analysis,"
  published in *Review of General Psychology*, 2007, 11 (1): 31–61.
2 In dialogical self theory, a distinction is made between different kinds of
  positions. *Opposite positions* refer to any pair of polar opposites without the
  assumption of any dialogical or monological relationship between them.
  For example, dependent is the opposite of independent in a purely descrip-
  tive way, like white is the opposite of black. A *counter-position*, however, is
  a relational term in the sense that one position is a dialogical or monological answer or reaction to another position, as part of a process where one
  position *places itself* toward or against another position. For example, I as
  optimist can give an encouraging answer to another person who expresses a
  pessimistic point of view. In this case the two positions, optimist and pessi-
  mist, respond to each other as part of a social relationship. Or, to give a more
  monological example, I criticize another person whom I see as unreliable
  and tell him my opinion in a dominating way without giving him any chance
  to respond from his own point of view. Central to the present book is the idea
  that the processes of positioning and counter-positioning occur not only
  between people, but also within the self of one and the same person (e.g.,
  I encourage myself at the moment that I'm either pessimistic or I'm criticizing myself in a devastating way). In the context of the present chapter, it is
  relevant to observe that the processes of positioning and counter-positioning
  can also take place between global and local positions. For example, when
  I'm involved in contacts with individuals and groups of diverse origin in a
  globalizing world, I can experience this as an enrichment of my local position and see it as an important learning experience (dialogical reaction). It
  is also possible that, as a reaction to the flux and change on a global scale,
  I retreat into myself in a defensive way, closing myself off from the inputs of
  global discourses and interactions (monological reaction).

3 Dialogical self theory allows one to make a distinction between several closely
   related concepts, like uncertainty, anxiety, threat, confusion, and absurdity. *Uncertainty* is experienced when the person does not know from which
   position to answer in complex, ambiguous, or unpredictable situations. For
   example, I immigrate to another country but don't know which new experiences can be expected. *Anxiety* results when, in a situation of uncertainty or
   danger, the position from which to answer is lying beyond the range of available and accessible positions in the repertoire. For example, my boss tells
   me that I will lose my job and, distressed as I am, I don't know what to say
   and what to do. *Threat* is experienced when the person expects damage or
   loss of existing positions, but has, at the same time, positions available and
   accessible in the repertoire from which to respond to the threatening situation. For example, an adversary brings me to court and I'm at risk of losing
   the case, but I have it in mind how to defend myself. *Confusion* is felt when,
   in a situation that requires an adaptive answer, there are different positions
   from which one can respond, but is it not clear which position is the most
   adequate. For example, I expect the other to be serious when talking about
   an important decision but at some point he makes a joke that may be serious
   or not. Confusion typically exists when the person has a lack of knowledge
   about the actual position of the other in a situation where this knowledge
   is relevant to future action. *Absurdity* is experienced when the person finds
   himself in a position that has no meaningful connection with the other positions in the repertoire. For example, as a result of a mistake, I'm accused,
   imprisoned and interrogated as a criminal while knowing that I'm innocent.
   Note that the different definitions are inspired by Kelly's (1955) personal
   construct theory.

4 Although we talk of "cultures" and "cultural groups" for distinguishing purposes, we do not adhere to any unitary view of cultures but acknowledge their
   complex and variegated nature. In an increasingly interconnected world, it
   would be naive to believe that there exist cultures that could be defined in
   any homogeneous way. Typically, cultures are of a heterogeneous nature and
   composed of different sub-cultures that may overlap and contradict each
   other. Moreover, they are not to be separated from individual selves because
   these selves are able to oppose to them, innovate them or confirm them.
   Culture and self are making each other up (Hermans, 2001a), like society
   and self are making each other up (Mead, 1934).

5 There is a conceptual difference between discussion, conversation, debate,
   and dialogue. In a *discussion* people are involved in an exchange of knowledge or information and respond to each other from different positions with
   the focus on a particular topic that is at the centre of the exchange. In a
   conversation people exchange knowledge or information from different positions, but there is no particular topic on which the exchange is concentrated.
   While a discussion is focused on a particular topic, conversation is permitted to move into all possible directions. In a *debate* it is the intention of the
   participants to express a particular position and articulate it in its difference
   from or even in contrast to another position. The debaters are not primarily
   motivated to learn from each other but to defend and articulate their own
   positions. Participants involved in *dialogue* are explicitly concerned about

learning from each other and revising and developing their original positions. *Dialogue* is different from discussion, conversation, and debate in a number of respects: (a) there is an exchange between different positions in such a way that the original positions of the participants are changed and developed on the basis of the preceding phases of the interchange. More than conversation, discussion, and debate, dialogue has innovative potentials; (b) it takes place not only on the verbal but also on the non-verbal or pre-verbal level, whereas discussion, conversation, and debate take place on a verbal and linguistic level (see also Chapters 3 and 4); (c) more than discussion, conversation, and debate, dialogue creates a common space and leads to common experiences and insights. It should be added that the development of a common space is not restricted to experiences that are common or shared between different people. It can also be developed within the self of one and the same person who is involved in an innovative interchange with himself (e.g., in a creative process).

6   For an elaborate discussion of the notions of centralization and decentralization and the differences between a post-modern and a dialogical model of the self, see Chapter 2.

7   The society of mind metaphor was already proposed by computer scientist Minsky (1985), who considered the mind as a hierarchically organized network of interconnected parts that function together as parts of a society. There are at least two differences between Minsky's proposal and ours. First, Minsky used the metaphor to study the internal workings of the mind, whereas we are interested in the self as intensely connected with society at large. Further, Minsky proposed a model that is strongly hierarchical in the sense that only "agents" (positions in our case) at the highest hierarchical level are able to become involved in dialogical relationships with each other. Pairs of agents at lower levels of the hierarchy are not able to comprehend each other and are not dialogical at all. Although positions in dialogical self theory show some hierarchical organization (e.g., Josephs, 2002), they function in far less hierarchical ways than Minsky's model has suggested.

8   For power struggles between cultural positions see also Aveling and Gillespie, 2008, who studied the identities of young Turks in London.

9   Positions that are the result of biologically driven impulses can be considered as "organismic positions," as proposed by Lysaker and Lysaker (2008). They argue that the self performs basic elemental and biological functions, such as monitoring energy levels ("I'm feeling tired" or "I feel sexually attracted"), safety in one's environment ("I don't feel safe here") or flight–fight reactions ("I want to get out here!" or "I will kill him!"). Initially such positions arise typically at a pre-reflexive and pre-linguistic level, although they can receive linguistic expression after the sensation or emotion has already emerged. The conceptual advantage of the inclusion of organismic positions in dialogical self theory is that they reflect the importance of the process of being *positioned*. This process is neglected in conceptions that consider the self as centralized and the I as a leading site from which the self is organized and regulated. Such a conception is well in agreement with a modern model of the self (see Chapter 2) with its emphasis on control of self and environment. For a dialogical model of the self it is essential to acknowledge that the

self is not only involved in an active process of positioning but also subjected to moments and periods in which it is positioned by forces that are beyond its immediate control. As Lysaker and Lysaker argue, organismic positions can be taken up in post hoc dialogical processes (e.g., "I'm feeling too tired to go to the party, but he will be disappointed. Oh ... I will write him an e-mail with a nice message"). In this sense, organismic positions form a conceptual link between biological and evolutionary determinants on the one hand and social and dialogical responses on the other hand.

10 For a more extended treatment of features of "good dialogue" see Chapter 3.

11 The different concepts introduced in the present chapter allow us to make a distinction between "self" and "identity." These terms, well known in the social sciences, serve as umbrella concepts that are often used and defined in very different ways, according to the theories involved. We propose the self, in the sense of the dialogical self, as the central concept in the theory. In its most general sense, it can be defined as a dynamic multiplicity of positions or voices in the landscape of the mind, with the possibility of dialogical relationships between these positions or voices. Subordinated to this general conception of the self, three kinds of identity can be distinguished: (i) *personal identity* defined as a dynamic multiplicity of personal positions (e.g., I as a person who likes to travel in Sri-Lanka, visiting Buddhist temples, and is interested in the national politics of the country); (ii) *social identity* defined as a dynamic multiplicity of social positions or roles (e.g., I as a university professor, lecturing for students and giving presentations at international conferences); (iii) *cultural identity* as a multiplicity of cultural positions (e.g., I as raised in France, married to an Iranian women, and working for a German company). In agreement with the analyses in the present chapter, the three forms of identity are closely intertwined and can be seen as different aspects of the same dialogical self.

2 Self and identity in historical perspective: traditional, modern, post-modern, and dialogical models

> *The charm of history and its enigmatic lesson consist in the fact that, from age to age, nothing changes and yet everything is completely different*
>
> Aldous Huxley

Self and identity are both individual and social constructions. They participate in societies that are changing over time. The self in medieval times is not the same self as in post-modern times. There is no self-in-abstracto being subjected to external causation. As a historical construction the self is not simply externally influenced by the time in which it is living, but a process that is an expression of the time and space in which it evolves. Historical changes as intrinsic to the self-process are particularly recognized when self and identity are conceived of as *extended* in space and time. Whereas in the previous chapter we analyzed the self as extended in space, in the present chapter we focus on its extension in time. Historical changes are reflected in the *collective* aspects of self and identity. In order to articulate these changes and their implications for the self, we will distinguish three models that are associated with particular historical phases: traditional, modern, and post-modern. Elaborating on specific features of these models, we will discern a fourth model: the dialogical one that is the centrepiece of the present chapter.

Two remarks should be made in order to clarify the particular nature of this chapter. First, the different models do not represent purely successive phases in the course of history. Although they each find their origin in a particular phase in history, they are not exclusively bound to this phase. That is, the previous phase does not stop when the next starts. Rather, the previous phase continues when the next one begins to develop. As a consequence of their simultaneity, the different phases have the potential of generating selves and identities of a higher complexity than before. So, the term "post-modern" might erroneously suggest that this phase starts *after* the modern phase ends somewhere. However, this conception is seriously contested by the observation that during the post-modern phase the modern (and even the traditional phase, as we will argue) continue to exist. In this way the different phases produce selves that include elements originating from different phases, but, nevertheless, form hybrid combinations as a result of their simultaneity. For example, in our era we observe that people put a high value on their autonomy and individuality (modern self) but also participate in international networks using the most advanced communication technologies (post-modern). Moreover, as recent investigations show, current levels of superstitious behavior and beliefs (as just one aspect of the traditional self) are surprisingly high.[1] In this example, the complexity of the self is illustrated by the fact that superstitious individuals do not give up their autonomy and individual freedom, so typical of the modern era, and do not cease to use the internet to expose their experiences and share them with like-minded others, as typical of a post-modern society. As we will argue in this chapter, elements originating from different models of the self (traditional, modern, and post-modern), meet each other in a dialogical self that is characterized by relatively high levels of uncertainty with both positive and negative potentials.

Second, the assumption of reaching higher levels of complexity through history might not imply that the self is automatically enjoying increasing levels of quality or richness. Complexity and quality do not necessarily coincide. Different historical phases are associated with different emphases. That is, each phase has its specific perspectives, expectations, and values and, as a result of this emphasis or even exaggeration, other perspectives, attitudes, and values may be backgrounded, neglected, or even suppressed. For example, the connection with nature, so self-evident for the traditional phase, became backgrounded under the influence of urbanization, industrialization, and an increasing control of the environment as typical of the modern self. The more people achieve control of the environment, the less connected they feel with the nature of which they are actually a part. The backgrounding of this experience does not necessarily mean that it is lost. Certainly, in particular situations (e.g., making a long journey through a natural environment or being affected by a natural catastrophe) the experience of connection with or dependence on nature can return to our surprise, leaving an imprint in our memory forever. As this example suggests, the experience of being part of nature, as typical of the traditional phase, does not totally disappear during the modern phase, but can be dominated by an attitude of control and exploitation as typical of this phase. This relative domination of elements of one phase over elements of another phase may lead to an exaggeration of the attitudes, values, and behaviors from one particular phase over those from another phase but does not make them disappear entirely. As we will see in the present chapter, such an exaggeration implies that each model has not only its assets but also its *shadow sides*. However, relative domination of one model over the other, and the resulting exaggeration, do not exclude the *possibility* that elements of other models become foregrounded and form, together with elements of other models, combinations at higher levels of complexity. People living in post-modern technological environments and participating in a diversity of social networks can be, at the same time, concerned about the protection and restoration of the natural environment. Or, people living their ordinary lives in comfortable circumstances go for an adventure trip in the wilderness (but not without their mobile phone).

Three models of the self

In the following we first present a brief sketch of three models – traditional, modern, and post-modern – before we elaborate on these models in direct relationship with the dialogical self.

Traditional self

The traditional view of the world is one of totality, overarching unity, and purpose (Gier, 2000; Richardson, Rogers, and McCarroll, 1998). These values are expressed in myths and celebrated in rituals. This vision coexists with a cyclical conception of time, in marked contrast to the linear conception as typical of the modern period. The purpose of the traditional worldview is to sacralize the cycles of seasons and the cyclical procreation of animals and humans. At the same time myths and rituals facilitated the painful passage through periods of personal and social crises. They helped people understand death and violence, and inhibited the power of sexuality. In this model the human self is not an autonomous entity but rather an integral part of a sacred whole, which is greater than and even more valuable than its parts. Traditional worldviews consider people as living their lives on two levels: the ordinary, lower life where people satisfy their basic needs, and a higher, better kind of life which can only be achieved if one is able to realize one's proper telos or purpose in the cosmos.

Traditional society showed a strong hierarchical structure, with the Church and the king receiving their power from above and mediating the will of God to the people, who were expected to support it. A text on the walls of King's College Chapel (Cambridge, UK), a building completed in 1547, summarizes this structure in an eloquent way:

WHERE TWO WORLDS MEET
The people who built this chapel thought of the universe, the whole of what there is, as two-fold.

There is the world of *earth*.
The things that make it up,
from stones to people,
are visible and solid.
But they do not last forever,
and this world itself will pass away.
There is the world of *heaven*.
Its inhabitants are invisible and
spiritual. God, angels and saints
last forever. The heavenly beings
will judge the earth when it ends,
and meanwhile have supreme
power over it.
These two worlds are not sealed
off from one another.
There are *places* which are
thresholds between them.
Churches like this one,
make heavenly power available
on earth.
There are *people* in whom
the two worlds join. They are
supremely important in history.
Such are Jesus Christ and
his mother, the Virgin Mary
('Our Lady') above all; but also
prophets, saints, bishops
and *kings*.

> *The king's power came from heaven,*
> *but on earth it depended on the loyalty of his people*
> His authority was threefold:
> it came down from heaven
> and up from the people
> it carried along on earth by natural succession,
> and political achievement.

As this text suggests, the heavenly beings were seen not only as "eternal" but also as "supreme" beings who had the power to judge earthly people at the end of their path towards good or evil. As far as the heavenly beings addressed the people in their transient existence, it was more in the form of revelations, miracles, or commands than through dialogues. The God of the traditional model does not dialogue with humans – he wants them to obey. As long as they are incarcerated in their bodily existence, predisposing them to sin, they are expected to "support" the doctrines received from above, rather than be stimulated to contribute to them or co-develop them.[2]

As Gier (2000) and Richardson *et al.* (1998) have described, many traditional people also saw their bodies and their senses as a hindrance to spiritual life. The natural world as a whole is at most only a derivative reality from a higher spiritual reality that morally surpassed earthly existence. This view was characterized by an opposition between soul and body and, in its more extreme forms, by Manicheanism or gnosticism, according to which human beings are involved in a fierce battle between their spiritual and animal natures. Ethics and religion helped people to move from the lower to the higher level, which could only be achieved through significant self-discipline and self-restraint. The self is not yet a self-reflexive project in which the individual is engaged in a process of self-development and self-realization, but is rather guided by a belief in destiny and fate.

Reflection and evaluation   It is a risky undertaking to evaluate the "positive" and "negative" sides of a particular historical phase and its view on the self because we can only do so from our particular perspective. When we pretend to give a description and evaluation of the features of any previous phase, we can only do so from the perspective of our contemporary time, including its specific values, which implicitly direct and structure our perception and judgment of previous phases.

In the present time, when many people are in search of meaning and purpose and are longing for contact and union with something or somebody else, one may be impressed by the traditional view of the inclusion of the individual in a meaningfully ordered cosmos. It makes, however, no sense to romanticize the traditional phase as a whole because it was full of danger and suffering. One can think of the many wars, robberies, killing of the inhabitants of conquered cities, famines, floods, many incurable diseases, epidemics such as plagues and cholera, death penalties for people who deviated from the "right religion," the burning of witches, etc.[3] From a worldview, however, there was a sense that the world was organized as a coherent whole in which the individual self had a meaningful place, able to move from a lower state to a higher state, and in the belief that there was an afterlife that promised eternal salvation. There was a morality that was shared by most people of a community and that gave them a sense of certainty and security about matters of right and wrong, good and bad.

Looking back at the shadow sides of the traditional view of the self, contemporary people often refer to the overly moralistic attitude of that period and consider themselves, on the other hand, to be happy, and liberated from the overly restrictive religious dogmas and a hierarchical system that suppressed individual autonomy and freedom. The body was seen as something lower and inferior and the "desires of the flesh" were generally considered an obstacle on the path to salvation. Scientific discoveries were often declared to violate religious truths and, in extreme cases, cost the scientist his life. Deviations from moral or religious laws were not tolerated and could lead to death. Conceptions about life and death were dictated from above and were presented as eternal truths that were immovable and did not allow any deviation. Any upward mobility was prevented in communities where belonging to a particular class was determined by birth. Women were subordinated to men, men to clergymen, clergymen to higher religious authorities, and these authorities to God, resulting in a rigid social system that restricted (but not excluded)[4] societal innovation.

Modern self

The coherence and cosmic unity of the traditional phase move to the background during the modern phase. The modern view of the world became, under the influence of the Enlightenment, more and more dualistic. As Gier (2000) explains, it separates the outer from the inner, the subject and the object, self and other, fact and value, the is and the ought, science and faith, politics and religion, the public from the private, and theory from practice. In line with Descartes' rational thinking and quest for undisputed certainties, science and conceptual analysis became guiding principles in many areas of life as reflected by economic expansion, mechanized industry, unlimited technological progress and centralized bureaucratic administration (Gier, 2000).

From a philosophical perspective, the modern sense of the self can be described in terms of a "sovereign self" (Richardson et al., 1998) that has, as an ideal, permeated much of modern culture and shapes to a large extent the self-image of people living in advanced industrial societies. While the traditional self found its justification in the participation in a wider cosmic order, the modern self finds its justification in its own ground. It assumes an unprecedented autonomy, but does so at the risk of considerable alienation from the social and natural environment, emotional isolation, loneliness, and excessive competition (Richardson et al., 1998).

The modern self is no longer defined by its place in a meaningful cosmic order but becomes a self-defining entity, with a deep metaphysical abyss between the realms of the *internal* self and the *external* world. Sampson (1985) argued that the Western self, both in the minds of ordinary people and in many conceptions of mainstream psychology, could be described as a "container self" with the following characteristics: (a) there are strict and sharp boundaries between self and non-self; (b) the other does not belong to the realm of the self and is located as purely "outside"; and (c) the main attitude of the self toward the external environment is one of control. The exclusion of the other from the self is in contradiction with the classic formulations by James (1890), who proposed to study the self as "extended" to the environment. The conception of the self as extended was later supported by the theoretical and empirical work of Rosenberg (1979), who showed that the transition between self and non-self is not sharp but gradual, and of Aron and colleagues (2005), who found empirical support for the existence of the other-in-the-self. Rather than an inevitable conclusion on the basis of empirical proof, the container self seems to be representative of a cultural bias.

Forms of individualism   The emphasis on autonomy, as typical of the modern self, entails different forms of individualism. In their influential book *Habits of the Heart*, Bellah *et al.* (1985) have described developments of the self in North America, from the time of Thomas Jefferson's Declaration of Independence, in terms of growing individualism. The authors explain that individualism was gaining ground at a time when individuals acquired the freedom to form their lives on the basis of their own choice, freedom, and persistence. It was believed that individuals had the right to defend their own interests and to maximize their own income and profit. This form of liberal capitalism was justified by the assumption that, in a society in which each individual realizes his or her own interests, the "social good" would be automatically realized for the greater majority of the population. Bellah and colleagues described this attitude in terms of "utilitarian individualism," which was based on the belief that what is good for the individual is automatically good for society.

Somewhere in the middle of the nineteenth century utilitarian individualism became so dominant in North America that it evoked counter-reactions. A growing number of people objected to a life based on calculation of one's interests and hunting for material profit. Initially the protests came from women, clergymen, poets, and writers. They found that utilitarianism had insufficient room for human feelings and experiences emerging from the deeper layers of the self. This counter-reaction, partly inspired by the nineteenth-century romanticism in music and literature, led to an alternative form of individualism, which was labelled by Bellah and colleagues as "expressive individualism."[5] A poem written by Walt Whitman (1819–92, cited by Bellah *et al.*) conveys the spirit of expressive individualism very well. The first line of the poem, which bears the name *Song of Myself*, begins: "I celebrate myself, I sing myself."

For Whitman success has not much to do with material profit. He was more interested in a life of rich experience, open to stimulating contacts with many people, enjoyment of both sensory stimulation and intellectual analysis and, above all, a life of strong feelings. In more recent times the spirit of the modern self is well expressed by the familiar term, the "self-made man" and by Frank Sinatra's song "I did it *my* way!"

Personal autonomy and strength of character as ideal characteristics of the modern self are strikingly portrayed in the film *High Noon* (1952), directed by Fred Zinnemann. On the day that the sheriff of a small community, masterfully played by Gary Cooper, retires from his job, he hears that a criminal, just released from prison, is on his way, together with his comrades, to the village with the intention of taking revenge on him. He is unpleasantly surprised to find that nobody in his community is willing to support him in his plans to stop the killers. After emotional discussions in the local saloon and church, people want him to leave the village. Even his wife asks him to choose, but his inner conviction and feeling for justice make him say, to everybody and to himself, "*I must do this.*" Standing alone and faced with a life-threatening challenge, he demonstrates an impressive firmness of character and, steered by his internal compass, he persists and finally succeeds in beating his dangerous opponent. The movie, an icon in the film industry of that time, can be seen as a typical example of a modern, inner-directed self, with its emphasis on personal goals, inner strength, overcoming resistance, personal achievement and heroism, masculinity, autonomy, future-orientation, progress, and control of the situation.[6]

Precursors of modernism   From a historical perspective, it can be asked when the modern self emerged. In their answer to this question, Richardson *et al.* (1998) stated that modern consciousness crystallized around a radically new conception of the self, brought about by the success of the scientific revolution in the seventeenth century and its philosophical elaboration by Enlightenment thinkers. However, as Gier (2000) has argued, modernism, as a movement from mythos to logos, has been going on for at least 2,500 years. Although it received its full expression in the Renaissance, its seeds are very old. In Greece, India, and China, the strict separation of fact and value, science and religion was proposed almost simultaneously by the Greek atomists, the Indian materialists, and the Chinese Mohists. Greek philosophy, in particular, embraced ideas that foreshadowed the modern model of the self. The Greek Sophists, for example, stood for ethical individualism and relativism and believed in the power of argument (make "the weaker argument appear the stronger"). The Sophists inspired Renaissance humanists to extend education not only to the aristocracy but also to the masses. Socrates, Plato, and Aristotle affirmed ethical individualism and rationalism, although they maintained teleology and the unity of fact and value (Gier, 2000). Apparently, the seeds of the modern self are very old and, although its representatives were often minority groups, they existed in times when the traditional model of the self was the dominant one.

Reflection and evaluation   As already said, we can describe and evaluate the self of previous historical phases only from the colored perspective of our present time. When we do so, the modern self can be considered from the point of view both of its assets and of its shadow sides. In its emphasis on personal autonomy and self-development, it has liberated us from the oppressive forces of hierarchical structures and the pretensions to dogmatic truth of the traditional period. It has brought more individual freedom and has enabled us to see life as a project for which the person, and not an overarching institution, is responsible.[7] The Enlightenment movement has given an enormous impulse to the development of reason and has stimulated science and technology as never before. There are, however, some serious shadow sides. The modern self, justified and stimulated by the Enlightenment movement, risks becoming encapsulated within itself. As a solipsistic consciousness it loses basic contact with the external environment and with nature and tends to transform this contact to an attitude of control and exploitation. It has eroded the intimate ties of traditional community life and has threatened the ecological balance of the entire planet.

Supported by the pretension to universality of the Enlightenment project, the modern project has manifested itself as expansive and explorative. In its spirit of conquest, it led to a world-wide process of colonialism and resulted, moreover, in the tragedy of slavery. Paradoxically, in its manifestations of colonialism and slavery, the Enlightenment project has undermined its core ideals of a unified mind and the universality of its project. By conquering other parts of the world and attempting to impose its own view of life on people with a different cultural origin, it has, in fact, led to the emergence of multiple identities that undermined the ideals of an internally unified mind. As Featherstone (1995: 11) argues:

... yet it is the fact that blacks are both inside and outside the development of Western culture within modernity which is the biggest problem. Gilroy (1993: 54) argues that slavery is the premise of modernity, something which exposes the foundational ethnocentrism of the Enlightenment project with its idea of universality, fixity of meaning and coherence of the subject. The problem is that it has produced members of society who are living denials of the validity of the project, whose existence within society, or capacity to be seen as persons or citizens was long denied. Yet black people are both Americans and black, or Europeans and black, and participate in a culture and set of collective memories which cannot be integrated with or limited to the cultures of the nation-states in which they reside. Their culture is African and Western and their identity lived through a form of 'double consciousness', formed from experiences which are both inside and outside the West, inside and outside modernity.

Both slavery and colonialism have inadvertently produced multiple identities. People immigrating to European countries or to the USA, from all parts of the world, develop multiple and hybrid cultural identities rather than selves that are unified or "purely integrated" in the host societies (e.g., see Bhatia's, 2007, study of the multiple and hybrid identities of people who immigrated from India to the USA).

Post-modern self

As Featherstone (1995) describes, the term "post-modernism" was first used to indicate a movement, centered in New York in the 1960s, that went beyond artistic modernism. Later it was picked up by literary critics and philosophers who detected similarities between the works of post-modern artists – paintings, novels, and architecture – and the writings of philosophers (primarily from France) which became known under the terms "post-structuralism" and "deconstructionism." The rapid transmission of information between Europe and North America drew in other intellectuals and social scientists, which resulted in the stretching of the concept of post-modernism toward an epochal shift: the decay and dissolution of modernity. The main features associated with post-modernism, summarized by Featherstone (1995), are the following: (a) a movement away from the universalistic ambitions of master-narratives with their emphasis on totality, system, and unity, and towards an emphasis on difference, otherness, local knowledge, and fragmentation; (b) a dissolution of symbolic hierarchies that imply canonical judgments of taste and value, towards a collapse of the distinction between high and popular culture; (c) a decentralization of the subject, whose stable sense of identity and biographical continuity give way to fragmentation and superficial play with an endless stream of images and sensations; (d) a tendency towards the aesthetization of everyday life, which was facilitated both by efforts within the arts to dissolve the boundaries between art and life (e.g., pop art, Dada, surrealism) and moves toward a consumer culture in which a veil of images is wiping out the distinction between appearance and reality.

Although he rejected the application of the term to his own work, Michel Foucault (1980) is generally seen by many as one of the main representatives of the French school of post-structuralism. Mainly in his later work, in which he was interested in the fundamental relationship between knowledge and power, he undermined the idea of universal truth. He argued that what is assumed to be "true" is highly dependent on the language community in which it is considered to be valid. A particular truth regime is contingent on specific historical circumstances, as indicated, for example, by the radically different visions of psychiatric disorders and corresponding treatments in the course of history. In different times different conceptions are seen as representing "the truth" whereas they are, in fact, determined by the social influence of dominant social groups and institutions in a particular historical period. What is assumed to be "true" is, in fact, an expression of the power structures of a particular community. Truth is not to be considered in terms of a correspondence between a particular theory or idea on the one hand and an "objective reality" on the other hand, but is constructed by institutions and social groups that have the power to *define* particular ideas as true or not. Conceptions of truth are not necessary but relative: a specific form of knowledge which is true in a particular time or under specific social conditions can, depending on changing circumstances, be replaced by other forms of knowledge. Truth is not absolute and universal but relative and dependent on the power structures of language communities.

In the field of psychology, post-modernism and corresponding ideas of post-structuralist thinkers have gained ground in past decades. One of the main representatives of post-modernism in psychology, Gergen (1991), has observed that new technologies make it possible to expand one's circle of relationships with an ever-growing range of other persons, up to a point of "social saturation." Whereas the modern self is seen as organized around a personal essence or inner core, the post-modern self is distributed in a multiplicity of incoherent and disconnected relationships. They pull us in a myriad different directions and invite us to play a variety of roles. In order to characterize the post-modern self, Gergen refers to the famous line in a poem by W. B. Yeats, written in 1919 in the aftermath of the First World War: "Things fall apart; the centre cannot hold." The self is simultaneously pulled into different or even opposed directions and, as a result, it becomes strongly decentralized, losing its inner coherence and stability.

The self is populated by a plurality of voices that make it difficult or even impossible to speak from one single voice that is seen as the "proper" or "right-minded" one. In agreement with the post-structuralist philosophers, Gergen cast doubts on the typically modern terms such as "reality," "authenticity," "true," "essential," "valid," "correct," and "ideal" that have, in his view, no transcendent foundations. Instead, he characterizes the post-modern self in terms of "multiphrenia," suggesting that it is split into a multiplicity of self-investments up to the point of fragmentation. He sees multiphrenia not as a form of illness, but as a historically contingent condition that provides possibilities for adventure and ways of playing with an abundance of roles, characters, and voices.

In post-modern times, change and flux are seen as fundamental. The self is considered to be *protean* (Lifton, 1993). The protean self is capable of changing constantly in order to adapt to present circumstances. Some may see change as reflecting one's true self, others may argue that there simply *is* no true self. Changes come unexpectedly and often form no coherent pattern. The idea that there is a "real me" that is identifiable throughout life is abandoned. Identity is "created" by outside forces. One of the most potent forces in this process of creation or construction is language with its ability to define and control. Life is like a story or text that is being written and rewritten constantly. Self and identity are no "reality" but the result of definitions (Anderson, 1997; Wade 2007).

The specific state of mind typical of the post-modern self can be succinctly formulated by a fragment from T. S. Eliot's *The Love Song of J. Alfred Prufrock* (1917; cited by Gergen, 1991):

> And time yet for a hundred indecisions,
> And for a hundred visions and revisions,
> Before the taking of a toast and tea.

Rather than by a hero with purpose, long-term goals, and inner conviction, so typical of the modern self, the post-modern self is better expressed by the characters of *Monty Python's Flying Circus*, a satirical and surrealistic comedy that deals with the idiosyncrasies of British life and ironically alludes to political affairs. The satire reflects the specific post-modern invitation: to carry a clown on one's shoulder, always ready to step out of any serious character (Gergen, 1992).[8]

Precursors of post-modernism Like the modern self, the post-modern self also has its precursors that vary widely in origin and thought. Three of them, Nietzsche, Dewey, and Freud, are mentioned briefly. As Lysaker and Lysaker (2002) note, Nietzsche claimed that the self can be best described as a "common wealth" or "a social structure composed of many souls." He depicted the individual person as a "subjective multiplicity" and suggested the analogy that human beings are no more single selves than Great Britain is a single people. The individual and Britain have in common that they are both composed of disparate elements that can neither be combined at their root, nor synthesized without remainder. Nietzsche rejects the existence of any overarching self and sees it rather as an ensemble, driven by desires and habits, that is located in the same body but lacks any overall integration.

Dewey (1929), mentioned as another precursor of post-modernism (Ingraham, 2007), confronted what he called the "quest for certainty." He challenged the idea that "the scientific method" provides a route to certain knowledge. In agreement with his post-modern successors, he considered this quest as a means of coping with the fundamental uncertainty of the activity of knowing. For Dewey knowledge is a verb: the activity of understanding and interpreting. What really matters is the process of *knowing* rather than the body of actually uncertain, equivocal knowledge that is produced. In marked contrast to the Cartesian search for absolute knowledge, we see in Dewey's work a preoccupation, not with the production of a body of knowledge, but rather with knowledge, including self-knowledge, as a never-ending process of interpretation and realization that has to face its intrinsic uncertainty.

Although Freud remained committed to various aspects of the Enlightenment project, he nonetheless rejected the Enlightenment notion of the centered, unified subject. His tripartite model divided personality into the ego, id, and superego, and into the conscious and unconscious. With this differentiation he rejected the idea of a unified subject that is centered in itself, fully self-conscious and self-transparent. Later Lacan (1977) expanded on Freud's critique of the unitary and autonomous ego and argued that, by asserting the ego's mastery of the world, the idea of a unified ego separates the ego from the world and creates a comforting shield from reality. This protecting shield imposes a false unity and rigidity on the self that hides its multiple and fragmented character.[9]

Reflection and evaluation Post-modernist theories are a favorite topic for hot discussions and they are often criticized for their philosophical assumptions (e.g., Habermas, 1987; Weiss and Wesley, 2007). Although it is hazardous to evaluate historical phases that still in part continue into the present, we can mention some pros and cons of post-modernism, with special attention to self and identity. On the positive side, post-modernism has contributed to liberating the self from its imprisonment within the walls of a centralized and stable structure, with sharp boundaries between inner and outer, with a strong emphasis on control and with pretensions to universality. In contrast, the self, as a decentralized process, becomes more open to the influences of historical circumstances and the surrounding world. The impacts of history, language, language communities, social conventions, globalization, networks, and technology are taken as serious topics relevant to the understanding of our experiences as members of a contemporary globalizing world. As a result of its decentralization and openness, post-modernism has been of significant value to the process of emancipation. In accord with post-modernist views, feminist theories have stimulated women to broaden their role-repertoire beyond traditional constraints and improve their participation in society. Post-modernism has also facilitated sexual freedom and variation beyond the masculine ideals and patriarchal social structures of modernism, and has considered homosexuality and lesbianism as neither abnormal nor objectionable on moral grounds. In more general terms, by its sensitivity and openness to the multiplicity and flexibility of the human mind, post-modernism has the merit of contributing to the liberation of selves and identities beyond the hierarchies and restrictions of the "grand stories" of societal institutions. It also sees life and work as less heavy and less serious by giving room to humor and play (Wittel, 2001).

Post-modernism also has its apparent shadow sides. As a counter-reaction to the absolute truth pretensions of modernism, post-modernism has embraced a relativistic stance, often leading to an "anything goes" attitude that forms an obstacle to the search for values that transcend the preferences of particular individuals, groups, and cultures. It should be noted that the relativism of the post-modern phase and the ethnocentrism of the modern phase have in common that they both block an active search for values and truths that can be exchanged and possibly shared by different cultural communities. While modernism does so by its ethnocentric attitude, post-modern theories do so by emphasizing difference, heterogeneity, and multiplicity to such a degree that their relativity thesis does not provide an epistemological basis for a meaningful dialogue about commonalities between groups or cultures that go beyond such existing differences, heterogeneities and multiplicities. It also does not present a solid basis for an *engaged* agency that is at the heart of the dialogical self.

Another limitation of post-modern theories is what is often called their "pessimism" or "lack of hope." One of the inherent problems of post-modernist theories is that they emerged to a large degree as a criticism of modernism and, as a consequence, are as one-sided and suffer from the same degree of exaggeration as their object of criticism. Against the optimism and utopian expectation of unlimited progress typical of modernism, they swing to forms of pessimism and even hopelessness in their future outlook as a result of their persistent doubts about progress. This worldview may subdue the enthusiasm and the optimism people need in order to strive for the improvement of their situation and the realization of a better world.

Finally, against the stability and continuity of modernism, post-modernists respond with a one-sided focus on change, flux, and discontinuity. For psychologists this creates a problem because it is well known that constancy and change, like continuity and discontinuity, do not exclude each other and may well coexist in the development of the individual person (e.g., Chandler *et al.*, 2003; Thomae, 1968). In addition, we can see on the global level a need for the coexistence of change and stability . Technologically advanced means of transportation, closely affiliated with post-modernism, enable people to cross the borders of countries and cultures. There is, moreover, a growing army of expatriates and immigrants and people in diaspora all over the world. This has not only stimulated travel but also led to the experience of "spatial dislocation." In sharp contrast to the stability of place typical of the traditional and, to a lesser degree, of the modern self, the post-modern self experiences locations as "places of transition." People are somewhere, in order to go to another place, and again to another place. This may result in a lack both of rootedness and of feeling at home in a place to which one becomes attached. As discussed in Chapter 1, this lack of feeling rooted and at home creates tensions with basic biological needs such as safety, belonging, and stability.

Simultaneity of the traditional, modern, and post-modern self

The reasoning in this present chapter is based on the assumption that the different phases are not purely successive and mutually exclusive. Rather, the previous phase continues when the next phase starts. In their simultaneity the different phases lead to selves and identities of higher complexity, with the consequence that a diversity of dialogical relationships between elements originating from different phases become possible. An autobiographical example may illustrate this process.

An autobiographical memory   One of my own memories (Hubert Hermans) shows how self-positions from traditional and modern origin became engaged in an internal dialogue:

I received my primary school education in the 1940s and 1950s of the previous century from teachers who were living as religious brothers in a monastery located in the neighborhood of the house of my parents. The education was strictly Catholic. Every morning the brothers, clothed in their dark habits, started their lessons with prayers followed by religious instruction and biblical stories in which they emphasized the normative implications for the everyday life of the pupils. They told us about the heavenly rewards that were promised for "right behavior," but also about the hellish punishments that waited for us if we lived a life of sin and lack of self-discipline. In accordance with the teachings, I believed that the Catholic religion was the "only true one" and that all other religions and world views were erroneous. However, when I was 14 years old, a sudden insight emerged from my own thoughts. Sitting alone in silence at home, I became immersed in a thought that came somewhere from the deeper layers of my mind. It came to me as a sudden awareness and had the character of a "flash" as Kohnstamm (2007) would call it. The thought took this form: *"When the representatives of other religions are as convinced about the truth of their beliefs as we are, then we can never have the only true religion."* This thought was not something which I remembered as coming from somebody else. It felt as though it came from me as a separate being, from the inner realms of my own mind and as the product of my earlier thinking and exploration. The thought was as precious as it was inescapable and it has left indelible traces in my mind ever since. Certainly, I was aware of the contradiction between my personal thought and the religious doctrines and dogmas of the Church, supported as they were by my beloved parents. Yet the thought did not make me an "unbeliever" or an "atheist." Rather, the contradiction evoked a continuing internal dialogue over the years, transforming the traditional religious beliefs of my early youth into a more personal quest. I became what one could call an "agnostic with a religious suspicion." Neither my interest in logical and scientific thinking nor my quest for spirituality disappeared over time. Instead, I remained committed to both of them for the rest of my life, although I never was able to resolve – what I saw as – their mutual tensions and conflicts. Rather, these tensions and conflicts functioned as an incentive to continue exploring both the field of science and spirituality.

Looking back on that described moment of insight, I realize that the education which I received from my teachers had two facets. As teachers of language, mathematics, history, and other subjects, they stimulated in their pupils the development of reason and rationality, faculties that are at the heart of the modern self. At the same time, they adhered to an orthodox religious view that, not very different from Dante's medieval worldview about heaven and hell (see Van Halen and Janssen, 2004), reflected basic elements of the traditional view of self and world. In my thought as described above I spontaneously applied the capacity of reason to traditional religious beliefs, leading to a tension-loaded dialogue between two *I*-positions, "I as a thinker" and "I as religious." The thought can be seen as representing a "dominance reversal" (Hermans, 1996b) of these positions: The religious position, strongly supported by my educators up till then, had to give way to the thinking position as precious for my autonomous self. At the moment of the reversal the thinking position was applied to content that had hitherto belonged to the exclusive domain of the religious position, which led to an interrogation of the religious beliefs by reason, so to speak. Although the thinker was the dominant party during the continuing dialogue, the believer did not disappear but was rather transported into a more open and (re)searching spiritual position.

Fate or self-reflexive project? The belief in fate or destiny is a central concept for the traditional self, because it directly concerns one's place in the cosmic order. In an insightful article Adams (2004) offers a critical discussion of Giddens's (1991; 1992) view that reflexivity is the most important characteristic of the modern self: for people today the self is a reflexive project in the sense of a continuous interrogation of one's past, present, and future. In this view, developments in the modern phase of history are often illustrated by contrasting them with established practices in traditional societies. In Giddens's (1991) own words: "There is no non-modern culture which does not in some sense incorporate, as a central part of its philosophy, the notions of fate and destiny ... to live in the world of high modernity is to live in an environment of chance and risk ... and the reflexive making of history. Fate and destiny have no formal part to play in such a system" (p. 109; cited by Adams, 2004).

It is Adams's (2004) purpose to demonstrate that spiritual awareness, including belief in fate and destiny, is not an exclusive characteristic of a traditional society but also of the modern self in contemporary society. He refers to the immense popularity of books and self-help texts that function as spiritual guides and are widely read by people of all educational levels. He pays particular attention to one of these books that he sees as illustrative of the literature he has in mind – James Redfield's *The Celestine Prophecy* (1994). In this book nine revelations of spiritual "insight" are gradually disclosed in the context of an adventure narrative. These insights, in later versions of the book complemented by tenth and eleventh insights, are peppered with references to concepts of fate that are presented to the reader as leading to spiritual awakening and unfolding. By 1996 the book had already been reprinted twenty times in the USA and had sold over a million copies. Since then its popularity has spread through many other countries in the world and has led to groups who meet and discuss its principles. There are also audio-versions, an "experiential guide," a number of follow-up books, websites, a monthly *Celestine* journal, and a full-length feature film with the same title as the book.

More generally, the contemporary concern with spirituality is manifested in a variety of cultural forms. Recent films such as *Love Actually*, *Sliding Doors*, and *Serendipity* can be seen as variations on the theme of destiny and fate, suggesting that romantic pairing is "destined" despite a series of obstacles that are initially blocking the way to union. Destiny and fate can well go side by side with modern self-reflexive awareness and can be exemplified by a variety of developments in popular culture, such as the popularity of "deep ecology," the resurgence of paganism, and many new age practices such as Wicca, witchcraft, divination (e.g., tarot cards, runes, I-Ching), past-life recovery, meditation, and visualization. Some of these practices come from Eastern cultures and are adapted for our time. Feng Shui, for example, originally a Chinese custom, is now a popular practice in the West, even used by some real estate agents to improve sales of products. This practice is concerned with the ordering of objects in one's living space. If one orders the objects according to certain rules, it is believed that this encourages the events in one's life to take a particular path. It is assumed that there is a connection between the action of the individual and a mysterious, transcendental power (Adams, 2004).

It is Adams's (2004) intention to argue that it is unnecessary and even undesirable to emphasize one side of the reflexivity/faith dualism as underlying Giddens's (1991) work. In contrast to such a dualism, discourses of faith do not necessarily exclude heightened self-reflexivity. Rather, the two may live in a creative tension as positions in a multi-voiced self. Such a view is in support of a pluralized notion of the self that acknowledges contradictions, tensions, and disagreement as typical of normal functioning. The self as a polyphony of affect-laden voices might accommodate both the self as a project and the belief in destiny and fate as self-positions involved in dialogical relationships. As Adams (2004) says:

the analogy with multiplicity, contradiction and polyphony is an admirably complex and experientially relevant means of grasping how non-reflexive and reflexive capabilities might interplay in a contemporary self which *is* constantly seeking to establish trust and continuity, amongst other processes, in numerous complex ways. In the context of a pluralized self, then, concepts of fate, and the need for faith, are here argued to be persistent factors in the achievement of self-identity. (p. 403, emphasis in the original)

In accordance with Adams's observations and arguments, we see the notions of faith, destiny, and fate as phenomena that were prominent in the traditional phase of history but continue to play a central role in the modern and even post-modern phases. The combination of a traditional self as believing in destiny and fate and a modern self as engaged in self-realization and self-reflection leads to a more complex self in which different or even opposed voices create contradictions and tensions that are not necessarily problematic or unhealthy but rather normal and healthy. Faith as emanating from the traditional self contributes to a sense of continuity and stability of the self needed to survive in a period in which change, flux, discontinuity and uncertainty are more prominent than ever before.

The upsurge of ego-documents and the democratization of history The multi-voicedness and dialogical nature of the self are expressed not only on the interface of the traditional phase and the modern phase, but also on the interface of the modern and post-modern phase. This can be exemplified by two phenomena – the explosion of ego-documents and the democratization of history. In an article titled "The immortal ego," Jurgens (2005) discusses the upsurge of weblogs and reality TV as allowing many to place their egos on show in the public domain. Her article was inspired by the establishment of the *Bibliotheca Biographica*, a "lasting digital library" of memories and personal stories that together offer a personally flavored time picture of the present. Participants who are motivated to leave something of themselves for future generations are given a "writing niche" which is accessible via the website of the library.[10] Jurgens argues that this project has a considerable chance of success because of two developments: the explosive growth of ego-documents and the democratization of history.

In earlier (modern) times, the self was seen as something that was located in the realm of intimacy and relatively isolated from the public domain. This changed, however, in the latter part of the twentieth century, when the web was increasingly becoming an outlet for the growing amount of ego-documents. Whereas in earlier times, people wrote their experiences in a personal and private diary, in the digital era participants write their documents for a larger audience and bring them into the public domain. The private becomes public. Like weblogs, reality TV enables a growing number of people to achieve fame. An example is the TV programme *Big Brother*, which allows viewers to watch the people, with whom they can easily identify, living together for a while. Fame is no longer reserved for stars, but potentially accessible to everybody. The "fifteen minutes of fame" of Andy Warhol seem to come within everyone's reach, provided the person is willing to allow him- or herself to be on display.

The democratization of history can be seen as another phenomenon at the interface of the modern and post-modern phase. In the past the recording of key events was largely mediated by reporters and officials who were charged with documenting and explaining the world. However, as Cascio (2005) observes, this is no longer the reality. The blog entries by people who witness a terrorist attack, the camera-phone photos of the aftermath, the Wikipedia accumulation of facts, in combination with the globally collaborative and personal nature of the internet, provide abundant documentation of how everyday individuals respond to history-making events. Millions of people have online journals accessible to anyone who is interested. Millions carry cameras wherever they go, allowing the recording of events as they happen. We have entered an era where millions are now amateur historians.

Many people write books and novels about their families and about the history of the locations where they were born and brought up. Even when these are not officially published, modern technology like the internet gives almost everybody the chance to present him- or herself as a historian with a high degree of uniqueness and considerable visibility. Many people are able to present their more or less artistic film creations at *You Tube*, a website with an impressive growth. In July 2006, the company reported that more than 100 million videos were being watched every day and 50,000 videos were being added per day in May 2006, increasing to 65,000 by July.[11]

As the French post-constructionists have argued, we have left behind the era of grand stories that were shared by large institutions and to a large degree determined people's thoughts and moral views. The rise of ego-documents and recent developments, such as weblogs, books about family members, TV programs like *Big Brother*, and video-websites like *You Tube*, show that the mega-stories have been replaced by the small stories of ordinary people who have become historians of their own lives. As autonomous beings with their own views, personal projects and unique stories, they are typical representatives of the modern phase of history. However, at the same time, they participate in national and international networks, using highly developed communication devices and being involved in a great diversity of contacts over the borders of countries and cultures. As such, they are typical representatives of the post-modern phase. At the interface of these phases, a multi-voiced dialogical self emerges that is engaged in the construction of personal stories and projects and, at the same time, shares these stories with a great variety of others with whom the self is connected temporarily or more permanently.[12]

Selves and identities: organismic or historical developments?

In the present chapter the relationship between the different phases – traditional, modern, and post-modern – is central. What is the precise nature of this relationship? How can we understand "development" of the self across centuries? In order to address these questions, we make a distinction between two kinds of development of the self, organismic and historical, so as to articulate the specific features of the concept of development on the collective level. For comparative purposes we refer to Wilber's (1997) conception of development of collective systems because he works, like we do, on the assumption that the different phases in the development of the mind are not only successive but also simultaneous. Let's have a look at his conception in more detail.

Wilber (1997) assumes that "what is a whole at one stage becomes merely a part of a larger whole at the next stage" (p. 40). In order to explain this assumption he refers to Arthur Koestler's notion of "holon," which can be summarized thus: what is a whole in one context, is part of a wider whole in another. For example, in the phrase "the bark of a dog" the word "bark" is a whole composed of individual letters, but a part with reference to the larger phrase. On the basis of this notion, Wilber sees development in terms of unfolding hierarchical networks, "because you first have to have molecules, *then* cells, *then* organs, *then* complex organisms … The *more holistic* patterns appear *later* in development because they have to await the emergence of the parts that they will then integrate or unify, just as whole sentences emerge *after* whole words" (p. 41, emphases in original). In order to further articulate his view, he makes a distinction between two kinds of causation. In "upward causation" the lower, less holistic levels influence the higher more holistic levels. But just as important is "downward causation," which refers to the influence or control of the higher levels on the lower levels. The author summarizes his conception of development in this way:

In any developmental or growth sequence, as a more encompassing stage or holon emerges, it *includes* the capacities and patterns and functions of the previous stage (i.e., of the previous holons), and then adds its own unique (and more encompassing) capacities. In that sense, and that sense only, can the new and more encompassing holon be said to be "higher" or "wider." Whatever the important value of the previous stage, the new stage has all of that plus something extra (more integrative capacity, for example) and that "something extra" means "extra value" *relative* to the previous (and less encompassing) stage. (pp. 41–2, emphases in original)

We fully endorse Wilber's claim that a particular phase in history includes the patterns and functions of the previous stage and adds to that phase its own unique patterns and functions. However, we have serious doubts when he considers cultural and historical phenomena in terms of an organismic metaphor. The central point of our argument is that an organismic metaphor, considering development as a series of stages that develop to *ever* higher levels of integration, may neglect the apparent shadow sides of the different phases in the history of self and identity.

The question is whether organismic metaphors are applicable to the social and cultural aspects of historical developments. In order to address this question, we have to look at the differences between organismic and social phenomena. An important characteristic of a social point of view is that individuals, groups, and cultures, developing their identities, are involved in processes of exchange and relative domination that are not well expressed by organismic metaphors. As anthropologist Clifford (1988) argues:

> Groups negotiating their identity in contexts of *domination* and *exchange* persist, patch themselves together in ways different from a living organism. *A community, unlike a body, can lose a central "organ" and not die.* All the critical elements of identity are in specific conditions replaceable: language, land, blood, leadership, religion. Recognized viable tribes exist in which any one or even most of these elements are missing, replaced, or largely transformed. (p. 338; emphasis added)

With Clifford, we take the view that the study of self and identity requires acknowledgment of the existence of other groups as intrinsic parts of social exchange and domination. Individuals and groups are not only different from each other but also recognize these differences and like or dislike them, agree or disagree with them, and support or reject them. Individuals and groups can form unifying coalitions but they can also be involved in relationships of mutual conflict, disagreement, and distrust. When they communicate with each other, they do so by using signs, symbols, and language. Moreover, one individual or group can dominate or silence the other so that the dominated party has no chance to express or develop its specific potentials. It is even possible, as the above quotation from Clifford suggests, that identities can lose a central element or transform it (e.g., a change from institutionalized religion to individualized spirituality) and not "die." In summary, notions that give a central place to the *other* as intrinsic to a dialogical conception of self and identity, such as sign-mediated interchange, social power and dominance, opposition, and conflict are not adequately explained by organismic metaphors.

The prominence and exaggeration of positions

Based as they are on the notion of growth, organic metaphors are also not very well equipped to explain the apparent shadow sides of the traditional, modern, and post-modern phases as discussed earlier in the present chapter. The existence of shadow sides suggests that historical change and development implies not only progress but also regress, not only integration but also disintegration, and not only richness but also poverty. In the course of history, we reach higher levels of development in some respects, but fall back in other respects. One needs not agree with all of Benedict's (1934) anthropological assumptions in order to acknowledge one of her central theses: each culture chooses from the large range of human potentialities a more limited number of characteristics, which become the leading traits of the persons living in that culture. When we transpose this insight to the social and historical domains, we see that the different phases (traditional, modern, and post-modern) represent different cultures, or different phases in the development of one culture, each with their own preoccupations, values, practices, and exchange patterns. Each phase selects and emphasizes particular elements from a larger range of human potentialities and makes them dominant over other elements. In terms of dialogical self theory: *different phases make different positions prominent, but at the same time neglect, suppress, or move to the background other positions.*

This prominence thesis has two implications. First, different phases emphasize different positions to the extent that *positions, when exaggerated, create their own shadow sides.* For example, the traditional self emphasizes collectivity and dogmatic truth to the extent that deviation from the norms is not tolerated and even severely punished. In a later period, the modern self gives such a high premium to personal autonomy and freedom that collective values and norms may become neglected or even dismissed, at the risk of loneliness. Again later, the post-modern self emphasizes change and flux to such a degree that fundamental needs for stability, continuity, and safety are under threat.

A second implication of the prominence thesis can be summarized as follows: *positions that were prominent in a previous phase are not totally removed from the repertoire but, in so far as they are neglected, dominated, or suppressed, are backgrounded, with the possibility of becoming, under facilitating conditions, prominent in a later phase.* When these "older" positions are revitalized, a broader position repertoire emerges with the possibility of dialogical relationships between the different positions. As we have emphasized in the first chapter, the process of globalization offers "travel" to many local cultures, different from the one in which we live. This travel offers not only the potential to broaden and enrich our position repertoire but provides, through comparison, a critical awareness of the shadow sides of our own culture or a re-evaluation of its positive sides. In similar ways, comparison of our present era with previous historical phases enables as to see both the possibilities and the limitations of an identity that is characteristic of a particular historical phase. Such travel has an implicit message: historical developments of self and identity do not move spontaneously to higher and higher levels of integration, like organisms do. Rather, they confront us with the strengths and weaknesses of the different "faces" of the self as associated with different historical periods and, as such, create conditions for *learning from history.*

Learning from the traditional self

The architects of the value system proposed by the theorists of the French Revolution thought that if a social system is based on one value only, the system would degenerate. So, if there was freedom only, people would not see and treat each others as equal . If there was equality only, personal initiative and freedom would be suppressed. If there was brotherhood only, this would entail the risk of a suffocating collectivity without much possibility for competition and achievement. However, considering the values as parts of a *pattern*, the shadow sides of one value would be mitigated and corrected by the presence of the other ones. Similarly, central elements of the different models of the self could be combined into patterns, in order to construct a position repertoire with the potential of preventing the exaggeration of one of its elements. We propose that the three historical models of the self provide elements that together could complement each other as parts of a broad and flexible position repertoire that takes into account both the merits and the shadow sides of the separate models.

One of the central elements of the traditional model is the conception that the self is basically ethical because it is always embedded in a larger whole in which the human being realizes a moral telos. In a dialogical conception of the self a moral stance follows from the consideration that the "other" is an intrinsic part of an extended self. As Richardson *et al.* (1998: 510) formulate: "Dialogic relations are always fundamentally ethical because in them we always are either acknowledged or ignored, understood or misunderstood, treated with respect or coerced." Not only dialogue, but the self also can be seen as basically moral enterprises, as Taylor (1989: 27) concludes in a thorough philosophical investigation of the development of the self in the course of history:

to know who I am is a species of knowing where I stand. My identity is defined by the commitments and identifications which provide the frame or horizon within which I can try to determine from case to case what is good, or valuable, or what ought to be done, or what I endorse or oppose. In other words, it is the horizon within which I am capable of taking a stand .

Indeed, in society we appear before others and take a moral stance. However, the other does not have an existence purely outside the self. In the "society of mind" we also take a moral stance in addressing the other as part of an extended self. So, as part of a dialogue within the extended self, we take a stance toward another part of the self, which is respected or not, is silenced or not, and can be expressed or not.

Another aspect of the traditional self which is of potential value to the dialogical self is the central place for belief or faith. It would be erroneous to conceive of the traditional and the modern as mutually exclusive. As

Adams (2004) has argued, traditional elements, such as destiny, fate, and faith, coexist with the emphasis on reason and rationality as characteristic of the modern self. It would likewise be erroneous to see tradition and the post-modern self as mutually exclusive. Rather, the change, flux, and uncertainty of post-modern life give extra shine and value to traditional events, recurrent festivals, and the stability of the expected. (See also the value of "ordinary positions" as recurrent and stable aspects of the self in the age of globalization as discussed in Chapter 1; and see the discussion in Chapter 1 of immigrants who in their adaptation to a new culture give a high value to their culture of origin.)

The connection with the environment and with nature is another central feature of the traditional self, as we have discussed earlier in the present chapter. In dialogical self theory, the connection with the other and with nature is expressed in the inclusion of the other as part of an extended self. The other is not simply outside the self but an intrinsic part of it. Moreover, the dialogical self is conceived as an embodied self (see Chapter 4) and as such part of the broader natural world, as expressed, for example, in the sentence "I'm part of the rainforest protecting itself" (Bragg, 1996: 95).

Learning from the modern self

We can learn from the modern self that the individual is appreciated as independent and autonomous and as having thoughts and actions that are not reduced to the workings of outside agencies. No longer part of a rigid hierarchy and subordinated to an absolute authority, the modern self is free to set its own goals and to develop a personal life-narrative (McAdams, 1988). As a *subject* the self is not only able to give meaning to itself as an *object* but also to develop itself as a *project* (May, 1975). In realizing and developing the self as a project, human beings manifest themselves as agents with a high degree of autonomy.

People in the modern phase conceived their selves as no longer controlled by external forces but, as agentic subjects gifted with reason, able to control their environment and themselves. However, reason and control do not exclude the possibility of receptivity. The coexistence of control and receptivity was expressed in a succinct way by Angyal (1966) when he described the self is a "part-whole." As a "whole" the self is striving for autonomy, that is, expansion through assimilation and control of the environment. As a "part" the self is oriented to homonomy, that is, a longing to fit in with the environment and participate in something that is larger than itself, such as a feeling of union with a social group, nature, or supernatural being. Whereas autonomy is expressed in the desire for superiority, acquisition, exploration, and achievement, homonomy is expressed in specific motives such as the desire for love, interpersonal contact, aesthetic pleasure, and religious experience. Angyal sees the two orientations as mutually complementary: a healthy person develops both orientations rather than one of them. As this and other conceptions show (see Hermans and Hermans-Jansen, 1995, for review), control and receptivity do not contradict each other but are mutually complementary (see also McAdams' 1985 distinction between power and intimacy). As autonomy and homonomy go together in the sense that they can alternate in the same individual, so the attitude of control of the modern self and the attitude of receptivity of the nature-bound traditional self can coexist in the same individual.[13]

Turn-taking behavior is an essential feature of verbal and linguistic variants of dialogical exchange. For efficient turn-taking behavior it is required that the interacting parties are able to move in a flexible way from the position of speaker to the position of listener and back. Whereas the speaker is in relative control of the content and form of the exchange, the listener is invited to be receptive as long as the speaker has the turn. In situations where a modern model of the self is predominant, speaking is more stimulated and encouraged than listening, leading to frequent interruptions or monological digressions. In such situations, speaking is the rule while listening is an art to be learned.

Dialogical self theory recognizes the relevance of autonomy and control of the self but not in the sense of a self-contained individualism. Rather, the self is extended to the world and to the other person in particular. A distinction can be made between *I*-positions that are typical of the autonomous parts of the self and *I*-positions that are expressions of the homonomous parts. For example, I as ambitious, I as rational, I as expansive, or I as controlling are examples of autonomous positions. Examples of homonomous positions are: I as open, I as receptive to art, I as enjoying nature, I as loyal to my group. Similar examples can be provided for positions in the external domain of the self leading to a variety of dialogical or monological relationships (e.g. "As an enthusiastic scientist I'm discussing the possibility of a common project with my inventive colleague," or "As a spiritual person I cannot have any meaningful contact with my very practical father. We are in different worlds").

Learning from the post-modern self

In contrast to the internally unified and essentialized modern self with its sharp boundaries between inside and outside, the post-modern self is subjected to strongly decentralizing forces and "distributed" into a variety of directions. As a consequence, the self emerges as a multiplicity of parts contingent on a variety of changing situations that make the self "multiphrenic" or fragmented. Dialogical self theory recognizes the relevance of decentralizing forces and the multiplicity and heterogeneity of positions, but makes a distinction between centralizing and decentralizing forces (Chapter 1). It is assumed that the self is able to make both kinds of movements. As subjected to decentralizing forces (e.g., the influence of globalization), the self is populated by an increasing density and heterogeneity of changing positions that are a challenge to its coherence and continuity. At the same time, the self is able to make centralizing movements aimed at the integration of the diversity of positions and the inclusion of positions that have a sufficient degree of stability and continuity. The dialogical self can be seen as a "substantial, yet multiplicitous" self (Falmagne, 2004), based as it is on the notion of "agency-in-diversity" (Hermans, 2001a).

The recognition of otherness in the self is one of the aspects of the post-modern self that is of central importance to the dialogical self. The notion of otherness (the other-in-the-self) gives access to the concept of alterity that has direct ethical implications. As involved in dialogical relationships with the actual other and the other-in-the-self, the alterity of the other is acknowledged when she is seen, approached, and appreciated from her own point of view, history, and particularity of experience. Expanding on the work of Levinas (1969), Cooper and Hermans (2007) have argued that in a well-developed dialogical self not only is the alterity of the positions of the actual other appreciated, but so also are the positions in the internal and external domains of the self.

A great advantage of the post-modern self, and of post-modernism in general, is the attention given to dominance and social power. For the dialogical self this has the important implication that power differences between individuals, groups, and cultures are, to a significant degree, reflected in the relative dominance of particular positions over other ones in the organization of the self. Given the acknowledgment of agency, dominance between positions is not to be seen as a *pure* reflection of power and dominance relations in society, as the self is able to respond to societal structures from an original point of view. Power relationships in society can be reflected in the self, but, at the same time, the self is able to construct counter-positions from an original point of view. These counter-positions can also develop on the collective level, as exemplified by feminist and ecological movements.

One of the often mentioned features of post-modernism is its relativism. As an attack on the modernist pretension to universal truth, post-modernists have emphasized the loss of the great stories and have argued for relative truth as localized, dependent on language communities, and changing with historical circumstances. Apart from the philosophical dis-cussions that spring from this view, it is a common observation that, with the retreat of larger institutions and their corresponding truth regimes, people can no longer rely on broadly shared truths and values. In soci-eties with a strong degree of individualization, experiences and values become differentiated. This leads to a situation in which "my experience" or "my view" is different from yours and becomes subject to interchange in which not only agreement but also disagreement plays a prominent role, and in which commonalities are more the result of interchange than as simply given. In a globalizing world, truths and values are increas-ingly becoming visible in their differences and contradictions and need exchange and negotiation in order to create clarity, reduce uncertainty, and arrive at common decisions where needed.

Traditional, modern, and post-modern selves: from time to space

Riesman, Denney and Glazer (1950) were among the first authors to discuss a distinction that shows a striking parallel to the distinc-tion between traditional, modern and post-modern models of the self (for discussion of Riesman's work in the context of identity we follow Cote, 1996). Riesman *et al.* distinguished three "character types" that he labeled tradition-directed, inner-directed and other-directed. The *tradi-tion-directed* character type is typical of traditional rural societies, in which relationships with significant others are controlled by careful and rigid etiquette, and learned by young people during years of intensive sociali-zation. This character type is heteronomous, that is, subject to external forces and domination: there is little choice and the apparent social need for an individuated character type is minimal. Corresponding to the mod-ern model of the self, the *inner-directed* character type emerges as a person with inner convictions and personal goal orientations. As a reaction to the disruptive influences of early industrialization – with its typical geographi-cal mobility, urbanization, capital accumulation, and mass production – individuals are socialized by the development of an inner "compass" that helps them to set their own goals and to find their own ways of life. Inner-directed individuals exercise choice and initiative and are stimu-lated to make careers. The third character type, *other-directed*, arises under conditions that resemble a post-modern (or late-modern) society, which emerged when the means of mass production were developed. It emerged at a time of increasing abundance so that the "scarcity psychology" of the inner-directed became supplanted by the "abundance psychology" of the other-directed. In the post-modern society, the over-production resulting from technological advances leads to heightened consumerism. As a consequence, a post-modern society needs consumption on a large scale in order to avoid capital accumulation. In Riesman *et al.*'s view, the lack of inner moral standards and increased other-orientation experiences entail uncertainty regarding the question of whether the "right" things are done and said. As an answer to this uncertainty, consumption is used as a way of identifying and expressing one's loyalties and relationships. Consequently, the other-directed character is sensitive to others – to their opinions and their approval. Early in their lives individuals learn to constantly monitor the social environment to ensure that their consumption patterns conform to the accepted standards, especially with regard to appearance and behavior. Certainly, the other-directed person strives to meet goals, but those goals shift according to the standards set by others (Cote, 1996; Riesman *et al.*, 1950).

Riesman *et al.*'s work, published almost sixty years ago, shows a remarkably sharp insight into the developments of the time, particularly as it heralded the post-modern, or other-directed, models of the self. However, as we will try to show, the situation in the world at the beginning of the twenty-first century requires further elaboration of their distinction: it needs a dialogical context.

Traditional societies, internally homogeneous and externally distinctive, can coexist well together on the same planet, as long as they do not violate each other's borders. The present post-modern, globalizing world society presents a very different picture. As a result of massive immigration, the facility of transport, diaspora, world-wide economic transactions, ecological problems and disasters, political instabilities, and transnational military operations, large-scale border crossings are taking place in many parts of the world. As a consequence, cultures with different historical origins are living together in the same space. Contemporary citizens live in an interconnected but internally differentiated society with an increasing likehood of tensions and conflicts. Such tensions, often leading to escalation of hostility between political groups, and sometimes even to political murders, show how sharpened and contrasting positions can lead to violence – most conspicuously in the phenomena of international terrorism and widespread suicide bombings that arouse intense emotions, not only in the relatives of the victims but, as a result of contemporary media communication, in living rooms all over the world. It can be asked whether it is possible to consider these phenomena from the perspective of self and identity construction. We are aware of the complex nature of these phenomena and we do not pretend to give any comprehensive explanation, but it is our view that a dialogical analysis of the historical models of the self may contribute to their

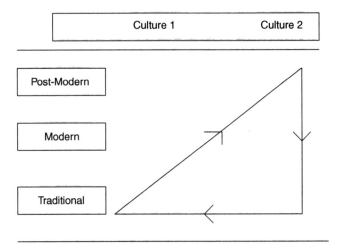

Figure 2.1 Culture 1 challenges Culture 2

understanding. In order to achieve this understanding it is necessary to *place the temporal models* of the traditional, modern, and post-modern selves *in a spatial context.*

Spatializing the temporal models of the self: the "triangle of global misunderstanding"

The three models of the self can be spatialized by placing them in front of each other as shown in Figure 2.1. The starting point is that individuals, groups, and cultures are not entities in themselves characterized by particular traits or features, but they are involved in processes of globalization and localization. Selves and identities are culture-inclusive but, in their turn, cultural groups are increasingly globalized. That is, cultural groups meet each other on a global level and, consequently, they understand or fail to understand each other, and do or do not endorse each other's values. When individuals, groups, or cultures meet each other, they do so on the basis of particular premises and worldviews. Dialogical relationships are possible only if the premises of the participants allow each other sufficient space and basis for negotiation and exchange. What then happens when cultural groups with different worldviews meet each other on the global level and what are the implications for dialogue? We address this question by an example of a misunderstanding that is taking place on national and global scales.

A well-known and widely discussed topic is the emergence of extreme right parties in several European countries (France, Belgium, the

Netherlands, and Austria) in the past decade. Substantial immigration in these countries, particularly from Islamic parts of the world, is generally seen as one of the main causes. As Ignazi (2003) has argued, citizens of these countries who were in favour of a hierarchically organized and homogeneous society have been lacking a political home for long time and finally found it in right-wing parties. Order and authority, shared values and norms, and national identities are centrepieces of these parties. Often they demonstrate a longing for what they see as the well-organized and coherent communities of a lost past. These features show a striking similarity with what we have described as the traditional model of the self. Why do people, living in a post-modern phase of history, favour a traditional model of their (political) identity? An answer to this question is given by Betz (2004), who attributes the success of extreme right parties to the increasing uncertainty and anxiety about the unknown. As a result of the processes of Europeanization and globalization, certainties seem to have disappeared and developments in the labor market are seen as a threat to people's standards of living. Therefore, they experience the incoming streams of immigrants as a danger and as destabilizing of the existing order in society. This threat is fueled by the fact that many immigrants have backgrounds that are seen as very different from the mainly secular host cultures, or the hosts adhere to religions (if they do) that are very different from those of the immigrants. The existing political parties in the middle of the political spectrum have no adequate answer to these anxieties and uncertainties and, as a consequence, cannot function as an alternative for the voters.

There are undoubtedly many possible reasons why existing political parties have no adequate answer to the uncertainties of contemporary life. In the context of the present chapter, we will focus on one particular reason that refers to a process that, in our view, is taking place at the interface of the different models of identity as described earlier. This reason goes beyond existing political parties and finds its origin in the loss of universal truth and grand stories as typical of the modern model of the self – a loss common to the modern and traditional models in that they both offer forms of certainty. The modern model does this in the form of universal truths, the traditional model in the form of an encompassing, hierarchical order with shared norms and values. In contrast, relativism characterizes the post-modern model. Relativism allows an immense variety of subjective truths and stories, dependent on individual, societal, and cultural differences and changing circumstances. One of the problems of the post-modernist model is that it does not offer the certainty, safety, and continuity that people want, on the basis of their biological needs, as discussed in Chapter 1.

The problem of the party system of European and other countries involves, on a deeper level, the increasing tension between globalization and basic biological needs of continuity and safety. This can be exemplified by the dramatic events of 9/11, which were followed by other attacks from political extremists who, in many but not all cases, gave religious justifications for their deeds. The problem for political parties of Western countries is that the post-modern phase with its typical relativism does not provide an adequate answer to the absolute truth and value claims by extremist political groups. The turn to extreme right political parties can be seen as filling a gap that is created by the lack of certainty and direction intrinsic to the post-modern identity model.

In our view, the process described above can be further analyzed as a "global misunderstanding," depicted as a movement represented by the triangle in Figure 2.1. Many immigrants of orthodox religions have worldviews that show strong similarities with the traditional identity model, such as the need for hierarchy, homogeneity, authority, order, direction, and certainty (the traditional position of Culture 1). In our contemporary era, dominated by the post-modern model, many citizens of the host country do not feel able to meet this challenge, because answering from the perspective of a post-modern model (the post-modern position of Culture 2) does not enable them to answer with a "counter-certainty" that would give them sufficient safety and direction in life. As a consequence, they answer by falling back on the certainties of an (implicit) traditional model, responsive as they are to the demagogic strategies of political leaders of extreme right parties, who give them the certainties they miss in the leaders of a more moderate kind. Ironically, the leaders of extreme right parties and their followers find their resources in an identity model (the traditional position of Culture 2) that is the same as the one to which they are opposed, emphasizing the need for hierarchy, homogeneity, authority, order, direction, and stabilized homogeneous identity. Culture 2 answers the challenge of Culture 1 with another version of the *same* model, while having the subjective conviction that they are "entirely *different*." Because the opposing groups both express a need for absolute truths and strong certainty, they are at risk of escalation and, according to some rather pessimistic commentators, a threat to the democratic functioning of society. Because this problem is part of the process of globalization, we speak of a "global misunderstanding."

As we have tried to argue, the spatialization of the temporally ordered models of the self has the potential of revealing some of the problems and misunderstandings of our time. This can be summarized by bringing some insights of Chapter 1 and the present chapter together: *because of its inherent relativity the post-modern model fuels traditional models as forms of defensive localization.* The conclusion is that the post-modern model of the self, although it comprises some elements relevant to a dialogical approach, does not provide, as it is, a sufficiently strong model for the realization of dialogical relationships between different individuals, groups, and cultures. As proposed earlier, there is a need for another model, a dialogical one, that elaborates on elements of the existing models, but transforms them in such a way that new avenues are opened for the realization of more productive and constructive relationships not only between different individuals and groups but also within the individual and herself. We will elaborate on this view in the rest of the book .

Summary

Whereas in the previous chapter the self was described as extended in space, the present chapter was devoted to the self as extended in time. Both globalization and localization (spatial development) and historical precursors of self and identity (temporal development) are seen as implying collective voices that are not simply outside the individual self but rather constituting parts of it. Three models of self and identity, associated with different historical phases, were distinguished: traditional, modern, and post-modern. Features of the *traditional self* are: distinction between a lower and imperfect existence on earth and a higher and perfect existence in the afterworld, body and senses as a hindrance to spiritual life, the existence of a moral telos, social hierarchy, authority, dogmatic truths, and connection with the natural environment. The *modern self* was discussed in terms of autonomy, individualism, the development of reason, the pretension to universal truth, strict and sharp boundaries between self and non-self, an attitude of control of the external environment, a separation of the outer and the inner, the subject and the object, self and other, fact and value, the is and the ought, science and faith, politics and religion, the public from the private, and theory from practice. The *post-modern self* was described as a movement away from the universalistic pretensions of master-narratives with their concern with totality, system, and unity, towards an emphasis on difference, otherness, local knowledge, and fragmentation; a dissolution of symbolic hierarchies with their fixed judgments of taste and value towards a blurring of the distinction between high and popular culture; a far reaching decentralization of the subject, whose stable sense of identity and biographical continuity give way to fragmentation and superficial play with an endless stream of images and sensations; a tendency towards the aesthetization of everyday life (e.g., pop art, Dada, surrealistic transformation of reality); tendencies towards a consumer culture; the dependence of "truth" on language communities; and the important role of social power behind definitions of what is true and not true, right and not right. It was demonstrated that the formulation of the three models is not entirely new, as they have their precursors in ancient times or in recent history.

Strong emphasis was placed on the assumption that the different historical phases are not purely successive but rather simultaneous in the sense that the previous phase continues when the next phase is starting. We exemplified the simultaneity of traditional and the modern elements by referring to the coexistence of reason and the belief in destiny and fate, as typical of the contemporary self. The simultaneity of the modern and post-modern models of the self was illustrated by the upsurge of ego-documents and the "democratization of history." It was argued that this simultaneity creates interfaces in which more complex selves and identities can emerge. In this context a distinction was made between organismic and historical development and objections were raised against a conception of history as a developing organism that is reaching higher and higher levels of integration. As a reaction to this view, we explained that a dialogical conception of the self recognizes not only centralizing movements, that refer to the integration and continuity of the self but also decentralizing movements that refer to its multiplicity, diversification, and fragmentation.

Being aware that any evaluation of historical developments is risky as it is colored by a contemporary perspective, we gave an overview of what we see as the assets and shadow sides of the different models. For example, as assets of the pre-modern self the connection with nature and the existence of community-based meaning and morality were mentioned, whereas the strong hierarchical order, the overly moralistic attitude and restrictive religious dogmas were seen as shadow sides. Reflecting on the modern self, we considered the emergence of personal autonomy and self-development that liberated us from the oppressive forces of hierarchical structures and the dogmatic truth pretensions of the traditional period as assets. Shadow sides of the modern self were described in terms of the self as encapsulated within itself with the risk of loneliness; the loosening of the basic contact with the external environment and with nature; the dualism between self and other; and the exaggerated attitude of control and exploitation that has eroded the intimate ties of traditional community life and has threatened the ecological balance of the entire planet. As assets of the post-modern phase we mentioned the liberation of the self from its imprisonment within the walls of a centralized and stable structure; openness to the influences of historical and social circumstances and recognition of the impact of history, language, language communities, social conventions, globalization, networks and technology; the broadening of the role-repertoire of women beyond traditional constraints and the improvement of their participation in society; sexual freedom and variation beyond the masculine ideals and patriarchal social structures of modernism; more sensitivity and openness to the multiplicity and flexibility of the human mind and more room for humor and play. As shadow sides we described the relativistic stance leading to an "anything goes" attitude; the lack of an epistemological basis for a meaningful dialogue between groups or cultures; pessimism and lack of hope; persistent doubts about progress; and a one-sided focus on change, flux, and discontinuity, resulting in a lack of rootedness or feeling at home. On the basis of these considerations we discussed how a dialogical view of the self can profit from this analysis of assets and shadow sides.

Finally, a spatalization of the temporally ordered models of the self was proposed. We argued that, under the influence of globalization, the different models of the self coexist in contemporary society and that an interface emerges where different views of the self meet. In an age of increasing immigration, traditional, modern, and post-modern selves and identities are *confronted with each other* and show fits or misfits. We analyzed, as an example, the impotence of European political parties in the middle and left of the political spectrum to give an adequate answer to the growing popularity of extreme right parties. We argued that this impotence is the consequence of the gap that exists between the relativism of post-modernism and the cosmic value and truth pretensions of traditional worldviews. We argued that this gap leads to a "global misunderstanding" and that a model other than the existing ones, a dialogical model, is needed to meet the challenges of a globalizing society.

NOTES

1 In a UK superstition survey Richard Wiseman found that current levels of superstitious behaviour and beliefs in the UK were surprisingly high, even among those with a scientific background. Touching wood is the most popular UK superstition, followed by crossing fingers, avoiding ladders, not smashing mirrors, carrying a lucky charm and having superstitious beliefs about the number thirteen. Moreover, superstitious people tend to worry about life, have a strong need for control, and have a low tolerance of ambiguity (www.richardwiseman.com/resources/superstition_report.pdf), accessed 2008).

2 In order to understand the hierarchical nature of traditional societies a distinction is required between the early period in which humans lived as hunter-gatherers and the later period in which they developed the practice of agriculture. As Binmore (2005) has argued, we can learn much from the

study of contemporary hunter-gatherers, like the African pygmies, Greenland eskimos, Australian aborigines, Paraguayan Indians, and Siberian nomads in order to better understand the circumstances in which our own ancestors lived. In these societies decisions are not imposed by a powerful leader with a stabilized and institutionalized power position. Rather, decisions are made on the basis of mutual negotiations with fair play as an important moral principle. People who put themselves in the position of "boss" or "leader" are corrected by ridicule or social isolation. These egalitarian relationships changed when, with the emergence of agriculture, societies became more hierarchical. At some point in time, groups claimed a particular place as their property and started to store food. Becoming vulnerable to attacks from rivals, they armed themselves in order to protect their property. This resulted in a division of labor in which an elite group had the task of protecting the precious places and, as a result, the members of this group received more power than others. Along these lines, societies became more hierarchical, with leaders who had the power to make decisions for the group as a whole and to dominate others in their daily lives. A million years in which our ancestors lived as hunter-gatherers is a very long time in comparison with the approximately 10,000 years in which they lived as agriculturalists. Our origin as hunter-gatherers has, according to Binmore, produced in us an "egalitarian nature" that is suspicious of the concentration of power in one person or group. Since agriculture started to change our selves and social relationships dramatically, we have lived in a "cultural, hierarchical cage" or, in terms of dialogical self theory, we are at risk of living in a "societal *I*-prison." The abuse of power to which people are often exposed since society became hierarchical is experienced as conflicting with their egalitarian nature that prefers negotiations to take place on the basis of fair play and justice.

3 For the relationship between religion and violence, see Girard (1979).

4 See, for example, the development of science in the Middle Ages: www. en.wikipedia.org/wiki/Science_in_the_Middle_Ages.

5 Central to Carl Rogers' and Abraham Maslow's interests were notions such as self-fulfilment, self-growth, and self-expression. They assumed that when a person is able to reach the higher levels of self-actualization or self-fulfilment, they are able to express their unique capacities and participate in the higher values of beauty, truth, and goodness. Humanistic theories fit well with the ideals expressed by the proponents of what Bellah and colleagues (1985) call expressive individualism. From a dialogical perspective we can ask whether humanistic psychology pays enough attention to the other person as part of an extended self and sufficiently acknowledges the alterity of the other person as part of the self. A related problem arises from the assumption that inner potential is part of an internal blueprint that is innate and only waiting to be expressed under the influence of a facilitating environment. This idea of "psychological growth" is comparable to a flower that contains all its inner potentials in its seeds and will blossom, given sufficient water, food, and light. The other-in-the-self, as one of the central ideas in dialogical self theory, brings elements to the self that are not necessarily implied by an internal blueprint or genetic program but are *added* as constitutive elements as a result of innovative dialogues with other people or with oneself.

6 The film *High Noon* makes frequent use of movement along straight roads. The hero is continually moving in linear ways from one point to the other, always accompanied by his gun as a symbol of strength and control of the situation. By these linear spatial movements, the film reflects the goal-orientation and sense of progress typical of the modern self.

7 The modern self has paved the way for a dialogical conception as it allows two autonomous positions that can become engaged in a process of exchange in which one voice, by its nature, does not prevail over the other voice. As the Enlightenment produced democracy, the modern self has generated the conditions for dialogue with oneself. However, the modern self is not "internally" multi-voiced and dialogical. It can only respond as an undivided and internally consistent unity which is, according to the Cartesian conception, totally clear and transparent to itself, without any darkness, internal division, multiplicity, or spatial opposition.

8 By its emphasis on multiplicity, language, history, and power, the post-modern model has made a significant and invaluable contribution to the development of a dialogical model. However, by its far-reaching decentralization and dismissal of the agency of the self (e.g., the death of the author), it is not able to account for the self as an original source of meaning production and reproduction. As such it is more relational (e.g., one emerges from each encounter as a different person) than dialogical (e.g., meaning production and innovation as contributions from the self to the world).

9 See science.jrank.org/pages/9748/Multiple-Identity-Critique-Subject.html

10 Each historical phase has its typical space. The traditional self can be characterized by a church that reaches out above all the neighboring houses of the village and has a pulpit that suggests that the Word is coming from above. Whereas the traditional space is vertically structured, the modern self needs a horizontal movement. This self can be represented by the production hall of a modern industrial building. People work in a goal-oriented way on a product in linearly constructed buildings on the basis of clear criteria for economic progress. A typical example of a post-modern space is the airport of a metropolis. Travellers move in very different and even opposite directions, without knowing where each other is going. Walking through the numerous airport shops, they consume the latest best-seller of a popular author, and during their flight they watch a film that gives them some distraction. The dialogical self is best exemplified by an international conference. Participants from different countries and cultures meet each other and exchange ideas and experiences from their own point of view. They anticipate learning from each other and, in the best case, they go home enriched by new experiences.

11 Wikipedia, 21 December 2007.

12 Cote (1996) assumes that in a post-modern society (he uses the term "late modern") individuals invest in a certain identity (or identities) and engage in a series of exchanges with other actors. This stands in contrast to the restrictions imposed on individuals of earlier societies where identities were more constrained both in repertoire and flexibility. He proposes the term "identity capital" in order to denote what individuals "invest" in "who they are." To be a player in the "identity market," one must establish a stable

sense of self which is bolstered by social and technical skills in a variety of areas, effective behavioral repertoires, psychosocial development to a more advanced level, and associations in key social and occupational networks. In this description Cote brings together, in our view, post-modern elements (e.g., identity market; social and occupational networks) and modern elements (e.g., stable sense of self).

13 In a personal comment on the present chapter (8 July 2008), Frank Richardson suggests that the "control or be controlled" orientation of modern life seems to squeeze out receptivity. As a critical response to the work of Angyal (1966), Richardson speculates that autonomy and receptivity may not really be balanced as equal partners, but rather that the experiences and meanings of receptivity ultimately *serve* autonomy or self-expression, a largely *modern* orientation.

3   Positioning theory and dialogue

A person cannot help thinking of himself as, and even feeling himself to be ... two people, one of whom can act upon and observe the other. Thus he pities, loves, admires, hates, despises, rebukes, comforts, examines, masters or is mastered by, 'himself'.

C. S. Lewis

One of the starting points of this book is that the self and identity can only be properly understood when their spatial and temporal nature is fully acknowledged. Therefore, we started this book by exploring self and identity as part of a globalizing world (space) and as part of a changing collective history (time). In the present chapter we develop a theoretical framework that takes these spatial and temporal processes into account. From a spatial point of view, we will describe the extended self in terms of a spatially organized position repertoire. From a temporal point of view, we will elaborate on the view that the dialogical self is located at the interface of different models of the self: the traditional, modern, and post-modern models.[1] In our discussion of the similarity between the post-modern and the dialogical model of the self, we will focus on the *multiplicity and differences* of positions. In agreement with the modern model, the dialogical self takes into account the *coherence* and *continuity* of the self. Finally, from the traditional self the dialogical self learns that there is a moral purpose, expressed in the *moral valuation* of the multiplicity and alterity not only of the position repertoire of other people, groups and cultures but also of the different positions in the self. This exploration will provide a basis for the formulation of the main features of "good dialogue."

Difference and contrast in the self

One of the fascinating phenomena in the study of the self is the fact that human beings develop relationships not only with other people but also with themselves. Particular relationships that emerge *between* people can also emerge *within* the self. For illustrative purposes, let's

120

consider four examples: self-conflict, self-criticism, self-agreement, and self-consultancy.

Self-conflict

In the case of self-conflict two positions or voices can push the individual into different or even opposed directions. A certain amount of inner conflict or "being of two minds" belongs to the everyday life of most people. It can be very transient and "small" as when we take some time to consider the menu in a restaurant, but can become more prolonged and serious when we are involved in a "war of voices" as, for example, in a situation of divorce or applying for a new job. In the latter cases, the consequences of following one of the voices and not the other one has far-reaching behavioral consequences and important implications not only for ourselves but also for the people around us.

In a situation of divorce, for example, partners often go through a period of inner turmoil. Conflicting voices struggle for priority, often leading to behavior that may be surprising or unexpected in the eyes of the partner and even oneself. A man who is left by his wife may say: "I don't understand her behavior, because some days ago she said to me that she loved me!" However, the husband is not aware of the intense and long-standing inner conflict on the part of his wife. The struggle of the voices leads to a period of instability in which the quick alternation of incompatible voices leads to very different and contradictory statements or actions. At the moment his wife says to him that she loves him, her loving voice ("I want to stay") becomes dominant and pushes conflicting voices to the background or even silences them. However, the conflicting voice can be silenced only for some time, because it cannot be "deleted" from the self entirely. Emotionally charged as it is, it can be pushed to the background but not excluded from the self for ever. At any moment it can become prominent again, depending on situational changes or spontaneous fluctuations in the self. After a period of seeming peace, the background voice ("I want to go") suddenly comes back and overpowers the other voice, driving the person to a separation. Such inner conflicts and periods of instability become less intense when one of the voices becomes more permanently dominant over the other or when the two voices find a common basis of agreement.

Apparently, there are very different kinds of conflicts. Some of them can be so serious that the person cannot function well for long without high psychological costs. On the other side, removing *all* conflicts from the self, if possible at all, would be at the cost of its creative potential.

Conflicts may bring the self into a field of tension, contradiction, or disagreement that may, however, have beneficial consequences for its functioning. Let's illustrate this by the case of a person who describes his work as a minister and psychotherapist in terms of conflicting voices:

In me the psychotherapist and the minister are sometimes badgering each other. Says the therapist to the minister "I don't see you as a professional helper. You have no obligatory supervision or additional training. During your study leave, you have your sleep out and nobody criticizes you when you limit your study to the newspaper." The minister has to take a moment to recover from this confrontation, but then answers "You are right, that is the absurdity of my position. While you are adapting to the norms of this world, I represent another reality that is very different. A strange kind of love which I do not always experience as love. This is also relevant for professionals, you know! Because all your supervision is a waste of effort, when you cannot love your clients. Did your Freud not say this somewhere?" The therapist answers "Does your pastoral work lead to scientifically valid results, is it evidence-based?" "God save me," the minister responds, "Love is not measurable. Therefore, I do not get observable results as you do, which in one way is a problem. Therefore, my people are not requested to pay ..."[2]

The result of this internal dialogue, expressed as an exchange between two people, does not result in a "disappearance" of the tension between the two positions. Rather, the field of tension functions as a platform where they alternate in a process of turn-taking. Instead of being "resolved," the conflict is clarified and each of the two positions is accorded a specific meaning in comparison with the other. The writer is able to distinguish between the concerns of the two positions and to articulate their differences and tensions.

Certainly, when the intensity and frequency of an internal conflict increase, the effect may be exhausting and the conflicts become maladaptive, as many therapists have observed. However, internal conflicts, like any internal tension or contradiction, may be a source of productive self-reflection, self-exploration, and self-dialogue and even lead to creative insights or activities. As such, internal conflicts have an adaptive function in the self and stimulate further development. Dialogue includes not only agreement but also disagreement, and not only harmony but also conflict (Hermans, 1996a). The processes of globalization and localization, as discussed in Chapter 1, often lead to internal conflicts and contradictions. Moreover, the increasing multiplicity and diversity in the self as typical of the post-modern self, as discussed in Chapter 2, entail contradictions and conflicts in the self. In light of the developments in the collective voices of our time, it should be emphasized that conflicts are not to be understood as antithetical to the concept of dialogue. It is the nature of the conflict and the answer it receives from the self that makes it adaptive or maladaptive (see Chapter 6 for conflict resolution).

Self-criticism

Self-criticism typically results when we compare our acts with particular standards set by ourselves or others and notice that they are not reached. Self-criticism is not a purely cognitive activity because it co-exists with self-evaluation. When we do not reach the standards, we tend to evaluate ourselves in a negative way. In a research project on self-criticism, Whelton (2001) selected a sample of college students according to their level of self-critical vulnerability to depression. He studied how they criticized themselves and how they responded to their criticism after an exercise in which they imagined an experience of failure. He found that those with self-critical personalities showed more contempt for themselves in their self-criticism than those of a control group. Moreover, he found that the self-critical students displayed less resilience in the face of the criticism. They were less assertive, sadder, more submissive and more ashamed than the students of the control group. As these results suggest, strong degrees of self-criticism are associated with strong emotions that color self-evaluations in negative ways.[3]

Despite the apparent observation that a high degree of self-criticism can have a detrimental influence on a person's well-being and good-functioning, it is not intrinsically maladaptive. Mild forms of self-criticism are part of everyday life and are often expressed in short statements when people are involved in a task that requires their full attention. As Lewis (2002) observed, people express self-criticism by short statements or words like "too bad!" or "stupid!" Such critical expressions are not necessarily a disadvantage when performing a task, but, rather, are normal forms of self-evaluation and self-correction. Self-criticism can be impulsive and momentary as the "stupid" example suggests, but it can also be part of a longer and more intense process of critical self-reflection, as when a person "retreats" into him- or herself for some time and engages in a critical examination of his or her actions.[4] Such critical examination can be part of a productive "life-review" (Butler, 1975), a process that is characterized by the progressive return to consciousness of past experiences. As part of the reflexive process, unresolved conflicts can be surveyed and perhaps reintegrated. People who enter a life review, often the elderly, confront themselves with their past failures and this may lead to feelings of anxiety and guilt and even to depression. However, they can also make creative use of their self-reflection when they think through what to do in the time that is left and how they can productively learn from the biases and failures of the past.

Whelton and Greenberg (2004: 113) elucidate the two sides of self-criticism in subtle ways:

A puzzling fact about human reflexivity is the extent to which self-awareness is imbued with self-evaluation and, for many (perhaps most) people, self-attack and self-condemnation. An immense amount of pain is generated in people by themselves, by the ways in which they passionately berate themselves for perceived shortcomings and flaws. This is a central and basic instance of a division of the self into two parts. A very basic and still largely unresolved issue is to explain how this process is adaptive and fundamental to the self and how the benign and functional aspects of it differ from the ravages of self-imposed psychological abuse.

As this quotation suggests, self-criticism is not intrinsically unhealthy, dysfunctional, or detrimental for one's well-being. Depending on the intensity, frequency, emotional quality, and the situation in which it emerges, it can be considered either adaptive or maladaptive.

Self-agreement

Making agreements with oneself is a phenomenon that, like self-conflict and self-criticism, can be considered an expression of a mind that deals with itself in reflexive ways. Although it is a rather neglected phenomenon in the psychological literature, it is valuable to see it as another example of how the mind acts upon itself.

Self-agreement can be considered as a form of positioning toward oneself in which individuals judge and reward their own actions. As Kenen (1984) has argued, self-agreement has the potential for internal social control and for creating social order in the self. Whereas social control and order can be created by an ongoing process of negotiation between two or more individuals or groups, agreement and negotiation may perform an analogous function in the domain of the self.

In her empirical research Kenen (1984) found support for three types of self-agreement: (i) *self-promises* occur when individuals have decided to make an agreement with themselves about something they will or will not do (e.g., "I just thought of the benefits and I just started ... so I decided to get my act together and try to lose the weight"); (ii) *self-persuasion* arises in those cases where individuals try to persuade themselves but seem to articulate only what the "persuading" side is saying. Although the partner in the dialogue does not verbalize its position to any great extent, the dialogue is articulated well enough to allow an agreement to be reached (e.g., "I talked myself into it by saying, 'think how good you'll feel when you reach your goal and look forward to your reward'"); (iii) *self-bargaining* occurs when two or more positions, consciously articulated by different aspects of the self, are appraised by each side in an effort to reach an agreement that different sides can live with, a process most nearly analogous to an interpersonal negotiation (e.g., "I talked to myself. It was as though I was at a bargaining table with myself." "I always reason with myself … It is always difficult – since I know myself only too well and would not be able to fulfil an outlandish promise. So my 'deal' is always made within realistic expectations and time boundaries").

On the basis of her results, Kenen (1984) concluded that self-agreements may enable individuals to interact effectively with themselves, resulting in a negotiated order with effective internal social control, where the one part of the self is regulating another part. Apparently, controlling or regulating one's own conduct can be dialogical or monological. It is monological when one part forces the other part to do something that the other part does not want, with the first part not willing to listen to the second one. It is dialogical when a decision emerges by a "democratic" negotiation between the different parts with a workable outcome as a result. Individuals can choose to regulate their acts in dialogical ways because they can imagine both their own actions and others' responses to them so that both can be taken into account. Social control can operate internally as individuals need a sense of a reasonably ordered internal social world so that they are better equipped to choose a certain course of action.

Self-consultancy

Self-consultancy is another form of activity of the self in which there is a basic similarity between addressing another person and addressing oneself. When we are confronted with a difficult problem or when we pose a puzzling question to ourselves, we are sometimes not able to give an immediate answer and need time to consult ourselves. Self-consultancy is also typical of situations in which we have to take a decision that has important implications for our future and/or that of significant others. We need some time to "walk around" with the problem or question, waiting for some meaningful answer. Sometimes we need longer to find an answer or some advice that is not immediately available. Self-consultancy occurs when we are in need of a high-quality answer that gives direction to our future behavior or suggests how we might cope with a particular problem. The outcome of self-consultancy often emerges from the lower levels of consciousness. One may go to rest with a particular question in mind and awake in the morning with the right answer. The process of self-consultancy is, however, not entirely unconscious because it is highly influenced by and dependent on the questions posed by the conscious mind. A creative answer or piece of advice results from a prepared mind.

Self-consultancy is one of the largely unknown processes that occur at the interface of the conscious and unconscious levels of the mind.[5]

Some people use systematic procedures of self-consultancy in which they interact with themselves as if they are interacting with another person. Lovell (2000: 356–7), a consultancy expert, is in the habit of consulting himself in the following way:

Practitioners can act as consultors to themselves. I find I can do this by describing to/for myself what I need to consult myself about. Sometimes I do this in the first person but I find that it helps to objectify things and to induce the consultancy dynamic if I use the third person singular: "George said … or "Lovell did … or "The minister/chair/worker felt…" The form of address depends upon how good or bad I am feeling about myself, things that have happened and what I have done.

Moments of self-consultancy and self-interrogation can also take place in a very sudden and transient way. Consider the following, which is attributed to George Bernard Shaw: "A Native American elder once described his own inner struggles in this manner: 'Inside of me there are two dogs. One of the dogs is mean and evil. The other dog is good. The mean dog fights the good dog all the time.' When asked which dog wins, he reflected for a moment and replied, 'The one I feed the most.'"[6] In this text the man is suddenly confronted with a difficult question that he cannot answer immediately. The words "he reflected for a moment" suggest that his attention shifts from a directly accessible to a less accessible part of his self that has to be consulted or interrogated. In order to reach that part, he needs some time to "make up his mind" in order to find the appropriate answer. The question invites him to start a process of self-interrogation and leads him to a part of himself that seems to be a source of wisdom. His answer gives the reader the feeling that there is some deeper meaning revealed that was not available during the running speed of the conversation, but could only be reached by pausing in the midst of the turn-taking process.

Self-consultancy and self-interrogation are acts of listening to oneself that require a certain degree of receptivity to the messages that the self offers after it is consulted about a particular problem, question, or task. An adequate answer is not provided as a result of impatient effort and it will not emerge when the person wants to speed things up and presses himself to give an immediate answer. Such an answer, if it comes up at all, will be premature or lack the quality that one hopes for. A high degree of openness to the present moment is required because it cannot be predicted when the answer will arise and what its content will be. The part posing the question is a different part of the self from the one providing an answer, and its difference, speed, and particularity should be recognized. In order to facilitate self-consultancy, it is necessary to

slow down or even interrupt the ongoing speed of the turn-taking process. Self-consultancy and self-interrogation require some silence to give
the answer a chance to emerge. This "preparing" silence is relevant to
consultations both with other people and other aspects of the self.

The relation of the mind with itself and its extension to the environment

Phenomena like self-conflict, self-criticism, self-agreement, and self-
consultancy suggest a basic similarity between the relationships among
people and the relationship between different parts of the self. Two or
more people can be involved in a conflict, criticize each other, make
an agreement with each other, or consult each other. In similar ways
the self can be involved in an unresolvable conflict with itself, reply to
an internal criticism, make an agreement with itself in order to correct
undesirable behavior, or consult itself when faced with a difficult problem or question.

Comparison between processes that take place within the self and
between different selves should take into account that they are analogous but not identical. They can never be entirely identical because the
different parts of the self are located in the same body. Indeed, two
people who are involved in serious conflict may decide to avoid each
other for the rest of their lives and move to a different part of the world.
Certainly, a person can avoid inner conflict, but the location of this
conflict in the same body and brain makes the nature of the avoidance
different from conflict between people. Similarly, one person may e-mail
another person to ask for a consultation. The other, however, may simply refuse to give an answer. This is different from a normal case of self-
consultancy, where the party who asks for a consultation is located in
the same body and is part of the same neurological system as the party
who is addressed. Therefore, parts of the self are, generally speaking,
more directly accessible to each other than are parts of society – unless
some parts of the self are entirely dissociated or disowned (often leading
to psychological problems). Despite the differences between external
and internal relationships, phenomena such as self-conflict, self-criticism, self-agreement, and self-consultancy suggest the existence of a
basic similarity between the way people address themselves as part of
a society and the way different parts of the self address each other as
participating in a society of the mind.

Addressing parts of an extended self Following James's (1890)
detailed exposition of the self, the dialogical self is explicitly formulated

as an extended self. This implies that the self is composed not only of internal positions, but also of external positions, that is, positions that are part of the extended domain of the self (e.g., "my teacher" or "my parents"; or combined positions such as "my uncle who was always my adversary"). What are the implications of this view for the phenomena under discussion? In order to answer this question, it should be clear that we have discussed the four types of self-dialogue in terms of relationships between positions within the internal domain of the self. Taking the extended nature of the self into account, we should recognize that they also occur between internal and external positions.

A person who is involved in a serious conflict with a colleague is walking around with emotionally charged memories of the heated conversation with him some days previously . He not only rehearses parts of the conversation, but also regrets what he himself actually said and imagines what he might have said in order to more sharply rebut the objections of his colleague that he regards as incorrect and even unfair. As part of an extended self, the colleague ("*my* colleague") belongs to the external or extended domain of the self. Consequently, the conflict with this colleague, as far as it plays a vivid role in the reflexive activity of the self, is to be identified as a *self-conflict* in the extended sense of the term. In similar ways, one could describe the criticism one gives or receives as part of a discussion with a significant other, as far as it plays a role in one's memories, imaginings, and expectations as *self-criticism* in the extended sense of the term. Likewise, someone can make an agreement with a significant other as part of the self, when in her imagination she promises something to the other, or persuades the other to do or not to do something, or is involved in an imaginary process of bargaining with the other. In that case we speak of *self-agreement* in the extended sense of the term. It is also possible that a person consults, in her imagination, a significant other (e.g., a teacher, a parent, or a supernatural being), or is consulted (e.g., by a colleague) in order to receive or give guidelines for future behavior. In such instances we speak of *self-consultancy* in the extended sense. In other words, the processes that we have described earlier as occurring between internal positions can also arise between internal and external positions.

The described forms of dialogue can also exist between two or more external positions in the self. A person may be "full" of memories of a recent *conflict* that she witnessed between a good friend and his wife, vividly imagining what is happening between the two and having anxious fantasies about the future of the couple. Or, somebody may be struck by the harsh *criticism* a good friend has received from a teacher, and disagrees in his mind with the passive reaction of the friend towards the teacher, regretting that he did not defend himself and take a more self-affirming stance. Or, a person has good memories of an *agreement* made by two close friends after they have stopped talking with each other in a period of serious conflict. Or, a father is happy when he imagines his daughter *consulting* a good teacher who could give her valuable advice concerning her future studies.

In summary, conceiving the self as extended implies that phenomena such as self-conflict, self-criticism, self-agreement, and self-consultancy take place in the position repertoire as a whole, that is, not only within the internal domain, but also within the external domain and between the internal and external domains. Not only is the self extended, but so too are its relationships. Along these lines the way is paved for a dialogical view that liberates the self from a conceptual imprisonment in forms of encapsulated autonomy so characteristic of the modern model of the self. Moreover, the notion of dialogue, as applicable both to the society at large and the mini-society of the self, transcends any intrinsic dichotomy or conceptual separation between individual and society.

Before we elaborate further on a dialogical view of the self, it is necessary to deepen the nature of the differences in the self. How far do they go and what do these differences look like? How can we understand a "distributed" mind that is yet dialogical?

Differences between parts of the self

In line with the post-modern model of the self, the dialogical model emphasizes not only the multiplicity of positions and voices but also their *differences*. For a full recognition of differences, it is required that what seems to be a unity or unified process is deconstructed in its difference and variation. A classical example is Plato's analysis of thinking as a dialogue between two voices:

I have a notion that, when the mind is thinking, it is simply talking to itself, asking questions and answering them, and saying yes or no. When it reaches a decision – which may come slowly or in a sudden rush – when doubt is over and the two voices affirm the same thing, then we call that 'its judgment'. (Theaetetus, 189e – 190a; see Blachowicz, 1999 : 184)

Plato shows here that what seems to be an act performed by just *one* unified thinker, can be seen as a meeting between *two* different voices. In order to distinguish such differences, one needs to make a transition to a level of analysis at which differences appear where unity seems to rule. A dialogical view of the self requires an analysis that shows how the different parts or positions of the self can become "coherent" or "unified" without giving up their differences. In order to avoid the pitfall of "premature unity," it is necessary to acknowledge the existence of a basic diversity in the self that underlies any form of coherence or unity. Dialogue needs difference and diversity as its fertile ground. In order to explore this ground, it is helpful to complement Plato's view of dialogue with recent developments in psychology and affiliated sciences.

Self-plurality and otherness[7]   In recent years, "self-plurality" theorists (for an overview see Cooper and Hermans, 2007; Hermans and Dimaggio, 2004; Raggatt, 2007; Rowan, 1990; Rowan and Cooper, 1999) have argued that the existence of multiple selves or identities within one individual is by no means limited to cases of severe psychological disturbance. From a phenomenological perspective, for instance, Cooper (1999) has argued that human beings, when experiencing emotions or thoughts that are inconsistent with a pre-established sense of self, may switch into an alternative concept of who they are. A person who perceives himself or herself as calm, for example, on experiencing rage may "flip" into a sense of self as righteous or aggrieved, resulting in an alternative identity that is incompatible with the previous one.

Evidence for the existence of self-plurality comes from a variety of sources. Drawing on self-report data, Lester (1992) has shown that around 84 percent of students are able to describe several sub-selves in their mind, with an average of three to four stated selves per student. In our own research (Hermans, 1996a; Hermans, Rijks, and Kempen, 1993) we invited some people, without any psychiatric history, to look at themselves from the perspective of an "imaginary other" (e.g., "a guide who helps me find my way in life" or "a protecting father"). When looking at themselves from that position, they produced self-narratives that were very different, both in content and affective properties, from the ones that resulted from their ordinary position (see also Puchalska-Wasyl, Chmielnicka-Kuter and Oles, 2008). Evidence for the existence of multiple self-concepts is also provided by Rosenberg and Gara (1985), who showed that people's self-descriptions (for instance, "psychologist," "historian," "overeater") tend to cluster around a smaller number of higher-order identities (see also Raggatt, 2000 for similar findings). Numerous clinical case studies of these types have demonstrated that many clients will spontaneously describe themselves in pluralistic ways (Hermans and Dimaggio, 2004; Rowan and Cooper, 1999).

Evidence for self-plurality comes also from studies on hypnosis. Hilgard (1977) demonstrated that subjects under hypnosis, who were instructed to become deaf to all sounds, did not flinch when wooden blocks were banged close to their heads, and, once their hearing was restored, failed to report having heard any sounds. However, when asked to speak from "a part of themselves" that had been listening and processing the information, they could fully recall the sounds. Such findings suggest that participants can simultaneously process the same event in two radically different ways. Similar findings have been reported from neuropsychological research on "split-brain" patients with a severed corpus callosum that prevented signals being transmitted between the different sides of the brain. In one study, for example, Gazzaniga (1985) exposed only the right half of a patient's brain to a terrifying fire safety film. Because the speech-processing module is located in the left half of the brain, the patient was unable to verbalize the content of the film. However, the patient still reported feeling afraid and nervous after seeing the film, suggesting that her anxiety was caused by the activation of an emotional, non-verbal module in the right brain hemisphere. Such findings support the view that the brain is to a large degree modular and pluralistic.

The findings reported above suggest that the trajectory of the self is not only towards sameness and identity. Alongside it, and perhaps instead of it at times, is a movement towards difference and diversity. And although such an understanding of the self is not unquestionable (see, for example, Braude, 1991), the degree of dissociation and dis-identification that can be experienced between different "personality states" suggests that, at the very least, the difference "within" the self is on a continuum with the difference "outside." As Spinelli (1994: 345) points out, dis-identifying with a particular mode of experiencing may actually take the form of attributing it to another. As an example, he refers to a fundamentalist lay-preacher who, on experiencing sexual arousal in the presence of particular members of his religious commune, attributed these feelings "to a temporary possession by Satan." Apparently, we can experience elements of our own being as mysterious, enigmatic, and transcendent to our 'self' just as we can experience the being of another person. For Cooper and Hermans (2007) this is reason to describe the differences within the self in terms of "self-otherness," just as we can talk of the otherness of another person.

From a contemporary inter-subjective standpoint, the self is riddled with the mysterious and alien otherness of others. That is, other beings exist within selves: through the language and tools that we use (Bakhtin, 1973; Heidegger, 1962; Vygotsky, 1962), through the interiorization of cultural and individual voices (Hermans, 2001a), through the multiple roles that we adopt (Gergen, 1991), and through our ethical obligation to the other's call (Cohen, 2002; Levinas, 1969). Despite the relational nature of the self, important aspects of the self may be dissociated or separated. Aspects of the self, like the vulnerable child or the shadow, are "disowned" (Stone and Winkelman, 1989) or "suppressed" (Hermans, Rijks, and Kempen, 1993), treated as "exiles" (Schwartz, 1995), or as disrupting the continuity of the self (Levinas, 1969).

To describe self-difference and self-otherness is not to suggest that this difference exists within a self-contained, isolated monad. Rather, in terms of dialogical self theory, it is to suggest that this otherness penetrates the self from the most explicitly "external" realms to the most seemingly "internal" ones, whether carried in the voices and positions of others-in-the-self or through the less obviously internal ones that can easily fuse with positions in the external domain (e.g., "I talk to my own children in the way my mother used to talk with me"). In other words, otherness is everywhere (Cooper and Hermans, 2007).

Whereas the notion of "otherness in the self" is used to indicate the presence of the other in the most intimate realms of the self, the notion of "othering" has to be sharply distinguished. It is often used in social sciences to indicate that particular units, such as human beings, meanings, ideas, social organizations, and ideological systems are maintained in their apparent internal unity through an active process of opposition, hierarchization, or exclusion (Cahoone, 1996). Other units are classified as foreign or "other" through realizing a hierarchical dualism in which one unit, typically the one to which one belongs, is privileged or favored, whereas the other is devalued in one way or another. For example, in his well-known work *Orientalism*, Said (1978) contended that European countries have not only conquered the East politically, but also appropriated the interpretation of the Orient's history, culture and languages in highly biased ways. In their construction of Asia's past, they adopted a perspective that takes Europe (and the male) as the norm and the "exotic" or "inscrutable" Orient as a deviation. Western publications about the Orient depict it as an irrational, weak, and feminized "other," in contrast to the rational, strong, and masculine West, a contrast that derives from the need to create differences between West and East in the form of immutable essences. There seems to exist a basic similarity between a "strange" culture (different from "my culture"), a "strange" person (different from "myself"), and a "strange" aspect of the self (different from "what belongs to me"). The resemblance is that they are subjected to the process of othering, resulting in a split or separation that prevents or undermines any dialogical relationship. A fundamental challenge for any dialogical conception of the self is the consideration that the self is deeply penetrated by "otherness-in-the-self" whereas, at the same time, it wants to confirm its own identity by the process of "othering." Before we address the question of how the self can deal with this basic split, we first want to deepen the relationship of the mind with itself from a philosophical perspective.

Differences in positioning

To what extent is a dialogue between the different parts of the self possible? How can one part of the self address another part? What is the nature of the answer given by the self to itself? Such questions have to be addressed in order to gain some insight into the dialogical nature of the self. Let's start with a brief exploration of the relationship the mind has with itself.

From a philosophical perspective, Blachowicz (1999) analyzes the processes that take place when the mind is proposing something to itself. It seems, he reasons, that I represent my thoughts to myself and I typically do so by expressing them in some perceptual medium, such as an inner voice, written speech, drawings, a diary, etc. When I do so in a procedural way, I'm able to hold on to them more completely and with more certainty. For example, when I'm planning to buy a piece of furniture, I can make a preliminary sketch of it and ask myself whether this is what I want. When I'm not satisfied with what I see on paper, I reject it. The party who made the first sketch is doing the *proposing*, whereas the rejecting party is doing the *disposing* or criticizing. The same happens when I'm writing a poem, a letter or an e-mail. As soon as I have given something its first shape, then the preliminary product functions as the proposing party that meets the evaluation and criticism of the disposing party.

Whereas in the above example the process of proposing and disposing takes place within the self, it also can take place when the person receives *feedback* from actual external others. Hermans (1996a) presented the following example. An author submits a manuscript to a scientific journal and, as part of the review procedure, receives three helpful but critical comments, with the suggestion that the paper be resubmitted. The author, who is eager to see the paper in print, is confronted with some problems that he cannot immediately resolve. The author can only solve them if he or she takes the (disposing) positions of the reviewers into account in relation to his own (proposing) position. That is, the author, on the one hand, has to move between the several reviewers to check them on consistencies and inconsistencies, and, on the other hand, between the reviewers and his or her original proposing position as represented in the old manuscript. At first all these positions may sound like a "cacophony of voices" and can even cause a "transient crisis," but after some intensive interchange between the positions a new structure begins to emerge. In the course of this process the author may arrive at a point of *juxtaposition*, where the several views are simultaneously present and permit an overview, allowing possibile new and sometimes sudden insights to emerge. A new structure is appearing that may differ considerably from the original one. The final result is a thoroughly revised manuscript, in which the reviewers' suggestions are incorporated and answered. Due to this interchange, the original position of the author, as presented in the first manuscript, is significantly altered. The new manuscript is the distillation of a process, in which the original position of the author, the disposing positions of the reviewers, and the re-positioning of the author, are part of an open, dynamic, multi-voiced self.[8]

In this example, the process of proposing and disposing is quite complex, because the author receives feedback not from one party but from three . Despite this complexity, it shows that the disposals that were initially provided by some actual others (the reviewers) were later incorporated in the self as external positions which the author "walks around" with for some time and which challenge him to give an answer that was not available at the beginning. The disposing positions that came from outside were later included as part of the external domain of the self and created a new field of tension within the self, requiring a further development of the initial position as manifested in the original manuscript. In a more simple form this process occurs when we want to solve a problem by consulting an expert. The expert's advice is then incorporated in the self and leads to an ongoing process of self-consultation.

In order to articulate the nature of the interchange between the mind and itself, Blachowicz (1999: 182) compares it with the interchange between a witness and a police artist cooperating in producing a drawing of a suspect:

I propose viewing the 'dialogue of the soul with itself' as a series of proposals and disposals similar in function to the exchange between the police artist and the witness in their collaboration. The two parties represent the independent interests of meaning and articulation. At one moment we may possess a meaning but fail to articulate it; at another moment we may possess just such an articulation, but find that its meaning fails to correspond with our intended one. We talk to our self when we think, because only a dialogue where each side provides proposals and corrective disposals for the other can achieve a simultaneous satisfaction of these twin requirements.

For a well-functioning self, it should be added, the two parts are not *entirely* different. As Blachowicz (1999) observes, the partners have each other's skills in some degree. Each should partly share the capacities of the other in order to make the collaboration productive. This is similar to forms of cooperation in a societal context. Two people who are connected with each other in some way, such as husband and wife, employer and employee, guide and traveller, circus director and clown, bus driver and passenger, builder of a house and its occupant, need some knowledge and understanding of each other's contribution to the partnership to make the cooperation work.

When involved in a process of proposing and disposing, the self is confronted with its own differences and is in need of these differences in order to arrive at some point of clarity about itself. A dialogical self is based on the differences between the self and itself, and therefore it is necessarily in the process of positioning itself *toward* itself. It is not a unity in itself in any self-contained way. The philosopher Gadamer (1989) was aware of this when he wrote: "Because our understanding does not comprehend what it knows in one single inclusive glance, it must always draw what it thinks out of itself, and present it to itself as if in an inner dialogue with itself. In this sense all thought is speaking to oneself" (p. 422). In this context, Gadamer referred to the "imperfection of the human mind" in this way: "the imperfection of the human mind consists in its never being completely present to itself but in being dispersed into thinking this or that" (p. 425). The dispersed self is basically uncertain because it is never complete at any moment in time and needs "another part of itself" in order to arrive at some clarity in its relation to itself and the world. This uncertainty strongly contrasts with the Cartesian self that resulted from the search for complete certainty, expressed in the famous dictum *Cogito, ergo sum* ("I think therefore I am"). The Cartesian self comes out as "a self of reason completely purged of body and feeling, a self without shadows, a self totally transparent to itself, totally knowing itself, totally self-possessed, totally certain of itself" (Levin, 1988: 15).

Increasing differences in a globalizing world   We began the present chapter by referring to the importance of multiplicity and difference in the self as inspired by the post-modern model of the self. In the course of the chapter we presented arguments for differences in the relation of the mind with itself not only from the social sciences but also from philosophy. In line with these contributions, we claimed that differences are intrinsic to the mind when it addresses itself and we referred to the process of proposing and disposing as an articulation of these differences. It should be clear that the presented philosophical arguments are not exclusively related to the post-modern condition and the process of globalization. The internal dividedness of the mind is certainly not the result of a late historical development that we call post-modernism, but it is at least as old as the times in which Homer created his *Iliad*. In her treatise of "internal rhetorics," Nienkamp (2001) was interested not only in the heroes' conversations with their comrades or with the gods, but also, and even primarily, in their conversations with themselves. In one passage she refers to the internal struggle that took place in Achilleus' breast when Agamemnon threatened to take Briseis (a woman who was given to Achilleus as a prize) from him:

And the anger came on Peleus' son [Achilleus], and within his shaggy breast *the heart was divided two ways*, pondering whether to draw from beside his thigh the sharp sword ... or else to check the spleen within and keep down his anger. *Now as he weighed in mind and spirit* these two courses and was drawing from its scabbard the great sword, Athene descended from the sky. (p. 11, emphases by J.N.)

As this quotation and others suggest (see Nienkamp, 2001), the divided mind can be traced back to ancient times and seems to be inherent to the human condition. What we want to emphasize is that the post-modern model of the self, in its emphasis on difference and multiplicity, challenges and stretches this human capacity to the utmost. Post-modernity and globalization do not create difference in the self but enlarge them on historical grounds. Processes such as immigration, international exchanges, tourism, traveling, media-communication, border-crossings, and diaspora increase not only the number but also the difference and heterogeneity of positions in the self (see Chapter 1). This can be illustrated by the autobiographical notes of Josephs (2002), a German psychologist who worked initially in Germany, and later some time in the USA. She explains that in her usual cultural surroundings – Germany – she generally did not "hear" or feel her "German voice." It was backgrounded like anything that is taken for granted in the here-and-now. This changed, however, from the time she was in America:

in the US university where I worked for a while I had two 'German voices,' which were notably different. I was 'proud' to be a German psychologist given the fact that the intellectual roots of psychology come from 'my' country – a feeling I had never had when working at an ordinary German university. At the same time I wanted to hide that I was German because I felt ashamed, given the fact that a high percentage of students were Jewish. To make things even more complicated, it was exactly the Jewish students whom I met in person who approached me *not* as a German, but as an ordinary visitor. (p. 170)

This quotation shows that as a result of border-crossing, two positions ("I as proud" and "I as ashamed") became prominent that were earlier in the background and did not play, in referring to her nationality, any significant role as long as she was in her home country. However, as a German in the US the two positions became not only prominent but even conflicting.

We started the present chapter by delineating four phenomena that illustrate the relationship of the mind with itself: self-conflict, self-criticism, self-agreement and self-consultation. We described them as observable facts of a normal functioning self. In the context of dialogical self theory as influenced by the processes of globalization and localization and by the transition from modernity to post-modernity, there is something to be added that is of central concern to dialogical self theory: *self-conflict, self-criticism, self-agreement, and self-consultancy are based on a position repertoire that demonstrates an increasing density, heterogeneity, and changeability.* This implies that the increasing differences and complexities of the self require a dialogical capacity that is developed enough to cope with a broadened position repertoire in adaptive and flexible ways.

Remember the case of Hawa, the woman born in Turkey, who immigrated with her family to the Netherlands when she was 5 years old (Chapter 1). She was located in a field of tension and conflict between her Dutch position, which gave her considerable freedom to form her own life, and her Turkish position, which required her to give priority to the traditions of her culture of origin. What should she do when she met a new friend who was not acceptable to her father? Consulting her Dutch position would give her advice that was very different from that of her Turkish position. This required her to find a way to deal with this conflicting advice. Finally, she succeeded when she could see and accept that the two self-positions and their corresponding cultures were not intrinsically conflicting, but rather mutually complementary in the organization of her self. This made her two cultural positions sufficiently compatible to allow her to introduce her new Dutch friend to her father.

To summarize: In the present chapter we have dealt with the notions of multiplicity and difference, introduced by the post-modern model of the self that gives a central place to these notions. In order to gain a more basic insight into the notion of difference, we referred to some philosophical thinkers who argued that, in apparent contrast to a Cartesian view of the self, the mind is to some extent a "stranger" to itself. As partly unknown to itself, the mind has to inspect, critically interrogate and consult itself in order to arrive at a meaningful answer. We emphasized that differences in the self are not an "invention" of the post-modern model of the self. Rather, we are living in a phase of history, indicated by such diverse terms as "post-modernity" and "globalization," in which differences in the self are "stretched" as never before. When the self is supposed to function as a "society of mind," then this self becomes more heterogeneous and complex in parallel with the increasing heterogeneity and complexity of the society at large, with the consequence that the capacity to develop dialogical relationships between the different parts of the extended self is not only a philosophical given but also a historical necessity.

Unity and continuity in the self

An analysis of the self in terms of multiplicity and difference, however, cannot give a definitive and satisfying answer to the question of whether the self is coherent enough to function as a unity. When we assume that the differences in self and identity increase, then the unity and continuity of the self become an issue that is relevant as never before. The unity and continuity of the self, of central concern to the modern model, cannot be simply seen as something of the past. The word "post-modern" could erroneously suggest that post-modernity follows modernity. Contrary to this view, we have emphasized that the three phases of the self – traditional, modern, and post-modern – find their starting point in different phases in history, but, once emerged, they coexist over time and create an interface where they meet each other, leading to hybrid combinations of different life-styles, cultural identities, and local traditions. As we have argued, theories of the dialogical self could learn from history and examine to what extent valuable elements of the corresponding models can be incorporated in them.

The modern model is a great challenge to the dialogical self, because it poses, explicitly or implicitly, the problems of unity and continuity. How can there be unity and continuity in a mind that is governed by difference, diversity, and discontinuity? In aiming at a sufficiently coherent theory of the self, it would be naive to incorporate unity in the self in the same way as theories have done that were, or still are, direct expressions of the modern model. A dialogical theory is not part of a modern model but can certainly learn from it. The question is rather: What do unity and continuity look like in a self that is different from itself? Or, to put it even more basically: Can there be unity at all? And if there is any unity, what kind of unity is this? Such questions confront us with the challenge of conceiving unity and continuity in such a way that, from a theoretical point of view, these notions are sufficiently compatible with the basic diversity and multiplicity of the mind as discussed before.

In the next part of the present chapter we will discuss the unity of the self via four concepts that are central to dialogical self theory: (i) the concept of "*I*-position" that links the process of positioning and repositioning to the continuity of the *I*; (ii) the possibility of taking a "meta-position" that permits an overview of a diversity of other positions; and (iii) the possibility of engaging in a "coalition" of positions" in which different positions go together; and (d) the construction of a "third position," in which two other different positions merge or fuse.

I-positions and the appropriating self

James's (1890) chapter "The consciousness of self" has been a source of inspiration to many scientists who were interested in the exploration of the self at the interface of psychology and philosophy. As part of his analysis, James introduces the concepts of "appropriation" and "repudiation" ("rejection" or "disowning" in other parts of the text) that are crucial to understanding that the self is able to determine which parts ("constituents") it takes in and which parts it rejects.

A thing cannot appropriate itself: it *is* itself; and still less can it disown itself. There must be an agent of the appropriating and disowning; but that agent we have already named. It is the Thought to whom the various constituents are known. That Thought is a vehicle of choice as well as of cognition; and among the choices it makes are these appropriations, or repudiations, of its 'own'. (p. 340)

James attributes the agentic capacity of the self to what he calls the *I*: "The consciousness of Self involves a stream of thought, each part of which as 'I' can remember those that went before and know the things they knew; and emphasize and care paramountly for certain ones among them as '*me*,' and *appropriate to these* the rest" (p. 400). At other places in his text, James argues that not only the "me" but also the "mine" is appropriated, in this way depicting a self that is extended to the environment. This is expressed in his frequently quoted statement: "*In its widest possible sense*, however, *a man's Self is the sum total of all that he CAN call his*, not only his body and his psychic powers, but his clothes and his house, his wife and children, his ancestors and friends, his reputation and works, his lands and horses, and yacht and bank-account" (p. 291, emphases in the original).

The theoretical advantage of the notion of *I*-position is that it brings unity and continuity in the self, while preserving its multiplicity. The *I* is continuous over time: in the process of appropriation and rejection, it is *one and the same I* who is doing this. At the same time, the *I*, located in time and space and intrinsically involved in the process of positioning, is confronted with a wide variety of new positions and possible positions. As a reaction, the *I* appropriates some of them and rejects others. Those that are appropriated are experienced as "mine" and as "belonging to myself" and, as a consequence, they add to the unity and continuity in the self.[9]

From a temporal perspective, the appropriated parts contribute to the constancy of the self over time: existing positions receive an imprint as "I," "me," or as "mine" and as such they add to the unity and continuity of the self. Moreover, *new* positions are appropriated to an already existing group so that they receive the *same* imprint that was already available before. As a result of this appropriation, the self receives a sense of unity and continuity, despite its apparent differences.[10]

In agreement with James's conception of the self, we want to emphasize that the existence of differences in the self does not, in any way, refute the existence of unity and continuity (see also Chandler *et al.*, 2003 for a similar view). As James assumes that the process of appropriation brings unity and continuity in the self, we assume that the same act of appropriation creates unity and continuity in a self that is spatially and temporally "distributed." We would like to underline that, in conceiving the *I* as spatially and temporally situated, the *I* is not a "ghost in the machine" (Lysaker, 2006), but participates in a process of positioning and repositioning.[11]

However, the act of appropriation is not the only function of the *I*. As we will discuss in the later sections of this chapter, we go beyond James in one essential respect. We will argue that, in the present era, there are strong reasons to attribute to the *I* not only an appropriating function but also a *receptive* one. We will show that the self has potentials that cannot be sufficiently understood by the notions "appropriation" and "ownership" because they assume the existence of a *possessive* self. We will demonstrate that the receptive function makes experiences possible that are inaccessible to the appropriative function of the self. Let's first elaborate on the appropriative function of the *I*, *Me*, and *Mine*, from a spatial point of view and later address the receptive one.

Owning versus othering   In a study of self-extension, Rosenberg (1979) asked a group of children and adolescents whether they would experience an insult to a significant other as an insult to themselves. He found that, in the case that the insult was directed to their mother, 89% of the respondents said they would experience this as an insult to themselves. This percentage gradually went down when the insult was directed to their father (82%), their school work (67%), the school itself (50%), their hobby equipment (32%), and the state governor (24%). As these figures suggest, there is no sharp boundary between what the respondents perceive as "myself" and "not myself." The results rather suggest a gradual transition between the two areas. This gradual transition is further demonstrated by indirect forms of self-extension, that is, the extensions of the self of significant others. A mother or father can experience an indirect enjoyment when they see that their children have fun playing, or a "secondary" pride when they notice that their children are proud of their achievements at school. Such secondary forms of identification are also gradual, given the fact that people experience these feelings in more intense ways in relation to their children than to more remote members of their family or to the children of their friends. In other words, not only is the self extended by degrees, but the self also participates in the gradual extension of the self of significant others.

In apparent contrast to the permeable boundaries between "belonging to me" and "not belonging to me," is the already discussed phenomenon of "othering," which is characterized by sharp boundaries between "me" and "not me." It refers to a self that is preserved in its internal unity through an active process of opposition, hierarchization, or exclusion of the other. There seems to be a noticeable difference between Rosenberg's (1979) study that suggests a gradual transition between "me" and "not me," and the phenomenon of "othering," where a sharp boundary and even a separation is made in case of a person or group defined as "not me." This often coexists with the definition of the other as "lower than me" or as "inferior." In this respect, the self extends its "tentacles" quite gradually, but suddenly retreats and creates a separation as soon as it touches something unfamiliar or threatening. Certainly, there are degrees of opposition, rejection, and separation. However, even when these degrees are taken into account, the sharpness of the boundaries with rejected others contrasts impressively with the gradually decreasing or increasing degrees of intimacy that the self can experience in relation to others who are welcomed to enter its warm shelter.

The separation between "mine" and "not-mine" and their appropriation or rejection are certainly not mutually exclusive categorizations. The treatment of external positions is strongly dependent on the linkages with specific internal positions. This can by exemplified by the simultaneous presence of appropriation and rejection in relation with one and the same external other. In James's (1890: 295) terms: "As a man I pity you, but as an official I must show you no mercy; as a politician I regard him as an ally, but as a moralist I loathe him." Ambivalence toward the other finds its roots in different internal *I*-positions, typically expressed in "but-sentences." The internal position, on the one side of the "but," represents an act of appropriation, whereas the internal position at the other side refers to a rejection of the "same" other. The same person can be an intimate person at one moment, but a stranger at another moment in time. At one time we can even be located in a "divided awareness" of the other as familiar and evoking intimacy, whereas at another time the same person is experienced as unfamiliar or even strange. Ambivalence towards the other is rooted in the contrasting internal positions that evoke the different responses of appropriation and rejection.

The extending I: beyond the self-contained I   Appropriation and rejection as expressions of the agency of the *I* take place both in the relationship of persons with themselves and in the relationship with others. As soon as an internal position is appropriated, it becomes "owned" and receives a place as an accepted position in the self. Accepted positions become, to some degree, dominant in the organization of the self. As Stone and Winkelman (1989), Schwartz (1995), and Hermans (2001b) have demonstrated, some positions, like "I as strong," "I as active," and "I as assertive" are in our Western culture typically owned and accepted as parts of the self, whereas their counterparts "I as weak," "I as lazy," and "I as shy," are often disowned. Usually we identify with the "positive" positions and dis-identify with those that are devaluated as "negative."

As a result of this (dis)-identification, the positive ones become more dominant in the self so that it rejects the negative ones that may be seen as "not me" or "not belonging to me." Some *I*-positions are located in the vague and ambiguous border-zone between self and non-self which can be characterized as "identity-in-difference" (Gregg, 1991), that is, they belong and do not belong to me *at the same time*. For example, I'm aware that I'm sometimes jealous, but at the same time I do not recognize jealousy as "belonging to me." I reject parts of *my* experience. Despite the paradoxical nature of the transitional area between self and non-self, we propose, for conceptual reasons, to consider positions in this area as *I*-positions, despite the fact that the extent of *I*-ness or ownership may significantly differ between various positions.

There is a basic similarity between disowned positions in the internal domain of the self and those in the external domain. Particular significant others (e.g., "my always cynical colleague," or "my ex-husband who left me") can be disowned and subjectively defined as "not belonging to me." *Yet, from a theoretical point of view they are significant parts of an extended self,* as long as they are defined as "mine" and play a recurring and affect-arousing role in one's memory, imagination, and anticipation. Another person or particular aspects of him or her may be rejected ("My husband when he is drinking again") while this person is yet defined as "mine" and thus part of an extended self (see also James, 1890). It is paradoxical that the same aspect of the self can be rejected and yet be appropriated by the same self in a wider sense (e.g., "*my* enemy"). This paradox applies both to the internal and external domain. Like the external, the internal one is divided in two parts, aspects of myself that I experience as close, intimate, owned, and familiar, and others that I feel as distant, "not me," strange or alien, and disowned, with the simultaneous definition of all those parts as being part of the broader "me" or "mine."[12]

The division into owned and disowned parts of the self has an important conceptual implication. Not only internal but also external positions, as parts of an extended self, can have the quality of *I*-positions, that is, the other conceived as "another I." This point of view is consistent with Bakhtin (1929/1973), who remarked: "For the author the hero is not 'he', and not 'I' but a full-valued 'thou', that is another full-fledged 'I' (p. 51). Indeed, the identification with another person, an animal, or even an object (e.g., a piece of art in which I recognize myself) or nature (e.g., "I as a piece of earth that becomes aware of itself") can reach the point that the other is seen as part of an *extended I*. It is important to note that this *I* is not a self-contained, individualistic *I*, so typical of the modern model of the self, but rather an *I* that transcends the boundaries of the self as an isolated entity. The extended *I* is a contextualized *I* that is not alone but always together with, and even extended to, something or somebody else: the hero of a book, a friend with whom you identify, one or more of your children in whom you recognize yourself, a character in a film that reveals a hidden part of yourself, or the person you met only briefly but felt as if you had known him or her for a long time. For a highly developed person, such as the Dalai Lama, Buddha or Christ, even an enemy can be experienced as an accepted and valued aspect of the extending *I*, although the distinction between self and other and between *I* and *You* is not removed.

What we said earlier about the gradual transition between *me* and *not me* also applies to the relationship between *I* and *you* and between *I* and *we*. The extended *I* is not subordinated to the dualistic separation between subject and object, self and other, internal and external, so typical of the modern self. It transcends the restrictive borders between *I* and *you*, as demonstrated by the gradual transition between self and other, by the notion of the other-in-the-self, by the appropriation of particular parts of the self as owned, and by the definition of the other as "another *I*." In this way the notion of the *I*-position has, due to the workings of the *I*, a unifying function. It keeps positions together that otherwise would be dispersed in an undefined and unorganized space or would be excluded from the self as an isolated container. The *I* of the concept of *I*-position creates a certain degree of unity and continuity in the self in the extended sense of the term. Central in a dialogical model of the self, the term *I* is an extending principle that (re)opens the self to the world.

Positioning and culture   Consideration of divisions in the self as resulting from the processes of appropriation versus rejection is relevant from a cultural point of view. A culture that puts a high premium on strength, activity, assertiveness, and independence expresses at the same time a disdain for its counterparts in the connotation of their names. The term "lazy" is colored by the absence of the highly valued term "active," and the term "dependent" receives its specific negative connotation as a consequence of the positive valuation of "independent."

The cultural influence on the processes of appropriation and rejection of self-positions is discussed by Lindegger (2010), who is interested in the cultural situation of South Africa in the post-apartheid era. Building on Roland's (1996) comparative psychoanalytic work on Eastern and Western cultures, he analyses their differences in this way:

Eastern cultures (including Japan, India and China) are characterized by a strong sense of relatedness, flexible self/other boundaries, value placed on dependency rather than autonomy, communication of a subtle, intuitive, non-verbal style with an emphasis on empathy, a hierarchical quality to social relationships, and spirituality as a highly valued aspect of life. Interestingly, Roland's description of Eastern culture has much in common with African culture. In contrast, Western culture is characterized by a stress on individualism and autonomy *with dependency seen as pathological,* firm and well developed self/other boundaries, communication being explicit and verbal, relationships being seen as egalitarian and contractual, and spirituality being devalued and seen as regressive. (2010, emphasis added)

As this observation shows, the dominant term "independent," highly valued in the West, defines the opposite term "dependence" in a pejorative way. However, when dependency is positively valued – in the context of relationships with ancestors and significant others in cultures that attribute high value to their traditions – then the term "dependence" has very different connotations, which may lead to misunderstandings at the interface of the two cultures.

As culturally embedded and colored, the *I* is not an isolated agency hovering above the self determining and organizing it as from a control centre. It does not have an existence on its own, separated from time and space, and it is not to be perceived as a "homunculus." In order to avoid the homunculus problem and the ghost in the machine idea, the *I* can be meaningfully understood as *emerging* from individual development. The self is fundamentally positioned and arrives at a point at which it becomes aware of itself, and can eventually define itself, appropriating some parts of itself and the environment and rejecting other parts. The conception that the *I* emerges from the process of positioning and being positioned in time and space is in no way incompatible with the consideration that the *I* is able to appropriate and reject elements of self and environment. Once emerged, the self is involved in a process of appropriation and rejection and develops agency as the capacity to organize itself (for developmental arguments, see Chapter 4).

The positioned nature of the self becomes particularly apparent when we consider the influence of culture and society on the process of appropriation. Many positions that become my own were already in my social environment before I was born (e.g., my family name). When I was born, the people around me said "it's a boy!" rather than "it's a girl!" and the difference between these positions that are attributed to us are not just names but rather representative of value systems that largely determine our lives from a young age onwards. Usually "I as a male" or "I as a female" become included as ordinary *I*-positions in the self. As the result of societal and cultural definition and training, they become, like many other positions, "naturally" appropriated as ordinary parts of the self.[13]

When individuals move from one culture to another, their *I*-positions may be particularly challenged. The question is whether *I*-positions that "work" in one culture are also adaptive in another one. Intercultural contact may have the pleasant or unpleasant implication that new positions should be appropriated as *I*-positions. People born and trained in America or northern Europe may have learned to be "honest" in their contact with others, that is, to express their "true" opinion. For example, when they are involved in a common project with others belonging to the same culture, "I as honest" is included as an ordinary position in their repertoire. This might change if they work for some time in an eastern country, where "to be friendly" is more highly valued than "to be honest." This discrepancy creates a certain amount of stress in the individual, because the "natural" *I*-position, to be honest, has to be suppressed and replaced, at least in some situations, by one that feels "unnatural" – to be friendly but not honest in all social situations. However, this position is required by the other culture but not sufficiently appropriated by the *I*. After some time and depending on the flexibility of the self, the person becomes able to include "being friendly" as an *I*-position in the repertoire. As this example suggests, cultural adaptation requires not only a reorganization of the repertoire but also the appropriation of positions that are adaptive in that particular culture.

Hard versus soft versions of multiplicity   Over time, we as authors have had many discussions with colleagues about the multiplicity of the self, and about the notions of positions and voices in particular. We were impressed by the fact that these discussions were often quite principled and sometimes even emotional. One of the central questions was this: Is it possible that the voices of the self have a dialogue with each other? Some colleagues could live very well with the idea that they had different parts and that these parts could engage in a kind of dialogue. Other colleagues, however, experienced difficulties in conceiving *parts* of the self engaged in dialogue with each other. Responding to an article submitted by one of our colleagues, one of the reviewers objected very strongly to the idea that the self is multiple in the sense of functioning as a multiplicity of parts involved in dialogue:

There is a question from a neuro-scientific point of view: how does each voice, each mini-self, end up with its own capacity for internal speaking and hearing unless they are sharing some basic mechanism? It seems untenable that new neural connections arise for each voice that emerges, which suggests that they might indeed be part of a single "self," whose job it is to talk and listen to itself. If so, the description of the voices may need to be modified – are they different actors (which is how they are currently portrayed) or one actor playing multiple roles (much like a one-person theatrical performance)?

This excerpt was a reason for the same reviewer to make a distinction between hard and soft versions of multiplicity. The hard version assumes that parts of the self function in autonomous ways and are capable of establishing direct relationships with each other without the intervention or mediation of any integrating agency. The underlying idea is that the self can be conceived of as a society of autonomous positions which are to a large degree decentralized. The soft version assumes that the different positions need the workings of some agency that links the different positions or voices and is able to create some unity and continuity, bringing aspects of the self together in something that is more than the sum of its parts. It is our view that the notion of multi-voicedness or multi-positionality can coexist very well with a self that acknowledges the working of the *I* as a guardian of a certain degree of unity and continuity in the self. This implies that the inclusion of the *I* in its agentic and appropriating activities favors a soft version of multiplicity. This conclusion is based on the distinction between two kinds of movements in the self: (i) decentralizing movements (e.g., the process of globalization) leading to increasing density and heterogeneity of changing positions and posing a challenge to the self's coherence and continuity; and (ii) centralizing movements aimed at the establishment of a certain degree of unity and continuity in the multiplicity of positions. By acknowledging both movements (for elaboration see Chapter 4), the dialogical self can be seen as a "substantial, yet multiplicitous" self (Falmagne, 2004).[14]

The unifying influence of meta-positions

Whereas *I*-positions contribute to the unity and continuity of the self by the act of appropriation, meta-positions do so by the act of self-reflection. Consider the example of a tennis player involved in a game. As long as she is in the game, the best she can do is to concentrate fully on the action. Any form of self-criticism or self-doubt would interfere with the quality of her performance. As long as she is fully engaged in the moment of action, she is just *in* the position of the player and in her performance. She merges with the action and there is not much room for self-reflection. As soon as she finishes the game, she begins to reflect, that is, she thinks critically *about* her performance as a player. Did she do a good job or not? At this level she evaluates her play and is satisfied or dissatisfied about what she has accomplished. As a result of this evaluation, she may decide to improve her skills or to follow a different strategy next time. As long as she is involved in self-reflection on this level, she thinks of herself in the position of tennis-player only. However, she can move to a higher level of self-reflection, where she places her position as tennis-player in the context of other positions. That is, she may begin to reflect about her future. Will she continue to invest her best efforts in tennis? Does she want to make a career? Does she go for Wimbledon or not? At this broader level of self-reflection she explores the connection between her position as a tennis player and some other significant positions, for example, as a mother, as a wife, or as a student gifted in languages. As part of this profound exploration, she talks about her concerns with a good listener or wise advisor. She may be, for some time, engaged in processes of self-conflict, self-criticism, or self-consultancy. Finally, she comes to a point where she can make the "right decision" as an act of self-agreement. In summary, the I can move to three levels: (i) being purely engaged *in* the position; (ii) reflecting *on* this position; and (iii) taking a broader position (meta-position) from which a greater range of other positions is considered. Although the second level represents a meta-position in the restricted sense (moving *above* the position at hand while staying in touch with it), the term is usually reserved for an indication of the highest level (moving above a broader range of positions).

Specific features of meta-positions   A meta-position, sometimes also described as an "observing ego" or "meta-cognition," has some specific qualities: (a) it permits a certain distance[15] from the other positions, although it is attracted, both cognitively and emotionally, toward some positions more than others (e.g., "I as critical" or "I as introspective" or "I as ironic"); (b) it provides an overarching view so that several positions can be seen simultaneously and their mutual relationships become visible;[16] (c) it leads to an evaluation of the reviewed positions and their organization (e.g., "I discovered that some positions have been seriously neglected in my life up till now"); (d) it makes it possible to see the linkages between positions as part of one's personal history or the collective history of the group or culture to which one belongs (e.g., "I'm becoming aware of the limitations of the culture in which I was raised"); (e) the individual becomes aware of the differences in the accessibility of positions (e.g., "I became aware that my playful side, which was quite prominent when I was young, became less accessible as I grew older"); (f) the importance of one or more positions for future development of the self becomes apparent; (g) it facilitates the creation of a dialogical space (in contact with others or with oneself) in which positions and counter-positions engage in dialogical relationships; (h) it gives a broader basis for decision making and for finding one's direction in life (Hermans, 2003; see also Georgaca, 2001).

A meta-position is not to be considered a "control centre" of the self or an agency that guarantees the unity and coherence of the self in advance. In order to avoid this confusion, it should be remembered that a meta-position is typically influenced by one or more internal or external positions that are actualized at the moment of self-examination. Moreover, depending on time and situation, different meta-positions emerge. That is, a talk with a good friend leads to another meta-position, with different content and perspectives from a conversation with a psychotherapist.[17] Finally, as each position has its horizon, so a meta-position, although it permits meaningful linkages between a variety of positions, has its limitations and is far from a "God's eye view." These limitations are the consequence of the assumption that multiplicity precedes unity or synthesis of the self. Note that one is positioned, sometimes in unforeseen ways, by others so that the positions in which one is placed can only later become appropriated and integrated as part of an organized whole (Hermans and Kempen, 1993).[18]

From a metaphorical perspective, a meta-position can be compared with a committee of which the members (like positions in the self) aim at an overview of processes that are taking place in the organization (like in the self as a whole). Within the committee there are frequent interchanges in which different points of view are presented and compared. As usual, some members are more influential than others and have more impact on the decision-making process (like the critical or the enthusiastic one). However, as in a democratic process, the contributions of all the members are welcome. When they become engaged in a creative interchange, the final conclusion or decision profits from the contributions and ideas arising from different perspectives, and from a common base supported by the position repertoire of the majority of the members or of all of them.[19]

Meta-position in a globalizing world: out of place Meta-positioning is not a purely individualized process. The voices of other individuals, groups, and cultures are involved. An example is the autobiography *Out of place* by Edward Said (1999), in which he reflects not only about his name but also about the different cultures in which he was involved. As Bhatia (2002) describes, Said struggled with his hyphenated, postcolonial identity as a Palestinian-Egyptian-Christian-Arab-American, a diversity of cultural positions that, as he reflected, were loaded with many tensions. He was born a Palestinian belonging to a Christian minority, living in an Arab country. He received his education in colonial Cairo in a British school and later went to America. In his autobiography he reflected about his confusing name that combined the English name Edward with the Arabic name Said:

> Thus it took me about fifty years to become accustomed to, or, more exactly, to feel less uncomfortable with, 'Edward,' a foolishly English name yoked forcibly to the unmistakably Arabic family name Said ... For years, and depending on the exact circumstances, I would rush past 'Edward' and emphasize 'Said'; at other times I would do the reverse or connect these two to each other so quickly that neither would be clear. The one thing I could not tolerate, but very often have to endure, was the disbelieving, and hence undermining reaction: Edward? Said? (Said, 1999: 3–4).

In this excerpt Said reflects about his name in which two identities which he thought highly incompatible were brought together. The experience of his name, as well as the training that he received in the English school in Cairo, expressed his experience of dislocation. The British staff of the school positioned the Arab boys as a "distasteful job" or as "delinquents" who needed regular discipline and punishment. There was a handbook with rules that were used to make the Arab boys become like the British, which led the boys to resist:

> Rule 1 stated categorically: 'English is the language of the school. Anyone caught speaking other languages will be severely punished.' So Arabic became our haven, a criminalized discourse where we took refuge from the world of masters and complicit prefects and anglicized older boys who lorded it over us as enforcers of the hierarchy and its rules. Because of Rule 1 we spoke more, rather than less, Arabic, as an act of defiance against what seemed then, and seems even more so now, an arbitrary, ludicrously gratuitous symbol of their power. (Bhatia, 2002: 68)

This quotation, and Said's work more in general, shows how a "cultural meta-position" includes some elements of the notion of meta-position as discussed before: taking a distance from other positions and reaching some overarching view from which the specific positions are considered in their interconnections. Words like "arbitrary" and "ludicrously gratuitous" express not only a strong evaluation but also suggest that Said's meta-position is strongly influenced by his more specific critical position. It brings, moreover, different (cultural) positions together and considers them as part of his personal history in the context of collective history (e.g., the English school in Egypt).

   The second quotation shows that power, one of the significant concepts in the post-modern model of the self, is clearly involved. The relationship between the English staff and the Arab pupils was different from the familiar hierarchical relationship between teachers and pupils within the boundaries of a single culture (e.g., an English school for English adolescents). It was a relationship of power that put one culture, the

English, including its language, above the other one, the Arabic, with the consequence that the Arabic boys developed forms of counter-power. These power relationships colored Said's multi-cultural identity as suggested by the problems he experienced concerning his name. Power relationships and differences in society do not simply "surround" the self, but infiltrate the most personal domains of the self (Callero, 2003).

Said's example also shows the theoretical relevance of the concept of positioning. As a verb it shows the dynamic aspect of the process of receiving, finding and taking one's place in a field of social relationships. There is an active *placing* of oneself in a particular relationship with somebody or something else and in a particular relationship with oneself. A significant theoretical advantage of the concept is that it can also be used in the passive form: being *positioned* by others, *being placed* by others and oneself. From his birth Said was positioned as a Christian-Palestinian and, under the influence of his parents, received, moreover, a mixture of an Arab and American identity. Placed in this field of contradictory and incompatible positions, he became involved in a process of appropriation and rejection that led him to identify with particular positions (e.g., Arabic), more than with others (e.g., English and American). This process in which he adopted them as *I*-positions was emotionally loaded and required life-long effort.

Said's autobiographical notes suggest that a meta-position is not isolated from the process of globalization and localization. His moves to different localities in the course of his life not only resulted in a higher density of cultural positions but also created larger differences and even contradictions in his repertoire. This suggests that a meta-position at the interface of different cultures is challenged by a higher density, stronger heterogeneity, and even incompatibility of positions, and, as a consequence, its complexity is enhanced. Yet this does not preclude the emergence of new meanings in the self, even when the meta-position is infused with contradictions and a high level of uncertainty. Commenting on Said's autobiography, Bhatia (2002) remarks:

The memoir enables him to enter into dialogical reflexivity with the different parts of his diasporic selves, thereby reworking and reconstituting the varied parts of 'Edward-Said' in a way that *new meanings about his identity are established.* Such an effort to rework the different parts of one's culture, heritage or ethnicity does not entail a movement to assimilation, marginalization and/or separation and integration in a new culture. Rather, as Said's memoir demonstrates, living in the diaspora is like being in a zone where all the contested parts of the self are constantly negotiating and renegotiating with each other. For the diasporic self, there is an ongoing, simultaneous dialogical movement between the *I* positions of feeling at once assimilated, separated and marginalized. (p. 69, emphasis added)

As this excerpt suggests, the perception of tensions, conflicts, contradictions, and incompatibilities is a fertile basis for the innovation of the self in particular and for creativity in general. Rothenberg (1990), for instance, described creativity as a Janus-like process, in which one is simultaneously conceiving multiple opposites or antitheses side by side and simultaneously. In a similar way, a (cultural) meta-position filled with contradictions and opposites creates a "Janus head" as an important condition for creativity, with the difference that there can be more than two heads.

Finally, Said's memoirs illustrate that a meta-position, like a life-review (Butler, 1975), can take the form of an *autobiography* or *self-narrative*, in which the person reflects on past events, performances, and experiences and on their interconnections as parts of a personal and collective history. A special case is the autobiography written from the perspective of the other-in-the-self. One of the first examples in the novelistic literature, later followed by many others, is Gertrude Stein's *The Autobiography of Alice Toklas* (1933). In this work she describes her memories, but told from the perspective of Alice Toklas, her partner, housekeeper, typist, and editor of her books. Stein thus writes her autobiography in the third person, creating an external perspective that reveals the way she sees herself as viewed by a significant other. Within the same work, this external view is combined with her internal perspective, from which she tells how she sees herself. In their combination the two angles allow a more comprehensive picture of the person Stein is. In dialogical terms, two different meta-positions are assumed, one from Toklas, the other from Stein, enabling the one position – implicitly or explicitly – to respond to the other position, complementing it, and agreeing or disagreeing with it (Hermans and Kempen, 1993).

In summary, a meta-position has three functions: unifying, executive, and liberating. As *unifying* it brings together different and even opposed positions so that their organization and mutual linkages become clear. In its *executive* function, it creates a basis for decision making and directions in life that lead to actions that profit from its support from a broader array of specific positions. As *liberating*, it acts as a stop signal for automatic and habitual behavior arising from ordinary and well-established positions. Considering them from the broader perspective of a meta-position increases the chances for innovation of significant parts of the self.

Coalitions of positions

Contributions to the unity and continuity of the self arise also from "coalitions of positions." The assumption here is that positions do not work in splendid isolation but can cooperate with each other, much like the way people cooperate in society at large. When they work together in coalitions, they form particular combinations that may significantly contribute to the unity and continuity of the self.

Typically, people organize their repertoire in such a way that two or more positions or voices dominate the repertoire (Hermans and Hermans-Jansen, 2004; Honos-Webb et al. 1999). That is, dominant positions usually have their companions, helpers, satellites, and auxiliary troops that together form stabilizing forces in the internal and external domains of the self. When a particular coalition becomes maladaptive or detrimental to one's well-being, the question is whether such a coalition can be changed or developed in such a way that a more adaptive or flexible coalition emerges. In this respect, we can learn from change processes in psychotherapy where strategies have been devised to modify stabilized or rigid coalitions.

Changing a maladaptive coalition: case example   At first sight, it may seem reasonable that therapists are doing well if they try to strengthen desirable positions and weaken or even remove undesirable ones, so that the former attain a more dominant place in the repertoire. Yet this is not necessarily the best strategy, because it is based on an unproductive good–bad dichotomy. The crucial question is how to make constructive use of the potentials of "undesirable" positions as contributions to more desirable coalitions. That is, how can a position that is experienced as "negative" be taken up in a coalition that, as a whole, is experienced as "positive." The point is here that a position is not desirable or positive in itself, but as part of the team of positions to which it belongs in a particular situation and time. Let's illustrate this with an actual case.

Fred, a 50-year-old man, suffered from burnout symptoms after a long period of over-demanding himself in his work situation. He described himself as a "persistent doubter," referring to his enduring anxiety about making decisions, particularly when he had to decide if a job was "finished" or not. In order to study his self in more detail, the Personal Position Repertoire (PPR) method (Hermans, 2001b) was applied in order to study not only the content of his positions but also their organization. It appeared that three positions were particularly significant during the time of the investigation: "the doubter," "the perfectionist," and, more in the background but very important to him, "the enjoyer of life." The last position was an enduring feature of his personal history, but was apparently suppressed by the dominant coalition between the doubter and the perfectionist, the latter position compensating for the anxiety aroused by the former.

After some sessions client and therapists[20] made a discovery that was crucial for the subsequent phases of the therapy. They found that the problem of the perfectionist could be resolved when Fred delegated tasks to other people at the right moment. He learned to contact other people in order to cooperate and even to delegate some tasks when doing a job, instead of completing a task entirely on his own. After more than a year of practicing, it was decided to investigate his position repertoire again. The most significant finding was the emergence of a new coalition, between the perfectionist and the enjoyer: he had learned to do a "good job" and even enjoy it, without making too many demands on himself. The new coalition was strong enough to push the doubter to the background of the self-system. Whereas the perfectionist had formed a coalition with the doubter in the first investigation, the perfectionist seemed to side with the enjoyer of life in the second one. The emergence of this new coalition enabled Fred to work with more pleasure than before and to cooperate more easily with other people. This case suggests that it is, in principle, possible to remove a particular position (the perfectionist) from an unproductive but dominant coalition (perfectionist and doubter) and combine it with another, more desirable, position (the enjoyer), with the result that the new coalition (perfectionist and enjoyer) is even more beneficial than the desirable position (enjoyer) alone (for details of method and case see Hermans, 2001b).

Apart from any psychotherapeutic change, the creation of coalitions can be part of everyday life. This is illustrated by the case of a woman who had for a long time been averse to practical work, leading to over-full and chaotic cupboards and wardrobes, things left at the wrong places in the house, the dishes not done, etc. She persisted in this behavior because she positioned herself towards others and towards herself as "I'm not practical and I don't even want to be." However, when she met a partner and they began to live together, she wanted to change this. Being very interested in art, she discovered that doing practical things in an artistic way (e.g., arranging things in the kitchen as an aesthetic composition) helped her gain more pleasure in activities that had previously been distasteful to her. Moreover, her position as a partner, sharing an apartment, stimulated her to become more engaged in creating the necessary order. From a theoretical point of view, we see in this example that a negatively experienced I-position (I as practical), including its associated behavior, can be changed by adopting it as part of a new coalition (with "I as artistic" and "I as partner"). Apparently, the latter positions were together strong enough to give the practical position a new, more positive, meaning resulting in a change of behavior. As this example suggests, behavior modification can be realized by adopting an undesirable or maladaptive position as part of a new coalition, provided that the other members of the coalition are different enough, in history and purpose, from the adopted position and dominant enough to determine the behavior of the coalition as a whole.[21]

Enjoyment of life as a cultural phenomenon   Coalitions of positions and their reorganization are phenomena that can be observed on the individual level and also on the societal level. As part of a longitudinal large-scale research project on social-cultural developments in the Netherlands, Felling (2004) was particularly interested in three kinds of values: *economic* (referring to the value of one's occupation in society), *familial* (referring to the value of one's membership of a family), and *hedonistic* (referring to the value of enjoyment of life). Studying the changes in these values in the period 1979–2000, he and his colleagues found that familial values decreased significantly, economic values remained more or less constant, while hedonistic values strongly increased. Even more relevant to our present purposes, he found that the correlation between economic and familial values decreased, while the correlation between economic and hedonistic values increased in the same period. The former correlation can be expressed in the sentence, "I work in order to be able to support my family," while the latter correlation can be articulated by the sentence, "I work in order to have an enjoyable life."

The three values in Felling's research project can be translated into three corresponding *I*-positions: I as a worker, I as family member, and I as an enjoyer of life. The changing correlations can be translated into changing coalitions, with the limitation that such patterns of correlations can do no more than suggest hypotheses. Whereas in the beginning of the period under study the position "I as a worker" formed a coalition with "I as a family member," at the end of the period the position "I as worker" became engaged in a coalition with "I as an enjoyer of life." In Felling's terms (2004) these changes indicate a continuing process of individualization as a collective, cultural phenomenon.[22] So, when many people nowadays embrace the position "enjoyer of life" then, from a sociological point of view, this phenomenon may well represent long-term changes on the collective level.

The increasing prominence of the enjoyer of life   Some positions are particularly suited to enter into a coalition with other positions. The "enjoyer of life" is such a position. It can be combined with a broad array of other positions. The "coalition-prone" tendency of the enjoyer results from what Allport (1961) once described in terms of "functional autonomy": a particular form of behavior that was originally engaged in for some other reason, may later become an end it itself. For example, whereas originally food served the function of satisfying a biological need, it later took the form of abundant dinners, consumed even when there is not an urgent need for food. Or, hunting as a means of gathering food, became an exciting leisure activity; dress as a means to protect the body, has become a way to display one's body in expensive costumes and lingerie, or, at the beach, in almost nothing. Fight, as a means to attack or as defence, found expression in economic competition and led to an enormous gaming industry. Sexual contact as a biological need became – as a result of the increasing use of contraceptives – a way to experience intimacy or pure pleasure, with a variety of drugs and stimulants available that can be used to intensify and prolong the experience. Travel, needed for nomads to find new environments for food and basic biological needs, was transformed into tourism as the biggest industry in the world. Last but not least, work, originally heavy, intense, or even dangerous, and necessary to earn one's bread, became a form of self-fulfilment and a way to achieve social recognition (Van Spengler, 2008).

The examples above represent developments over centuries, showing that many activities, as a result of their functional autonomy, became ends in themselves and, as a consequence, produced positions that tend to be combined with enjoyment or happiness in a variety of ways, such as: "I as enjoying a good dinner with friends," or "I as an enthusiastic member of a hunting club," or "I as exposing myself in the latest dress fashion," or "I as liking to play *City of villains* (or any other more recent version of the endless series of computer games), or "I as enjoying sex" (e.g., in combination with video-contact with another couple), or "I as liking to take my vacations in East-Asian countries." Apparently, the position as enjoyer is suitable for forming coalitions with a great variety of other positions.

The coalition-prone quality of the "enjoyer" is further stimulated by consumerism, mentioned as one of the characteristics of post-modernism (Chapter 2). The movement from production-oriented to consumer-oriented capitalism has led to the world-wide marketing of brand names and uniformity of tastes resulting in a flattening of differences between products. Barber (2004) goes so far as to speak of a growing "ethos of infantilization" that makes kids consumers, and consumers kids. There emerges a uniformity of consumer behavior across the different developmental ages, which he expresses in neologisms such as "kidults," "adulescence," or "twixters."

Post-modernism appears to include paradoxical elements: it can be described, under the influence of the French post-structuralist philosophers, in terms of differences and variety, but under the influence of consumerism in terms of increasing uniformity. The former trend manifests itself in the broadened range of positions from which the "traveling" world citizen can choose, whereas the latter trend manifests itself in forms of enjoyment that run the risk of becoming flattened and lacking any experiential depth. For philosopher and sociologist John Stuart Mill (1863/2004) the difference in quality of enjoyment or happiness was reason to distinguish between "happiness" (he had in mind intellectual and moral pleasures) and "contentment" (he thought of physical pleasures), claiming that the former was of a higher value than the latter.[23] Evaluation in terms of "higher" and "lower," Mill adds, can only be made by people who have experience of *both* of them. His examples, however, may be based on a hidden mind–body dualism when he defines intellectual pleasure as "higher" and physical enjoyment as "lower," and this view contrasts with the fact that for many people sexual pleasure with a loved one can be experienced as a very "high" form of enjoyment. Therefore, it seems more meaningful to make a distinction between "deep" and "superficial" forms of enjoyment. The deeper level of enjoyment, as experienced in satisfying work and in intimate relationships, is felt as more enriching and leaves more enduring traces of satisfaction in the mind than the more superficial level of enjoyment that results from consumerism. In this way we can understand that decorating one's house in a personal way or becoming engaged in volunteer work in the service of society represents a deeper level of enjoyment than buying sex or seductively advertised sex-associated products.

In summary, in the course of history the position of "enjoyer of life" has become increasingly prominent in the lives of many people. It has become a typically coalition-prone position, allying itself with a great variety of other positions. The phenomenon of consumerism, as a product of a consumption-oriented liberal capitalism, entails the risk of flattening the quality of the enjoyment. Given the strong differences between types of enjoyment, it makes sense to distinguish between deeper and more superficial forms of enjoyment.[24]

The third position: beyond conflicts

When two positions are involved in a conflict, they can find, under specific conditions, a *conciliation* in a third position that is able to lessen and mitigate the conflict between the original positions. At the same time, the third position has the advantage that the energy, originally invested in the resolution of the conflict, can be used in the service of the development of a third position. We will show that the introduction or development of such a position exerts a unifying influence on the self. Let's discuss this process, referring to some examples.

Rosanne's mission In an extensive case study, Brazilian investigators Branco, Branco, and Madureira (2008) describe the story of Rosanne, a 25-year-old woman who defined herself as lesbian. She had a stable romantic relationship with a 22-year-old girlfriend, despite the fact that she was still living with her parents. In an interview with one of the investigators, it became clear that the Catholic value system was a cornerstone in her life. Three specific *I*-positions were particularly prominent in Rosanne's life: she as a Catholic, as a daughter, and as a lesbian. Her internal conflict focused on the Catholic daughter *versus* the lesbian woman. The purpose of the investigators was to show the creative strategies Rosanne used to weave a relative self-integration out of strongly contradictory beliefs and values. Such reconstructions enabled her to arrive at a conciliation of the conflicts and contradictions between her two opposing worlds: the traditional society and the gay community.

During the interview Rosanne said that members of gay and lesbian groups usually came from problematic families and that she saw herself as an exception to this rule. She described her own family as "normal" and "well-structured," referring to the absence of divorce, drugs, and problems with the police. She was part of a family where her father worked and her mother stayed at home, describing it as a traditional well-structured family, despite the lack of affective, positive communication among its members. Although she participated in the lesbian community, she continued to go to church: "If I was out of the Church, it would be much worse!"

At one point she decided to contact a priest and tell him about her problems:

I have already told a priest about my orientation and everything, but he said ... he made a lot of questions, you know ... like, why I was hanging out with those people and that and that ... this sort of thing. Then, I started to think like ... Well, am I doing any harm to anyone? That's OK the Church has its dogmas, its laws, if you want to be part of it you have to follow them ... But ... I told myself, yes ... in Church ... like, God says you have to give love, to receive love, that is, that tender thing, you know? ... You are with somebody, you don't wish to do any harm, you are giving love when the person needs it ... that is, needs someone ... you are there, to help, you don't mean to do any harm. Why is that wrong? ... You see? And ... well ... that's the way I see it, that's the way I understand things. Then I started to think like: I go to Church ... to strengthen my spiritual side, because I miss, I need it, if this part of me is feeling bad, I feel bad ... (Branco *et al.*, 2008: 32)

Rosanne was well aware of the Church's view on homosexuality. However, becoming involved in a process of self-persuasion ("But ... I told myself ... "), she constructs arguments to justify herself as a good Catholic person, though homosexual, elaborating on a "personal theology" in which her religious values and her private, personal life are merging. She tries to find in religious virtues the anchor that she needs to bridge the gap between the two incompatible worlds which she feels are tearing her apart.

As Branco *et al.* argue, the issue of power needs to be highlighted. Her positions as a Catholic and as a daughter of her parents are dominant in her repertoire, and under the influence of the institutionalized power of the Catholic church in Brazilian society. So, she is in need of strategic processes that bridge the gap between her two worlds and interconnect her socially opposing *I*-positions in a way that provides a significant coherence and consistency, taking into account dominant positions as reflections of societal power structures. In the course of her self-reflections, she discovers that this is possible by constructing the position of a *missionary*. At some point she starts to talk about herself as a Christian woman who helps forsaken and lost people, including many gays and lesbians, living aimless in a difficult world. She feels that her mission may help people to think about their lives and change them in order to better fit traditional and Christian values, practices, and beliefs. In her own words:

> Our family is a structured family ... no divorced parents ... Well, that's what I ... hum ... and something else, I also try to help, when I am with someone ... kind of ... we, like, if I am seeing someone ... I even avoid ... going ... to the person's place, 'cause I start ... I can't ... I see things, like, this way ... see ... for example, an ex-girlfriend of mine, she didn't talk to her brother, she furiously hated him ... Then, I went, it's not like that, you know. ... You ... well ... then, I took her to Church, like, you know how to deal, you cannot force the person, push the person, she goes if she wants to, but you know how to deal with things like that. Until one day, she bought a gift for her brother, you know, she came to me and said, Rosanne, I bought a shirt to my brother. Like, that was the way she showed me she was doing something for him, see? Then, you know, you start to ... want to help people, because in such groups ... there are a lot of people that are there just for *oba-oba* ... ("oba-oba" in Portuguese means something like 'meaningless fashion' or 'silly fun'). (Branco *et al.*, 2008: 34–5)

Rosanne's deepest concern was "doing good", according to the values of Christianity and this seemed to represent an increasingly dominant position in her self. From this position, she wanted to see herself as a missionary. By considering gays as "lost souls" to be rescued and guided, she found a good reason for her presence in the gay community. Located in the field of tension between two groups of positions (she as a daughter of a Catholic family and she as a member of the lesbian community) she finds a strategy for dealing with intensely conflicting *I*-positions by developing a "third position" (she as missionary). The third position reconciles to a significant degree the conflict between the original positions and has a unifying influence on the self. At the same time Rosanne derives energy from the two conflicting parts of her self and invests it in the third position. In this way, she develops a strong *motivation* for becoming engaged in a new activity that is supported by a broader array of positions in her self.

   The pianist: the unifying influence of art   The film *The Pianist* (2002), directed by Roman Polanski, is a historical account of the Polish pianist Szpilman, who succeeds in avoiding deportation to a concentration camp by hiding himself from 1939 till 1945 in different places in Warsaw. Near the end of the film there is an impressive scene, in which the pianist, who is hiding in one of the ruins of the heavily damaged city, is discovered by a Nazi officer. When this man asks him whether he is a Jew, Szpilman answers "yes." The officer then asks him what he does for his living. Szpilman answers that he is a pianist. Then the officer takes him to a room with a piano and asks him to play something. The pianist sits and hesitates for a while. Then he plays, in that desolate space, a Chopin ballade. The officer listens, leaves, and comes later back with a food package for the pianist, even giving him his military coat as a protection against the cold.

   The film is moving not only because of the surreal contrast between the macabre character of the ruins and the sublime quality of the music, but also because of the beauty of the sounds that fill the empty space and bridge the gap between the Nazi and the Jew. The power of the music pushes their oppositions to the background. For some time at least they are able to meet each other in a third position, which lifts both up to some higher level. Music and art in general are communication devices *par excellence,* able to reconcile divisions and oppositions.

   It might be asked which position it is that figures in the film as a "third position." Is it an internal or an external position? Is it possible to give it a name? The viewer is impressed by the speaking power of the film and of the scene of the piano playing in particular, but is not very well able to give a name to the unifying position. It is not clearly defined but certainly very powerful. The transcendent power of the music is both internally and externally unifying. Much of the power of the position is that it is of a non-verbal quality, and is understood on a deeper emotional level that the viewer of the film seems to understand very well. When we say that it is an "artistic" position, then it is certainly one that goes beyond the boundaries and even conflicts between individuals, nations, and cultures. Art has a unifying impact that transcends cultures. People from different cultures can love the same Chinese porcelain, African music, Arabic architecture, Japanese marshal arts, and Indian dances. Art has the potential to cross boundaries and provides a fertile soil for third positions that reach beyond institutionalized power differences, political opposition, and military violence.[25]

Being black and white at the same time: the case of Griffin   John Griffin's classic on racism, *Black like me* (1960), was analyzed in the context of dialogical self theory by Barresi (2008). This story takes place in 1959, in the early phase of the civil rights movement, when alienation between whites and blacks in the southern parts of United States was at its peak. At that time, the white journalist John Griffin altered his skin color and spent a month traveling in the south, experiencing first hand what a black man experienced every day of his life. Initially his "black" and "white" identities were so different that there was no "sympathy" between them. However, in the course of time he overcame the dichotomy of two opposing positions, and acquired a personal identity that was neither white nor black, but just human.

As Barresi (2008) argues, many American whites believe that they can sympathize with a black perspective. However, they see black experience from a dominant white "first-person" perspective and the black identity from a "third-person" perspective and, as a consequence, their view is limited in scope. Griffin was an exception, not only because he was more sympathetic with the blacks than most other whites, but also because, being in a black body, he actually acquired knowledge from a first-person perspective about what it is like to be in the social position of a black person in America. What he saw was an ugly picture, one that he met with not only in the looks of hate and racism of other whites, but also when he looked at his own black image in the mirror for the first time. What he saw was shocking:

Turning off all the lights, I went into the bathroom and closed the door. I stood in the darkness before the mirror, my hand on the light switch. I forced myself to flick on the switch.

In the flood of light against white tile, the face and shoulders of a stranger – a fierce, bald, very dark Negro – glared at me from the glass. He in no way resembled me.

The transformation was total and shocking. I had expected to see myself disguised, but this was something else. I was imprisoned in the flesh of an utter stranger, an unsympathetic one with whom I felt no kinship. All traces of the John Griffin I had been were wiped from existence. (Griffin, 1960/1996: 15)

For a while, Griffin's self-consciousness is of a dual sort. As a white self he was conscious of being in the strange unlovable body of the "other." As a black self he entered into a world he had never experienced before, with unknown dangers and threatening rules (e.g., "As a black never look at a white woman!"). In this world he had to learn quickly in order to survive. The two positions were not yet on speaking terms. He was flipping from one to the other, experiencing first hand the black identity that had to learn in order to survive as a black person in the southern

United States, while, as a white identity, watching with the curious interest of an observer the new world he was entering.

The relation between the two identities takes a crucial upward turn when Griffin meets a black man while hitchhiking in Alabama. The man asks him to stay with them and his family for the night. Griffin discovers that the family is in many ways like his own family, with several children close in age to his own. He talks with the family about his own family and he experiences how similar the two families are, and yet how different as a consequence of their skin color. Reflecting on this meeting he writes:

> It was thrown in my face. I saw it not as a white man and not as a Negro, but as a human parent. Their children resembled mine in all ways except the superficial one of skin color, as indeed they resembled all children of all humans. Yet this accident, this least important of all qualities, the skin pigment, marked them for inferior status. It became fully terrifying when I realized that if my skin were permanently black, they would unhesitatingly consign my own children to this bean future. (Griffin, 1960/1996: 112)

Griffin arrived at a point where he went beyond the duality of his black and white identities. He achieved a more general human position that ignored, or rather subsumed, the two very different social identities into a third position. Later, in his final essay on racism, Griffin wrote:

> The emotional garbage I had carried all those years – the prejudice and the denial, the shame and the guilt – was dissolved by understanding that the Other is not other at all.
>
> In reality, the Us-and-Them or I-and-Thou dichotomies do not exist. There is only one universal We – one human family united by the capacity to feel compassion and to demand equal justice for all.
>
> I believe that before we can truly dialogue with one another we must perceive intellectually, and then at the profoundest emotional level, that there is no Other – that the Other is simply Oneself in all the significant essentials. (ibid.: 212)

As Barresi's (2008) analysis shows, power differences between blacks and whites, particularly at the end of the 1950s in the southern United States, are reflected in Griffin's dual identity and in the painful effort he had to make to arrive at a point where he could reduce the deep conflict between the incompatible positions. Finally, he could reach a third position in the form of a "generalized other" ("I as human") that was able to transcend significantly the two conflicting cultural positions.

In summary, we referred to the notions of unity and continuity in the context of dialogical self theory. We were stimulated to do so by the central place the same notions have been given in the modern model of the self. In our view, discussion and inclusion of these notions in dialogical self theory is a necessity. However, it is not our intention to consider the modern idea of unity as similar to the dialogical one. Dialogical self theory acknowledges multiplicity, and multi-positionality in particular, as a cornerstone of the self. Given this multiplicity, we have argued for unity and continuity in terms of combination and integration of positions, at the same time recognizing and maintaining their relative autonomy. In order to elaborate on the idea of unity-in-multiplicity we discussed the unifying effect of *I* in the concept of the *I*-position. Similarly, we dwelt upon the concepts of meta-position and coalition of positions, and on the existence of a third position. Central to our argument here is the thesis that, in the context of the dialogical self, unity and continuity are not features of a self-contained entity, but possibilities and even necessities of selves and identities that are extended to a world that is living increasingly at the interfaces of cultures and, as such, are part of historical and globalizing processes.

The self as part of a field of awareness and the "notion of good dialogue"

The traditional self, as described in Chapter 2, has at least two central features: it is part of a wider cosmic order and it is basically moral. As explained earlier, in putting forward our view of the self, it is not our intention to "copy" elements from the three models (traditional, modern, and post-modern), but rather to consider them as sources of inspiration and transform significant elements of them as parts of a dialogical self. Therefore, in the remaining parts of the present chapter we will explore to what extent the dialogical self can be seen as part of a wider order and to what extent it is of a moral nature. Specifically, we will introduce three concepts that are relevant to the further development of dialogical self theory: (i) the concept of "composition," which emphasizes larger patterns of positions rather than their specific relationships, and offers the possibility of an artistic view of the self; (ii) the concept of "depositioning," which refers to the capacity of the self to move beyond a particular position or group of positions and to participate in a broader "field" of awareness; and (iii) the concept of "good dialogue," which is based on the moral consideration that it is good to develop dialogues between and within people who are positioned in very different ways, yet who are part of an interconnected world society.

Composition: from specific positions to pattern

The notion of space is central to dialogical self theory, in contrast to the Cartesian view that space (*res extensa*) is outside the self (*res cogitans*). This is expressed in the central notion of "position," a spatial term that carries the implication that when there is a position, there are also *other* positions. All these positions are imagined to be located in a space, given the consideration that space is not only physical but also metaphorical and experiential. The assumption of space as being both *in* the self and in the world has the potential to transcend the dichotomy between the inner and outer and the internal and external as the metaphor of the society of mind transcends the dualism between self and other. Along these lines, we would like to explore processes that take place when the boundaries between inner and outer and between self and other become highly permeable and open to a wider field of experience.

Before we discuss the possibility of an enhanced receptivity of the self, let's first take a look at changes in perception when it is altered by drugs. This introduction will lead then to a discussion of a broader "field of awareness."

Opening the doors of perception   In his book *The doors of perception*, Aldous Huxley relates how the perception of spatial relationships dramatically changed after he took mescaline. In a vivid and sensitive way, he describes the flowers and books in his room:

The really important facts were that spatial relationships had ceased to matter very much and that my mind was perceiving the world in terms of other than spatial categories. At ordinary times the eye concerns itself with such problems as Where? – How far? – How situated in relation to what? In the mescaline experience the implied questions to which the eye responds are of another order. Place and distance cease to be of much interest. The mind does its perceiving in terms of intensity of existence, profundity of significance, *relationships within a pattern*. I saw the books, but was not at all concerned with their positions in space. What I noticed, *what impressed itself upon my mind* was the fact that all of them glowed with living light and that in some of them the glory was more manifest than in others. In this context, position and the three dimensions were besides the point. Not, of course, that the category of space had been abolished. When I got up and walked out, I could do so quite normally, without misjudging the whereabouts of objects. *Space was still there, but it had lost its predominance.* The mind was primarily concerned, not with measures and locations, but with being and meaning. (1957: 14, emphasis added)

There are three elements that find expression in this quotation. First, the specific physical position of the objects and their location in space becomes less dominant (e.g., "I ... was not at all concerned with their positions in space"). Second, rather than specific positions or their two-way relationships, an encompassing pattern of positions becomes important. Third, this experience cannot be well described in terms of "appropriation" or "ownership." Rather, the experience "comes in" and is *received* by an open mind (*"impressed itself upon my mind"*). The experience cannot satisfactorily be described as "mine" (*my* perception, or *my* creativity) because this would not give enough weight to the observation that there is a mind participating in a wider field of awareness. In fact, there is a widening and opening of the self with highly permeable boundaries that are not strictly demarcated from the environment.

Rollo May on creativity and Martin Buber on mysticism In comparing May's (1975) work on creativity and Buber's work on dialogue, Hermans (1994) observed an emphasis on both *receptivity* and *encounter* in the views of both authors. May, primarily but not exclusively interested in artistic creativity, writes: "Obviously, poetic and creative insights of all sorts come to us in moments of relaxation" (p. 104). However, he immediately adds: "They come not haphazardly, however, but come only in those areas in which we are intensively committed and on which we concentrate in our waking conscious experience" (ibid.). A well-known example is Albert Einstein, who wondered "Why is it I get my best ideas in the morning while I'm shaving?" The answer is that often the mind needs the relaxation of inner controls for the relevant ideas to emerge. Many artists and scientists have observed that ideas come at a break in periods of voluntary effort. In May's terms, "It is as though intense application to the problem – thinking about it, struggling with it – starts and keeps the work process going ... but the insight often cannot be born until the conscious tension, the conscious application, is relaxed" (1975: 66–7).

In his influential study on dialogue, Buber (1970) also emphasizes the attitude of receptivity. In his view, the *I* is a member of a pair that manifests itself in two fundamentally different ways: as *part* of an *I-You* relationship (subject–subject relationship) and as *part* of an *I-It* relationship (subject–object relationship). The term *I* is not a single word but, rather, part of the word pair *I-You*. This pair has to be distinguished from another word pair, *I-It*, which indicates a completely different attitude toward the world. Only in the *I-You* relation is there an encounter. When the *I* stands in relation with a *You*, the *I* exists, as a living being-as-a-whole, in the present. The *You* as the other is encountered by the human person as an independent other, yet addressed in a relation. Although the *I* and the *You* remain the same beings over time, they manifest different forms in each new encounter as parts of a new *I-you*. No encounter repeats itself in the same form. In Buber's view, the encounter between *I* and *You* is unthinkable without a receptive attitude, which is the cradle for emergence of deeper meaning.

The *I* as part of the *I-It* relation is an objectifying, rather than a dialogical *I*. The term "*It*" signifies an object of observation, classification, thinking, or using, but it is never an actual being-as-a-whole. The *It* is the result of a single fact of observation. Even the universe may be constructed as an objective totality. However, as an objective reality, the *It* is only an abstraction from the living experience of the human being living *with* nature.

The attitude of receptivity is part of the experience of ecstasy, clearly present in both May's work on creativity and Buber's philosophy of encounter. May pays attention to the phenomenon of ecstasy when he relates the experience he had as a student when confronted with contradictory results in his research findings. Walking to the subway, after he had put the problem aside, he found the solution. At the moment of breakthrough *"everything around me became suddenly vivid."*

I can remember that on the particular street down which I walked the houses were painted an ugly shade of green that I normally would prefer to forget immediately. But by virtue of the vividness of this experience, the colors all around were sharpened and were imbedded in my experience, and that ugly green still exists in my memory. The moment the insight broke through, there was a special translucence that enveloped the world, and my vision was given a special clarity. I am convinced that this is the usual accompaniment of the breakthrough of unconscious experience into consciousness. Here is again part of the reason the experience scares us so much: the world, both inwardly and outwardly, takes on an intensity that may be momentarily overwhelming. This is one aspect of what is called ecstasy – the uniting of unconscious experience with consciousness, a union that is not *in abstracto*, but a dynamic immediate fusion. (1975: 64)

Buber also emphasizes that the special qualities of the object become manifest, not when we "take" it or "appropriate" it but when we "encounter" it. If an object becomes part of an *I-You* relationship, it is perceived as a "light." In the encounter, things in the world become a *You* that expresses them in their uniqueness. This *You*: "fills the firmament – not as if there were nothing else, but everything else lives in its light" (1970: 126). In the *I-You* relation, the boundaries between subject and object, so typical of the moments of ecstasy, are transcended, and the object "enters" the subject: "Sea and rivers – who would make bold to separate here and define limits? There is only the one flood from *I* to *You* ..." (ibid.: 155–6). In discussing the relation between *I* and *You*, Buber explicitly refers to "the ecstacy of unification" (p. 135).

Symbols as facilitating receptivity   Symbols play a central role in creativity and in mysticism. Strikingly, both May and Buber use the symbol of the tree as one of their main examples. May (1975) refers to Cézanne, who experiences "being grasped by the tree." The painter is impressed by "the arching grandeur of the tree, the mothering spread, the delicate balance as the tree grips the earth – all these and many more characteristics of the tree are absorbed into his perception ..." (pp. 87–8). May emphasizes that the tree in Cézanne's perception is more than the sum of all the aspects: "This vision involves an omission of some aspects of the scene and a greater emphasis on other aspects and the *ensuing rearrangement of the whole*; but it is more than the sum of all these" (p. 88, emphasis added). Moreover, the concrete, unique tree is formed into the essence of the tree: "However original and unrepeatable his vision is, it is still a vision of all trees triggered by his encounter with this particular one" (ibid.). The tree, as painted by Cézanne, is a "speaking" tree, and in this speaking, something comes into being that did not exist before: "Thereafter everyone who looks at the painting with intensity of awareness and lets it speak to him or her will see the tree with the unique powerful movement, the intimacy between the tree and the landscape, and the *architectural* beauty" (ibid., emphasis added).

For Buber also the tree may invite an encounter: "it can also happen, if will and grace are joined, that as I contemplate the tree I am drawn into a relation, and the tree ceases to be an *It*." In this encounter, the tree impresses the viewer as an articulated and patterned whole that participates in a larger whole: "Whatever belongs to the tree is included: its form and its mechanics, its colors and its chemistry, its conversation with the elements and its conversation with the stars – all this in its entirety." In this encounter, the tree becomes manifest in its uniqueness and exclusiveness: "The power of exclusiveness has seized me" (ibid.: 58).

From a comparison between May's treatment of creativity and Buber's depiction of mysticism, we can learn the following: (a) both of them are interested in the notion of "encounter" that can be seen as a unifying form of dialogue;[26] (b) they put a strong emphasis on the attitude of receptivity towards the environment, suggesting that the *I* does not appropriate things from the environment and brings them within the boundaries between "me" and "not me." Rather than a possessive self, there is an opening self that is constituted by a dialogical environment of which the self is a part and that has something to offer that is not *accessible to the appropriating I*. Both authors are aware of the potential of the *I* to let the environment speak as "another *I*," with whom it is possible to engage in a dialogical relationship; (c) both authors suggest that, when the environment is approached in a dialogical way or receives a chance to "speak to us," it manifests itself as part of a *wider whole* of which the individual feels a part. This wider whole manifests itself in particular when it is mediated by symbols: when the person enters into a dialogical relationship with the environment, it reveals itself not only in its forms but also in the beauty of its colors, in its intensity and depth; (d) the authors refer to the patterning of the environment in terms of "architecture," "rearrangement," and "firmament." The specific positions of things is less important than their inclusion in a pattern; they receive their meaning as part of an articulated and more encompassing whole.[27]

When positions in the self become part of a patterned whole that is wider than the ordinary limits of the self, the emphasis shifts from the specific positions to the spaces *between* them. They become part of a *composition* in which the specific positions are taken up in their simultaneity. This composition can be the result of an artistic or scientific activity leading to the experience that one is part of a wider, meaningfully ordered whole. It can be found in any top, flow or peak experience that liberates the person from being locked up in any "*I*-prison," and that allows them to go beyond stress, taken up as the self is in a broader "field of awareness."[28]

Picasso, particularly in his cubist period (influenced by African art), started to look at his objects from different angles and juxtaposed these perspectives in one and the same painting. His well-known multi-leveled faces and multiple profiles express an intense attention to architecture and patterning. In such works we find a breaking down of the sharp separation between painting and the environment, as expressed in the dissociation of the contours of his painted people and objects. As Diehl comments:

... his [Picasso's] main interest is in the major problem of creation which he instinctively chose: *Combine and assemble various pictorial elements*, obtain their true junction on the canvas, attain the internal unity of painting (which Cézanne already defined) and achieve a degree of cohesion which enables him closely to associate the whole universe, *throwing down frontiers or traditional distinction between man and all that surrounds him.* (1977: 46, emphasis added)

In this quotation, as in previous ones, there is an emphasis on composition ("Combine and assemble ... elements"). We want to emphasize the importance of composition not only in works of art, but also in the organized position repertoire of the self. Self-reflection consists of a "subject" (the self-reflecting *I*), an "object" (the *me* and *mine* as the object of self-reflection), and a "project" (the way one organizes one's self across time). Our proposal is to consider the object and the project as artistic compositions of positions or as a narrative construction that is designed and redesigned over time. In viewing the self in this way, several features are highlighted: (a) there is a multiplicity of parts or elements (internal and external positions as part of an autobiographical story); (b) this multiplicity can be seen as a pattern in which the specific relationships between positions become less prominent than their spatial organization; (c) this organization can be viewed and appreciated from an artistic point of view; (d) as a composition the self is extended beyond the strict boundaries of its internal positions, like in a cubist painting where the boundaries between the object and its environment become blurred (see Diehl's quotation above); (e) viewing the self as an artistic construction can transcend the dualism between "positive" versus "negative," "pleasant" versus "unpleasant," or "good" versus "bad"; (f) considering the self as an artistic pattern creates a subjective experience of a broader space, opening wider horizons of experience and making the mind more receptive; (g) there is special attention to the spaces *between* the positions, rather than to positions in their isolation; compare looking at a painting along the dimension immersed–detached – zooming into a detail isolates this detail from the composition and focuses attention to one part of the work only, while zooming out and considering the pattern as a whole takes the spaces between the parts into account; this way of looking enables the individual to discover places where there is no position but where there could or should be one; (h) as a composition the different parts of the self are brought together in an act of "juxtaposition" so that new "bridges of meaning" can emerge.

It is not only in creative works in art that we see a lessening of the sharp boundaries between object and environment, between subject and object, and between self and other, but we can also find it as a central feature of mystical experiences. We will explore some of these experiences in order to learn from them so that we can better understand the process of depositioning.

The depositioning of the I

In a treatment of the relation between mysticism and consciousness, Forman (1999) discusses three forms of mysticism: one that he calls the "unitive mystical state" where there is a sense of becoming unified with a wider external environment; a second one, called the "dualistic mystical state" in which awareness is typically experienced as unbounded and expansive silence, while the individual remains conscious of the surrounding world; and a third one described as "pure consciousness," referring to an inner silence characterized by the absence of sensations, thoughts, or perceptions, a state of nothing but consciousness. For illustrative purposes we give one example of each state. The "unitive mystical state" is well illustrated by a report from Krishnamurti who wrote down his experience in 1922:

On the first day while I was in that state and more conscious of the things around me, I had the first more extraordinary experience. There was a man mending the road; that man was myself; the pickax he held was myself; the very stone which he was breaking up was a part of me; the tender blade of grass was my very being, and the tree beside the man was myself. I also could feel and think like the roadmender and I could feel the wind passing through the tree, and the little ant on the blade of grass I could feel. The birds, the dust and the very noise were a part of me. Just then there was a car passing by at some distance; I was the driver, the engine, and the tires; as the car went further away from me, *I was going away from myself*. *I was in everything*, or rather *everything was in me*, inanimate and animate, the mountain, the worm and all breathing things. All the day I remained in this happy condition. (quoted by Forman, 1999: 375, emphasis added)

In this state the person feels united with objects, animals, and people that are usually perceived as "outside." The self is extended to "everything" and this everything is far beyond the limits of the environment defined by the ordinary *I* as *mine*. The *I* is more receptive than appropriative, "rather everything was in me." The experience of space is not lost (e.g., "the car went further away") but is felt as strongly expanded beyond the individual who is far from self-contained. The expanded consciousness is like a "field."

Another type of mystical experience is the "dualistic mystical state." One of the examples is from Forman's own experience:

This began in 1972. I had been practising meditation for about three years, and had been on a meditation retreat for three and a half months. Over several days something like a series of tubes (neuronal bundles?) running down the back of my neck became, one by one, utterly quiet. This transformation started on the left side and moved to the right. As each became silent, all the noise and activity inside these little tubes just ceased. There was a kind of a click or a sort of 'zipping' sensation, as the nerve cells or whatever it was became quiet. It was as if there had always been this very faint and unnoticed activity, a background of static, so constant that I had never before noticed it. When each of these tubes became silent, all that noise just ceased entirely. I only recognized the interior noise or activity in these tubes in comparison to the silence that now descended. One by one these tubes became quiet, from left to right. It took a couple of weeks and finally the last one on the right went *zip*, and that was it. It was over.

After the last tube had shifted to this new state, I discovered that a major though subtle shift had occurred. From that moment forward, *I was silent inside*. I don't mean I didn't think, but rather that the feeling inside of me was as if I was entirely empty, a perfect vacuum ... (Forman, 1999: 370)

The author describes this experience as silence that is explicitly associated with awareness. This awareness can emerge on a permanent or semipermanent basis. Silence is at the core of this state, even while the person remains conscious of the outside sensate world. However, unlike the unitive mystical state, there is an experienced dualism between the inner silence that is conscious of the world but primarily finding its essence in itself, and the environment as being outside. Forman's descriptions suggest that this state is oceanic, unbounded, and expanded beyond the body, but the heart of the experience is an omnipresent inner silence. The oceanic feeling finds its core in itself, in a state of silence, emptiness, or as if being in a "desert," while in the unitive mystical state there is a far-reaching feeling of unity and identification with the broader environment.

The phenomenon of "pure consciousness state" goes one step further in the sense that there is an absence of sensations and thoughts. It can be found in a description in James's (1902/2004) *Varieties of religious experience*, where he describes how St Teresa of Avila (1515–82) experienced her "orison of union" as part of her mystic marriage with Christ:

> During the short time the union lasts, she is deprived of every feeling, and even if she would, she could not think of any single thing ... She is utterly dead to the things of the world ... I do not even know whether in this state she has enough life left to breathe. It seems to me she has not; or at least that if she does breathe, she is unaware of it ... The natural action of all her faculties [are suspended]. She neither sees, hears, nor understands. (quoted by Forman, 1999: 365)

In James's account there is, for her, an absence of sensory stimulation, memory, cognitive activity and even understanding. She becomes oblivious of her own body and all things around her. In contrast to the unitive mystic state, pure consciousness becomes awareness in itself, devoid of all mentally and sensory content. Instead of focusing on any content, the *I* reaches a state of pure awareness.

Depositioning and the Receptive I   The three mystical states described above can be seen as constituting three steps from specific *I*-positions to the *I* as awareness. In the unitive state there is an experience of unity with a wide variety of objects, organisms, and persons in the environment, to a point of full identification. The *I* is no longer located or imprisoned in a specific position with all its concerns, memories, and anticipations, but able to leave any position and to move freely from one to the other in an enlarged space. The three states can be compared by placing them on the dimension immersed–detached. In the unitive state the self is fully immersed in the environment. In the dualistic state the *I* becomes a form of awareness, with silence at its core, that is at a distance from everyday life, yet remaining conscious of it. Forman calls it "dualistic" because the person is living in "two worlds." A third step is represented by the pure consciousness state, characterized by an absence of mental content. Even further than in the two previous states, there is a depositioning of the *I* as being at distance, even separate from, any content.[29]

The three states have to be distinguished from what we have earlier described as a "meta-position," in which we see a first indication that the *I* is able to "leave" a specific position, to rise above it, and even to look at a number of positions and their interrelationships from a certain distance. However, despite the fact that the *I* has some overview of a variety of positions, it remains attached to and influenced by specific positions in the self. The *I* is clearly bound to the content of the positions and, despite some distancing, remains constrained by them. In the three described states of awareness, on the other hand, the *I* is no longer located in a particular position or meta-position. The particular positions, their overview, and their interconnections are no longer of central concern to the *I*. Rather, the *I* merges with other positions in an enlarged environmental space (first state), becomes part of a widened space of silence (second state), or becomes a form of pure consciousness (third state).

It is noteworthy that in all three states of awareness, the familiar experience of space becomes transformed and the spatial boundaries even recede. At the same time, all the experiences can be described only by making use of the metaphor of space. Even St Teresa, who was supposed to be in a state of pure consciousness, could express her experiences only by using spatial metaphors, as expressed in her book *The interior castle*. Whereas the dialogical self makes use of metaphorical descriptions of space, the fields of awareness create the need to speak of a "paradoxical space": the *I* leaves the ordinary self-space and participates in a broader awareness that can, in its turn, only be articulated and expressed by using a spatial metaphor, be it on a different level of experience.

Central features of the three states are the openness and receptivity of the self, the high permeability of its boundaries, and its becoming part of a larger whole. The question is, what is this larger whole? In the traditional model of the self it was the wider cosmos in which the individual self was meaningfully ordered. As argued in Chapter 1, we are living increasingly in a globalizing world in which the boundaries between different selves, groups, and cultures are challenged as never before. The globalizing world is far from being "meaningfully ordered," as the many international, interregional, intercultural and intercontinental problems demonstrate. As far as there is an order, it is not a given but rather a challenge that can only be met at the interfaces between individuals, groups, cultures, and also at the interface of the individual and himself or herself. In our view, this challenge needs to consider the *I* as a broader field of awareness. Is there an argument for this thesis?

Whereas large-scale problems in earlier times, such as floods, earthquakes, and uncontrollable disease, were typically caused by nature, many problems today are, partly or entirely, caused by humans and have, moreover, global implications. Pollution, warming of the earth, the depletion of natural resources, the waves of immigration and the resistance they meet, international terrorism, and the tensions between ethnic and religious groups are cases in point. In our view, *an increasingly globalizing, interconnected world society is in need of a self that learns to be part of an expanded field of awareness.* That is, self-contained identities are not well suited to work on such problems, because their strict boundaries are too sharp and their extensions too limited to feel solidarity with people and the environment on a global scale.

It would, we think, be a misunderstanding to suppose that states of expanded awareness are the exclusive domain of people who are "gifted mystics," or that they are exceptional phenomena mentioned only in the literature. In a minor form they can be part of the experiences of everyday life. Some people have access to such experiences when they reach, after a long walk, a mountain top with a view of a fabulous landscape; others when they enjoy great music or art that transports them beyond their daily routines; again others when they have an extraordinary experience of love; or when they have accomplished something, alone or together, that gives them the feeling that they are rising above themselves; or when they experience a broadened awareness when feeling part of a group that brings together people from different religions, ethnic groups, or cultures. At such moments our lives are intensely and *broadly* filled with meaning and, even when we experience it as "extraordinary," we feel most *close* to ourselves. Positions in our selves (including others-in-the-self) that are usually not immediately accessible, are coming to the surface. The self–other boundaries become more open and we feel part of a larger whole. For some people such exceptional and valuable moments are a reason to make decisions to choose a different or new direction in their lives. Such extraordinary experiences can extend our selves into a larger field of awareness that expands the horizons of the ordinary positions in the self. They also have the potential to break through, temporarily or more permanently, the "inner walls of the self" that are expressed in the form of categorizations and judgments of others. As Nouwen observed:

I have had a few moments in my life in which I felt free from all judgments about others. It felt as if a heavy burden had been taken away from me. At those moments I experienced an immense love for everyone I met, heard about, or read about. A deep solidarity with all people and deep desire to love them broke down all my inner walls and made my heart as wide as the universe. (1994: 60–61)

The existence of "inner walls" of the self brings us back to a more fundamental theoretical issue: the agency of the self. The preceding considerations lead us to propose that the *I* is *not only appropriating but also receiving*. The appropriative function of the *I* suggests an organizing *I* that brings elements to the self that did not belong to it before. Moreover, the *I* repulses or removes elements from the self that are felt as not belonging there. In this way, we understand that the *I* calls particular things or persons "mine," including them within the boundaries of the self that can be opened or closed, depending on the judgment of the *I* about particular elements as "fitting" or "not fitting." Considering the self as appropriating and rejecting fits very well with a utilitarian view of the self as "owner of certain goods," a conception that would be very well in accord with the idea of the self as a container. It suggests, moreover, that the self as "possessing" considers itself a master who has the content of the self and its organization under its control.

The *I* as receptive is very different from the *I* as appropriative, because elements are received *beyond* the agency of the self. The self does not appropriate it but receives it as a gift, challenge, or destiny. In these cases, the agency is not in the *I* but in the other as another *I*. By attributing a receptive function to the *I*, agency is brought to the surrounding world so that dialogical relationships between self and world have a chance to emerge. As we have seen in the preceding sections, becoming part of a wider field of awareness is engaging the *I* in a way that goes beyond the appropriative function of the self. You cannot "own" the love you receive from a loved one, or be the possessor of a great aesthetic experience, or even control your "own" creativity. This is not to deny that in love affairs the appropriating and receiving functions can alternate, as expressed in the different expressions "you are mine" versus "I'm yours." However, becoming part of a broader field of awareness seems to move the appropriating function to the background, so that the *I* is invited to fuse with the wider field, where it gives up, transiently or more permanently, its appropriative and controlling aspirations. The restricted *I* becomes an enlarged *We*.

From a theoretical point of view, it makes sense to bring the notions of "position" and "*I*" together in the composite term "*I*-position." As positioned, the self is localized in space and time, that is, as part of a globalizing world and a collective history. As a receptive *I*, it has the potential to become part of a broader field of awareness. It is the suggestion of the present chapter that in the concept of *I*-position, the self, although bound to space and time, has the potential to become more than what is included in the modern expression "I'm myself."

The concept of the *I*-position acknowledges the autonomy of the individual as typical of the modern model of the self and as celebrated for a long time by Western cultures. Autonomy has received a place in the present theory by the conception of the self as "a dynamic multiplicity of relatively *autonomous I*-positions in the landscape of the mind." At the same time it allows, via the notion of *depositioning*, the exploration of more collective versions of the self as they are prominent in all those cultures (e.g., Asian, African, South American) that celebrate we-experiences (with other people, ancestors, and nature) that make people feel part of a more encompassing whole. In these cultures *I*-positions function, more prominently than in Western cultures, as *we*-positions or as a meaningful part of them. In this sense, dialogical self theory and the notion of the *I*-position in particular promises to provide a conceptual link between different cultures in a globalizing world. Rather than dividing the world into individualistic and collectivistic cultures (see Hermans and Kempen, 1998, for criticism), we are in need of concepts that *bridge* them and are applicable to both of them. The concept of *I*-positions is, in our view, a candidate that is well equipped to contribute to such a task.

What is good dialogue?

In this final part of the chapter, we will focus on the main features of "good dialogue," taking into account the concepts discussed in the present and previous chapters. When we talk about "good dialogue," we do so in the expectation that dialogue can contribute to a minimal coherence in an otherwise fragmenting world without falling back on the self-contained unity typical of the modern self. Dialogue is *not only* something to be studied, but represents a moral and developmental purpose: an activity that is desirable and valuable when people want to learn from each other and from themselves in the service of a further development of self and society. With that purpose in mind, we will concentrate on the follow-ing features of good dialogue: (a) it is innovative; (b) it has a sufficiently broad bandwidth; (c) it recognizes the existence of misunderstanding; (d) it creates a dialogical space; (e) it takes into account the alterity of the other and also the alterity of the different parts of the self; (f) it takes into account the existence of power-differences; (g) it has an eye for the dif-ferences between dialogical genres; (h) it has the potential to participate in a broader field of awareness and leaves room for silence.

Dialogue is innovative   In the literature, the concept of dialogue is sometimes broadly defined, at other times in a more restrictive way. The broad definition considers dialogue as identical to communication and, with reference to the self, internal dialogue includes every form of internal communication or activity, including rumination. In a more restrictive sense, dialogue is considered as something that is not simply given, but has to be learned and developed, although its precursors can already be observed early in life (see Chapter 4). In the restricted sense, dialogue in the self is a developmental process and an active learning-via-interchange that gives an impetus to the self. That is, it introduces elements into the self that were not there before the dialogue took place and, once introduced, are experienced by the participants as valuable.

There are three reasons why we advocate a definition of dialogue in a restricted sense. First, when dialogue is considered identical to communication, a conceptual difference between the two concepts is superfluous. When scholars of communication say that is it not possible to NOT-communicate, the implication would be that it would not be possible to NOT-dialogue. Dialogue then would be identical to *every* form of communication, resulting in a conceptual inflation of dialogue. When the concept has no constraints, it becomes "everything" and loses every focus. Second, when one sees dialogue as identical to communication the conceptual difference between dialogue and monologue becomes, if not impossible, at least problematic. When dialogue is "everywhere," then, consequently, a monological relationship between people would be seen as a form of "dialogue," resulting in a confusion of the two concepts. Third, treating the two concepts, dialogue and communication, as identical would have the detrimental implication that dialogue as a moral aim and developmental purpose would be undermined. To put it strongly, it could be said that Hitler communicated with his audience, but it is highly questionable if he was involved in a dialogue with them.

Question and answer, as well as agreement and disagreement, are central processes in a dialogical relationship. However, as already said in Chapter 1, a disagreement between two parties can easily produce a defensive reaction on the part of one or both of them, with the result that they simply repeat what they have said before and don't learn from each other. The same can be said about question and answer. When a speaker is posing purely rhetorical questions and is not interested in the response from the side of the listener, the answer is already implied in the question, limiting any learning process. Indeed, question and answer, like agreement and disagreement, are included in dialogue but dialogue in a well-developed sense consists of something more than that. This "more" is the innovative element. Dialogue is innovative when the participants are able and willing both to recognize the perspective of the other party in its own right, and to adapt, revise, and develop their initial standpoints by taking the preceding verbal and nonverbal messages of the other into account. This innovative impact can vary from new insights that result from a creative exchange between partners involved in a common project, to the vague and undefined feeling that members of a group may have when they sense something emerging that they find valuable and important, but that they cannot, or not yet, articulate. Innovation is also a central feature of dialogues in the self: self-conflict, self-criticism, self-agreement, self-consultancy and any other self-activity are dialogical only if they bring in an element of innovation or newness as a result of a productive process of interchange with oneself or with others.

The innovation of the self has its boundaries. When a person renews the self incessantly without arriving at a position with a certain degree of stability, a productive dialogue is impeded. Innovation requires not only change but also some stability in order to arrive at a point at which a position can become effective. One could compare a new position in the self with a new member in an organization. He or she requires some time to get acquainted with the new environment before being able to make a valuable contribution to the organization. A constant renewal of the self with a lack of any stability is symptomatic of the indecisiveness one can observe in a person who is looking for advice and consults one advisor after another. After every meeting he or she takes a new point of view in a never-ending flux of changes, never arriving at the point of certainty that is needed for decision and action.

Innovation as typical of dialogue in the self is lacking in the phenomenon called "rumination." In that case one or a few negatively experienced positions are dominating the self (e.g., "I as a failure," "I as guilty," "I as a loser," or "I as drinking too much"). Often these positions are connected with a limited range of external positions (e.g., "my critical colleague," "my angry father," "my boss who is not satisfied about me," or "my wife who doesn't understand me") that are experienced as feeding the internal ones. In ruminating, the *I* is severely constrained by a cluster of internal and external positions that are easily accessible, but that do not allow any exit. Typically, the person makes cyclical movements across these positions, again and again arriving at the same positions and becoming absorbed in their negatively colored memories, cognitions, and anticipations. In fact, such a cluster functions as an *I*-prison from which the person feels unable to escape. There is a tendency to become locked up in oneself and lose contact with the environment. Given the lack of any innovation and because of the rigid dominance of one or a few positions, ruminating is more monological than dialogical and there is an overall negative feeling. At the same time, positive positions (e.g., "I as optimist," or "I as active organizer of my life," or "I as having a sense of humor") are backgrounded and not accessible as long as the period of rumination continues.

Rumination can also take the form of co-rumination when two people, typically female adolescents who are friends, talk with each other about their problems. As Rose (2002) described, co-ruminating adolescents talk excessively about their problems in dyads. They do this frequently, discuss the same problem repeatedly, encourage each other, go into the details of problems, speculate about possible negative outcomes, and focus intensely on their negative feelings. Although these adolescents develop intimate friendships, co-ruminating may have the undesirable effect that internalizing problems (depressive symptoms and anxiety) increase. These results suggest that ruminating, even when with a friend, is different from a dialogical relationship, given its absence of innovation during the process of interchange, its repetitive character and inaccessibility of positive positions.

Dialogue needs a broad bandwidth   From a practical point of view it is not possible that all positions of the repertoire find an expression in one act of dialogue. Because the process of positioning is contingent on a particular situation, only those positions that are part of a working self that selects and activates positions relevant to the situation at hand will find a voice. On the other hand, dialogue can only function well when it has a sufficiently broad bandwidth, that is, it needs to be open to a range of different positions that are expected to be relevant to a particular dialogical relationship. Moreover, in order to facilitate dialogue, the bandwidth tolerated by each of the participants should not be very different. Take the example of a woman who cared for her mother during the last months of her mother's life. She had many conversations with her mother that gave her the feeling that they had an intense bond in which "everything" could be discussed. However, after her mother's death, she discovered that her mother's will included arrangements that she as a daughter felt were entirely at variance with the conversations before the death of her mother. This left her with the feeling that her mother had not said "everything," nor told her important things when she was still alive. In this example, the concept of bandwidth becomes relevant. Apparently, the daughter thought that the contact with her mother had a very broad bandwidth, but later concluded that the mother had written her will from particular positions (e.g., loving a particular person whom the daughter did not know) not included in the earlier talks between mother and daughter. In the experience of the daughter, the bandwidth of the dialogue was broader from her own side than, she felt, from the side of her mother.

With reference to the notion of bandwidth, there is a clear difference between formal and informal relationships, the latter usually having a broader bandwidth than the former. When a contact starts in a formal way and gradually becomes more informal, the bandwidth of the contact becomes broader, with the consequence that the participants interact from a wider array of positions. Somebody may be used to talking with his colleague about work tasks, but later, over a cup of coffee, one of them reveals that he is the father of a disabled child. This may or may not invite the other to talk about personal experiences.

The notion of bandwidth is particularly relevant to the concept of meta-position. An effective meta-position requires the inclusion of those positions that are relevant to a particular decision enabling the participants to consider a problem from different angles. Positions that are relevant to a particular problem do not remain out of sight and, consequently, lead to a decision that has a sufficiently broad basis in the repertoire.

Reference to the bandwidth of a dialogical relationship can also be fertile when distinguishing between self-positioning and self-presentation. In his classic work *The presentation of self in everyday life* Goffman (1959:28) explains that a person is motivated to convey "an impression of reality that he attempts to engender in those among whom he finds himself." He gives the example of a girl living in a dormitory who receives many telephone calls in order to impress the other girls with her popularity. *Self-presentation* aims at conveying an image of oneself to the outside world, in such a way that the addressees perceive this image as reality. *Self-positioning*, on the other hand, is concerned not only about the positions people wish to present to the outside world, but also about those that they take towards themselves. It should be noted that the latter may be entirely discrepant from or even contradict the former. The dormitory girl in Goffman's example may give many signs of her popularity to the outside world, but "internally" she may position herself as "somebody in whom boys are not interested" or even as "not worth attention." In such a case the two positions are dynamically related when the externally presented position may function as an overcompensation for the internal one. As we argued earlier, the self is characterized by oppositions, ambivalences, and ambiguities, in which a broad variety of positions play their part, not only those that are foregrounded as presentations to the outside world but also those that are backgrounded as "shadow positions" (Hermans, 2001b), "exiles" (Schwartz, 1995) or "disowned selves" (Stone and Winkelman, 1989) in the darker spaces of the self. Although backgrounded, they may nevertheless influence a person's behavior in significant ways, as many psychoanalytic theories have argued.

In summary, dialogical relationships can never include all positions of the repertoire at once. However, for a good dialogical relationship a sufficiently broad bandwidth is required in order to make positions or their coalitions "work" in a particular situation, and to enable the participants to take decisions that have a sufficiently broad basis in the repertoire. The more positions support a particular decision, the broader is its basis in the repertoire. It should also be taken into account that, when the bandwidth that different participants tolerate is asymmetrical between them, there is a risk that they find no common base for mutual understanding.

Dialogue recognizes misunderstandings Misunderstanding is not the opposite of dialogue but rather part of it. In a discussion of the relationship between self and other, Barresi (2002), building on Bakhtin's work, makes a distinction between *first-person information*, the experience that an individual has about his or her own activity, and *third-person information*, the experience that another person has about an actor when observing that actor in an activity. In order to fully appreciate a person's activity, some sort of integration of first- and third-person information is required. However, according to Barresi and Bakhtin, the actor never succeeds in integrating the two sources of information. When we are engaged in a social activity, we must combine *directly perceived* or first-person information about ourselves with *imagined* third-person information about ourselves (from the side of the other) in order to fully understand our intentional activity. Moreover, we must succeed in integrating *imagined* first-person information about the other person with *directly perceived* third-person information of the other person's activity in order to understand the other's intentional acts. This creates an epistemological problem that can never be fully solved. The fact that the two perspectives, imagined and directly perceived information, do not fully match creates a fertile ground for misunderstandings (e.g., in a conversation one parent says: "I'm surprised that you don't like our new son-in-law." The other parent answers: "He reminds me of my disliked brother, who used to make such jokes." However, the parents were not aware of each other's view before their exchange so that they ended up with a misunderstanding). It is never certain that my imagined information about the other's behavior is identical to the directly perceived information about the other's behavior from his or her point of view. We engage in dialogue in order to exchange and compare our viewpoints and we may even arrive at common viewpoints and decisions, but the two points of view will never match entirely. Therefore, misunderstanding is intrinsic to dialogue and can never be avoided entirely. Dialogue cannot be realized without the recognition of the existence of a basic epistemological uncertainty.

A related source of misunderstanding follows from the distinction between the other-in-the-self and what is defined as the "real other." In fact, the other-in-the-self is a notion of the other that never can fully coincide with the "real other," because the real other has his or her own perspective that never fully coincides with the notions that exist about this other person. Nevertheless, *exclusive truth claims* about the other do not recognize this distinction because it is in their nature to see the imagined other as identical to the other as he or she "really is." Failing to see the difference, intentions are attributed to the other that may be entirely different from the other's own perspective, but this difference is not made visible because the exclusive truth claim is blind to any difference between imagination, interpretation, and assumption on the one hand, and "reality" on the other hand. Such truth claims often have the form of general statements such as "in contact with women a man always wants ...", or "when you come from that culture, we know that you ..." Such claims do not acknowledge the *perspective* from which they arise, including its limited horizon, and they are, therefore, not open to acknowledging that there *may* be another perspective that leads to another opinion, experience, or observation. The person who makes exclusive truth claims does not allow space for others to express the way they position themselves. As a consequence, productive dialogue is impeded or even impossible when one or both parties are guided by the pretension that their "truth" matches objective reality. Dialogue becomes possible only when parties involved in interchange acknowledge that there are more possible perspectives from which a particular topic can be considered. Any absolute truth claim denies the existence of multi-perspectivity and therefore blocks the innovative potentials of dialogical activity. Behind the reality-claim of many assertions are often unnoticed misunderstandings.

As Van Spengler (2008) observes, many religions have, in the service of reaching maximum certainty, produced sacred books that were written by people who have elevated them as the word of God. This has resulted in exclusive truth claims that have led to intolerance, discrimination, coercion, persecution of deviants, wars, and terrorism. Such phenomena that have colored history with blood are *expressions* of the lack of dialogue and, at the same time, *produce* situations in which dialogue between the different parties cannot evolve. Dialogue is possible only if there is *space* for another position that can function as a starting point for productive disagreement, agreement, negotiation, contradiction, ambivalence, and conflict. One of the great achievements of the Enlightenment was the belief in tolerance and respect for human dignity which has led to the declaration of human rights. However, as we discussed in Chapter 2, the modern model of the self, greatly influenced by Enlightenment philosophers, suffers from a dualism between self and other, resulting in a conception of the self where there is no intrinsic place for the other. We see it as a promise of a dialogical view that the other is included in the self as part of a social process. However, dialogue can only work when it acknowledges the distinction between the other-in-the-self and the actual other. This distinction can be made only if, instead of exclusive truth claims, there is room for the existence of different and contradictory perspectives that function as starting points for meaningful dialogue.

Even if multi-perspectivity is acknowledged, dialogicality does not automatically evolve. For innovative dialogue an interface is required where positions (including the other-in-the-self) can be exchanged and compared with positions of the actual other (including the other-in-the-self on part of the actual other). On the interface of the different perspectives of self and actual other, misunderstandings can be observed, discussed, and corrected. In order to create a productive interface, it is required that the parties involved in the dialogue take their starting point *in the present*, that is, they are open to the information that is presented in the here and now, rather than being led or misled by conceptions of each other built up in the past or anticipations of their points of view imagined in the future.

Dialogue needs a dialogical space   When two or more people are increasingly involved in a dialogue, they feel the emergence of an invisible common space in which they feel accepted as dialogical partners and feel the freedom to express their experiences from their own point of view. Being in this "dialogical space" (Goolishian and Anderson, 1992; Hermans, 2003; Reichelt and Sveaas, 1994) the participants are open to each other's experiences, although these may be very different from their own. The bandwidth of the space is broad and a diversity of positions and experiences can be expressed. The participants typically feel a strong sense of sharing and have the impression that the space is *between* them and connects them.

Disagreements, conflicts, and even shadow positions don't exclude the emergence of a dialogical space. Take the example of a team of professionals who meet at regular times. To the annoyance of his colleagues, one member is regularly absent, because he hates meetings and decides not to join. The other members discuss his behavior and most of them conclude that it is unacceptable. The leader of the group, highly respected by his co-workers, takes the position of the dissident member and tries to convince his colleagues that he is of special value to the team because of the creative quality of his work. Finally, the team agrees to accept the absence of the dissident member but, they ask him, in return, to write a report, a task that most other members dislike. The deviant member, on hearing this, feels accepted in his shadow position ("I as hating meetings") and writes the report with pleasure. In this example, there is initially no dialogical space between the deviant and his colleagues because he separates himself from the group by his refusal to be present and, in turn, he is separated from the team by the other members who see his behavior as unacceptable. However, from the moment that a solution is suggested and agreed to, there emerges a dialogical space between the members of the group and the deviant, who feels respected for his particular qualities. Moreover, the members and the deviant find each other by creating a "third position" ("engaged deviant") that reduces the conflict between the original positions ("non-engaged deviant" versus "conforming team member"). Generating the third position creates more space in the team members to the benefit of all of them, for a longer or shorter time.[30]

In this example, we see that the emergence of a shadow position, disowned by the team, and maybe also by the deviant himself, threatens the sucessful functioning of the team and works in a destabilizing way (decentralizing movements). However, from the moment the team was willing to take the behavior of the deviant into consideration and to suggest he performed an alternative task, integrating forces (centralizing movements) are at work, enabling the team to find a new equilibrium.

Positions or, more dynamically formulated, ways of positioning, can be seen as "concentrations of energy" that require a specific *place* in which they can come to full expression. A manager who positions himself as ambitious likes to occupy a large room in the main building of a company, a person inclined to meditation wants to be in a quiet place without distraction, the humorous person likes to make jokes in the party room, the adolescent who desires an ecstatic experience visits a disco, and the person inclined to piety enters a holy place. By visiting such places, people evoke or attempt to evoke corresponding spaces in their selves. There is not only a multiplicity of positions, but also a corresponding multiplicity of spaces.[31] Positions need a fitting physical place and a corresponding space in the self for expression and development. The problem with shadow positions is that places for expression are less available and less accessible as long as the person himself or the social environment rejects these positions and fails to provide space for them. Therefore, a dialogical space is challenged by the introduction of shadow positions while, at the same time, the inclusion of such positions in this space is a way to give it expression and to use its energy as part of a productive coalition of positions or the construction of a third position (see the example of the deviant group member).

The affective dimension is particularly important for the construction of a dialogical space. The space can easily disappear when somebody is not in tune with the affective dimension or the atmosphere of the space.[32] Suppose a person tells someone that his son has recently died. The respondent then asks only factual questions (where? when? how?) but does not express, verbally or non-verbally, any attention to the feeling dimension. The speaker will not feel sufficiently understood and may be discouraged from continuing to talk about his experiences and his feelings in particular.

Dialogue respects alterity Respect for alterity is the moral feature of dialogue *par excellence*. In its most general sense, alterity refers to the otherness of the other and its recognition as intrinsically valuable. Dialogue is a pre-eminent form of relationship that takes alterity into account (for extensive review see Simão and Valsiner, 2007). Alterity implies the discovery, acceptance, and even stimulation of the differences between self and other in dialogical relationships. This refers not only to the actual other in general, but also to *the other in her multiplicity*. The self, as well as the other, is multi-voiced and deserves in this multiplicity space for expression. This statement applies not only to the functioning of the self in one and the same situation, but also to the self as manifesting itself in successive situations. That is, the multiplicity of the other can take the form of expressing one position at one moment and another position at another moment. This "temporal multiplicity" on the side of the other is seriously reduced as long as the self is in need of stability and continuity, a need that is also important in the external domain of the self. Given this need, the self over-stabilizes the other-in-the-self, entailing the risk that contact with the actual other is constricted to a rigid position that limits the movements of the actual other from one to another position.[33]

It is necessary to emphasize the significance of widening the space for the multiplicity of the other, because, as a result of prejudices, stereotyping, stigmatizing, and judging, the perceived other is often reduced to one position only. There is the basic problem of egocentricity in the self that means that one is willing to acknowledge the multiplicity of one's own self, while reducing the other-in-the-self, as equated with the actual other, to one or a few positions only. As we have argued in Chapter 1, biological survival needs (e.g., stability, safety, and self-maintenance) have the tendency to reduce the position repertoire. The same needs also play a significant role in the reduction of the multiplicity in the perception of the other. This creates a problem for the acknowledgment of the alterity of the other, because alterity implies not only the content of the positions but also their variation and multiplicity. In stereotyping or judging the other, it is often forgotten that the other has always "another side" or even "many sides."

The alterity of the other manifests itself in different forms. First of all, the actual other is different from the self, that is, the other has different positions. Even when the positions of two people are given the same name, the memories, expectations, and aims associated with them are different, given the fact that people have different personal and collective histories. Second, the positions of the other are different in their temporal manifestation: they can be different at successive moments or periods. Although there may be significant changes in the other's position repertoire in the course of time, the positions *attributed* to the other are perceived as being stable, with the consequence that the changes are not perceived or even denied. Third, positions on the part of the actual other are different from those of the self in their organization: the self of the other is not only multi-voiced, but this multi-voicedness also has another *pattern*. This can only be understood when giving others the opportunity to tell their stories from their own particular point of view, with attention to the specific way in which the implied positions are composed.

As Cooper and Hermans (2007) have argued, there is not only an alterity in the world around us, but also inside us: the positions within the self deserve attention and recognition in their otherness. It is legitimate to talk of a "self-alterity,"[34] just as one can talk of the alterity of another person. In the cited publication, the authors (Cooper and Hermans, 2007) have presented reasons for going beyond Levinas's (1969) characterization of the self as sameness, towards an understanding of the self as having an internal diversity and alterity. In developing the notion of self-alterity, the authors were careful to avoid the pitfall of reducing the inter-subjective foundations of a Levinasian worldview to a kind of intra-psychic psychologizing. They explicitly emphasized that the notion of self-alterity should be seen as an extension of "other-alterity" rather than as an alternative to it. Even the most "internal" self-experiences are infused with something of the non-self. From that perspective, it should be noted that self-alterity like other-alterity is characterized by the recognition and valuation of the differences, multiplicity, and changes of one's own positions.

The recognition of alterity and its realization in dialogical relationships finds itself in a field of tension with the notion of identity in the sense of sameness over time. In striving for identity, stability, and continuity, the self wants to remain the same despite successive identifications with others. In the service of the need for continuity, the alterity of the other becomes subordinated to dominant self-positions. The other can even be used, to take a term from Bakthin, as a ventrilocutor, expressing the opinions, views, and even experiences that originate from dominant positions in the internal domain of the self (e.g., "He says that you ...", or "Everybody says that ..."). Apparently, the recognition of the alterity of the other implies certain identity costs. The alterity of the other continuously challenges a stabilized self-identity, undermining its pretension of certainty. Therefore, the recognition of the alterity of the other, and even of the different parts in the self, requires a certain tolerance for uncertainty. This tolerance should be a central part of "alterity-learning." Such a form of learning requires a balance between the need for a clear and sufficiently stable identity on the one hand, and, on the other, the necessity of recognition and incorporation of alterity as part of productive dialogical relationships.

The recognition and processing of alterity is problematic because of the natural human tendency to remain in the "comfort zone" of the self, that is, a set of ordinary positions that are perceived as familiar and to which one continually tends to return. Such positions give the person the feeling of safety, stability, and continuity, and tend to become dominant in everyday life. The existence of a comfort zone can be observed not only in the spaces of the self, but also in the way people behave in physical space. They tend to return to the places where they have already been and where they feel at ease: the same chair, the same restaurant, the same route for a walk, and the same holy places. A similar attachment can be observed in the workings of the self. There is a tendency to "visit" the same positions in the self repetitively. Not only do we do this in the internal domain, but in the external domain also we find ourselves addressing others-in-the-self that are familiar and to which we tend to return in our memories, thoughts, and fantasies (e.g., a picture of a deceased family member or a figure who is revisited in one's fantasies). Returning to familiar positions gives order, continuity, and safety.[35] On the other side, the continuity and familiarity of positioning in routinized ways form obstacles to acknowledging the alterity of positions. Alterity needs some deviation from the stable routines of everyday life and requires a certain amount of innovation in the self, but this is not always welcome, particularly when it is conflicting with one's favorite identity positions. Therefore, dialogue can take alterity into account only when selves and identities are open to the uncertain inputs of the less familiar aspects of the positions of both others and of oneself.[36]

It should be added that repeating visits to the same place does not necessarily mean that the self becomes routinized. It is certainly possible to visit the same place several times, but to do so from different positions. For example, one may visit a particular place and enjoy it from an artistic position, later going back to the same place but accompanying a loved one, and, again later, going there out of nostalgia. The same place can be visited from different positions, opening different spaces in the self. It is even possible to experience the same place as fresh or new from the perspective of the same position (e.g, being sensitive to the richness of variations from an artistic point of view).

Dialogue needs the acknowledgment of power differences Dialogue in its innovative potentials can flourish in a good talk between friends, colleagues, and acquaintances and in any relationship where power differences are not too large and participants are able and willing to construct a common dialogical space in which they allow themselves to be influenced by the several parties involved. This statement has two implications. First, dialogue can evolve only on a voluntary basis. When somebody is forced, by some authority, to engage in a dialogue, it is not very probable that such a person, in this situation, can contribute to the emergence of a dialogical space with freedom to move in different directions. Second, in the case of a dialogical process in an organization or institution, the social positions of the participants should be taken into account. When power differences are too large, the information initially given in a positive atmosphere could, at some later time and in a different situation, be used or abused by the person in power for other purposes. This is not to say that dialogue between parties differing in power is not possible. It is just to emphasize that such differences put constraints on the openness required by good dialogue.

Generally, differences and opposite views between individuals, groups, or cultures are a fertile basis for engaging in a dialogical relationship. However, it would be a naïve assumption to see people located in different or opposite positions as representing *equally strong* parties able to disagree or to express their different points of view. Many different and opposite positions are loaded with power differentials. In a masculine society the position "female" may be seen as lacking the positive aspects attributed to males. Or, in colonial or post-colonial times, the colonizers may see the representatives of an Eastern culture as "childish," with the implicit assumption that these "children" lack the positive qualities that the "adult" colonizers attribute to themselves. Or, in a society where being young is highly valued, being "old" is perceived as "over the hill," "out to pasture," "finished," or "an old rock." Opposites are embedded in historical and cultural circumstances so that the dominant position paints the opposite one with its own color. The consequence is that the opposite one is not perceived in line with its own quality, merit and history and, as a result, is prevented from contributing to a dialogue from its original point of view. Moreover, power differences are, to some degree, incorporated in the self, as different theorists have described, using terms such as "internalization" and "introjection." As a result, the polar opposites and how they are evaluated are not only influential in the relationships between people but also within the self. Women, old people, representatives of oppressed cultures or ethnic groups, often see *themselves* as lacking the positive connotations of the dominant term of opposites.

Although social power limits dialogue, the self is able to produce forms of counter-power. It is one of the great insights of Mead (1934) that selves are not only representatives of society and conform to existing institutional structures, but are also able to *create* them. Mead was well aware of the problems that arise when social process is limited to the internalization of the attitude of the other within the self. Had he restricted this process to internalization only, the self would be no more than a copy of external social roles and the members of society no more than "slaves of customs." There would be no innovations that would bring social changes in society and renew institutions. Being aware of this problem, Mead introduced his distinction between *I* and *me*:

> I have been undertaking to distinguish between the "I" and the "me" as different phases of the self, the "me" answering to the organized attitudes of the others which we definitely assume and which determine consequently our own conduct so far as it is of a self-conscious character. Now the "me" may be regarded as giving the form of the "I." The novelty comes in the action of the "I," but the structure, the form of the self is one which is conventional. (1934: 209)

In Mead's view, social rules and conventions of the generalized other are placed in the *Me*, whereas innovation derives from the *I*. He gives the example of artists who are usually seen as unconventional. He does not consider artists are complete "outsiders." They accept certain rules of expression, as, for example, did the Greek artists who were, at the same time, innovators and supreme artisans in their society. They introduced an originality that made their contribution unconventional.

Mead's insight is relevant to understanding the relationship between power differences and innovation in the dialogical self. Societal power differences certainly have a pervasive influence on human relationships and on the dynamics of the self. They put serious limits on the bandwidth of dialogical relationships, both between the participants in a dialogue and within the dialogical self. On the other hand, the *I*, as an agentic force in the self, is able to create counter-positions in the self that can give a corrective and even innovative answer to the positions that are, from a historical point of view, dominant, established, or even "ordinary" in social or societal relationships. Moreover, as many examples in history have demonstrated, innovators and critics are often able to create coalitions in which different selves meet each other in order to set common goals and create counter-forces to established positions in society.[37]

Dialogue takes differences between genres into account   Dialogue is not an abstract process that takes place apart from time, space, customs, and traditions. In the course of history, societal and institutionalized groups create their own specific ways of communication. A frequently used term to indicate a more or less stabilized way of linguistic interaction is "speech genre" (Bakhtin, 1986) referring to a particular style, thematic content, and compositional structure of communication.

Speech genres are highly dependent on the time and the space that determine their content and structure. Genres are very diverse because they are contingent on the situation, social position, and the nature of the interrelations of the participants in the communication. The expression "you are crazy!" sounds "normal" in an informal chat in a café, but it would sound strange and be considered unacceptable if uttered during the defense of a doctoral degree at a university.

Misunderstandings may emerge when two parties in communication use the *same* phrase or word, but give these words a different meaning as if speaking in *different* speech genres. Misunderstanding is complete when the participants are unaware of this difference. Take the following example. A professor at a Dutch university invited a Japanese colleague to work on a common project. This included discussions and the use of the library. After a few days the professor was called by an official of the city who asked what the Japanese colleague was doing at the university. The professor answered that his colleague was here to "work" on a common project. Two days later the Japanese colleague was officially told that he must leave the country within three days because he had no permit to "work" in the country. It appeared that the term "work" had an entirely different meaning in the bureaucratic language of the official from the everyday language of the professor. If the professor had used the word "study" instead of "work" there would have been no problem at all. Thus, the same word can have different meanings in different genres, often leading to unwelcome surprises and misunderstandings. Therefore it is relevant in dialogical relationships to be aware from which genre a particular person is speaking.

Change of genre by the same person can also be misleading when the speaker is aware of the change but the audience is not. A well-known example is Bill Clinton, who under oath denied that he had "a sexual affair" with Monica Lewinsky, and said in a nationally televised White House statement: "I did not have sexual relations with that woman." This statement later became famous for its technical truthfulness but deceptive nature, based on differences in the definition of "sexual relations." Later, Clinton admitted that he had lied and that he had had "inappropriate intimate contact" with Lewinsky, but denied having committed perjury because, according to him, the legal definition of "oral sex" was not included in "sex" *per se*.[38]

The examples described above suggest that a dialogical relationship between two parties in communication can only evolve when (a) the genre in which the communication takes place is shared by both parties; (b) they take into account that the listener understands the words of the speaker according to the meaning defined by the genre in use; (c) they explicitly indicate a possible shift to another genre.

Dialogue is facilitated by awareness and silence   It is expected that dialogue will profit from engagement in a broader field of awareness. Participation in this field makes people more receptive than when they are limited to the processes of appropriation and rejection. Closely associated with the receptive attitude is the increasing permeability of the boundaries of the self, resulting in an open self that is more willing to accept the alterity of the other parties than when participants are experiencing themselves as separated from them.

Because of its unifying potential, participation in a broader field of awareness facilitates the accessibility of specific positions in the other and in the self. It is, moreover, easier to get access to a greater variety of positions and to move out of them. In particular, the experience of unity with a broader field, facilitates a clear identification with, and, at the same time, a flexible movement across, a multitude of positions. The excerpt from Krishnamurti, quoted earlier, serves as an illustration of this process. It shows vividly how the author could move fluently across a great variety of positions in the field. In this state the self is neither fixed or imprisoned in one particular position nor overly attached to it. There is an experience of a free space in which the *I* can move flexibly from one to the other position without losing contact with any of them.

At the same time, the "unitive state of awareness" gives a certain depth to the experience of movement between the various positions in the field. This strongly contrasts with the movement between positions characteristic of the post-modern self. In the latter case, locations are experienced as "places of transition," where people are moving to a place in order to go to another place, and again to another place, often resulting in an experience of "spatial dislocation" and a lack of rootedness. The experience of participating in a field of awareness is of a very different kind. Rather than moving from one place to another as a form of dislocation, the person experiences *all* places as part of a unified field. In contrast to the superficiality that may result from moving quickly across a variety of places, participation in a field of awareness gives rise to an experience of depth and results in clarity, rest, and a feeling of belonging to a larger whole.

Silence, rather than speaking, is a central feature of the field of awareness. In general terms, silence can be experienced in very different ways. In everyday communication, it is often experienced as the absence of words. Silence in this sense can be a painful experience when participants feel that they are supposed to talk without any break. This kind of silence is often felt as undesirable and in need of being filled by anything than silence. However, silence can have a very different meaning: being fully present in the actual situation without any distraction from interfering thoughts or verbalizations. In this form, it creates space in the self and in the other and has the potential of bringing people closer together than is possible by words or explicit communication only. Silence in the latter sense is indispensable for participation in a field of awareness.

From a dialogical point of view, there is a remarkable difference between the process of turn-taking as typical of explicit communication and participating in awareness. While turn-taking is typical of verbal dialogue, silence can be felt as a non-verbal form of dialogue. While in turn-taking the participants alternate in speaking and listening, in the experience of silence "receiving" and "sending out" are brought closely together and even coincide. When silence becomes part of a common field of awareness, successive turns give way to *turns that coincide*. The coincidence of giving and receiving is not only part of the rather exceptional experience of common awareness, it can also be observed in the rituals and practices of everyday life. When two people are shaking hands, touching each other, caressing each other or kissing each other, giving and receiving are not successive as a form of turn-taking, but fuse in the same act. As part of a field of awareness, silence becomes a deeper kind of dialogue in which the participants feel that they participate in something wider and greater than their limited selves. They experience themselves as part of some larger composition.[39]

Summary

Inspired by the three models of the self, traditional, modern, and post-modern, we focused in this chapter on some of the main concepts of dialogical self theory. In response to the term "difference," central in the post-modern model, we dealt with the multiplicity and differences in the self and showed that actions that take place between people (e.g., conflicts, criticisms, making agreements, and consultations) occur also within the self (e.g., self-conflicts, self-criticism, self-agreements, and self-consultations), demonstrating the self as a society of mind.

We observed that the other is not outside the self but rather an intrinsic part of it. That is, self-conflicts, self-criticism, self-agreements, and self-consultancy take place not only within the internal domain of the self, but also between the internal and external domain and even within the external domain (between others as parts of the self). It was our intention to show that there is no sharp separation between the internal life of the self and the "outside" world, but rather a gradual transition. This, however, contrasts with the phenomenon known as "othering," which is characterized by its rather sharp demarcation between the self and the other. Surprisingly, the transition between self and other is gradual in some situations, but sharp in others. The dimension open–closed is crucial for understanding and permitting dialogical relationships.

We argued, on the basis of the philosophical literature, that, faced with problems and questions, the mind does not simply coincide with itself, but rather *needs itself* in order to arrive at some clarity about itself and the world. The mind is involved in a series of proposals and disposals that reflect the basic "imperfection of the mind." This imperfection strongly contrasts with the clarity and unity of the Cartesian conception of the self.

Reflecting on the concepts of unity and continuity, so central to the modern model of the self, it was our concern to make them fit with a dialogical conception of the self that acknowledges the existence of differences, multiplicity, and discontinuity. This was expressed in four concepts: (i) *I*-position: we argued that unity and continuity is brought into the self by the capacity of the self to give positions (as representing the multiplicity of the self) an "*I*," "*me*" or "*mine*" imprint. As positioned in time and space, the self is multiple and changing. However, as belonging to one and the same *I, me* or *mine*, unity and continuity are created in the midst of multiplicity; (ii) *meta-position*: the *I* is able to leave specific positions and move to a meta-perspective from which the specific positions can be observed from the outside, as an act of self-reflection. We discussed in detail the main features of meta-positioning as an observing or meta-cognitive activity; (iii) *coalition of positions*: positions do not work in isolation. As in a society, they can cooperate and support each other, in this way creating strong forces in the self that may dominate other ones; in this context we discussed the prominent place of the "enjoyer of life" in contemporary society; (iv) *third position*: a conflict between two positions can be reconciled by creating a third position that has the potential of unifying the two original ones without denying or removing their differences. From this perspective, we discussed the case of a lesbian woman in Catholic Brazil, Roman Polanski's film *The Pianist*, and the case of Griffin, a white man who lived for some time with a black identity.

In response to the notion of "one's place in a meaningfully ordered cosmos," central in the traditional model of the self, we discussed the possibility of the *I* as becoming involved in a process of *depositioning*. This led to a discussion of the concept of *composition*, where the emphasis is not on the specific differences between positions but on their encompassing pattern. We illustrated this concept by analyzing the mescaline experience described in Aldous Huxley's book *The doors of perception*, and the concern with patterns in the paintings of Cézanne. In this context, we also explored the similarity between Rollo May's treatise of creativity and Martin Buber's exploration of the *I–You* relationship.

As strongly unifying forces we discussed three forms of awareness leading to a far-reaching depositioning of the *I*: (i) a unifying form of awareness where the *I* is able to identify itself with a great variety of positions, at the same time being free from them; (ii) a "dualistic" form of awareness where the *I* is strongly detached from specific positions, while remaining conscious of their existence (however, not identifying with them as in the unifying awareness); and (iii) a form of awareness that is characterized by an absence of any sensory experience. In all these forms of awareness silence – not in the sense of absence of words but rather as being fully in the present – is a constitutive part. In these forms of awareness, dialogue evolves not as successive turn-taking but as simultaneous presence.

Stimulated by the moral nature of the traditional self, we finally discussed the main features of "good dialogue" as a moral and developmental purpose. Nine features were outlined: good dialogue is *innovative*; it has a certain *bandwidth*, referring to the range of positions allowed to enter the dialogue; it acknowledges the unavoidable role of *misunderstandings*; it creates a *dialogical space*; it recognizes and incorporates the *alterity* not only of the other person but also of other positions in the self; it recognizes the importance of societal *power* differences as reflected by positions in the self; it recognizes the existence of different *"speech genres"* and their role in misunderstanding and deception; it has the potential to stimulate participation in a broader *field of awareness* and its composition; and it profits from *"speaking silence."* We included the notions of awareness and silence in this list in the expectation that an increasingly globalizing, interconnected world society is in need of a self that transcends the limits of the modern encapsulated self and may learn from the experience of being a part of a broader field of awareness.

NOTES

1 In the present chapter we discuss the temporal dimension of the self, beginning with the *collective* level. In Chapter 4 we will deal with the development of the self on the *individual* level.

2 J.-J. Suurmond, Zo ga ik mijn therapeutische gang, omringd door zeethutten en heksen [In this way I proceed as therapist, surrounded by sweat huts and witches]. *Trouw*, July 28, 2005 (authors' translation).

3 Self-criticism has also been used for political purposes. Under some totalitarian political systems (e.g., in communist countries) important party members who had fallen out of favor with the elite were sometimes forced to participate in "self-criticism" sessions. They had to produce either written or verbal statements detailing how ideologically mistaken they had been, and were obliged to affirm their new belief in the party ideology. However, self-criticism was not a guarantee for rehabilitation and offenders were nevertheless often executed.

4 Everyday life is full of "dialogical fragments" that accompany our experiences and behavior from moment to moment, such as, "No meat? That's bad, no, it's good, I'm on a diet," or "Shall I ask him, no, he's busy, shall I ...," or "want to stop this, yes, okay, fun to walk a bit and..." Such fragments – short,

often incomplete, impulsive and very transient – are often sublingual, inchoate, and almost not heard and they typically take place at a low level of self-awareness. When we are explicitly attentive to our experiential stream or when we slow down our usual speed of life and particularly when we feel that such transient fragments are not capable of solving a particular problem at hand, they rise to higher levels of awareness and have the potential of developing into explicit dialogues (e.g., self-negotiation, self-criticism, self-conflict, self-agreement, or self-consultation). For some theorists (e.g., Stern, 2004), this is reason to invite people to intensified self-awareness of the present moment under the assumption that awareness of dialogical fragments on a micro-level has the potential of promoting dialogical processes on a macro-level of awareness.

5 That many decision-making processes take place, in large part, on an unconscious or subconscious level, has been convincingly demonstrated by many neurological and social psychological experiments. Despite all this evidence, it is not at all clear to what extent dialogical processes that lead to decision making are conscious or unconscious. Typically, a workable solution to a problem requiring a decision emerges after putting a *question* to oneself on a conscious level. When one starts a decision-making process with a question, there is already the beginning of a conscious dialogical process. Moreover, making a decision, even when it is in large part the result of unconscious processing, requires a certain amount of conscious preparation. Important decisions, like creative ideas, are most often the result of a "prepared mind," that is, one is "walking around" with a problem or question for some time before a solution is found or a decision is made. Part of this preparation takes place on a conscious level. The question to what extent decision-making processes are conscious or unconscious is further complicated by the fact that there are different levels of consciousness or unconsciousness rather than a razor-sharp boundary between them.

6 www.answers.com/topic/self-conflict

7 In this section we summarize some of the works discussed by Cooper and Hermans (2007).

8 Dialogical relationships, both between different selves and within one and the same self, are often expressed in sentences that include the words "but" (referring to the existence of an opposite position), "although" (referring to the existence of a background position), and "maybe" (referring to the existence of a possible position).

9 Recent research has suggested that much of our experience of unity and continuity is illusory. This is well illustrated by Ehrsson, Spence, and Passingham's (2004) study of the "rubber hand illusion" in which (healthy) participants hid their right hand beneath a table while a rubber hand was placed in front of them, suggesting that the fake hand was part of their own body. Both the rubber hand and hidden hand were simultaneously stroked with a paintbrush while the participant's brain was scanned with the use of functional magnetic resonance imaging. In eleven seconds, on average, the participants began to experience the rubber hand as their own. The stronger this feeling was, the greater the activity recorded in the premotor cortex. When, after the experiment, the participants were asked to point towards

their right hand, most of them reached in the wrong direction, pointing towards the rubber hand instead of the real one that was hidden under the table. Apparently, the brain, confronted with a discrepancy between visual and tactile information, reacts with a "multisensory integration" of an illusionary kind. The tendency of the self to overly unify the multiplicity and heterogeneity of experiences in daily life, can also be discovered by systematic self-reflection. Hubert Hermans made notes of his experiences during one full day and discovered that his notes revealed a much greater variety of discontinuous thought patterns, unpredictable emotions, and mood changes than he noticed after a usual day without systematic self-reflection. The central role of discontinuity has been especially articulated in models of the self based on meditation practice. According to Hayward (1999:389) "awareness of finer levels of perceptual processing seen in meditative training shows discontinuity of experience". Apparently, we experience, even within short moments, more multiplicity and discontinuity than the untrained mind would expect. This leads to the question how far we can go, and want to go, beyond our illusion of unity and continuity in order to become sensitive to our apparent multiplicity and discontinuity without becoming fragmented.

10 For extensive discussion of the dialogical self in the context of James's and Bakhtin's contributions, see Barresi (2002).

11 Throughout this book, we use the general term "position" that includes the more specific term "I-position." The reason is that one may be positioned by another person or by society without the self being aware of it or before the self becomes aware of it (e.g., a child being discriminated against on the basis of class, skin color, or religion before becoming aware that he is evaluated by others on the basis of such categorizations).

12 Studying some texts that clients had written about themselves, Hubert Hermans selected for each client a particular sentence and invited the clients to indicate the *psychological distance* they experienced between their *I* of the present moment and the words "I," "me," "mine," and referents to other people mentioned in the selected sentence. He found that some (but not all) other people mentioned in the sentence (e.g., a good friend) were experienced as more close to the *I* of the present moment than the words "I" and "me" in the text. For example, the word "him" in the sentence "I regret that I insulted him" may be more close to the presently experiencing *I* than the world "I" in the sentence "I insulted him unjustly"). Apparently, there are moments or situations where I feel closer to another person than to myself. Such findings suggests that it is possible that I appropriate another person as closer to myself than "I myself." This refers to highly permeable boundaries between the internal and external domains of the self.

13 A notable exception is the phenomenon of *transgender*, where the "assigned gender" (the identification by others as male or female based on physical sex) does not match one's "gender identity" (self-identification as male, female, both or neither). Transgender individuals may be positioned as male or female by society but they do not appropriate this gender definition as their own. Some of these people feel the gender, assigned on the basis of their genitals, is a false or incomplete description of themselves and,

consequently, they feel it as not "belonging to me" (www.en.wikipedia.org/ wiki/Transgender). In this case the societal definition does not match the personal one and, as a result, the gender position is an assigned or attributed position but not felt as their own.

14 A similar discussion between proponents of unity and multiplicity has taken place in cultural anthropology (see Van Meijl, 2008 for review). In her article "The illusion of wholeness" Ewing (1990) argues that individuals continually reconstitute themselves in response to internal and external stimuli so that different situations lead to "new selves." Individuals construct these selves from an available set of self-representations that are contingent on the context and mutually inconsistent. The individual is generally not aware of these shifting selves, so that the experience of wholeness and continuity is not undermined. In Ewing's view the experience of personal continuity and wholeness is illusory. Ewing's view is criticized by another anthropologist Quinn (2006), who presents arguments for the unity of the self. She supports her view by referring to LeDoux's (2002) neuro-scientific theory of the "synaptic self." In this conception the self is seen as "a unit," but not as "unitary." The sense of unity emerges as a product of neural systems acting in concert to achieve integration, but the integration is never perfect (Van Meijl, 2008).

15 A meta-position can be described as a succession of some specific movements: moving back, standing still, and bending slightly forward, like a painter does when, after working on a part of the painting, he moves back and examines the art work as a whole with attention to the interconnection of its parts. In this way, the viewer creates a certain distance, while being at the same time in touch with the work. In making these movements along the dimension detachment–immersion the act of meta-positioning can be seen as a spatial and dynamic description of what we usually call "self-reflection."

16 We say here explicitly "*some* overarching view" in order to emphasize that it is not possible to see "all" positions in one glance. The dialogical self functions, in practical life situations, as a "working self." Only part of the repertoire becomes prominent and engaged in dialogue, depending on the requirements of the situation at hand. Yet there are clear individual differences: the meta-position of some people has more "bandwidth" than that of others. The meta-position has a broad bandwidth when it is able to encompass a large number of heterogeneous positions.

17 Self-reflection is not to be understood as a purely internal "introspective" act but as a process in which actual others and the other-in-the-self are constitutive elements. Introspection, as a form of internal self-reflection without direct involvement of the other, is implicitly or explicitly based on a modern model of the self with its dualism between self and other (see Chapter 2).

18 In some instances people can become positioned by others in sudden and unwelcome ways, as illustrated in the film *Rebel without a cause* (1955), directed by Nicholas Ray, in which James Dean plays the role of a boy who is challenged by the leader of a youth gang to engage in a game. This game requires each of the two competitors to sit in his own car which are placed side by side. When a signal is given, they accelerate fullly and drive at high

speed in the direction of a cliff edge. Before the car reaches that point, the driver can jump from his car, but the one who leaves his car first loses the game, and is seen by the others as "chicken." This challenge created for Dean a *position-dilemma*: if he refused, he would be seen by his comrades as a coward; if he accepted the challenge, he could be a hero, but for this he had to risk his life. Finally, he accepted the challenge and won the game.

19 Some theorists avoid the term "part" when referring to the multiplicity of the self. The term "part" would suggest the functioning of a mechanism, like the parts of a car. Therefore, they prefer to speak of a "member" of a team or group of positions. When we use the term "part" of the self, we have in mind a part that is actively *participating* in a (dialogical) self.

20 The therapists were Els Hermans-Jansen and Hubert Hermans, who cooperated in applying the PPR-method in this case.

21 Note that coalitions of positions are not limited to the internal domain of the self. They can also emerge in the external domain. For example, a manager perceives the members of his team as a highly cooperative group, unaware of the hidden animosity that actually exists between some of them. Or, a person suffering from paranoia, may see a conspiracy between people that actually does not exist.

22 The concept of *individualization* has to be distinguished from the concept of *individualism*. Whereas the latter is a phenomenon on the level of the individual (see the work of Bellah *et al.*, 1985, as discussed in Chapter 2), the former is a typically sociological concept that refers to societal processes that work *toward* individualism.

23 www.en.wikipedia.org/wiki/John_Stuart_Mill.

24 The enjoyer is not the only coalition-prone position. Other positions too are of this nature. In a post-modern era with its typical attitude of relativism, positioning oneself as "ironic" or "humorous" is often a way to express the view that nothing is absolute and serious enough to have the status of "objective truth" or the final word. Generally, humor has the effect of undermining an established position and its place in an existing order by (a) caricaturing the position, that is, exaggerating it to such an extent that even the most serious position becomes ridiculous; (b) reversing the position, that is, bringing it from the one to the other end of a pair of polar opposites (e.g., the king becomes naked, the president a beggar, and an ape sits on the throne). Carnival makes an abundant use of both caricature and reversal.

25 We emphasize the opening of boundaries in the context of a discussion of the modern model of the self with its emphasis on autonomy and boundaries closed to the environment. This is not to deny that there are circumstances in which it is necessary to protect one's boundaries and to close them. For example, some people in power use the word "we" to mark a collectivity over which they want to exert authority, suggesting that their we-statement is supported by all the people included in the we-definition. The people who are included in the definition may find it necessary to close their boundaries against the power-holder and develop forms of counter-power for the sake of defense or survival.

26 We speak of a "unifying" form of dialogue because in this book we use the concept of dialogue in a broader sense. It attends not only to the unifying

aspect of dialogue, but also leaves room for differences, contradictions, disagreement, conflict, oppositions between different selves and different aspects within the self. Such differences and disagreements are considered as "invitations to dialogue," and they do not necessarily disappear when dialogue evolves. Dialogical partners can co-construct a common dialogical space in which they agree or disagree and become involved in a common exploration of their conflicts.

27 Research suggests that there are cultural differences in perception of patterns. Masuda *et al.* (2008) tracked the eye-movements of two groups of students while they looked at photographs. One group were American-born graduates of European descent and the other group Chinese-born graduate students who had come to the US. Each picture showed a clear central image placed in a realistic background, such as an animal in a jungle. It was found that the American students spent longer looking at the central object, while the Chinese students tended to dart around, taking in the context. This research suggests that Americans tend to break things down in an analytical way, focusing on putting objects into categories. By contrast, East Asians have a more holistic view, looking at objects in relation to the whole.

28 The concept of "*I*-prison" is based on the consideration that any specific position is experienced as limiting or blocking when it is not possible to find an exit from this position. The "natural" process of positioning and repositioning assumes a movement from one position to another as a dynamic feature of life. Even when a position is initially experienced as pleasant or enriching, it can, when the transition to another position is blocked, become experienced as a "prison." In addition, the experience of "stress," which is particularly felt when the person is actually located in one position but feels that he *should* be in another one, is an example of being locked up in an *I*-prison.

29 The paradoxical nature of the two first forms of depositioning is that the person is able to leave all specific positions, being at the same time *in* them and *liberated* from them, and has the capacity to move freely from one position to another. In this sense the process of depositioning is the experiential opposite to feeling constricted in an "*I*-prison."

30 As this example suggests, shadow positions or disowned positions are part not only of the internal domain (e.g. "I as jealous") but also of the external domain of the self (e.g., "the guy who evokes my disgust").

31 The existence of a multiplicity of spaces opens up the possibility of studying *conflicting spaces* in the self, just as it is possible to study conflicting positions. Take the example of a person who was brought up in a village, but hated living in the conservative milieu of the place. While still a child he wanted to live in a large city, and later actually moved to a metropolis where he enjoyed the intellectual and modern atmosphere. However, at some point the company for whom he worked required him to move to a small city in another country. From then on, he felt imprisoned because, in the experience of his self, the small city took him back to the village of his youth from which he had always wanted to escape. The move to the small city actualized the conflict between two spaces in his self, the village-space and the city-space.

32 Atmosphere refers to the generalizing affective quality of a particular environment as it influences the affective tone of the self and fills the space *between* its positions (like the fog in a landscape). The feeling tones of atmospheres show enormous variations: a small village is attractive by its intimate atmosphere, a horror movie is exciting by its weird atmosphere, a difficult meeting can inhibit people by its tense atmosphere, and the place of a mass massacre is abhorrent by its depressing atmosphere. A dialogical space is typically characterized by an accepting, open, and stimulating atmosphere. Atmosphere is similar but not identical to mood. Whereas atmosphere refers to the broader environment, including its impact on the self, mood is restricted to the affective tone of the self coloring the space between the positions. Mood is also different from emotions. Whereas emotions are conceived in tems of specific and transient *I*-positions (Chapter 5), mood refers to the more generalizing affective tone of the self as a whole and is typically less transient than emotions. It has a more field-like character.

33 Because the self of the actual other is, in principle, as multi-positioned or multi-voiced as one's own self, the other can potentially be interiorized as more than one position in the self. Different *internal–external connections* may emerge in the organization of the self: as a son I experience my father as "my loving father"; as practicing bowling together, I see him as a "my mate in sport"; but when it comes to political issues, I consider him as "my opponent." Nevertheless, the perceived multi-voicedness of the other may be considerably reduced when I approach the other in one way only. For example, in contact with some people, I notice that the conversation always ends up in an intellectual discussion, but I'm aware that this results from my own strongly developed intellectual position. A practical way to gain an impression of the actual multi-voicedness of the other is to look at the nature of the contact between the other and the others around him. Every other has *satellites of others* around him who trigger different positions in his self. For example, I notice that the person whom I see as a typical intellectual, is making fun and sometimes even acts as a clown when with other people. More simply, tell me who your friends and enemies are and I know your multi-voicedness.

34 We prefer the term "self-alterity" in the present text, although in the text referred to (Cooper and Hermans, 2007), the term "self-otherness" was used. We do this in order to avoid confusion with the notion of "other-in-the-self" discussed earlier in this chapter.

35 Ordinary positions are not only part of the internal domain of the self (e.g., "I as father" or "I as liking to drink a beer at the end of the afternoon") but also part of the external domain (e.g., "that is a nice guy" or "you are a familiar customer here"). When such ordinary positions become very dominant in the repertoire, they may reduce the openness of the self to new or less familiar aspects of self and other and also to their alterity.

36 Routinized positioning in the comfort zone without variation and innovation can arrive at a point where it becomes an "I-prison" creating the need to escape. This typically leads to the need to develop a new position or realize a new coalition of positions.

37 Note that in this book four functions of the *I* have been described: *self-reflexive, innovative, appropriative,* and *receptive.* In our view, all four functions are necessary for an adequate understanding of the workings of the dialogical self.

38 www.en.wikipedia.org/wiki/Monica_Lewinsky.

39 The relationship between mysticism and morality is clearly inconclusive. As Jones (2004) observes, the spectrum of views is very broad. On the one hand, there are scholars who are convinced that mysticism and morality are incompatible. Some argue that mystics are inherently selfish in their self-centered quest for enlightenment and that the values underlying this quest preclude a concern for others. At the other end of the spectrum are scholars who argue that mysticism is necessary for a concern for others or is even the origin of it. Only mystical experiences permit an escape from the self-centeredness of our everyday life and, in this rather extreme view, only mystics can be truly compassionate and moral. Given these mutually exclusive views, it is far from certain that the participation in a field of awareness in itself leads to "good dialogue." Therefore, all the other features of good dialogue have to be taken into account.

4   Positioning and dialogue in life-long development

The well bred contradict other people. The wise contradict themselves.

Oscar Wilde

Positioning and dialogical activity are not simply given but the result of complex developmental processes. In the present chapter we want to discuss some processes that are crucial for understanding the emergence and development of a dialogical self. What are its precursors and early manifestations and in what ways does it develop in the course of time? When we pretend that the dialogical self is not only social but also embodied, how is the body expressed in the process of positioning and repositioning and in forms of dialogical activity? Under what conditions is the dialogical self involved in a progressive process and under what conditions in a regressive process? Such questions are central to the present chapter, which is divided in three parts. In the first part we describe some forerunners and early manifestations of the dialogical self. The second part is organized around the central role of "promoter positions" that are particularly relevant to understanding how the self is stimulated to reach higher levels of development. In the third and final part, we present a model that is useful in explaining the progressions and regressions of a dialogical self in development.

Precursors and early manifestations of a dialogical self

In the first part of this chapter it is our purpose to demonstrate that the embodied nature of the dialogical self is expressed in early processes of positioning and repositioning and that the social nature of the self is rooted in pre-linguistic and non-verbal forms of interaction. We will focus on some phenomena that are crucial for understanding the social and embodied nature of the dialogical self, starting with the processes of "imitation" and "provocation."

Imitation, provocation and inborn subjectivity

Imitation in the visual field, like echoing in the auditory field, can be seen as a precursor of dialogical activity. The study of neonatal imitation is a field that is particularly relevant to understanding the developmental basis of the dialogical self. Usually, neonatal imitation refers to the variety of a young infant's facial, hand, and finger movements and vocalizations, typically studied in a laboratory environment shortly after an experimenter has modeled the same behavior to the infant. Much of this research is inspired by the pioneering work of Maratos (1973), and Meltzoff and Moore (1994) who have demonstrated that from birth onward infants are capable of imitating tongue protrusion modeled by an experimenter.

The tongue protrusion experiments by Nagy and Molnar (2004) are particularly relevant to the emergence of a dialogical self. Looking for the mechanism of neonatal imitation these researchers discovered that newborns are not only capable of responding to tongue protrusion by an experimenter, but also able to take the initiative during this interaction. There exists not only neonatal imitation but also neonatal "provocation," where newborns spontaneously produce previously imitated gestures while waiting for the experimenter's response. Apparently, infants are not only capable of responding to a model by imitating, but also able to provoke an imitative response. A psycho-physiological analysis showed that imitation was accompanied by heart-rate acceleration, while provocation was accompanied by heart-rate deceleration, suggesting different underlying mechanisms. As the researchers explain, heart rate deceleration is an index of orientation, attention, recognition, and stimulus expectation, whereas heart rate acceleration signals the preparatory arousal before and during tongue movement imitations. The investigators concluded that, "These findings may constitute a laboratory demonstration of the first dialogue ..." (2004: 54). Indeed, the succession of imitation and provocation can be considered as precursors of turn-taking behavior and exchange in terms of question and answer, as typical of later dialogical processes.[1]

As Nagy and Molnar (2004) argue, imitation is not a purely cognitive process that appears, according to Piaget's (1978) theory, at the end of the first year. Rather, neonatal imitation is one of the many social skills that are expressions of an inborn inter-subjectivity, including preference for humanlike faces, emotional expressions, and extremely rapid learning of how to identify the mother's voice and her face or odour. As a wide variety of ethological studies have demonstrated, several human behavioral patterns are universal, including basic patterns of communication and basic facial emotional expressions (see Nagy and Molnar for review). This suggests that imitation as a precursor of dialogical activity is an inborn form of inter-subjectivity.

In the course of development, imitation becomes an even more social activity than it is immediately after birth. This was demonstrated in an experiment by Rochat (2000), who investigated the propensity to reproduce tongue protrusion in a group of 1-month-old and 2-month-old infants under two conditions. In one condition the experimenter modeled tongue protrusion with a still face and then paused for some seconds without any interaction with the infants. In the second condition the experimenter interacted with the child, during and after the tongue protrusion, and actively engaged the infant in proto-conversation. It was found that the infants responded to the two conditions in different ways. The 1-month-old babies generated an overall increase of tongue protrusion in the still-face condition, compared to the communicative condition. In contrast, the 2-month-old infants increasingly showed tongue protrusion in the communicative condition. Apparently, for the 2-month-olds tongue protrusion is dependent on a stimulating social context. Infants appear increasingly sensitive to the relative communicative tuning of the social partner. These findings are in agreement with the general observation in developmental psychology that the second month of life marks the emergence of inter-subjectivity and the active sharing of experiences with social partners.

A clear sign of growing inter-subjectivity in the period between 1 and 2 months is the socially elicited smiling in face-to-face interactions with social partners around the sixth week of life. In that period infants start to smile in response to social stimulation. Smiling emerges as a sign of mutuality and signifies an affective tuning to the other. This sensitivity and sharing leads in turn to a responsive attitude in the caretakers who develop different, enriched ways of interacting with the infant (Rochat, Querido and Striano, 1999).

The child seems to have an inborn inter-subjectivity, as was already proposed by Bruner (1983) as a basis for language acquisition. He posited the existence of a Language Acquisition Device (LAD), with the social environment acting as a Language Acquisition Support System (LASS). Before any LAD is able to "generate linguistic hypotheses," the social procedures found in pre-linguistic communication must function adequately. Children have a natural tendency towards mutual attention and agreeing on reference ("referential inter-subjectivity"), which is expanded by a device for acquiring language. This inter-subjectivity entails a sensitivity towards, for example, "a patterned sound system, to grammatical constraints, to referential requirements, to communicative intentions, etc." (Bruner 1983: 31). Caretakers treat their children as proper partners in a hermeneutic process of communication and do so as if the infants understand.[2]

Pseudo-dialogues, memory, and imagination

For the emergence of dialogical relationships between mother and child, so-called "pseudo-dialogues" are a phenomenon of interest. Using stop-frame and slow-motion microanalysis of films and videotapes, developmental psychologists have observed that mothers and infants are involved in turn-taking behavior from the moment the infant is born. Sensitive as they are to the reactions of their children, mothers respond to the sucking pattern of their babies from birth onward. When the baby sucks, the mother is quiet. However, when the baby pauses, she often talks to him and touches him, addressing the baby with a combination of verbal and non-verbal signs. It seems that the mother treats the baby's bursts of sucking as a "turn," responding with a dialogically structured pattern (Kaye, 1977). During this rhythmic process of turn-taking, the mother waits for an *imagined* response from the baby as Newson (1977) and Stern (1977) have described: she acts *as if* the baby is involved in an actual process of turn-taking.

At some later point in development, the infant actually answers with babbling and the incidence of this reaction increases contingently with the mother's responses. By the time the baby is a year, she is generally able to give some real responses. When there is an expectant pause, the baby vocalizes and pseudo-dialogues change into more developed speech acts (Newson, 1977: 57):

BABY: (turns attention to top)
MOTHER: "Do you like that"?
BABY: "Da"!
MOTHER: "Yes, it's a nice top, isn't it"?

When children are 2 to 3 years of age, they seem to converse not only with their parents and siblings, but also with an *imagined* interlocutor (Garvey, 1984). Young children, not yet being able to "think" silently in words, as most adults do, use language to rehearse or rework a prior conversation. In familiar surroundings they rework memories of earlier events, amuse themselves, and use language to direct their own actions. Garvey (1984) recorded a variety of vocalizations and speech from 28-month-old Sarah during a nap period. They ranged from quiet murmurs to grunts, squeals, and intoned babbles; from humming to snatches of songs, rhymes, and counting. Sarah talked to a doll, had a "telephone conversation," described her own activities (e.g., "I'm putting my socks on"), and gave accounts of her playing with toys. As these observations suggests, memory and imagination enable the child to "evoke" others (e.g. dolls and family members) and introduce them as parts of their extending selves.

Returning to pseudo-dialogues, the phenomenon of rhythmic turn-taking as typical of a pseudo-dialogue exemplifies the central importance of non-verbal and pre-linguistic communication for the development of dialogical relationships. Dialogue is broader than linguistic dialogue. In fact, much dialogue between people, including adults, develops through body language, facial expression, smiling, gazing, vocalizations, intonations, and gestures. Non-verbal dialogue can also include dance, drum beating, ballet and music, and many forms of artistic activity. Even actions can be symbolically loaded as, for example, a parent punishing a child as a sign of disapproval. Mead (1934) was aware of the relevance of non-verbal communication, when he introduced the notion of "gesture" in his theory of symbolic interactionism. Thus, the conception of dialogue comprises both verbal and non-verbal elements and, as such, reflects its relevance to a psychology of globalization in which people from different cultures use both forms in their communication as part of their dialogical histories (Lyra, 1999).[3]

Giving and taking

Giving and taking between mother and child in the first year of life can be considered non-verbal forms of dialogue, as Fogel (1993) has argued. When the mother gives a toy to the infant, she brings it into the visual field of the child and moves the object in such a way that the infant is invited to open her hands before receiving the toy. It is as if the mother says, "I offer you a toy – do you want it?" The infant, in turn, orients her body to the toy and opens her hands as if to say, "Yes, I want it."

The interaction between mother and child, as exemplified by the process of giving and taking, has a clear dialogical structure, although the child is not yet able to use language. It is evident that the infant does not understand the words produced by the parent, but is able to understand the intonations and the meaning of the gestures. Moreover, the intonations and gestures that are exchanged between parent and infant can be understood as sequences of question and answer. In a similar way, Fogel (1993) demonstrated that when the mother reaches out to help the baby into a sitting position, the forces exerted by mother and child wax and wane in a co-regulated manner. When the mother pulls the child into a sitting position, she feels the infant's force increase. She then responds to this increase with a decrease of her own force. In turn, the infant increases her own force as a response to the decreasing force of the mother. Fogel describes these co-regulated movements as non-verbal invitations to the child to change her position, and sees the action of the child as a cooperative response. Even when one describes such movements in terms of co-regulation and not yet as sign-mediated dialogue, such co-regulated activities work as a bodily foundation for dialogical activities. As early joint actions they prepare later dialogical activities in which mother and child are involved in explicit forms of sign-mediated interchange.

As Bertau (2008) has noticed, the notion of reversal is first found in Vygotsky's (1929) account of interiorization, described as a movement that enables the child to take the role of the other toward herself so that she achieves control of her own behavior. In this process, speech functions as a semiotic means employed first by another person and then by the self, an early ontogenetic manifestation of reversibility. Children's pretence play also can be described in terms of a "reversal" that takes place when children behave as if they are other people, in this way introducing other people and objects in their spaces of imagination. The phenomenon of reversal allows us to understand what Vygotsky (1999) had in mind when he argued that consciousness is a "social contact with oneself." It also enables us to understand that pretence play facilitates the development of a theory of mind, that enables the child to take the other's perspective. By doing as if one is the other and by simulating the other's speech and actions, one learns to understand his thoughts and experiences. The introduction of the other at the interior level and the simulation of his speech allows the exploration of *different* points of view. These observations led Bertau (2008) to notice a kind of paradox: the child is fundamentally *oriented* towards the other, at the same time *disregarding* the other. The child increasingly participates in a commonly shared world, while simultaneously "retreating" into an interior world of cognition and imagination, in which the other is reconstructed and recreated. In a sense, the child develops as a Janusian being able to face in two directions, approaching the other and leaving the other. This bi-directionality also qualifies dialogical relationships: dialogues with others take place in two spaces: the *exterior* social space where the other actually is moving me to the outside; at the same time, I can only understand him and dialogue with him when I myself retreat into a metaphorical *interior* space, where I recreate him so that I can understand him better than before.[4]

Joint attention: the 9-month miracle

A step of utmost significance to the development of a dialogical self is made when the child, by 9 months of age, starts to perceive and understand others as *intentional* (Rochat et al. 1999). She begins not only to understand the other as intentional but also to view objects in the environment *from the perspective of the other*. This can be observed when the adult, involved in a conversation with the child, points with her finger to an object in the environment. The child does not look at the finger, as it used to do earlier, but looks in the direction in which the adult is pointing. This represents a capacity of the child that can be well described as "joint attention," a phenomenon highlighted as "the nine-month miracle" (Tomasello, 1993). From that moment on, learners do not just direct their attention to other individuals and their behavior as separate from objects in the environment and not to objects in the environment as separated from others, but they are actually beginning to see objects as the other individual sees them, that is, from the other's perspective. The child is learning not simply *from* another but rather *through* another (Tomasello, 1993).

The phenomenon of joint attention is particularly relevant because it changes the perception of objects in the environment. Prior to the age of 9 months, the infant is only capable of engaging with an object *or* with a person, the object not being part of their interaction. After 9 months, however, a radical change takes place, because from then the infant is able to coordinate object and person. In this process, gazing is not simply common or mutual but a true form of perspective taking (Bertau, 2004; Tomasello, 1993).

A significant moment for the development of a dialogical self is when the joint attention between caretaker and child is directed not only to objects in the environment, but to the child itself, resulting in a form of *self-reflective attention*. This attention is not a direct perception of the child of herself, but rather an *indirect* perception of herself, that is, through the perspective of the caretaker. From now on, the child is able to learn about herself via the perception and intention of the other toward her (Bertau, 2004; Tomasello, 1993).

In our view, joint attention has important affective implications that deserve special consideration. When the child is doing something that is forbidden by the mother, she will say, "Bobby, you are naughty!" When the mother sees him doing what she particularly likes, she rewards him by saying, "Bobby, you are sweet!" Mothers and caretakers utter these sentences with corresponding intonations, facial expressions, and rewarding or punishing behaviors. The child is placed, and feels himself placed, in two affect-laden positions that he interiorizes in his self as "Bobby-naughty" and "Bobby-sweet". That is, the child knows himself, via the external positioning by the mother, not only in a cognitive but also in an affective way. The child learns to distinguish between actions that bring him into the naughty position and those that bring him into the sweet position, and he even learns what he can do in order to move from the negative to the positive position. Being "sweet" or "good" versus being "naughty" or "bad", both basic affective positions in early childhood, are powerful instruments used by parents in the process of socialization and education. As parents repeatedly place the child in these positions in a variety of situations, the positions become rooted as affectively laden parts of the self that become more or less stabilized depending on the further development of the child.

Depending on the frequency, intensity, and duration of the reactions of the parents, some positions, positive or negative or combinations of them, become more dominant in the self than others. When the child is repetitively and intensely placed in a negative position by the parents or caretakers, this position becomes more rooted and dominant in the self than when he is primarily placed in a positive position. As the result of joint attention and its affective tuning, the child cannot escape the (affective) view of the other towards himself. Self-reflection is not an act of the child as separated from the other. Also the (beginning) dialogue of the child with herself is no longer a dialogue with herself within the borders of a self-contained entity. Self-reflection and self-dialogue develop *via* the other and include the perception, intentions and emotions of the other and the child's reaction to them. Along these lines the phenomenon of joint attention paves the way for inclusion of the other-in-the-self as a constitutive part of the self's extension to the world.

Role playing and the emergence of new positions

The extension of the self is further stimulated by role-play, one of the most important learning experiences for young children. In this activity imagination, joint attention and exploration, including self-exploration, can go well together. It provides a rich array of opportunities for experimenting with new positions and their inclusion in the self.

In an analysis of role-play in the context of dialogical self theory, Fogel *et al.* (2002) give the example of 17-month-old Susan and her mother playing with a lion puppet. They have played with this puppet many times in the past. In previous sessions the mother has always played the role of the agent, the lion (e.g., roaring, scaring, and tickling), while Susan has always played the role of the recipient (e.g., being scared, being tickled). At some point, Susan tries to put the lion on her own hand for the first time and activates it as if she wants to scare the mother:

Mother and Susan are sitting on the floor. Mother hides the lion and Susan follows the lion, looking for it. Suddenly, the "lion" comes out of his hiding place and "roars!" Susan screams and steps back. She stares at the lion for a few seconds. She then abruptly grabs the puppet from the mother's hand and tries to pull it off. The mother resists and makes the lion move and scream, "No! No!" After a short and playful fight, Susan is able to slip the puppet off mother's hand. She smiles and explores the puppet. She turns it around looking for the opening to put her hand in. The mother comments, "Oh, *you* are gonna do it!" Mother helps her to put the lion on her hand. Susan smiles and says, "Roar!" Mother laughs and comments, "Scare mom." Susan then carefully observes the lion. She turns the lion toward her own face and makes it open its mouth. She first smiles and then watches the lion, astonished. She looks surprised and a little confused. The mother intervenes: "Ahh! You scared me!" Susan then moves the lion toward mother and says, "Roar!" while smiling. Mother pretends to be scared, screams, and then comments, "Scare mommy." (2002: 200)

In their comment on this excerpt, Fogel *et al.* explain that Susan is experimenting and playing with a new position and its corresponding emotions. She explores these emotions as she physically embodies the lion with her hand. She moves from the role of the child to the role of the lion-adult and vice versa. Although she gets confused for a moment, she is able to act in both roles. She is able to leave the first position and enter a new one, a process that involves imagination beyond perception. A new voiced position exchanges information with the old one, resulting in a more complex and narratively structured self.

Placing Susan's play in a broader theoretical context, Fogel and colleagues make clear that the presence and the voice of the mother constitute a fundamental pole of the dialogue. If the mother had been absent, the child would not have been able to go through the process of self-exploration and self-extension. But from now on child and mother continue this game in further sessions, with new variations and innovations. The child, after she has learned the play from the mother, is able to continue playing it in the absence of the mother and interiorizes the lion as a position in relation to other positions represented by dolls and imagined significant others.[5] Gradually, the child feels the new position as something of her own and appropriates it, as she can easily identify with it and feel it is something that belongs to her. That is, the new role is interiorized and appropriated in the self as an *I-position*. A similar process of including new *I*-positions takes place later in life when the child becomes a pupil at school, a member of a sports club, a friend of a college student, and, as an adult, married. In these situations, as-if positions as exercises in free-play develop into socially defined positions in institutionalized structures, where they are guided by rules and subjected to social expectations.[6]

Mead's distinction between play and game   The emergence of joint attention and role-playing marks the transition from direct perception to *indirect* perception of the world and the self. The perception is not directly from the child to the world, but indirectly, that is, from the child to the world *via* the mother. This indirect perception was already reflected in Mead's (1934) seminal discussion of the capacity of the child to "take the role of the other" and view the world and herself from that perspective. Elaborating on the capacity of role-taking, Mead maintained that, in the genesis of the self, the child goes through two developmental stages: play and game. In the *play stage*, children learn to take the attitude of particular others towards themselves. Playing the role of the parent, teacher, or policeman, children address themselves as a parent or a teacher, and arrest themselves as a policeman. Play thus represents being another to the self: "The child says something in one character and responds in another character, and then his responding in another character is a stimulus to himself in the first character, and so the conversation goes on" (1934: 151).

Mead, interested as he was in the relationship between self and society, introduced his well-known concept of the "generalized other" as necessary to understand the basic rules of games. In his view, the play stage represents an important step in the development of children in taking the attitude of significant others toward themselves. However, they lack in this stage a more generalized and organized sense of themselves. Therefore, the *game stage* is required to develop a self as part of an organized society. Whereas in play children take the role of discrete others, in a game they are required to take the role of *everyone* else involved in the same activity. Moreover, game situations typically include different roles that have a definite relationship with one another. Playing a game requires the participants to be able to take *all the roles* as an organized arrangement. Even a simple game, such as hide-and-seek, requires a child to alternate the roles of "hunter" and "hider" and to know these roles in their mutual relationship. More complicated game situations are provided by baseball, football, tennis, and many other sports that are organized around detailed and specific rules.

Mead's analysis suggests that play leads to the introduction of specific, discrete positions in the self, whereas game introduces more general positions in the self (the generalized other). The latter type of position is necessary for a society that is in need of social rules which organize the relationships between positions and which are shared and understood by all the participants of a (societal) game. However, as Ritzer (1992) observes, Mead's theory lacks a macro-sense of society in general, and institutions in particular, in the way that theorists such as Marx, Weber, and Durkheim have outlined. Interested, as he was, in the *unity* of society and the "objective" attitude of the generalized other, he did not elaborate a systematic theory of macro-social conflicts, social differences, and ethnic- and gender-based inequality. In fact, Mead's theory represents a "homogeneous society" metaphor, with a heavy emphasis on micro-social game-like processes. From the perspective of globalization, we would like to add that the "generalized other," like social and emotional rules (see Chapter 1), has become a more complex phenomenon in a world-society that has led to the emergence of a variety of interfaces between cultures. At these interfaces, different and even conflicting rules, that "worked" within the boundaries of relatively isolated groups or cultures, have lost their meaning as general principles on a world scale. Given the processes of globalization and localization as intimately related developments, world citizens are challenged by the possibility and even necessity of developing "joint attention" together with people from different cultural and historical origins. The basis for learning to cope with this broadened bandwidth of joint attention is, in our view, not only in the school but also and even primarily in the early contact of the child with parents and caretakers.

Dialogical frames

When the linguistic capacities of children allow more sophisticated forms of turn-taking, mothers enter dialogues with their children in routinized ways (Bertau, 2004). The interaction with the mother often takes the form of a conversational training that is characterized by a high number of questions. In this training the questions are first of all a communicative appeal to the child but they will soon lead to a dialogue in which the child introduces her own voice.

In a study of interrogative forms in the interactions between mothers and children, Holzman (1972) shows the existence of dialogical frames. In these frames the child has not only taken up her role in the conversation – knowing when to pose a question and when to give an answer – but has also understood the role of the other with whom she is involved in the conversation. Studying the interactions between mothers and their 2- to 3-year-old children, Holzman gives examples of conversations that show alternating initiatives on the part of parent and child:

(1.) Mother (M) starts and initiates child:
    M: "What's the baby's name?" (child's doll) (p. 318)

(2.) Child (C) starts, mother is pseudo-starter; child initiates mother in order to initiate herself:
    C: "What's that?"
    M: "What is that?"
    C: "Shoe lace." (p. 326)

(3.) Child is self-starter and initiates himself
    c: "What dat?"
      "A trailer."
      "Dat's a cow."
      "Dat a barn."
      "Dat's a street." (p. 331)

As Bertau emphasizes, the voice of the mother is of primary importance as the first initiator of the conversation. She shapes the position of her dialogical partner as a participant in the dialogue as she is the most active speaker at the beginning. After the mother is the main initiating partner in the dialogical pattern, the child gradually becomes a more and more active partner in the conversation, and the point may come when she takes over the initiative. What the child is acting out playfully here becomes quite important as a self-questioning technique for several problem-solving activities. The child is posing a question to which she knows the answer, but she poses the question and gives the answer as part of a routinized dialogical frame. Along these lines, early mother–child dialogues lead to the inclusion of an exchange structure supported by the actual voices of the participants involved in a process of positioning and counter-positioning. This self-questioning technique functions as a developmental basis for the later processes of self-consultation, self-agreement, self-criticism, and self-conflict.

As Bertau (2004) has shown, the above excerpt demonstrates an important phase in the emergence of a dialogical self: there is somebody who is competent as a conversational partner and via whom the self is driven into dialogicality. Continued perspective-taking can thus be understood as a process in which the attention of others on objects becomes part of an ongoing dialogue. The self then emerges from a commonality of attention. The infant is increasingly aware of the other's attention and intention as *belonging to the other* and, moreover, incorporates them in a common view on the object. This attention and intention thus function as central organizers of the dialogue between the partners and later between the child and herself. As Vygotsky (1987) has argued, human cognition is fundamentally social in the sense that the initial outer, shared, and verbally mediated activity is later interiorized in the self. He observes that the child is talking to himself as he talked to others: "In our view, something similar happens when the child begins to converse with himself as he previously conversed with others, when, speaking to himself, he begins to talk aloud in situations that require it" (Vygotsky 1987: 75; see also Bertau, 2004). The interiorization of the dialogue with the other, into the self, functions as a developmental basis for the dialogical relationship with the other-in-the-self.

The emergence of self-space and self-boundaries

The dialogical self is not only social but also spatial. That is, social positions are at the same time spatial positions. The theory put forward here proposes a dialogical approach based on positioning theory (see also Raggatt, 2007). That is, the processes of positioning and repositioning are basic to the process of dialogue with others and oneself. Therefore, the dialogical self can only be properly understood when two of its defining features are taken into account: its spatial nature and the emergence of boundaries. The notion of "position" is spatial and implies the existence of other positions (e.g., counter-positions). They are not entities in themselves that can be studied as isolated things. Rather, they are part of a field that stretches between them. This field is loaded with some tension, not in the sense of a conflict but as part of an orientation towards something or somebody who is "there," and who can respond in a way that is only partly predictable. A position or, more dynamically formulated, the act of positioning receives its meaning always as part of its dynamic relationship with one or more other positions involved in a sign-mediated interchange between self and other or within the self. At the same time a position assumes the emergence of some boundary. It can only exist when it can be spatially distinguished from other positions. That is, there are particular boundaries between them, boundaries that can vary on the dimension open–closed. In the following sections, some phenomena directly relevant to the spatial nature of the self and its boundaries are explored.

Spaces of protection and safety   From birth onward children receive or create a space of protection–warmth–security in which they experience comfort and feel safe. They receive it when they are involved in intimate contact with the mother who holds them close to her own body, so that they can feel her touch and her warmth. When they are alone, they create an intimate space by hunching themselves forward into their own bodies and putting their thumbs in their mouths. Even before birth they touch themselves and are supposed to feel some pleasure, particularly by touching their genitals. Practically all children have a strong preference for small places and actively create them, for example by crawling under a chair or behind a sofa. They hide themselves in a wardrobe, or enjoy making a den or a hole in the ground, or other small places that give them a particular sense of well-being and excitement.

Personal space and anxiety for strangers   The child not only has a preference for small, protected, and intimate physical spaces, but also develops an *invisible* space that extends beyond the borders of the body, a so-called "personal space." In order to understand the concept of personal space, it should be clear how it differs from "territory." An important feature of personal space is that it accompanies the individual's movements when he goes from one place to another, whereas territory is fixed in a particular place. Burgoon and Jones (1976:131) define personal space as: "The invisible volume of space that surrounds an individual ... an invisible, dynamic, and transportable space the site of which is governed by the individual ... at any point in time." As Horner (1983) has argued, personal space is not marked by rigid boundaries, but its borders fluctuate according to various social, psychological, and organismic conditions. The boundaries become semi-permeable when a certain degree of familiarity exists with the person who enters the space. In other words, boundaries are not fixed, but are to some degree flexible, depending on the nature of the relationship with other people.

A concept that is similar to "personal space" is the so-called "self-boundary structure" (Fisher and Cleveland, 1968). Over the course of time, people develop a "behavioral space" that separates them from what is "out there." The self-boundary structure functions as a screen, which the individual carries with him at all times and can interpose between himself and the outer situation at any time. A well-developed self-boundary structure is needed for a feeling of safety. As Straus (1958) has proposed, a person's experiential space can be divided into safety and danger zones. In normal functioning there is a clear differentiation between the two zones so that, in the case of impending danger, the individual can retreat to the safety zone. In maladaptive functioning (e.g., in a state of all-pervasive anxiety), however, the distinction has disappeared and space is experienced as dangerous in an undifferentiated way.

There is evidence that the development of a personal space and a self-boundary structure coexists with the onset of what has been called "stranger anxiety" during the second half of the first year of life. The young child begins to realize that a stranger has the potential to intrude on his personal space and, as a result, he becomes fearful of all strange people who approach him, particularly in the absence of a caretaker (Horner, 1983).

From the age of 4 to 6 months, anxiety may be clearly observed. When an unfamiliar person appears, the baby frowns, takes a deep breath, turns away, or may even cry (Bronson, 1972). The intensity of the infants' reactions, ranging from wariness to intense fear, depends on their interpretation of the stranger and the situation (e.g., who else is present? how does the stranger act?). Given the *semi-permeability* of personal space, the child will not react with intense anxiety when the parents or other familiar people are present (Bronson, 1978).

As suggested earlier in this book, the concept of the dialogical self is conceived of as an embodied self. The embodiment of the self finds its basis in the assumption that space is not simply outside the self but also in the self (see also Jaynes, 1976, who has treated the self metaphorically as a "mind-space"). In the course of development the child interiorizes people, animals, and objects that have an existence in physical space, as positions in a self-space. This space is not an empty space but highly differentiated in terms of positions. These positions are located in "safety zones" or "danger zones," the latter representing a zone of increased uncertainty. Some people who are felt as threatening when entering one's personal space, are placed in the position of "stranger." This position becomes interiorized in the external domain of the developing self and is located in its "danger zone." From that moment on, there are "walls" in the self that demarcate people or groups that were placed in the safety zone or the danger zone. The individual becomes able to "close the doors" for people who are perceived as threatening. In the course of time the personal space develops into a "collective space," in which the individual feels allied with others in defending the boundaries of their house, street, district, region, country, culture, and all that they define as exclusively belonging to them. In this way, the development of personal and collective space can be seen as a precondition of later xenophobia, stranger anxiety, and defensive localization, as discussed in Chapter 1.

The existence of boundaries is necessary for the development of an open dialogical self. Such a self exists only when the child, and later the adult, is able to make a distinction between "my position" and "your position" in the course of a dialogue and, moreover, to see the difference between what "I have to contribute when it is my turn" and "what you have to contribute when it is your turn." I can only know what is my position and contribution to the process when I'm able to see not only the difference between your position and my position, but also to distinguish the two positions in *consistent* ways during the process of turn-taking. If my position is not clearly distinguished from your position and the two positions become mixed up, a dialogue in the sense of the development of my and your original positions, on the basis of subsequent steps in a turn-taking process, would be impossible and lead to confusion. For the same reasons, a dialogue between two positions as parts of a multi-voiced self can only meaningfully develop when the distinctions are sufficiently clear and consistent in their follow-up. A well-functioning dialogical self requires, moreover, sensitivity to the present moment of dialogue so that images built up on the basis of past interactions can be transcended. Only in this way can the self be sufficiently open to the present intentions and experiences of the actual other. Boundaries and their openness are defining features of a dialogical self.

For a dialogical self, as extended to the environment, two distinctions are relevant: (i) between internal and external positions and (ii) between the image of the other (as external positions in the self) and the actual other. The first distinction prevents the person confusing his internal positions with the image of the other (e.g., the image of the other as a projection of one or more internal positions). The second distinction is necessary in order to prevent the actual other being "covered" by an image of the other that does not correspond with the real intentions of the actual other (e.g., when the actual other is perceived on the basis of an enemy image). Those real intentions are accessible only if the person is continually aware that the image of the other is not necessarily identical with the intentions of the actual other and that dialogue is needed to correct that image. Such a dialogical attitude requires a tolerance for uncertainty as a necessary condition for an open dialogical self.

Turning points in body positions

The way the environment is perceived depends strongly on the position of the body. This is what Neisser (1988) had in mind when he proposed his concept of the "ecological self" that exists by virtue of its embodiment and location in space. The perception of objects in the environment depends directly on the information about the location of one's own body in that environment. Moreover, perceived information about the environment gives, at the same time, information about one's own position in space. This view is supported by the room experiments of Lee and Lishman (1975), in which an observer finds himself in a room in which the end wall recedes. The discrepancy between the visual information and one's place in the room causes a loss of stability and, as a correction, the observer tends to fall forward. The reverse effect takes place when the observer is in a room with an approaching wall. Such experiments suggest that one's physical position in space has direct repercussions for the way the environment is perceived and vice versa.

In the light of the ecological nature of the self, there are four moments in the development of body position and body movement of the young child that are significant for understanding the process of positioning and repositioning in space: rolling over, crawling, standing, and walking. By 6 months most babies are able to *roll over* from front to back and back to front. This is a bodily repositioning that gives the child a view of the world that is entirely different from when they were lying in the other position. Moving to the front position gives the child a frontal view of the environment and, if the distance permits it, objects can be actively grasped and moved toward the body and to the mouth in particular. The objects can be moved from "there" to "here" and back and, moreover, from "not felt" to "felt" and back.

Most babies from 6–12 months start *crawling*, a complex action that requires the simultaneous and coordinated movement of both arms and legs. This movement makes it possible to approach something out of reach and touch it. Babies are now placed in a field of tension that unfolds between what is reachable and what is not reachable. A dynamic and linear field is stretched between "here" and "there" and the baby is able to make movements from one to the other, able to reduce or increase, by her own motor skills, the distance between the two positions.

The first attempts to *stand upright* can be detected from the time that the child is about 4–5 months old. Standing can only be successful when infants are able to gain control over their legs and, moreover, to develop a good balance. Often with adult support, but finally alone, they are able to straighten their legs and stand up, holding on to a stable object for support. When they do so there is a constant risk of falling down. Whereas crawling enables the infant to move on the horizontal plane, standing up makes it possible to explore movements on the vertical plane. While crawling makes it possible to get acquainted with the opposite pair of "here" and "there," standing stimulates the child to explore the opposite pair of "high" and "low."

In combination, the bodily movements of crawling, standing, and, at some later moment, *walking*, create for the child a space that is highly dynamic in the sense that it becomes a structure in which the child can move from one position to another. In this way the child is able to go, by his own force and effort, into different directions and back, thereby constructing a multi-directional spatial environment. In this way, basic movements such as rolling over, crawling, standing, and walking can be seen as turning points in the movement development of the child, enabling him to reposition himself in such a way that a multiplicity of bodily positions and perspectives on the world become possible.

We emphasize the role of the body and body movements because they function as the physical basis for the metaphorical movements in a multi-positional self. As Johnson (1987) has argued, metaphors are deeply entrenched in the human mind and are reflected in basic "image schemas," such as verticality and horizontality, which find their origin in the form of our body. Moving along such dimensions helps us to structure the environment and make sense of the events that take place in our surroundings. A verticality schema is used to employ an updown orientation. We stand "upright" or "lie down," climb a staircase, wonder about the level of the water, and ask how tall our child is. A horizontality schema helps us to employ a here–there orientation. We "go to our house," "leave a place," or "push something away" that bothers us.

However, an image schema is more than an expression of a corporeal structure. It is also used as a metaphor for organizing our psychological understanding. Estimations of quantities are expressed in terms of verticality. We say: "prices are going up" or "the company's gross earnings fell." Such phrases are based on the concept that "more is up" although we are not aware of that. We employ a verticality structure as a physical basis for our mental comprehension, although there is no intrinsic reason why "more" should be "up." In a similar way, we use horizontal schemas to structure and understand our world. We say, "the project is in progress" or "this is too far from my view." Although there is no intrinsic reason to assume that improvement in a project is a form of spatial movement, we use a horizontal schema to conceptualize what is happening.

Apparently, a given image schema emerges first as a structure of our body, and is then figuratively developed as a meaning structure at more abstract levels of understanding. Likewise, the processes of positioning and repositioning, originally movements of the body, become a metaphorical way of looking at the workings of the self. Positions of central importance in the self can be understood in metaphorical ways. On a vertical plane we can find ourselves in a "top-dog" or "underdog" position, relevant as a basis of a power difference in the self (see also Chapter 1), and, in a related way, we imagine that the position of a winner, perceived at the top of society, is "higher" than that of "loser," perceived at the bottom of society. On a horizontal plane where we make steps towards or from something or somebody else, we can position ourselves as "close to" a significant other or as "alienated" from somebody, in this way reflecting psychological distances between ourselves and others. Moreover, dialogical relationships are based on metaphorically structured and embodied positions: we move to another position and back, going to and fro on a horizontal plane, and when we are more or less dominant in a dialogical exchange (e.g., by the amount of talk) we are moving up and down on a vertical plane.

The transition between bodily positions and the transition to the metaphorical use of these positions can be summarized in this way:

1. The child is lying on his back.
2. He rolls over.
3. He starts crawling.
4. He stands upright.
5. He walks.
6. He approaches another, older child who has a toy.
7. The younger child wants to have the toy but is not strong enough to get it.
8. Finally, the older child gives the toy and they play and converse with each other.

9. After some time they interiorize and appropriate each other as positions in their selves.
10. These positions influence and orchestrate their conversations, exchanges and actions in relation to other people.

Opposites like "up" versus "down" or "close" versus "detached" represent metaphorical dimensions that are rooted in the body. They give forms to our perceptions and experiences and show that we can move from the one pole to the other. We understand *contra*-dictions and *oppositions* in our conversations and exchanges with others and with ourselves, and we express our *ambi*-valences by saying "on the one hand" versus "on the other hand." Doing this, we use a horizontal dimension on which the positions are localized. Likewise, when we imagine the *suppression* of positions in ourselves or in the other (e.g., shadow positions) or see one position as *higher* or more important than another, we use a vertical dimension to give structure to our understanding of their relationships. The dimensions with their opposite poles and the (metaphorical) movements that are made between the poles are rooted in the structure and physical movements of the body. Therefore, the processes of positioning and repositioning are constitutive of the dialogical self as an embodied self.

Transcendent experiences in childhood

Between the opposite pairs "me" versus "not-me," and between "mine" versus "not mine," more or less permeable *boundaries* can be established. This was discussed earlier when we described how in contact with significant others, a "personal space" and "self-boundary structures" were demarcated. In the course of development, the child learns to make a clear distinction between parts of the environment that are typically "nearby" and "familiar," and other parts of the environment that are "far away" or "unfamiliar" or even experienced as threatening. There is, however, a particular class of experiences that has the potential to transcend such dichotomies and open the self to the environment to an unusually high degree. These experiences, which we have described in the previous chapter in terms of "participation in a broader field of awareness" can be found in childhood.

In a research project on "sudden flashes of self-awareness in childhood," developmental psychologist Kohnstamm (2007) was interested in experiences of children that reflect a sudden awareness of being an individual person as distinguished from others.[7] He collected autobiographical descriptions of "I-am-I experiences" as remembered by adults reflecting on their past experiences as children. Somewhat to his surprise, he also found descriptions of what he called "transcendental experiences," which were characterized by a loosening of the self-boundaries and a feeling of being part of some larger whole. A typical example is the report provided by an 82-year-old Dutch woman who remembered an event that went back to when she was barely 3 years old:

In the bed nook

I woke up and became aware of the fact that I was lying in the bed nook while the yellow flickering light from the small oil lamp cast shadows on and off and muted voices from another room were to be heard, and now and then a creaking noise (my brother, just barely one year old, had gotten a swing which our father had hung up in the laundry room; the thick cord made this noise). Suddenly, I was overcome by a strange, comforting sense of safety and security. I was lying here, and I belonged, I was part of the light, of the noise, of everything. I've never told anybody, but this kind of yellow light has always made me feel happy, like, for example, the lights from the old street lights in Paris. (2007: 149–50)

Such transcendental experiences might erroneously suggest that the child is open to such a degree that the boundaries of the self just disappear. In apparent contrast to this suggestion, are cases of transcendental experience that show that open self-boundaries and participation in a larger whole coexist with a clear I-am-I experience in which the child feels an autonomous person who has an existence separate from others. The following excerpt is from a 50-year-old man who wrote about an experience he had as a 9-year-old child:

I had celebrated my ninth birthday just a few days before and was in the playground where I would often hang out when all of a sudden I felt, *I am I, entirely for myself, only for myself, separated from the others and ultimately without any connection to them.* I wrote my name in the sand – a scene which is still clear in my mind – and I looked at it and felt myself as being entirely my own. I was looking at myself. It was like a brief, terrific high, an extreme intense feeling of independence, without any fear; rather, I was filled with pride and security. At this moment, the other children didn't matter at all, though I felt no animosity towards them.

This was a leap, an 'aha-experience', a feeling of abundance and completion, a feeling of being a part of the greater whole, which I felt as absorbing me, a feeling I've hardly ever had afterwards. I have never told anybody about the experience as I have here. (ibid.: 152, emphasis in the original)

With this and other reports, the author demonstrates that two orientations can go together: one which he characterizes as "I-am-I pride," a feeling of autonomy and independence, and another as participating in some larger whole, an increased contact with an intimate environment or with a loving nature or feeling in the lap of protecting gods. This suggests that the experience of autonomy and the existence of clear self-boundaries can go well with the feeling of participation in a larger field of awareness in which the stranger seems to disappear.

In discussing the results of his study, Kohnstamm refers to an investigation by Newberg, Eugene, and Rause (2001) who studied Tibetan Buddhists and Franciscan nuns, who reported regular transcendental experiences through meditation and prayer. Their brain pictures showed increased activity in the prefrontal cortex with a simultaneous reduction of activity in the posterior-superior parietal lobes at the upper back of the brain. In Newberg *et al.*'s view, the left part of this area is responsible for knowledge about the borders of one's body and the borders between self and environment. They hypothesized that during meditation these borders become blurred resulting in an experience of an infinite space with which the self merges. This experience is typically associated with strong positive emotions of joy and happiness that are attributed to the intense connections between the parietal lobes and the limbic system, our "feeling center."[8]

It is very possible, Kohnstamm speculates, that children are able to experience a blurring of their self-boundaries through the same brain processes as found in the studies on meditation. It is even possible that the child's brain is more susceptible to such border-crossings than the brains of adults and that the experiences which adults can only reach through the intense practice of meditation and prayer, arise spontaneously in children. Children are able, more easily than adults, to "switch off" their active mode of perception and behavior and arrive at a more receptive mode in which they experience themselves as part of a larger space.

In summary, the experiences of participation in a broader field of awareness, as reported in Chapter 3, can also be found in childhood. The reports typically emerge from the retrospective reflections of adults who remember, through their life, such events as extraordinary and precious moments. For dialogical self theory it is relevant to know that such transcendental experiences can emerge even when the normal self-boundary structures remain intact. The feeling of being an autonomous person, typical of the modern model of the self, can coexist with the experience or awareness of being part of a larger cosmic whole, typical of the traditional model.

Some theoretical considerations

Before continuing our exploration of significant dialogical phenomena in childhood and adulthood, we want to address three issues that require theoretical discussion in order to understand the nature of the dialogical self in a developmental context: (i) the connection between the social and the body; (ii) the connection between the social and the personal; and (iii) the difference between the concepts of voice and position.

Connection between the social and the body

The infant is a social being from birth onward. If this is so, what then is the relationship between the body and the social in the emergence of a dialogical self? The most general answer to this question is to refer to the intense interconnection between the social development of the child and the (metaphorical) movements of the body. When a mother is cold and distant towards her child in the first months of life, there is the risk that the child will feel insecure in its relationship with the mother and with other people. As a result of an insecure attachment, the child will experience obstacles when moving from a danger zone to a safety zone in the spatially structured self. As this description of movements in the self suggests, we propose to take the spatial and embodied nature of the self into account in order to understand the social development of the child. While social processes are taking place, the child is developing, at the same time, as an embodied self. That is, she will increasingly structure her experiences in relation to others and herself on the basis of spatial metaphors that have their origin in the form of the body and in the movements that are allowed by the body. As bodily located, the child is able to move (crawl, walk) away from the mother and to return to her. When the distance between the mother and the child increases, the child sooner or later feels unsafe and wants to return to the mother in order to feel safe again. When doing so, the child is typically moving on a horizontal dimension that is, at some later point in time, interiorized in the self as a metaphorical dimension stretched between the polar opposites of feeling *close* versus feeling *distant* in the relationship with the mother as a central other-in-the-self. The social dimension safe versus unsafe is, at some point in the development of the child, experienced in terms of the spatial and bodily dimension of close versus distant. Likewise, the child experiences the other, particularly adults, as bigger, and stronger than herself. At some point in time, she experiences herself as stronger, and greater than another child. These experiences represent differences on a vertical dimension that become metaphorically articulated in the form of significant self-positions such as "top-dog" (or winner) and "underdog" (or loser), the one placed and experienced as *above* the other. The social dimension that is stretched between the social opposites of being strong versus weak becomes experienced in terms of the spatial and bodily dimension that is structured between the opposites up versus down or high versus low. The original positions close versus distant and up versus down can be seen as part of a physical and spatial basis from which a variety of specific affect-laden positions emerge that are structured as polar opposites (e.g., the enemy as big, powerful, distant, and threatening versus my pussycat as small, close, and sweet).

The general idea behind these considerations is that social and bodily dimensions become increasingly intertwined in the development of the child and that sign-mediated interchanges with others lead to the construction of personal and social meanings in a spatially structured and embodied self. Self-positions are no abstract givens but emergent properties of a socially constructed and embodied self. Psychological positions emerge from social processes that are structured by the form and movements of the body and its basic opposites. In line with Vygotsky's (1987) view that the child begins to converse with himself as he previously conversed with others, we assume that the child experiences the positions in himself that he previously experienced in his embodied relationship with the other. The child converses with others on the basis of embodied positions: *during* the conversation the other is experienced, in relation to the self, as big or small, as threatening or safety-giving or as close or distant, and all these positions have their specific affective connotations.

The connection between the social and the personal

When we assume that self-positions are of a social nature, what then is personal in the self? Is the personal identical to the social? Is the personal to be understood as an "interiorization" of the social or is the personal more than that? In order to answer these questions, let's analyze the example of a boy who was positioned by others as an "outsider" or "deviant." At his birth, he was socially positioned as a "boy" and, as a cultural implication, he was expected, both by his parents and later, even more so, by his peers at school, to be "tough." However, this social positioning was clearly discrepant from his personal experience of being "different." As a very introverted boy who daydreamed all the time, absorbed by his fantasies, he did not meet the expectations of his teachers and peers and, as a consequence, they ridiculed him as "sleeper" and "dreamer," and treated him as an outsider. Initially, the boy, taken aback by this treatment, did not understand what was going on, but tried to survive in the environment of the school in which he was regularly the victim of bullying. However, at some later point in his school career, his achievements improved and he finished his primary school and later his high school and university with success. When he decided to follow an academic career, he remained a "dreamer," since this position never totally disappeared from his position repertoire. Thus, the outside world, and *also the boy himself*, continued to see him as a "dreamer" and as an "outsider." However, there was a point at which he realized that his outsider position, although a disadvantage and a loss of connection, was also a resource that transformed fantasy and dreaming into imagination and originality. After his university training, he became a staff member in a university department and decided to develop a method for assesing personal meanings that had not existed in his field until then. It felt rewarding to create an activity that was seen as "deviating" from the mainstream in his field, but at the same time as "contributing" to the same field. His fate, as an "eternal outsider," became his destiny, motivating him to create something from his personal point of view that, he hoped, would be of some value to society. Finally, he found out that being a "dreamer," in a position rejected by his social environment, later appeared to be a welcome resource for constructing something creative that was accepted and even respected by his professional colleagues, although his feeling of not being fully accepted as a member of a social group never disappeared entirely.

In this example, the position of being a boy is clearly socially defined, including the corresponding expectation of being "strong" and "tough." Even the position of an outsider was socially defined, but there was already the beginning of a personal element because, as an outsider, the boy found some tendencies in himself at variance with stereotypical social expectations. The position of "dreamer" was partly the result of a social and societal definition and partly the result of his personal outlook. He was put in this position by his social environment even before he was aware that he was "dreaming." In fact, he never thought of himself in this way until people in his environment made him aware of something in him that was different from others around him. After a time of being defined by (powerful) others as a dreamer, there came a period in which he started to see and *appropriate* this position as something that belonged to him and that he began to cherish as something valuable for himself and even for the society to which he belonged. From that moment on, the dreamer position became, more than ever, an *I*-position that was part of his self-definition and even felt an intimate part of himself. In this period, this position, originally attributed to him by people around him, became a very personal inclination. The dreamer, originally symbolizing a rejection by society, became his personal answer and choice, certainly after he discovered that "I as a dreamer" could establish a welcome and productive coalition with "I as creative." What was first a social definition later became his personal answer. Moreover, what was originally a disorganizing position, placing the boy outside society, later became part of a productive personal coalition, allowing him to find a respected place in society. The rejected dreamer became, in the long run, a respected scientist. After all, the respected scientist can be considered a "happy coalition" of social and personal *I*-positions.

As the example of the dreamer suggests, social definitions can become personal ones by their appropriation as parts of a personal position repertoire. Social positions are socially defined and organized while personal positions are personally defined and organized. The self typically emerges at the interface between these groups of positions. A social position, if appropriated, can become a personal one and vice versa (e.g., a very personal way of dressing can later become fashionable and incorporated in the position repertoire of other people). Society offers a series of social positions that may become personal at some later point in time and, conversely, some personal positions, including perspectives, ideas, and products, can be introduced into society and accepted as new social positions or as variations of existing ones. Thus they engender innovative elements in a society that would otherwise remain overly conservative (see also Mead, 1934).

Bringing together the personal and the social under the more general heading of positions has the advantage that any antinomy or separation between self and society, so characteristic of the modern model of the self, is transcended (see also Raggatt, 2007). If the personal was the exclusive domain of the self only, and the social of the society only, this would result in a self isolated from society on the one hand, and a selfless society on the other hand. In contrast, the self is society-inclusive and society is self-inclusive, like the self is culture-inclusive and culture self-inclusive (Hermans, 2001a). Recognizing this deep interconnection enables the dialogical model of the self to become more sensitive not only to the ways in which the lives of individual people are shaped by the society in which they live but also to the ways in which society and its history are made by the individuals and groups that are parts of it.

Social and personal positions can go well together in societies that tolerate personal investments in social positions. In those societies, social positions receive their *characteristic* features by their coalition with personal positions. When we say that somebody is a "teacher," we give only superficial information about the way this person is doing her job. More specifically, we notice that one teacher wants to define herself as an "inspiring teacher," another as a "teacher with a sense of humor," and again another as a "teacher who undertakes educational travel with his students." Typical social positions, such as teacher, father, employer, employee, professional and other roles that are defined by social expectations and prescriptions, receive their characteristic expression by their coalition with one or more personal positions.

The possibility of creating coalitions of social and personal positions can vary considerably between different kinds of society. In communist political systems, for example, social positions are, or were, often rigidly prescribed and constrained with a minimal contribution of personal choice and variation. Daily life was seriously restricted and controlled by the "party apparatus" that tried to regulate social life by imposing rigid rules and dictats so that individual freedom was seriously circumscribed and personal initiative discouraged. Private enterprise was almost excluded and deviations from the party norms could be severely punished. In such a political situation in which the system defines the person (or tries to do so), coalitions between personal and social positions were impeded or even made impossible.

In societies that celebrate individual freedom, there is, generally speaking, more space for coalitions of personal and social positions that fit with each other (e.g., establishing an official foundation with a personally formulated mission). However, in these societies there are also situations in which there is a clear misfit. When, for example, a catholic priest falls in love with a woman, his personal position of "being in love," and certainly its public expression, contradict the celibate status of his job. When the priest feels, as a result of his love, increasingly alienated from his celibate status, and perhaps from his position of being a priest as a whole, there emerges an irreconcilable conflict between his social and personal positions that may end with his exit from the Church. Apparently, there are situations in which social and personal positions conflict to such a degree that they may bring about important turning points in people's lives. The distinction between social and personal positions also has implications for the concept of motivation. The motivation for a particular *social* position (e.g. employee, employer, professional) tends to increase when this position becomes part of a coalition with a variety of *personal* positions, or when this social position itself becomes personalized to a considerable degree (e.g., "'My role in society feels like 'something of myself' or like it 'belongs to me'"). At the same time, this coalition should be sufficiently strong to form a counter-weight to other positions or coalitions of positions that are in conflict with it or could, in one way or another, undermine it (for the concept of motivation, see Chapter 6).

For conceptual purposes, it makes sense to explore further the relationship between the personal and social. In line with our preceding formulations, one may assume that the exterior becomes interiorized and the social becomes personalized. This process of interiorization is not to be understood as an internal "copy" of the social and exterior. The processes of interiorization and appropriation represent a *qualitative* change. The interior and personal adds something that is not or not yet in the exterior and social. It is even more than that: it is not only addition but also transformation. The exterior is reconstructed and recreated in the interior in such a way that the self has an original contribution that is not covered by any external social or societal process. The qualitative and irreversible change from the exterior to the interior represents the fundamental agency of the self. This agency is not only a source of personal development but also of societal development and innovation.

The difference between the concepts of voice and position

There is another issue that is in need of further clarification – the distinction between "voice" and "position." The distinction between the two concepts, often used interchangeably in the literature on the dialogical self, can be outlined on the basis of the preceding considerations. To briefly summarize our view: we see the concept of positioning as more basic in dialogical self theory than the concept of voice. For this thesis, we present three different arguments:

(1) Because the notion of voice as the instrument of speech is intrinsically connected with the use of language and signs, it should be noted that the person is already positioned long before he is using voice as a means of social interchange. At birth or even before, you are already socially positioned as a boy or girl, as white or black, as belonging to a particular family, as receiving one or more family names and one or more first names (see the discussion about the name "Edward Said" earlier in the chapter) and as destined to be dressed and trained according to the practices of a particular religion, ideology, or worldview (e.g., circumcised or not). All these factors can have a deep and often long-lasting impact on the further development of self and identity and they precede the moment that you explicitly say to others or to yourself "I'm ...", or "I feel ...", or "I notice ...";

(2) Very early in life, you are involved in a process of bodily positioning and repositioning, as in the activities of rolling over, crawling, standing upright, and walking. Moreover, the child is able to take different positions in space that give very different perspectives, and shows himself an active explorer of these positions (e.g., climbing a staircase, hiding himself behind a tree, covering himself with a blanket, etc.). As we have argued, such forms of bodily and spatial positioning and repositioning result in a multiplicity of perspectives and positions, before the child is actually able to use its voice to tell

what he experiences when seeing his surroundings from a particular perspective. Moreover, a position in its embodied manifestation implies the whole body, whereas a voice activates primarily the upper parts;

(3) You can be positioned and behave accordingly, without being conscious of the position in which you find yourself. Let's consider some empirical evidence in support of this statement. As part of their experimental research into dialogical self processes, Stemplewska-Zakowicz *et al.* (2005) asked students to discuss whether psychological knowledge could be helpful in passing exams. Some of them were instructed in such a way that they believed themselves to be in the position of an expert, whereas others received an instruction that made them believe that they were in the position of a layperson. In some experiments the students were positioned as expert or layman in a direct way (they both received the instruction that they were expert or layperson), whereas in another experiment students were positioned in an indirect way (their interaction partners were instructed that they were an expert or layman, but they themselves were not given this instruction). The investigators found that different positions produced different narratives (the students positioned as experts gave more advice than those positioned as laypersons). For our present purposes it is relevant that the experimenters found that even indirect ways of positioning showed this effect (although to a minor degree): students who were positioned as experts by their interlocutors but did not know that they were positioned as experts, actually gave more advice than those who were positioned, also in an indirect way, as laypersons. As this finding suggests, you can be positioned by others while not being aware that you are in this position, yet exhibit the behavior corresponding to it. Such forms of positioning, taking place on an unconscious or subconscious level, have not reached the level of explicit formulation, yet they influence what will be said or done from an implicit position.

On the basis of the preceding arguments, we conclude that the notion of "position," as an expression of the intrinsic embodiment of the self, refers to phenomena and processes that are more fundamental to the dialogical self than the phenomena and processes indicated by the notion of voice. As we have argued in this book, the processes of positioning and being positioned determine to a large degree which voices are actualized, what they have to say, and under what circumstances they are constrained in their expression. Due to their intrinsic connection, positions can be voiced so that people are able to tell explicitly about their experiences from a particular position and exchange them with other people and with themselves. Due to their linguistic capacities, people are equipped to further articulate, differentiate, and expand their position repertoire, connected as they are with other people from whom they can learn about themselves and the world on the basis of a joint stock of knowledge and experience.

The role of promoter positions

It would be problematic to conceive the development of the self in terms of a multiplicity of unrelated positions that each follow their own course. If the self consisted of a diversity of positions each showing their specific development over time, then a confusing cacophony of voices lacking any insightful organization would emerge. In order to understand the organization of the self from a developmental perspective, a particular concept, a promoter position, is needed for creating order and direction in the multiplicity of positions of the self. These positions focus particularly on the temporal aspects of the self and organize the self over longer time-frames.

Promoter positions (Valsiner, 2004),[9] have the following characteristics: (a) they imply a considerable openness towards the future and have the potential to produce a diverse range of more specialized but qualitatively different positions in the future of the self; (b) by their openness and broad bandwidth they integrate a variety of new and already existing positions in the self (by "integration" we mean that positions are reorganized in such a way that they result in a more adaptive self); (c) by their central place in the position repertoire, they have the potential to reorganize the self towards a higher level of development; and (d) they function as "guards" of the continuity of the self but, at the same time, they give room for discontinuity. Whereas continuity is guaranteed by their ability to link the past, present, and future of the self, a certain degree of discontinuity results from the fact that they function as a source of new positions. In this sense, promoter positions function as innovators of the self.

"Acceptance" as a promoter position in the internal domain

In order to illustrate the role of a promoter position in the internal domain of the self, we refer to a case-study, discussed in more detail by Hermans (2003). Before showing when and how the promoter position was constructed, we first give some background information about the person and about the procedure that was followed.

Leo, a 29-year-old man, contacted a psychotherapist after he was criticized by his superiors because of his "arrogant behavior" and lack of empathy towards his colleagues. In the same period, his partner broke off her relationship with him for similar reasons. As a reaction, he wrote an aggressive letter in which he accused her of being the cause of all of his problems. When his girlfriend then refused any further contact with him, Leo could not stop thinking of her and she increasingly became an obsession with him. He started to follow her and her new boyfriend around all day and terrorized them with frequent nightly telephone calls. His worries about his stalking behavior and the serious criticism he had received from his superiors were reasons for Leo to contact a psychotherapist.

The therapist (Els Hermans-Jansen in cooperation with Hubert Hermans as co-therapist) proposed that Leo explore his situation in terms of a position repertoire. This was done by providing Leo with a list of internal and external positions that he supplemented on the basis of his own experiences. Leo was invited to select and introduce these positions as part of the repertoire that he saw as relevant to his life and to investigate the organization of the repertoire via a matrix in which the horizontal rows referred to his internal positions, and the columns to his external positions (for details of the method, see Hermans 2001b). One of the positions in the internal domain was "I as a stalker," which was highly prominent in his relationship with his ex-partner Laura, who functioned as one of the most central external positions in his self. The intention of the therapist was to examine the meaning of the stalker by correlating this position with all the other internal positions in the repertoire. It appeared that the "stalker" showed the highest correlation with the "avenger" as two positions in the internal domain that were particularly prominent in his relationship with Laura.

In a further assessment of the repertoire, the therapist and Leo discovered a highly influential background position – the dreamer. Leo explained that this position was very important to his relationship with Laura, who had always been an ideal person for him. For the therapist this was a reason to explore, together with Leo, the relationship between the avenger and the dreamer as two relevant background positions of the stalker.

In an attempt to further explore the narrative content of the two positions, the psychotherapist suggested that Leo tell about some events from the perspectives of the avenger and the dreamer separately. This invitation led the client to consider the positions as different voices, each with a particular story to tell from a specific point of view.

The positions were explored by using elements from the Self-Confrontation Method (Hermans and Hermans-Jansen, 1995) by inviting the client to tell, from each position separately, about significant events or circumstances in his past and present, and expected events or circumstances in the future (e.g., hopes, plans, or anxieties). An example of a question about the past was this: "Has there been anything of major influence in your past life which still continues to exert a strong influence on you?" Client and therapist read this question aloud sitting side by side, taking spatial positions that symbolized a relationship of cooperation. The method invites clients to give their spontaneous associations which then leads, with the assistance of the therapist, to the formulation of sentences that each refer to a significant experience in the client's life. These sentences are written down on small cards so that they together form a spatial structure and can easily be compared and combined with other sentences. Similar questions are also asked about the client's present and future (Hermans and Hermans-Jansen, 1995: 35).

For illustrative purposes, we give two sentences that Leo articulated from the perspective of the avenger:

"When I have nothing more to lose, I enjoy destroying somebody; I derive some pride from that."

"When I have the feeling that somebody (my ex-partner) is not honest with me, and I discover this, I want to give that person a lesson, with verbal violence and with telephone calls ... I want to make somebody suffer."

These sentences, considered as "utterances" from a specific voice, refer to Leo's present. However, when he told his story from the perspective of the dreamer, an entirely different voice emerged, which went back to his past:

"I was fantasizing that I would later get a rich and easy life; I made high buildings with Lego."

"I am the reformer of the world, a well-known figure who traces criminals, a kind of private detective, a hero who attracts much admiration and attention."

After comparing the formulations from the two positions the therapist and Leo concluded that, from the perspective of the avenger, Leo's stalking behavior was an act of restoring his self-esteem which had been threatened by Laura's decision to end their relationship. From the perspective of the dreamer, this behavior could be understood as a way of attracting Laura's attention and to play the role of a hero in her eyes. Although the dreamer was experienced by Leo as opposite to the avenger, the dreamer played a highly significant role in his behavior towards his ex-girlfriend. The discussion between the therapist and Leo led to the insight that the stalker, the avenger, and the dreamer formed a coalition in which the avenger was aroused in an effort to restore the threatened ideals of the dreamer. In the service of the unrealistic dreamer and the self-affirmative avenger, Leo became a stalker.

A promoter position came to the fore when the co-therapist asked Leo the following question during one of the therapy sessions that followed the assessment of his position repertoire: "Can you mention a position that, in your view, will be relevant to your future development?" In order to help Leo answer this question, the co-therapist gave him the checklist of positions that he had earlier used to construct his own position repertoire. He then pointed to the position "I as accepting." In the discussion that followed, both Leo and his therapists felt that this position was valuable as an effective counter-weight to the narrow-minded attitude of the avenger and the unrealistic ideals of the dreamer.

In the phase that followed, Leo began to experiment with accepting himself and others in various situations. Some situations were quite difficult for him (e.g., accepting that his new girlfriend had talked with another man), whereas other situations were easier (e.g., accepting that a colleague at work had a different opinion about a particular subject). By discussing such examples with the therapist, Leo gradually learned to accept the fact that other people had their own opinions, wishes, and anxieties, and that it was important, to others but also to himself, to take these into account.

In order to check if the process of change was moving in the intended direction, the therapist and Leo decided to assess and evaluate the changes five months after the first assessment. In the meantime, the accepting position was so far developed that Leo was able to formulate some sentences *from the perspective of this position*. Here are some examples:

"When the accepting is not there, there are emotions: This attacking, short-sighted, reproaching kind of communication ... then I give room to the avenger."

"Whereas Johnson [previous employer] reacted somewhat amused to my self-image (dreamer), I see now that I get respect from Jackson [present employer]; for example, my suggestions are followed and I get respect from the administration."

In the first sentence, Leo refers explicitly to the avenger but he prefers to focus on moments when the accepting position is "not there" and to criticize the avenger from the outside. The formulation suggests that he is, from the perspective of his accepting position, aware of the narrow perspective of the avenger and somewhere accepts his responsibility for the emergence of this position ("... then I give room to the avenger"). In the second sentence, Leo constructs a coalition between the accepting position and the dreamer and indicates that the dreamer is no longer merely fantasizing and building "castles in the air." In contrast, the dreamer becomes *integrated* into the accepting position, which suggests that he feels able to develop more realistic ways of earning respect and attention.

In Leo's example, we see that there are three strongly interconnected positions that formed obstacles to the development of his self: the stalker, the avenger, and the dreamer. In an attempt to reorganize his position repertoire, a promoter position, "I as acceptant," was developed that in the course of time became strong enough to function as a healthy counter-position in the further development of his self. The question that directed Leo's attention to this position explicitly referred to Leo's future, suggesting that, in his perception, this position would be important for this future development. Rather than referring to a specialized position, "I as acceptant" seemed to be fertile enough to engender and influence a range of positions relevant to his future. The accepting position was, moreover, able to exert an integrating influence on the other positions that played a significant role in his present problems. In the sentences he constructed from the perspective of the accepting position, he established a connection between the accepting position on the one hand and the avenger and dreamer positions on the other hand. As a result of this (beginning) integration, his dreamer position lost much of its unrealistic and narcissistic quality, and became more focused on attainable goals. His formulations suggested that the accepting position helped him to cope with his aggressive feelings and childish fantasies and stimulated him to reach some higher level of development.

Shape-shifting in cultural anthropology

From a cultural-anthropological point of view, the workings of a promoter position can be observed in a phenomenon known as "shape-shifting," discussed by Gieser (2006) in the context of dialogical self theory. Shape-shifting refers to a process whereby people believe that they are temporarily transformed, either mentally or physically, into another being. One of the cultural groups who practice this ritual are the Kuranko people of Sierra Leone, who use shape-shifting to transform themselves into animals to give them a sense of power, control, meaning, healing, and identity. Shape-shifting is closely connected to a particular feature of the Kuranko culture: the tendency to spatialize internal events. Memory is seen as referring to something "far away" and the unconscious is represented by going into the darkness of the bush. Personhood does not reside in autonomous individuals but in social relationships. These social relationships extend clearly beyond fellow-humans. The Kuranko also have relationships with ancestors, spirits, fetishes, and animals, including totem animals. In this context, shape-shifting can be understood as an inward travel from the conscious into the unconscious, expressed as an exterior movement from town to bush, where the shape-shifter is going to identify with an animal. In particular, identifying with the totem animal of the clan (e.g., an elephant) empowers him to expand his possibilities and strength beyond the ordinary. After his return to the village, he is respected by the other members of the clan and may even receive the status of a hero, because he serves as a model capable of tapping the powers of the wild. Moreover, by his performance he has confirmed the moral bond between his clan's people and their totem animal.

From a theoretical point of view, Gieser analyses the process of shape-shifting as a dynamic relationship between two domains of the self: the internal and the external (or extended) domain. An external position (the animal as the object of identification) is transformed into an internal position ("I as animal"). As soon as the external position has been appropriated by the internal domain, it becomes so dominant that it suppresses all the other positions in the internal domain. In this phase of the transformation process, the power asymmetries between the positions are pushed to the extreme, resulting in a monological self. There is only one voice that reigns in the self, the voice of the person-as-animal. The shape-shifter believes that he has transformed himself into the reality of another being, which increases his strength and power to the utmost. After the period of shape-shifting, however, the new position loses its dominance and, receiving its place among a variety of other positions, it becomes a normal dialoguing partner in a multi-voiced self. The new position becomes stabilized as part of the repertoire, together with all the rewarding characteristics the shape-shifter attributes to it (power, control, and healing). Although the new position has lost its absolute dominance in the self, it has the capacity to subordinate and influence earlier positions that were characterized by marginality and powerlessness (Gieser, 2006).

The process of shape-shifting exemplifies how the self can be innovated and further developed by the introduction of a new position that functions as a promoter position. Through ritual approximation and temporary dominance of this position a process of appropriation and interiorization takes place that makes the shape-shifter strongly identify with the totem animal. Although it is highly dominant in the beginning of the process, it later becomes a dialoguing partner that influences and is influenced by a larger number of *I*-positions moving the self towards a new future.

Although their cultural context is highly different, there seems to be a basic similarity between the process of shape-shifting and the therapeutic process as exemplified by the case of Leo. In both cases there is a significant other who is introduced into the self as an external position, the totem animal in the one case and the therapist in the other. In the course of the process the new position becomes interiorized in the internal domain of the self: "I as powerful" in the case of shape-shifting, and "I as accepting" in the case of therapy. Once interiorized and integrated in the self, they start to influence other self-positions, leading to the innovation of the self as a whole. Moreover, as newly established parts of the self, they are able to influence other positions and even engender new ones in the future, integrating them at the same time.[10]

Promoter positions as integrating shadow positions

Promoter positions, going beyond the spur of the moment, have a certain extension over time and, as innovative and integrative energies, they facilitate and stimulate the development of the self. Typically, significant others – real, remembered, anticipated or imaginary – who enter one's life temporarily or for a longer period, serve as promoter positions. Inspiring figures in the areas of art, science, politics, novels, film, or music may serve as promoter sources, that open the self by their appeal to already existing *I*-positions and their potential to engender new ones. As a result of this openness, they are given a stabilized and influential position as other-in-the-self. Children and adolescents may become particularly impressed by a teacher who appeals to them not only in the context of learning and school achievements, but also and primarily as a person who touched them at a sensitive point in their lives. Such teachers or educators or other models receive the status of a promoter position and, once interiorized as others-in-the-self, they are, actually or in imagination, consulted when the person is in need of advice, direction, confirmation, or encouragement. Such figures serve as a compass, particularly when people are confronted with problems, choices, or decisions that require a new orientation in their lives. Significant others are particularly likely to become promoter positions when people are at a turning point in their lives or are in need of direction, encouragement, or advice. Meeting a new person or becoming part of a new group can engender a new promoter position, particularly when this person or group appeals to positions in the self that were hidden, neglected, or waiting to become actualized.[11]

Imagined figures as well as actual figures may function as promoter positions. Some people return, particularly in a period of stress or pain, to an image or picture of a deceased family member or a friend for support and advice. People with a religious or spiritual background often consult the picture, image, or statue of a Buddha, Christ, or holy person, and many people have daily dialogical contact with an image of God, whom they approach as the "ultimate promoter position." Depending on the influence of such a position, the consultation of imagined significant others can create a "position shift" similar to the imagined role reversal learned by the child in early childhood (Bertau, 2008). The result is that memories, thoughts, and emotions that are associated with existing positions change as a result of the different perspective. In most cases, the perspective offered by a promoter position of this kind offers a wider horizon[12] and creates a certain distance from the pressing problems of the moment, with the result that strong emotions are calmed and make room for different emotions or feelings. As many people can tell on the basis of their own experiences, imagined others as promoter positions have the potential to transform negative emotions into positive ones or to bring about acceptance of them as they are. They have, moreover, the power to enlarge one's experiential space in a way that the "walls" of limited or specialized positions can be transcended. Often a promoter position of this kind also functions as a meta-position that widens the horizons of the self. In addition, experiences described earlier as "transcendental" may open a "promoter field" with a strong integrating influence on a diversity of other positions.[13]

The most powerful promoter position is not the one that gives the most positive feelings, but rather the one that is able to integrate positive and negative feelings. Shadow positions or "disowned" positions are often associated with more negative than positive feelings and for many people it is a difficult problem to integrate them as *I*-positions in the self. Significant others, like a loving partner, parent, or friend or a dedicated therapist, are particularly able to integrate shadow positions as acceptable parts of a co-constructed self. Therefore, the most rewarding social relationships are not those with the most positive positions and feelings but the relationships that are able to cope with negative positions. The integration of shadow positions and negative feelings into a social relationship typically results in shared positive feelings and gives the relationship a broader bandwidth than before.

Promoter places

Places that have some special value for a person may be associated with a promoter position. Typically this is a place where a promoter position emerged or could be fully expressed. You may remember a place, village, city, region, country, or part of the world that made an indelible impression because you had an experience that was the beginning of a "new life," or because you see the place as the location of a significant turning point for your future. Such a place becomes, like a significant other, interiorized as a precious part of the self, and functions as a cradle for the development of new internal positions. Throughout one's life one returns to that place in imagination, associated as it is with feelings of inspiration or nostalgia. Some people actually make a "nostalgic jour-ney" in an attempt to find the "lost paradise again." Promoter places add significantly to the temporal structure of the self-space. Some places, like the remembered place, have an affinity with the past; other places, such as the house in which one lives or the place where one works, are affiliated with one's present life. Yet other places, associated with a future state of the self ("I would like so much to live there ...") may motivate and organize present activities.

Different models of the self show remarkable differences between the kind of places with which they are associated. The traditional model has an affinity for stable places, as expressed, for example, by the "*stabilitas*," one of the basic rules of the monastery tradition of Saint Benedict. The young monk who enters the monastery knows that he will remain for his whole life at the same place. As part of his initiation, an older monk shows him the place where he will be buried. The post-modern self, on the contrary, is affiliated with ever-changing places, as in the notion of "dislocation," suggesting that every place is a transitional place (e.g., vis-iting sites on the internet; tourist trips). One is somewhere in order to move to another place. Historical changes in the process of positioning and repositioning correspond with increasing changes in the stability of places in the self.

A multi-level model for the development of the self

The preceding considerations lead to the construction of a model that takes into account the central role of promoter positions in the development of the dialogical self. This model (see Figure 4.1) allows for the inclusion of several concepts and phenomena that are crucial for the progression or regression of the self and its organization in the course of time.

Overview of the model

The model presented in Figure 4.1 is made up of a number of circles placed on top of each other, representing different developmental levels of the self. There are three kinds of movements: progressive, regressive, and balanced. When the self is involved in progress, it moves up to a higher level of development; when it is in a process of regress, it moves down to a lower level of development. When it is involved in balanced movements, the self makes movements on one and the same level, with-out going "up" or "down." A central assumption is that "important life events" and, in addition, the way the self responds to these events, deter-mine the development of the self as a whole. It is further assumed that the

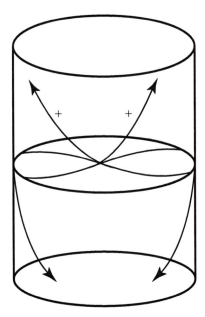

Figure 4.1 Multi-level model for the development of the self

progressive movements are facilitated by the availability and accessibility of promoter positions (indicated by + in the Figure). When, in the case of a disorganizing event, there is an opportunity for innovative dialogue with one or more promoter positions, the movement toward a higher level of integration is facilitated and stimulated. When the self arrives at a higher level, the same process is repeated with new opportunities and challenges. When, on the other hand, promoter positions are not available and accessible, there is a considerable risk that the self, in the case of a disorganizing event, moves down to a lower level of integration where the same process takes place again. The movements up and down do not correlate with age but are instigated by events, and the way the individual responds to these events, over the course of time. An individual may be involved in many upward or downward movements through a life.

On each level there are centering and decentering movements in the self, represented by the lemniscate[14] in the middle circle in Figure 4.1. *Centering* movements go in the direction of the center of the self, a hypothetical place of perfect integration, represented by the center of the circle. These movements work in the direction of order and integration. *Decentering* movements go away from the hypothetical center towards the periphery of the self, represented by the circumference of the circle. These movements disrupt or undermine an existing order and integration.

Each of these movements has its potentials and risks. Decentering movements, as expressed by the increasing multiplicity and diversification of positions, imply the possibility of innovation of an existing order in the self. However, decentering movements entail the risk of disorganization, chaos, and fragmentation when these movements become overly dominant in the self. Centering movements work in the direction of coherence, unity, and integration and restore the organization of the self when an existing order is challenged. When centering movements become overly dominant, the self is at risk of becoming rigidly organized, centralized, and inflexible. Both movements are indispensable for the functioning of the self and they can be seen as complementing each other, although one of the two may be–depending on the present state of the self and the situation at hand–predominant in a particular period. Together, they construct the self as unity-in-multiplicity or multiplicity-in-unity. The model is non-linear in the sense that the self may make at some periods in the development a progressive movement and in other periods a regressive movement. This makes the development of the self to a high degree dependent on the *context* (social, political, cultural, or historical) in which the self is embedded.[15]

The theory underlying Figure 4.1 assumes that it belongs to the nature of the dialogical self to be subjected, to a greater or lesser degree and in alternating ways, to centering *and* decentering movements. The idea is *not* that decentering events are alien to the self and necessarily affect or threaten the intrinsic unity and coherence of the self, as if the decentering movements themselves are outside factors that are extrinsic to the self. Instead, both movements, centering and decentering, are intrinsic to the development of the self. This statement has to be considered as following from the basic idea that, when the society becomes more complex and decentering, as the result of globalization (Chapter 1) and postmodern trends (Chapter 2), the self also, as a society of mind, becomes more complex and decentering. In accord with the reasoning put forward in Chapter 3, dialogical self theory is constructed in such a way that it incorporates both centering movements, emphasized in the modern model of the self, and decentering movements, emphasized in the postmodern model of the self, as equivalent movements in the self.

Apart from societal and historical arguments that emphasize the two basic movements as equivalent in the development of the self, they can be observed in the daily functioning of the self. Everyday events have, more or less, a challenging impact on the self in the sense that they change or disrupt an existing order – an argument or disagreement with a family member or colleague, an annoying e-mail contact, an unwelcome question or a sudden memory that seems to come out of the blue.

The self is not only subjected to decentering movements as a result of more or less abruptly changing circumstances, it is also in need of them. We desire adventure, need variation, and actively search for new challenges. Such events decenter the self to a greater or lesser degree. In its reaction to such changes, the self adapts to the new situation (e.g., just getting used to it) or by creating a new order in the self (e.g., by a clarifying talk with the other or with oneself). These reactions can be considered as (re)centering movements as a response to the decentering ones. On the other hand, when there is a long absence of decentering movements, the individual will respond to a lack of stimulation or to boredom by actively searching for new challenges or incentives. Apparently, decentering movements are needed to "feed" the self that would otherwise "dry up," while centering movements, on the other hand, are needed to bring a (new) balance and order in the self. In other words, centering and decentering movements are part of everyday life and tend to alternate in dialectical ways.

The difference between transition and crisis

Within the broad array of possibilities in the decentering movements, there is a difference to note between transition and disorganization. In the case of a transition, the self is confronted with a new, unfamiliar or even threatening situation that requires an adaptation or reorganization of the self. For example, children create imaginary figures in times of transition, as in Winnicot's term "transitional object" (1971). An inanimate object is transformed into an imagined animate being that serves as a companion in the transition from one state to another (e.g., from waking to sleeping). The adoption of such an object as part of a daily ritual helps the child to reduce heightened uncertainty during the transition.

In the literature about adolescence, a period in which many new positions require some form of organization, the notion of "transition" is frequently used. At first sight, some authors argue, adolescence looks like a turmoil of changes with growth spurts, the appearance of secondary sexual characteristics, the first menstrual period, sexual desires and experiences, homosexual thoughts, self-consciousness, abrupt mood changes, smoking, use of alcohol, and experimenting with drugs. In adolescence the I is confronted with a diversity of actual and possible positions that lack a stable organization. Sudden and unexpected shifts between divergent positions are typical of this developmental period. This is nicely exemplified by a girl looking at herself in front of a mirror (Clarke-Stewart, Perlmutter, and Friedman, 1988: 413):

Sometimes I look in the mirror and say to myself, "Okay, who are you *really*, Natalie?" I pull my hair back and put on makeup and look very sophisticated. That's one me. I let my hair fall loosely on my shoulders, put on a Shetland sweater, and that's another me. I write poetry and stay up late to watch the stars and planets through my telescope; that's another me. I get really involved in my chemistry homework and think I'll be a doctor, or I want to be a translator, or I want to be a foreign correspondent. There are almost too many possibilities – Natalie, age 17.

Although all such developmental changes, mood changes, and confusing possibilities of positions, when taken together, could constitute a crisis or serious disorganization, there is in the traditional literature on adolescence little support for this view. Empirical evidence suggests that the self, during adolescence, continues to evolve rather steadily (e.g., Savin-Williams and Demo, 1984). Burns (1979), who shares this opinion, criticizes Erikson (1968) for lending weight to the conventional but erroneous view that adolescence is a period of storm and stress. Erikson, suggests Burns, has over-generalized his findings, based on clinical analyses, to the adolescent population as a whole.

A disorganization or crisis of the self, some authors argue, is not so much caused by a particular developmental period, like adolescence or mid-life, but rather by particular life-events that affect core positions in the self. As Neugarten (1970) has argued, predictable, on-time events will not be unsettling when they arrive. Unanticipated events, rather than the anticipated, are likely to create a crisis. Major disorganizations are caused by events that upset the sequence and rhythm of the expected life-cycle, as when one loses a loved one or one's job earlier than expected.

When *core positions* lose their function in the organization of the repertoire, a disorganization of the self is particularly likely. A position is a core position when a large variety of other positions are dependent on its functioning. So, when a core position is changed or undermined, many other positions are changed or undermined too, so that the repertoire as a whole may become disorganized and overly decentralized. For example, when a student has centered his life around his university studies (i.e., where he lives, campus entertainment, contact with colleagues, respect from parents, future aspirations), a failure to complete his studies could cause a crisis because all of the other, more peripheral, positions will be shaken.[16]

From the perspective of the present theory, it should be emphasized that a crisis is not simply "caused" by an external event. Its appearance *also depends on the response that this event receives from the self.* A particular event, such as the unexpected loss of a significant other or one's job, may shock the self and create excessive decentering movements. However, as a response to such an event the self mobilizes centering movements that are intended to restore a disturbed balance. According to the present theory, such centering movements are facilitated by the presence of one or more promoter positions if they are well-developed and strong enough to face the challenge. From a long-term developmental point of view, centering and decentering movements are considered equally important for a well-functioning self. For making the actual movement up to a higher level of development, however, centering movements of the self, represented by the integrative strength of promoter positions, temporarily dominate the self. When promoter positions are absent or poorly developed, the chances that the self reacts with a crisis and regresses, for a shorter or longer time, to a lower level of integration, significantly increases. In a period in which the self is confronted with events that have a disorganizing influence, promoter positions have the potential to give an adaptive response that prevents an actual disorganization of the self, even when one or more core positions are at stake.

In the light of existing evidence in the psychological literature, adolescence, like mid-life, may be described as a period of transition, bridging one developmental period and the next one, rather than a period of crisis. Transition, of course, calls for *reorganization*. Rather than the breakdown of a core position, such periods represent the building up of a sufficiently stabilized and integrated position repertoire. An adolescent may go through a crisis after the divorce of his parents; or a person in mid-life may become disorganized when his child dies unexpectedly. It should be emphasized, however, that the response of the self in terms of disorganization or reorganization is co-determined by the existence and quality of promoter positions.

There is another factor that only recently received some attention in the literature about adolescence and should be taken into account: the increasing influence of globalization. Focusing on the psychology of adolescence, Arnett (2002) discussed the uncertainty resulting from globalization. He argued that in a globalizing world, people have to face the challenge of adapting not only to their local culture but also to the global society. In contemporary society, most people, and adolescents in particular, are developing bi-cultural or multi-cultural identities, implying that part of their identity is rooted in their local culture whereas another part is oriented to the global situation. As an answer to these decentering influences, some of them develop a hybrid identity, successfully combining global and local elements in a mix. However, Arnett observes, the global–local dynamics also cause an increase of identity confusion, particularly among young people in non-Western cultures. Because globalization often has a disorganizing impact on local cultures, some young people feel themselves at home in neither the local situation nor the global situation. Many children of immigrants, as well as refugees, asylum-seekers, or parents living in diasporas fall in this group (see also Mills and Blossfeld, 2003, who, in a large-scale research project in thirteen countries, found that groups at the bottom of society are at particular risk). Seen from this perspective, Erikson's (1968) thesis about crisis in adolescence receives confirmation, at least for some groups, but maybe for very different reasons than those he proposed – that it is not temporal (developmental) factors that lead to adolescent crisis but spatial (globalizing) factors.

The impact of globalization on self and identity is a reason for proposing a spatial complementation of traditional developmental concepts. Neugarten's (1970) argument that unanticipated, off-time events are more unsettling than predictable, on-time events is not only a temporal issue but also a spatial one. Globalization leads to border-crossings and discontinuities of space that may transform events, considered as on-time events within the traditions of local cultures, into unpredictable off-time events taking place in globalizing conditions. For example, in the case of a marriage, particular events and practices such as child-rearing and religious rituals are predictable and on-time as long as one lives within the boundaries of one culture with commonly shared traditions. However, marriage becomes more unpredictable when it takes place between people who are born and raised in different cultures, each with different expectations about child-rearing, education, finances, and social rituals. In such a case the existing order in the self may become disrupted because a core position (e.g., "I as married and expecting that my children will be raised according to practices of my own culture") is undermined and results in regressive movements of the self, unless there are promoter positions available and accessible that prevent such regression (for a methodology to investigate the organization of the position repertoires, see the case study of a husband and wife raised in different cultures, Hermans, 2001b).

Summarizing: two kinds of movements are basic to the self, centering and decentering. Within this context, a distinction can be made between transition and crisis. We suppose that transition leads, under the influence of centralizing forces, to a progressive development, whereas crisis implies the risk of a regressive movement of the self. Adolescence is a developmental period that is controversial as to whether it is primarily a period of transition or crisis. We have argued that, in answering this question, the process of globalization should be taken into account. Globalization, and the tension between globalization and localization in particular, produces decentering forces that may undermine core positions in the self, particularly when a threatening disorganization does not receive a counter-weight from the side of promoter-positions.

Positive disorganization of the self

It can be asked whether crisis or disorganization, as a form of far-reaching decentering, *necessarily* implies a regressive movement of the self. This issue is a fundamental one because it raises the question of how many resources the self has available to find an adaptive answer to situations in which one or more core positions are losing their function. The question also touches one of the essential features of the dialogical self, that is, its extension. How many promoter positions, in the internal as well as the external domain of the self, are available and accessible and what is their quality as facilitators of progressive movements? In the context of these questions, we want to introduce a concept that we see as promising for future theory and research on the developmental aspects of the dialogical self: the notion of "positive disorganization" (see also Dabrowski, 1964).[17]

Certainly, in a period of disorganization of the self, it is at risk of regressing to a lower level of integration. However, we assume that regression or progression strongly depends on the number and quality of the promoter positions that are available and accessible in the internal and external domains of the self. The extension of the self has the potential of broadening the range of possible positions with a promoter function that may introduce new resources into the self. *When the integrative power of a promoter position is strong enough, it is able to compensate for the disorganizing influence that results from the change or even loss of core positions.* Integration of disorganizing events at a higher level is possible when the external domain of the self is open and *receptive* enough for the introduction of promoters. People may find a promoter in the actual contact with an inspiring teacher, supportive friend, loving parent, husband, or wife. They may find it in the same figures, even when they are no longer actually available but are interiorized as others-in-the-self. In this way they continue to play a significant role as external positions who may be consulted at difficult moments in time and who give support, consolation, and strength to the person when he or she is in need of it. Many people have imagined significant others available as promoters, such as a Buddha, a Christ, a Mohammed, or any other religious or spiritual leader. Both in the external domain and the internal domain of the self, promoters are available or can be developed. Some are particularly relevant as resources of developmental progress and integration. As we have seen earlier in this chapter, the accepting position can have a significant integrative function because it has the potential to establish a coalition with a diversity of other positions. For other people, "I as never losing my sense of humor" has the same function, or "I as an enjoyer of life despite adversities" or "I as a fighter who never gives up." External positions can influence or even be transformed to positions in the internal domain. For example, a person remembers his inspirational father, who always said: "You always should go on and never give up," facilitating the development of "the fighter in myself." Or, a person may recite to himself, particularly at difficult moments, a quote from an influential book that strengthens particular internal positions at moments of adversity.

A central point that we want to make is that the *extension* of the self has the potential to open it up for the inclusion of external positions that may be developed as *promoters*. We consider such promoters able to stop or compensate for the detrimental influences produced by strongly disorganizing events. Such promoters may be powerful enough to *replace* core positions when these are losing their functions as integrating and organizing agencies. As such, they are able to construct coalitions with other positions strong enough to meet a disorganizing challenge. In such instances, disorganization that receives a dialogical answer from an influential promoter position can be experienced as positive and constructive, that is, as an enrichment and as a developmental achievement or gift. Disorganization of the self becomes a "dark period" with, at the end, a positive outlook.

Multi-level conflict in personal development

One of the reasons for proposing the model presented in Figure 4.1 is its sensitivity to the *oscillation* of the self between different levels of integration within a short period of time. Take the example of a depressive artist who was the victim of traumatic past events. He was admitted to a psychiatric hospital but, despite treatment, was never cured. At some point in time he found out that he was able to express his experiences in the form of paintings. He felt this activity as increasingly rewarding, especially since his work was well-received in the art world. As a consequence, he made a career as an artist, although his depression never disappeared. Is he functioning at a higher *or* lower level of development? From the perspective of the model presented here, there are reasons to assume that he developed to a higher level as an artist, but to a lower level as a depressive patient. As a result his self functions at different levels of integration, depending on the position evoked by a particular situation and his reaction to it.

The possibility that the self can function at different developmental levels gives rise to the distinction between two kinds of conflict, labelled "uni-level" and "multi-level" conflict (Dabrowski, 1964). The former kind of conflict is familiar both in everyday life and in the social sciences. It is a conflict between two positions at the *same* level of integration. For example, an employer has to take a decision that affects the life of a friend in a negative way. This leads to a conflict in the self in which one position ("I as employer") is felt as detrimental to the other one ("I as a friend").[18] This type of conflict differs from a multi-level conflict, where a position located on one level is in conflict with a position on *another* level. This occurs when a particular position is more developed than another one, while the less developed "lower" position is interfering with the more developed "higher" one. Take the example of an ambitious professional who was always trying to reach the absolute top in his field. As long as he was young and felt that there was enough time ahead to realize his aspirations, the combination of "I as a professional" and "I as being ambitious" functioned as a happy coalition. However, when he grew older and approached the end of his career, he found out that it was time for him to reorient himself. He decided to become a mentor and started, with great pleasure, to give advice and supervision to his younger colleagues. He experienced this job and the rewarding contact with younger people as an enrichment of his personal development. However, his lifelong ambition did not disappear and was not fulfilled. Moreover, his ambition of "reaching the top" had no longer a constructive function in his work as a mentor, because he felt it as his task to be concerned about the future career of his colleagues rather than realizing his own ambitions. He had discovered that he was sometimes quite jealous of some of his successful younger colleagues and he increasingly felt his ambition was a stumbling block for his further development. In this example, his decision to give a twist to his career brought him to a higher level of integration because he found a new position that allowed enriching resources in himself to surface. However, his ambitious position did not develop correspondingly after it had lost its productive function. Rather, it became, more and more, a "shadow position" that he increasingly felt he "disowned." The two positions–being a supportive and wise mentor on the one hand, and, at the same time, feeling locked in the *I*-prison of his earlier ambitions on the other hand – were involved in a multi-level conflict.[19]

Multi-level conflict and the process of globalization The phenomenon of a multi-level conflict is particularly relevant to understanding the process of globalization on the level of the self. As argued earlier, globalization leads to an increasing density, heterogeneity, and changeability of positions in the self, unless the self shows counter-movements to these processes (as discussed in Chapter 1). As a result of border-crossings, heterogeneous elements are introduced into the self. Different positions, originating from different social and cultural backgrounds, show different developmental trajectories. Such trajectories are part not simply of a unified personal development, but rather of a diversity of social and cultural situations, each with their own traditions, values, expectations, and emotion rules. Such differences not only create a diversity of positions in the self, but also influence the speed, direction, and flexibility of the developmental trajectories of different positions. When those trajectories show significant differences in speed, direction or flexibility, the increasing tension between the different positions results in a multi-level conflict.

An example of a multi-level conflict emerged in the case of Hawa (Clarke, 2004), to which we referred in Chapter 1. Remember that she emigrated from Turkey to the Netherlands when she was 5 years old and at the age of 30 suffered from burnout. As part of an assessment by a psychotherapist she told different self-narratives, from her Dutch position and her Turkish position, with a severe conflict between the two. From the perspective of her Dutch position, her social development was central, and expressed in her frequent contacts with Dutch friends, a development that she experienced as positive and rewarding. However, as the daughter of a Turkish father she was confronted with social and emotion rules that she experienced as blocking her social development when living in the Netherlands. From the perspective of the developmental model presented here, she experienced her Dutch position as making progressive movements, whereas she felt her Turkish position as making regressing movements. However, in the course of psychotherapy, she discovered that her Turkish position also had positive aspects and was more beneficial to her development than she had realized earlier. After a period of conflict between the two positions, she found that they were instead mutually complementary and both welcome parts of her self. In terms of the developmental model presented here, it may be concluded that experiencing the two cultural positions as mutually complementary, rather than involved in a seemingly irreconcilable conflict, stimulated both positions, as part of an adaptive coalition, to a higher level of integration. As the case of Hawa suggests, it is possible to reconcile positions involved in a multi-level conflict, in such a way that they move together to a higher developmental level. In order to realize such a movement, promoter positions are needed as important facilitators. In Hawa's case, the psychotherapist fulfilled this role.[20]

We can ask what kind of social figures are particularly relevant as promoters in a globalizing society with its typical border-crossings, cultural diversity, and social and psychological tensions. We consider the following criteria relevant to define adequate promoters: (a) they have knowledge about different cultural groups, including their history, values, and normative rules; (b) they have a positive attitude towards other cultural groups and are willing to take their constructive potential for the development of the self into account; (c) they are critical not only of particular cultural practices, values, and rituals that belong to other cultures, but also of those of their own culture; (d) they are sensitive and open to different cultures as parts of one and the same self that includes a multiplicity of cultural positions; and (e) they are willing and able to foster dialogical relationships between people from different cultural origins and between different cultural positions in the self.

Social figures as promoter positions foster development as part of productive dialogical relationships. However, dialogical relationships have their potentials but also their constraints. When people feel that, as part of an exchange, their central positions are undermined or threatened, the innovative impact of dialogue is limited to more peripheral positions or to peripheral aspects of central positions. When, for example, the life of a person is organized around a central religious or political position involving inflexible dogma or rigid party rules, he or she will probably not give up this position or change its basic nature when invited into a dialogical relationship. When, however, central positions are open, questionable, or uncertain in the eyes of the individual, dialogue has the potential to contribute significantly to a reorganization of the self as a whole.

The double face of dialogue is that it has both decentering and centering potential. It is decentering because every new meeting with another person, even with a familiar one, may involve pleasant or unpleasant surprises and, as such, it decenters the self to some extent or even disorganizes it. At the same time, dialogue has the power to centralize experiences that were decentering at an earlier moment (both movements as represented by the lemniscate in Figure 4.1), moving the self up to a higher level of integration. Promoter positions are integrative forces *par excellence*, that, as part of a productive dialogue, stimulate the self in progressive ways.

Summary

The present chapter is based on the proposition that, in order to understand the workings of the dialogical self, it is necessary to have insight in its developmental origin. We began by describing some phenomena that can be considered precursors or early manifestations of the dialogical self. Referring to some experiments on tongue protrusion, the phenomena of imitation and provocation were analyzed as innate precursors of dialogue. So-called pseudo-dialogues in early mother–infant relationships and the role of imagination and memory were also discussed. The acts of giving and taking in the first year of life were treated as important non-verbal early manifestations of dialogue. A decisive moment in development is when joint attention, at the end of the first year of life, enables the child to perceive objects from the perspective of another person. This capacity makes it possible for parents or caretakers to point to the child herself as a common focus of attention. This discussion led to the conclusion that self-reflection and self-knowledge take place, from the beginning, in indirect ways (via the other) rather than in direct ways. We also pointed out the relevance of role-playing for the inclusion of new positions in the self and, building on Mead's well-known distinction between play and games, discussed the notion of the generalized other. We argued that this notion was based on a homogeneous society metaphor, but that it was less relevant to understand the uncertainties typical of a globalizing world where different social rules meet at the interface of different cultures.

We continued the discussion of the precursors of dialogue by referring to "dialogical frames," that, as question and answer sequences, are initially used in the interaction between parents and children and later used in the process of self-questioning by the child. The self-questioning technique functions as a precursor of self-consultancy procedures as discussed in Chapter 3. Central to understanding the spatial aspects of the dialogical self is the emergence of a personal space as an invisible, dynamic, and transportable space in the first year of life. Semi-permeable self–other boundaries are typical of a personal space indicating the relevance of the dimension open–closed for the development of the self. Particular attention was given to transcendental experiences in childhood, which are characterized not so much by a disappearance of self–other boundaries, but rather by their high permeability. The implication of the notion of open space for the dialogical self was discussed.

Because the dialogical self is considered as an embodied self, the development of the body and its corresponding movements (rolling over, crawling, standing, and walking) were analyzed as leading to important turning points in the way the world is perceived. This led to a discussion of the metaphorical implications of the body and its movements for the emergence of self-positions. Two main dimensions of the body, each with their polar opposites, were discussed: the vertical dimension (up versus down or top-dog versus underdog) and the horizontal dimension (here versus there or close versus distant). In line with this analysis, the connection between the body and the social and, moreover, between the social and the personal was explored. In addition, the difference between the notions of "voice" and "position" was analyzed.

A central place in this chapter was given to "promoter positions," which are distinctive by their openness towards the future development

of the self, by their potential to produce a diverse range of more specialized positions, and by their power to integrate and synthesize other positions. Two examples were fully explored: the emergence of the position "I
as acceptant" in the course of a psychotherapeutic process, and, from a
cultural-anthropological point of view, the phenomenon of "shape-shifting," which refers to the process of identification with a totem animal.
The similarities between these two seemingly disparate examples were
discussed on the basis of dialogical self theory.

Finally, a model for the development of the dialogical self was presented
with the focus on three kinds of movements: "progressive movements"
that stimulate the self to a higher level of integration; "regressive movements" that bring the self to a lower level of integration; and "balanced
movements" that are characterized by movements that do not, or do not
yet, lead to any progression or regression. Within the category of decentering movements a distinction was made between transition and disorganization and, elaborating on the latter phenomenon, the concept of "positive
disintegration" was introduced, referring to the existence of crisis as a
potentially progressive movement of the self. In this context, the integrative power of promoter positions was emphasized and we argued that they
have the potential to compensate for the disorganizing influence resulting from the change or even loss of core positions in the self. Elaborating
on the model presented, it was argued that multi-level conflicts are particularly relevant to the process of globalization. When the developmental trajectories of positions emerging from different cultural backgrounds
are different in their speed, direction, or flexibility, one cultural position
can be experienced as progressive while another one is felt as regressive,
resulting in a multi-level conflict. Promoter positions have the potential to
transform a multi-level conflict into a form of integration so that serious
conflicts lose their overwhelming prominence. The main features of promoter positions, able to function successfully at the interfaces of cultures,
were summarized.

NOTES

1 Imitation is not limited to physical movements. Newborn infants at an average of 36 hours of age were able to display facial expressions of happiness,
sadness and surprise when they were imitating an actress demonstrating
these expressions (Field *et al.*, 1982).
2 For a discussion of Bruner's model and its relation to Ludwig Wittgenstein's
middle and later work see Nicolaj Richers' article "How did they do it?
Language Learning in Bruner and Wittgenstein." www.bu.edu/wcp/Papers/
Lang/LangRich.htm.
3 In this context, Schore (2004) refers to the relevance of the right hemisphere
of the brain for non-verbal forms of dialogue. On the basis of a review of

recent neuro-scientific literature, he argues that empathy, identification with others, and more generally inter-subjective processes, are largely dependent upon right hemisphere resources, which are the first to develop. In apparent contrast to the conception that linguistic processes are typically associated with the left hemisphere, he emphasizes the critical function of the right hemisphere for the development of a dialogical self. Early social interactions are critical to non-verbal forms of the self and, in turn, these events impact the later development of a more complex dialogical self.

4 Referring to Vygotzky's work, we sometimes use the term "interiorization," whereas in dialogical self theory as a whole the concept of "extension" is central. These terms represent opposite movements. Whereas interiorization suggests a movement from the outside to the inside, extension implies a movement from the inside to the outside. We see this more as a formulation problem than as a conceptual problem. From a conceptual point of view, it is evident that one reaches to the outside in order to bring something inside. Like a hand that stretches out in order to take something from the environment, the developing self reaches out to the environment in order to incorporate something. In other words, the two movements imply each other in any interactional or dialogical relationship between self and world.

5 "Imaginary friends" or "imaginary companions" also play an important role as external positions in the dialogical self of many children. In a large-scale research project with approximately 1,800 children between the ages of 5 and 12 years, Pearson *et al.* (2001) found that 46.2% of them reported having imaginary friends. These findings were unexpected as previous studies suggested that imaginary friends are generally experienced by fewer, much younger children.

6 The notion "interiorization" is rooted in the Vygotzkian socio-cultural tradition, while the notion "appropriation" is proposed by William James in his writings about the self. In their historical origin and in their psychological meaning the two notions are not identical. In the context of dialogical self theory, we use the former notion to refer to the process that takes place when forms of positioning *between* self and the actual other develop into forms of positioning *within* the self, whereas we refer to the latter notion in order to describe the process of making a particular position one's own, which takes place when the *I* is able to incorporate that position as part of the self.

7 For a review of Kohnstamm's book, see Hviid (2007).

8 The relationship between brain processes and the blurring of self-boundaries was central in a study by Persinger (1987), who applied electromagnetic impulses to the temporal lobes of his adult subjects. The majority of his subjects reacted to this stimulation with the feeling that there was something or somebody "there." This being was sometimes experienced as a "God" or a "deceased loved one" or an "extraterrestrial being" or occasionally as a "self as outside of one's own body" (see also Kohnstamm, 2007).

9 From a semiotic point of view, Valsiner speaks of a "promoter sign." From a positional and dialogical point of view we prefer the concept of "promoter position." In its description we expand on the insights presented by Valsiner.

10 The development of promoter positions can also be achieved via specific meditation exercises. In the tradition of Tibetan Buddhism, meditation procedures have been developed in which the person starts by focusing on his breathing. Then, he imagines the figure of Buddha in front of him and observes him in three positions – wisdom, fearlessness, and compassion – as reflected in Buddha's body, facial expression, and posture. Next, he imagines the Buddha to be above his head and from there entering his mind. He then identifies with him. In this way, the meditating person interiorizes the three qualities of the Buddha as internal positions in his own self (for alternative practices, see Rinpoche and Mullen, 2005).

11 An important feature of a promoter position is its integrative function. It should be noted, however, that the introduction of a new promoter position can have, initially, a dramatically disorganizing effect on the self as demonstrated, for example, by the phenomenon of religious conversions (James, 1902/2004). After the promoter position is appropriated or received as an established part of the self, it can start to exert its integrating impact.

12 Just as a position in physical space offers a limited view, positions in the self are limited too. Memories, needs, expectations, plans, emotions, action tendencies, and perceived skills associated with a particular position fall within its boundaries. A horizon opens a particular view on self and world and limits it at the same time. Depending on the course of development of a position, its horizon may advance or recede. For example, a professional sportsman preparing for the Olympics may feel that he has unlimited possibilities, given his strength and capacities. However, as he gets older, he is confronted with the inevitable decline in his performance level and he becomes aware of the necessity of giving other positions a more central place in his repertoire. He feels that he has to attend to the shrinking horizon of his position as sportsman and decides, for example, to become a coach. Doing so, he can "transport" the skills and experiences of his previous position (sportsman) to his new position (coach), in this way avoiding his previous position becoming, at a certain point, an I-prison that moves his self to a lower level of integration. From a more general developmental point of view, we assume that an adequate answer to the shrinking horizon of a particular position is to give a more central place to another existing position or even develop a new position in which the experiences, capacities and skills of the previous, shrinking position can be introduced and integrated.

13 The concept of meta-position (discussed in Chapter 3) is different from the concept of promoter position. A meta-position permits a simultaneous overview of other positions, while a promoter position engenders and integrates positions in their temporal manifestation. A promoter position is also different from a "third position" (as discussed in Chapter 3). A third position is able to reconcile two or more conflicting positions and has, as such, an integrative function. However, it does not necessarily have a temporal extension in the sense that it engenders a new position in the future.

14 The lemniscate is a mathematical symbol for infinity. The sign was devised in 1655 by mathemetician John Wallis, and named "lemniscus" (Latin: ribbon) by mathemetician Bernoulli about forty years later. The religious

meaning of the infinity symbol predates its mathematical origin. Similar symbols have been found in Tibetan rock carvings, and the infinity-snake, called ouroboros, is often depicted in this shape. In the world of tarot, it represents the balance of forces (www.altreligion.about.com/library/glossary/symbols/bldefsinfinity.htm).

15 We may ask whether an "*I*-prison," from which the person cannot escape, is the result of a predominance of centralizing or decentralizing movements. An answer to this question can be found when one takes into account that an *I*-prison is an isolated position located among other positions that have become inaccessible. An overemphasis of centralizing movements results in a rigid organization of the repertoire whereas an overemphasis of decentralizing movements ends up in feeling lost. In both cases there is an *I*-prison.

16 The notion of "core position" is introduced in order to clarify the *organization* of positions and should not suggest the existence of a "core self," as a basic *conception* of the self as a whole, characteristic of the modern model of the self.

17 Dabrowski (1964) who took the notion of positive disintegration as the centrepiece of his theory, considered psychiatric disturbances, such as depression and neurosis, as positive contributions to personal growth and even as preconditions for reaching higher levels of development. By going so far, his theory was not well received by most of his colleagues, but we consider his notion of positive disintegration as a creative idea that can well be incorporated into dialogical self theory, particularly in understanding the dynamics of centering and decentering movements and their contribution to the further development of the self.

18 In a developmental study of conflict resolution, Borsch *et al.* (2006) investigated the dialogical capacity of ninety-one Dutch children of 4–12 years old, by inviting them to play with puppets that represented three positions, "I as sweet," "I as naughty," and "my mother." The children were instructed to imagine a conflict they had had with their mother and to tell how the story developed and ended. The investigators studied both the external conflict between child and mother and the internal conflict of the children with themselves, as expressed in the stories told. In both parts of the study it was found that the dialogical capacity, in terms of the number of successful resolutions of the conflict, increased systematically with age. Moreover, it was found that in all age groups, girls demonstrated a more developed dialogical capacity than boys. The conflicts studied in this investigation can be considered as uni-level conflicts because they evolve at the same level of integration.

19 More generally, there are at least four challenges that a person has to meet during the process of aging: (i) *increasing discrepancies in the developmental paths* of different positions, leading to an increasing probability of multi-level conflicts. As a result of these discrepancies some positions become obsolete, disowned, or dysfunctional and require a reorganization of the repertoire; (ii) the *shrinking* of the repertoire as a whole, resulting from the loss of social positions (societal roles) and significant others so that the repertoire is less able to deal with a diversity of situations; (iii) *reduced*

flexibility, that is, an increasing "mental stiffness" that makes it more difficult to move from one position to another one; (iv) *reduced openness* to new experiences and new positions so that the repertoire becomes increasingly organized around a limited amount of "ordinary positions" that function as obstacles to its innovation. Note that this is not a description of the process of aging but rather a depiction of some challenges. It depends on the dialogical capacity of the person and on the development of relevant promoter positions whether these challenges are met or not.

20 As this case study exemplifies, there are some basic differences between dialogical psychology and narrative psychology. While narrative psychology sees positions, expressed in terms of characters, figures, or images, as parts of an encompassing narrative, dialogical psychology assumes that a person has a multiplicity of narratives to tell, depending on the positions that emerge in a particular situation. Every existing narrative can be shaken, undermined, transformed, or adapted by the process of positioning, repositioning, and counter-positioning in which the self is continuously involved. While in narrative psychology story is superordinate to position, in dialogical psychology any narrative is subordinate to the process of positioning. While in narrative psychology time is more constitutive than space, in dialogical psychology, time (Chapter 4) and space (Chapter 3) are of equal importance. While in narrative psychology, centering movements (leading to unifying narratives) are emphasized, in dialogical psychology centering and decentering movements represent alternating phases in the developing self (Chapter 4).

5   A dialogical view of emotions

Let's not forget that the little emotions are the great captains of our lives and we obey them without realizing it.

Vincent Van Gogh

As already argued in the context of globalization (Chapter 1) emotions are embedded in a social context and result from real, imagined, anticipated, or recollected outcomes of social relationships. In this chapter we aim to elaborate on this view by showing that emotions are part of an organized position repertoire and play a crucial role in the process of dialogue both between people and within the self of an individual. Special attention will be given to some affective implications of the traditional, modern, and post-modern models of the self. As part of the post-modern model we will discuss the phenomenon of consumerism as having important implications for the emotional lives of many people in contemporary society. Love will be discussed as a most relevant feeling to the dialogical self. Finally, a stage model will be outlined that can be used as a procedure for the dialogical change of emotions.

Emotions and self

This chapter is based on the assumption that there is an intense interconnection between self and emotion and their relation is understood as *bi-directional* (see also Morgan and Averill, 1992): emotions have an influence on the self and, conversely, the self is able to confirm or change emotions. Let's briefly elaborate on each of these directions.

Emotions necessarily involve the self. For example, in anger the self is perceived as affronted, in fear as threatened, in grief as diminished, and in love as reaching out to another (Morgan and Averill, 1992). An emotion leads not only to a particular perception of the self, but it also organizes the self so that it is prepared to give a response to the situation at hand. As Greenberg (2002) holds, emotions are foundational in the construction of the self and a key determinant of self-organization. In flight–fight situations that arouse strong emotions, the self is organized in such a way that it responds as a whole. When the self feels attacked, *all parts* are organized so that the self is ready to retreat or prepare a counter-attack. In such situations there is a biological or evolutionary tendency to give a response that maximizes the survival chances of the individual. A strong emotion receives absolute priority in the self and all the other parts are subordinated to the prevailing emotion. This is not a situation of perfect integration of the different parts of the self, but rather a reaction in which the self is organized around one emotion only. As LeDoux (2002) has argued in his neuroscientific theory of the synaptic self, the self responds in such situations not so much as unitary but as a unit.

In order to investigate the influence of emotions on the self, Hermans-Konopka and Hermans (2010) instructed a group of 120 participants to indicate the changes in their selves caused by fourteen different emotions. Participants were instructed to select verbs that expressed their experience of a particular emotion. The verbs were classified as positive or negative and the participants could select particular verbs in order to refer to changes in self-experience. For example, a participant could say: "anxiety is imprisoning me" or "joy is warming me." The results showed that love, joy, self-esteem, and tenderness led to the most positively experienced changes in the self, while inferiority, anxiety, weakness, and loneliness caused the most negatively experienced changes in the self. It was also found that within the group of negative emotions, anger led to the most positive changes in the self. This suggests that reacting to a frustrating situation with anger, makes the self feel more positive than when it reacts with fear, powerlessness, or disappointment.

Emotions do not only change the self, but the self is also able to influence and change emotions. As LeDoux (2002) has suggested, the brain has two circuits for producing an emotion, a lower and a higher one. The lower circuit is involved when the amygdala, an important part of the limbic system involved in the processing of emotions, senses danger and produces an emergency signal to the brain and the body. The high circuit, slower than the lower one, is involved when the danger signal is carried from the lower parts of the brain to the neocortex. Because the lower circuit transmits signals more than twice as fast than the higher one, the reflecting brain is not well able to intervene and stop the emotional response in time. We jump back from a suddenly appearing figure in the dark or shout at an inconsiderate family member before we have a chance to correct ourselves. In some situations it is adaptive to respond quickly (e.g., in situations of danger), while in other situations it is more adaptive to think before acting (e.g., taking the intentions of the other into account). From a psychotherapeutic point of view, it is important to make use of the higher but slower road in the brain as an attempt to transform particular maladaptive responses into adaptive ones (Greenberg, 2002).

We assume that dialogical processes also, certainly those that have the form of explicit turn-taking behavior, follow the slower pathways of the brain. In an exploration of the neural foundations of the dialogical self, Lewis (2002) emphasizes that the biological purpose of emotion is to give attention to those aspects of the situation that are in some way important to the organism and urge the production of actions in order to deal with them. However, he adds that the control of attention by emotion is reciprocally related to the control of emotion by attention. In his view, attentional states amplify, and then regulate, emotions by appraisal of their causes and the generation of plans to resolve them. From a neural point of view, the relation between attention and action-planning is mediated by the frontal and prefrontal cortices that regulate processes on the executive level of anticipatory attention and control. At this level higher-order processes of volitional attention emerge as a basis for behavioral plans and actions. Of particular significance to the dialogical processing of emotions is the orbitofrontal cortext (see also Schore 1994), a region at the very base of the frontal lobe that is tuned to rewards and punishments in the environment. This region has dense connections with the lower amygdala, which is responsible for fear, anxiety, and some kinds of anger. It is, moreover, connected with the temporal lobes where perceptual, including auditory, input is processed and integrated, and with Broca's area which controls speech production and reception. In this way, the cortex in its connection with the amygdala and the speech center provides the neural conditions for the perception and regulation of emotions and their articulation in speech. These neural conditions allow the dialogical self not only to receive emotional input but also to regulate and alter it. As many psychotherapeutic traditions have argued, talking about emotions allows the self, under facilitating conditions, to change them.

Emotions as temporary positions in the self

Every position has its particular affective color or connotation. Being in a dependent position feels different from being in an independent position. When I'm listening to music in a concert hall, I have different feelings from those I experience when I'm chatting in a café late at night. In such cases I'm positioning myself somewhere, or I feel positioned, and this feels "good" or "bad" or otherwise. Even in contact with the same person, I can position myself in different ways and the affective connotation of the changing contact varies correspondingly. When I meet a person for the first time, it may be that I position myself in a quite formal way, but as soon as the contact evolves, we both become increasingly informal.

Not only do positions have their specific affective connotation, but *emotions themselves can become ways of positioning*. In that case, they become ways of *placing* oneself towards others or oneself, or *being placed* towards others or oneself. The concept of "emotion work" (Hochschild, 1983) articulates the nature of emotions as ways of positioning. Emotions are not purely internal processes, but parts of a highly dynamic social and societal process of positioning. Depending on the positions in which people find themselves, particular emotions are expected to emerge, whereas others are expected to be absent or suppressed. Under the influence of position-related expectations, some emotions are tolerated, accepted, emphasized, exaggerated, or denied, whereas others are not. When a waiter creates an atmosphere for pleasant dining, he tries to do this by his presence and behavior, and the guests, from their side, open themselves to enjoy it. When a social worker makes a client feel cared for, he tries to let the client feel this care and the client allows himself to receive it. Such emotion work is typical not only of social positions in the line of social or societal expectations but also of expectations or requirements of a more personal nature. People act on their feelings when they let themselves feel sad, permit themselves to enjoy a reward they have given to themselves after a hard task, convince themselves that they may feel grateful for the things they have received in their life, imaginatively exalt their feelings of love, or put a damper on their love ("I'm trying to convince myself that it is better not to love him"). In all those cases, emotions are considered not as purely intrapsychic impulses or as physiological reactions that take place within the skin, but as integral parts of an agentic process of social or personal positioning. People position themselves in an emotion in relation to the environment or in relation to themselves ("As an independent who has everything she wants, I expect myself to be happy").

The example of a game of bowls may illustrate what it means to *position* oneself as emotional. Kraut and Johnson (1979) observed bowls players either from the end of the lane or from the area where the others were waiting to take their turn. From the first point, their immediate reaction was observed after a strike or a spare or a failure. From the second point, their behavior was registered as immediately communicated to the other players. The result was that in the second case far more nonverbal emotional displays were observed. So, the enjoyment, pride, or disappointment were more clearly expressed when the player turned his face to the other players than when it was directed to the other side. It may be assumed that the player experienced an emotion even before he turned his face to the other players, but he "positioned" himself as glad or disappointed when he *placed* himself in this emotion *towards* the others in the group. In his expression of the emotion and corresponding bodily and facial movements, he let the others know how "good" or "bad" he felt about it.

Placing oneself in a particular emotion can also occur in the relationship that one entertains with oneself. When I am in strong disagreement with a colleague, I may notice that I'm becoming increasingly irritated, but I do not show this irritation and do not maintain myself in this emotion, because I don't want to disrupt my good relationship with him. However, later when I am home again and think it over, I begin to realize how inconsiderate he was. I again feel the same irritation and it grows into an even stronger anger. At a certain point, I explicitly address myself in my feelings of irritation and anger and say to myself "I'm really angry with him." At that moment I position myself as angry (towards my colleague) in the relationship with myself. I'm aware of my anger and confess it is "there" in the relationship with myself. The consequence may be that I decide to invite my colleague for a talk again, and discuss more explicitly what I had hidden or suppressed during our earlier talk.

Positioning oneself in a particular emotion can be entirely invisible to other people in one's environment. A person who is seen by others as successful and admired for his contributions, sees himself as a failure, because he has set his standards so high that he is never able to meet them. Even when he never expresses this to the outside world (maybe with the exception of his therapist), he explicitly places himself in the position of a "loser," saying to himself, "You are a total failure." Sometimes, people position themselves towards the outside world in a very different way from towards themselves, and it may even be that they experience, successively, different emotions in different contexts. They may actually feel pride when receiving respect from others, while feeling "inside" a continuous dissatisfaction that never disappears even when "objective" parameters contradict the low evaluation of themselves.

The conception of emotions as a way of positioning has implications not only for the intensity of an emotion (e.g. "I'm so angry at him!") but also for the depth of the experience. In her study of airlines flight attendants, Hochschild (1983) observed that, in the context of economic competition, some airlines exhorted their attendants to smile more, and "more sincerely," at their passengers. However, the workers, opposed to these exhortations, responded to this speed-up with a slow-down, that is, they smiled less broadly, without any sparkle in their eyes, and cut off the smile more quickly. The conflict between the company and the attendants ended up in a "war of smiles." As this example suggests, smiling as an expression of "feeling friendly" can go more deeply into the self or remain at the surface.

As a result of the process of positioning, emotions are processes moving on a continuum between "superficial" and "deep." Feelings of affection or love may become deeper when a person is "standing still" and becomes aware of all the good things he has received from his partner. Sadness becomes more "owned" when one goes "into it," doesn't fight against it, and sees it as the "other side of one's emotional life" that, like the positive side, asks for attention and even care. Generally, self-reflection and dialogue with oneself are not activities that are directed to "emotions in themselves," that have an existence separate from these activities. Rather, emotions are clarified and deepened as a result of concentrated self-reflection and focused dialogue and, as a result, even acquire new meanings. As soon as emotions are reflected upon or shared with another or oneself, they reveal aspects that were not experienced before. Self-reflection and dialogue are not abstract processes that are directed to ready-made emotions. Self-reflection, like dialogue, may be critical, amused, quiet, accepting, or ironic and these qualities add or contribute something to the emotions that was not there before.

Positioning as consonant or dissonant with emotions

The term "emotion work" may easily be misunderstood. Apart from the fact that it sounds quite technical, it could suggest a one-way relationship between self and emotion, as if emotions can be fully controlled or changed by the efforts of the self. It could imply mistakenly that an emotion, like a piece of clay, can be modeled into any form that the *I* wants to give it. In order to rebut such a view it is important to investigate the process of positioning in a more differentiated way. This can be done by making a distinction between positioning in which the self is *consonant* with an emerging emotion, and positioning in which the self is *dissonant* with it. Consonance can be observed when the person positions himself in accordance with the specific experiential quality of the emotion. When, for example, I give space to my sadness so that it can reveal itself in its own experiential quality, then I position myself in consonance with the emotion. When, however, I position myself in a way that does not take into account the specific experiential quality of the emotion, there is a dissonant way of positioning. This can be observed when I actually feel unhappy but define myself as happy, wanting to escape from an emotion which I do not want to experience or tolerate when communicating with myself and others. Certainly, as we have argued earlier in this section, the process of positioning is able to amplify, enlarge, and even transform an emotion. At the same time, we should take into account that there are ways of positioning that acknowledge emotions in their own specific experiential tone (consonance), and other ways that neglect, reject, or suppress the specific experiential nature of a particular emotion. Along these lines, a theoretical view of emotions can be developed that puts a high premium on the experiential quality of emotions and, at the same time, takes the positional and social nature of self and emotions into account.[1]

Emotions as organismic positions

When we said in the beginning of the chapter that we assume a bi-directional relationship between self and emotions (they make up each other), then this implies that the self is, to a large degree, subject to the influence of emotions and can at times even be overwhelmed by them. Emotions "come up," gradually or abruptly, even when they are unwelcome (e.g., anger during a formal meeting or ceremony). When we conceptualize an emotional process in terms of positioning, we must acknowledge that we are not only *positioning* ourselves in an emotion (e.g., I position myself as happy), but also are *positioned by* emotions. We can become irritated even when we consciously want to be friendly and we can feel nervous and anxious even when we cannot find any "objective" reason for that. Apparently, the *I* is forced to be receptive when emotions come up in the self and "occupy" the space of the self.

In a profound discussion of types of positions, Lysaker and Lysaker (2008) propose a new concept, the *organismic position*, that can function as a bridge between biologically based tendencies and the functioning of the dialogical self. Talking about moments where we feel threatened, they say:

In these instances, the self encounters itself as it performs basic elemental functions, for example, monitoring energy levels or the relative safety of one's environment. Imagine a situation in which a fight or flight reaction occurs. In this instance, at a pre-reflective level, one senses oneself as threatened and responds with a strong disposition to either flee or confront the threat. Once again, one can interpret and respond to this encounter, but this is nevertheless an event in which one's being is disclosed to itself. It is part of the conversation. Neuroscience suggests that in flight–fight scenarios the brain functions quite differently. Higher cortical functions involved in the prefrontal cortex become less involved, yet there is still a self being experienced. People can be aware during those experiences and certainly deal with them afterwards. (2008: 52)

In line with the bi-directional relationship between self and emotion, the self is subjected to the urgency of organismic positions, yet able to evoke a counter-position which not only limits the influence of the organismic impulse, but may also lead the self into an internal conflict. Lysaker and Lysaker give the example of a group of male friends who are hanging around outside a bar. Suddenly, they are aggressively approached by another group of men. Startled and threatened, most of them feel a strong tendency to flee. However, those who feel an urge to flee, feel at the same time the pull of loyalty to their friends. They feel caught between the organismic position "I as threatened" and the more social position "I as a friend." Seeing the faces of their friends and feeling their loyalty make them stay. This example shows, according to the authors, how organismic positions can become involved in an inter-animating play with social positions. The organismic position produces an action tendency that, given its urgency, could lead to an impulsive flight, but actually this flight does not take place. It receives a counter-force from the part of a social position that eventually appears to be the most dominant one in this situation. The example suggests that action tendencies produced by organismic positions do not simply determine the self and its behavior, but become part of an interplay of positions at the interface of the biological and the social. In similar ways, the embodied self can be subjected to fatigue or to sexual impulses but, as soon as the self becomes aware of them, they meet other positions, personal and social, with their implied social rules and expectations. In as much as the organismic positions are felt by the self as incompatible with personal and social positions, this may lead to internal negotiations such as, "I feel exhausted, but as a colleague I'm expected to finish this document before tomorrow," or "I feel very attracted to her, but, because she is the wife of my friend, I have to control myself." Important emotions (like anger, anxiety, and sexual impulses) can be considered as organismic positions that are biologically and evolutionarily-based, yet they can be "lifted up" as dynamic parts of a multi-voiced self. Once admitted there, they find themselves at an interface where they meet personal and social positions as their adversaries or allies. The inclusion of the concept of organismic position into dialogical self theory enables a bringing together of the biological, the social, and the personal as parts of a multi-voiced self.[2]

The other-in-the-self as co-determining the nature of emotions

The conception of an emotion as a way of positioning has implications that go even beyond the purely internal experience of it. When the emotion is part of an *I–other* relationship, then the position of the other in the extended domain of my self *co-constructs the nature of the emotion.* For example, I'm angry with a person who accuses me of something, particularly when I'm convinced that I'm wrongly accused. Suppose that the same person accuses me a second time about the same thing and with the same words. Then, the anger that I experience the second time will be different in intensity and tone from the first time. I know and feel that he is accusing me *again*, and this "again" makes the emotion which I feel now no longer entirely the "same" emotion as earlier. It is very possible that the "again-awareness" makes me even angrier than before. It is also possible that, in the case of many successive accusations, I get used to the series of accusations and react with some form of indifference. In other words, the emotion is to a certain degree "colored" by its *positional history*, including the experience one has had with others on previous occasions.

An emotion is influenced not only by its positional history, but also by its *positional context*. An emotion caused by the behavior of another person is influenced by the extent to which the other is connected with other positions in one's repertoire. When a good neighbor leaves for another country and I'm aware that I probably will never see her again, I may be sad. However, when the person who leaves me is at the same time my husband, the father of my children, my lover and my sports-partner, then my sadness will be more intense, deep, and more persistent than in the case of my neighbor. Apparently, the intensity, depth, and duration of an emotion, evoked by an external position, is influenced by the density and variety of its connections with other positions in the repertoire.

Emotions are not only part of *I–other* relationships, they are also part of *I–me* relationships and their positional history and context influence them in ways that are similar to those of internal and external *positions*. Emotions, conceived of as internal positions, have a history in which they are preceded and coexist with a range of other emotions that co-construct their nature. A feeling of relaxation may be extra deep after a period of stress, risk, or danger and an emotion of anxiety may come as an unpleasant surprise when it occurs in a situation in which one previously used to feel quite safe. The same applies to the emotion of the other. My experience of anger or love on the part of the other is co-dependent on the history and context of the other as a position in my self.

Because the *I* is aware of the history and context of emotions, they emerge amidst a range of other emotions and feelings that influence them. Anger or irritation can emerge through the annoying behavior of a loved one, but the emotion is softened by the care one feels for this person. Or, a person who flushes in embarrassing situations, may feel anxiety in the expectation that it may occur again. Or, disappointment that one feels as a result of the neglectful behavior of another can be ameliorated by the awareness that one feels very grateful for all the benefits one has received from this person previously. Or, gratitude may be strongly felt when one knows about the sacrifices this person made in order to give you pleasure. Given the extension of the self over time, one knows about emotions and feelings that intensify, lessen, deepen, or change the emotion that is presently emerging in a particular situation.

Positions organized as a composition of stones

In order to study the organization of positions, including emotions, we developed a method in which positions are represented by stones that differ in size, form, color, and texture. Clients are invited to select from a large pool of stones those most likely to represent particular positions that are most prevalent in their lives. After the selection, they are asked to arrange the stones as a composition that fits the experience of the positions in the metaphorical space of their self. In this way, the spatial organization of the positions, that is, their mutual distance, separation, proximity, and, particularly, their centrality and marginality can be studied and discussed with the client.

One of our clients selected a group of stones that she organized in the form of a circle. Two of them, "I as anxious" and "I as angry" were placed at the periphery at a considerable distance from the other stones. The client explained that these positions were marginalized under the influence of another position, "I as critical," that was assigned a place near the centre of the circle. She made clear that the critical position was responsible for the suppression of the two other positions that were clearly "disowned" and had the character of "shadow" positions. Her critical and rejecting attitude towards her anxiety and anger caused these positions to be exiled, although the client felt, at the same time, that they were important parts of her self. When the therapist invited her to consider the composition of the stones as a whole and say more about the way they were organized, the client answered: "In order to be more myself, I need to move them." Saying this, she took the stone representing her critical position in her hand and moved it far from the center. Then she took the two stones representing her angry and anxious positions and moved them to a place near the centre. Doing this, she said: "This one [critical] must be moved away; when they [angry and anxious] are in the centre, I can be myself." As this sentence suggests, her emotions of anger and anxiety were not simply experiences in themselves, but rather were suppressed and seen as unacceptable from the perspective of her critical position. After moving them to the centre, she said that she felt "closer to herself," while before moving them she felt more distant towards herself. This suggests that the place of an emotion as part of an organized position repertoire influences the experience of the emotion as part of the self (e.g., as owned or disowned).

Stability and rigidity of emotions

In dialogical self theory, emotions are conceived of as temporary *I*-positions. They typically come and go. Emotions such as anger, sadness, and anxiety on the negative side, and joy, enjoyment, and happiness on the positive side, are typically contingent on events that are taking place and on the way the self responds towards these emotions. They can prevail temporarily in the affective domain of the self, but they typically fade away and make room for other emotions after some time.[3]

However, there are examples of emotions that are to some degree innate and so frequently aroused that they seem to have a trait-like character. For example, "neuroticism," one of the traits of the so-called Big Five, includes chronic anxiety, depression, nervousness, excessive emotionality, moodiness, hostility, self-consciousness, vulnerability, and hypochondria, all converging in this basic and general factor. Patients suffering from generalized anxiety and depression show elevated levels of neuroticism (e.g. Eysenck and Eysenck, 1985). Research has suggested considerable heritability estimates for the Big Five traits. In a large research project on monozygotic (identical) and dizygotic (fraternal) twin pairs, Loehlin, McCrae, and Costa (1998) obtained heritability estimates ranging from 51% to 58% for the Big Five traits, suggesting that basic traits, including neuroticism, are already, in the main, established from birth onward. Given the fact that a great deal of the research on the Big Five traits is based on self-reports, it is probable that neuroticism establishes a basis for self-definitions such as "I as fearful" or "I as anxious" representing self-positions of a chronic and stable nature.[4]

Anger is another example of a position that can, under the influence of significant life events, become stabilized and persistent over time. When transient anger becomes stabilized and rigid over time, it can become transformed into hostility. Murray (1962) provided a profound analysis of a type of personality organization characterized by persistent, outwardly directed hostility. He mentioned the following features of people with a so-called "satanic personality": (a) a secret feeling of having been harshly, treacherously, or unjustly deprived of what they feel to be well-earned benefits, rewards, and glory; (b) a basic state of alienation, resentment, and distrust; (c) a hidden envy coupled with overt contempt for the achievements of others; (d) repression of any guilt feelings;

and (e) the adoption of a strategy – slyness, evasiveness, subversion, or destructiveness – for venting their self-consuming hatred. A characteristic by which they are most easily identified is the absence of any capacity to experience or express love, gratitude, admiration, or compassion (Murray, 1962: 49). Murray's satanic personality is characterized by hostility as a generalized and chronic form of anger that can function as a basis for stabilized and rigid positions that are central in the organization of the self. (As further evidence for the stability of emotions, see also Lupton's (1998) notion of "emotional style," which disposes individuals to respond to a diversity of situations with a particular emotion.)

In summary, dialogical self theory acknowledges the existence of both transient and more stable emotions. The stability of emotions may be the result of genetic factors (e.g., neuroticism) or significant life events (e.g., frustrating experiences leading to a satanic personality).

The emotion of the other-in-the-self

Several emotion theories (e.g., Arnold and Gasson, 1954; Frijda, 1986; Lazarus, 1991) emphasize the role of *action tendencies* in emotions that can be understood in terms of readiness to act towards the environment in specific ways. Frijda (1986) expanded on this notion of felt action tendency and argued that at the core of an emotion experience is the awareness of action readiness (e.g., awareness of an urge to attack, run, or embrace), which includes a sense of urgency or impulse to behave in a particular way.

A common characteristic of the emotion theories mentioned is that they are cognitive or interactional rather than dialogical. In their discussion of emotions they give a central place to the appraisal of the situation. Depending on the way a situation is perceived and appraised, a particular emotion emerges. This appraisal seems to be based on a conception of personality or self in which the other has no place. The emotion is directed to the world and to the other as outside realities. As far as these theories assume – explicitly or implicitly – a self, this self shows a clear affinity with the modern model of the self in which the self functions as a monadic entity influenced by the other *but not constituted by it*.

A dialogical view in which the other is an intrinsic part of the self, has important implications for the elucidation of emotions as positions in the self. In such a view, the self experiences action tendencies not only towards the other but also from the other towards the self. Because the other is included as the-other-in-the-self, the self remembers, imagines, and anticipates action tendencies not only from the self to the other but also from the other to the self. The interchange between imagined, remembered, and anticipated actions from both sides is constitutive for the nature of the resulting emotion. That is, the emotion is not only self-exclusive but also other-inclusive.

The other-inclusive nature of emotion can be exemplified by a case that reflects many situations in everyday life. Person A has made an agreement with a colleague (person B) to cooperate on a common project in a situation of relative autonomy. They work together and both entertain contacts with a group of clients. After some time A criticizes B for the way he interacts with one of the clients. Person B, however, feels this as intrusive and reacts with anger about what he sees as unjustified criticism. As a reaction, Person A also becomes angry and accuses his colleague of rigidity and unwillingness to take his "fair" feedback into account. Person B now becomes even angrier than before and threatens to stop cooperating if A does not change his behavior. Then, A breaks their agreement in an upsurge of rage. Imagine that this escalation takes place in the course of a series of incidental meetings and telephone conversations. The anger and rage increase because both follow their action tendencies, exacerbated by vivid and emotional ideas not only about their own actions but also about those of their colleague. In more general terms, adaptive and maladaptive behavior results not only from the immediate perception of each other's actions but also from imagining each other's actions and reactions – something that is difficult to explain in terms of "appraisal." The notion of appraisal is not sensitive to the processes that are taking place *within* the self. The significant other as a position in the self does not exist in isolation but is dynamically related to other positions in the repertoire. In the example of the two colleagues, the persons involved in the conflict will explicitly or implicitly remember similar conflicts with other people in the past. These other people are included in the external domain of the repertoire and the emotions that played a role in the past are actualized by the present conflict and have an influence on it. The notion of "appraisal" does not seem sensitive to the position history and context of the other-in-the-self as connected to the present actual interaction with the other.

Emotion as movement in space

There is a close and intrinsic connection between emotions and movements as expressed by their etymological connection. The English word "emotion" is based on the Latin *emovere*, where *e-*, a variant of *ex*, means "out" and *movere* means "to move." Moreover, because the concept of emotion is closely related to movement, the notion of space is involved. Both movements and emotions are spatial.

Evidence for the conception of emotion and movement as spatial phenomena lies in the observation that emotions are expressed in the form of bodily movements and that, moreover, different emotions involve different types of movements. For example, joy broadens the experienced space and induces the body to make upward movements (e.g., jumping about playfully). Anxiety is related to the Latin word *angustus* which means "narrow," and, in a wider sense, "oppressive." This emotion significantly narrows the experience of space and typically triggers a movement of fleeing from, or, in some instances, fighting against. Anger hardens the body and produces a movement *against*, and contempt makes the person look down on another and produces a movement *away*. An emotion induces a particular spatial positioning of the body and is expressed in a particular movement in relation to the person or object that evokes the emotion.

Emotion as spatial movement: an exercise   In one of our workshops on emotional coaching, we invited the participants to remember or imagine a situation in which they experienced a strong emotion. They were invited to express this emotion as movements in space. After this part of the procedure, they were invited to imagine another emotion, very different from or even opposite to the first and express this emotion also as a movement in space. In order to introduce a dialogical aspect, the participants were invited to express the "message" of each emotion in a sentence, so that the nature of the emotion could be more deeply explored. In order to illustrate this process, we use the examples of two participants.

Example One.
A manager in a large company, 45 years old, described a situation in which she was with a colleague who criticized her openly in front of her team. She remembered that her first emotion was considerable anger, but this anger was blocked by anxiety. When she was invited to express this anxiety in movement, she restricted her movements and closed her body, with her arms crossed on her chest as if protecting herself. She seemed to restrain herself in her body, and was shrinking as if her body had become smaller. Overall, she seemed to be very small and tense. When she was asked to let her anxiety speak, she said, "You should not say anything because, if you do, he will leave and will not come back."

When she was asked to mention a very different or opposite emotion, she referred to happiness and expressed this by a series of opposite movements. Her body, and arms in particular, opened and made broad movements as if she was receiving something that was coming from the outside. Her breathing became deeper and more free and she made eye contact with the people around her. Her happiness gave the following message: "You have the right to be yourself and to say what you feel; there is nothing wrong with it."

Example Two.
The owner of a small company, 55 years old, was dissatisfied with the results of his business. He remembered a situation in which he was sitting in front of his computer, writing e-mails. The knowledge that his company was not successful made him feel totally powerless. He could not go on, and felt blocked and almost paralyzed. He experienced two emotions which were both prominent in this situation but felt very different from each other: anxiety and anger. Anxiety was clearly expressed in his body and movements. His body looked smaller and became immobile. He bent as if he was carrying a heavy burden on his back and his breathing was quick and superficial. He said that he imagined a rope around his belly that did not allow him to breath easily. His body looked frozen and his movements were blocked. From the perspective of his anxiety he said: "Look at yourself, how difficult it is for you, you had thought that you could do it, but you cannot."

When he expressed his anger, his posture straightened. It was as if he had become taller and he took up more space. He looked straight and quite tense. The message of his anger was: "You will manage it, you have freedom to do it, you have already done so much, you will do it again."

Different and opposite emotions are often expressed by different and opposite movements in physical space. We assume that such differences and oppositions are also present in the self-space. Emotions such as anxiety and inferiority restrict the self-space, while anger, hardening the body, fortifies it. Emotions of joy and happiness, opening the body to the outside world, lead to the expansion and enrichment of the self-space. Emotions organize both the physical and the metaphorical self-space. Some emotions take more space, others take less space, some emotions expand it, others let it shrink. These differences correspond with the way the space is felt. For example, feeling unsafe is associated with a space that is threatening and unlivable in, joy makes it bright and boredom makes it feel empty.

The body and bodily movements in space function as a physical basis for the metaphorical movements in a multi-positional self. Typically, people experience spatial differences in their relationships with different people. In some contacts the experienced space is small and there is not much opportunity to "move freely." The other person or group is experienced as "restrictive," "oppressive," or as "blocking" one's desires to go in a particular direction. In other contacts, the experienced space can be surprisingly wide. In the contact with such a person or group, one feels typically "free" to move in the desired direction or even to explore very different directions. In particular, contacts and activities that are felt as "inspiring" broaden the experienced space and widen the horizon in the self. In other words, those external positions that create space for the development of a variety of internal positions are typically experienced as space-enlarging and facilitating of a diversity of (metaphorical) movements in a variety of directions. Positions that have the meaning of a promoter in the self (see Chapter 4) are space-enlargers *par excellence*.

As the above examples show, emotions not only have bodily and spatial implications, but also have narrative and dialogical implications, that is, they have something to tell. Emotions, conceived of as *I*-positions, can assume a voice and can give a message. This message invites the person to adopt in a receptive mode and listen to the content of the message. This brings us to a discussion of some dialogical aspects of the process of positioning.

Messages of emotions and their restrictions

In order to arrive at a dialogical view of emotions, it is necessary to add an additional and fundamental element to emotions as processes of positioning. Emotions not only have their own experiential quality, as *I*-positions in a dialogical self, but they also have their own *message* to tell, that is, they can *address* self and others from their own specific point of view. For their part, self and others can listen to the message of an emotion or not and they can silence it or not. Self and others can also respond or not respond to the emotion and agree or disagree with it. It is at this point that social and cultural rules and conventions come in. Questions, responses, agreements, and disagreements are, to a large extent, influenced by social and cultural rules that allow people to speak or not speak directly from the position of a particular emotion. For example, positive emotions (e.g. "I like you" or "I admire you") generally receive more space for expression in social relationships than negative emotions (e.g., "I despise you," or "I'm jealous of your success"). As a consequence, many people have difficulties in accepting such emotions in themselves and others, so they cannot give an adequate response to them.

As a position in the self, an emotion becomes involved in monological or dialogical processes. Because in the present theory we conceive both emotions and the self as social, they are similarly subjected to cultural *restrictions* and *privileges* (Averill, 1997). When the expression of an emotion is forbidden in a particular social milieu, it does not leave much space for dialogical relationships. In many cultural groups an unmarried person is not allowed to express feelings of love toward a married one. Or, an adolescent who experiences homosexual desires is not allowed to express these emotions and, as a consequence, he is left alone with these feelings or even has to suppress them. When the adolescent despises this part of himself and rejects it, the relationship within the self is monological rather than dialogical. On the other hand, when people are privileged by social rules to experience and express particular emotions, they are more able to approach their emotions in dialogical ways. In Chapter 3 we referred to a woman, Rosanne, who lived as a lesbian in a conservative Brazilian milieu. She felt seriously constrained about sharing her feelings and experiences with others and was involved in a serious conflict between her Catholic and her lesbian position. Finally, in a lesbian community she found not only the space to express and share her feelings, but was also able to develop a "missionary" position that motivated her to help other members of the community who lived in deprived circumstances. As these illustrations suggest, social rules, restrictions, and privileges determine to a large degree whether emotions become part of monological or dialogical relationships.

Social rules and opportunities restrict or stimulate dialogical expression and the sharing of emotions, but in addition the intensity and persistence of emotions have implications for their dialogical expression and development. When an emotion is intense and persistent (e.g., an enduring depression or in the phenomenon of hostility, as a persistent form of anger), it may dominate the self to such a degree that self and others feel unable to give a response that would make a difference. It is as if the emotional person is not able to take into account any counter-message from the part of his self, from the other-in-the-self, or from the actual other. The emotion exercises a firm grip on the self so that it becomes monological as the result of the dominating voice of the emotion. When, however, the self is flexible enough and the emotion only temporarily dominant, there is sufficient space for the self and for the other to produce a counter-message to which the *I* is able and willing to listen. As the result of a dialogical relationship between self and emotion, the emotion can be changed or transformed, but this is not to be seen as a necessity. The emotion can also be confirmed and accepted in itself. When one is willing to take a dialogical view of emotions, one of the consequences is that self and emotion are equal "democratic" partners in this dialogue. Each party has the right to speak from its own point of view and one of the parties has not, a priori, more authority in the interchange than the other. Any final decision or outcome is the result of a preceding interchange. In this interchange emotions have their own "freedom of speech."

The difference between emotions and feelings

In the psychological literature, emotion and feeling are often distinguished. Many researchers distinguish feeling and emotion, where feeling refers to the subjective experience of the emotion. Izard (1990), for example, defines emotions as a system which has three main aspects: neurophysiological, expressive and subjective. Feelings are defined as the subjective, experiential aspects of emotions. However, in the context of the present theory, it seems worthwhile to articulate the difference between emotions and feelings in a dialogical context.

First-order phenomenology and second-order awareness

In a thorough comparison and analysis of different emotion theories, Lambie and Marcel (2002) argue that there are two kinds of emotion experiences, which they call "first-order phenomenology" and "second-order awareness." In the former case the emotion experience has phenomenological "truth," while in the latter case a person is reflexively aware of the emotional experience. For example, when the experience of anger takes the form of "he *is* a bastard" there is first-order phenomenology, while in the phrase "I'm angry at him" there is second-order awareness. The authors emphasize that the two forms of experience can also be directed to the self ("self-focused"). When I say "I'm a total failure," this is a first-order experience because there is a claim to phenomenological truth. This is different from the sentence "I feel inferior," which refers to a second-order experience. In the first case, the emotion experience refers to "how I am," while in the second case, there is a recognition and awareness that I experience the self in this or that way.

Although Lambie and Marcel favor a more restrictive conception of the self than the extended view proposed in this book, we find their distinction of the utmost importance for a dialogical view of the self. The reason is that an emotion experience as first-order phenomenology leads to a blurring of the distinction between the other-in-the-self and the actual other. This phenomenology implies the conviction that the way I define the other is not a matter of "my definition influenced by my emotions," but the other as he really is. Awareness that the other-in-the-self is an imagined other that never can fully coincide with the "real other" is absent as long as the self adheres to this phenomenology. It is not admitted and even not considered that the real other has his own perspective that never fully coincides with what is imagined about this other person. *Exclusive truth claims* about the other, implied by first-order-phenomenology, do not recognize this distinction because it is in their nature to see the imagined other as identical to the other as he or she "really is." Apparently, this phenomenology fails to make a distinction between imagination, interpretation, and assumption on the one hand, and "reality" on the other hand. As a consequence, productive dialogue is impeded or even impossible when emotion experiences are expressed with the claim that one's "truth" matches objective reality. Dialogue becomes possible only when parties engaged in an emotional interchange make a distinction between their spontaneous tendency to claim the truth and their self-reflexive awareness that it is their emotional experience that leads them to judge and evaluate reality from a particular position or perspective. In other words, in order to arrive at a point of second-order awareness, it is necessary to consider the influence of emotions as internal positions on the image of others as external positions in the self. When this awareness increases, there is more recognition of the difference between the other-in-the-self (external position) and the actual other. The inclusion of the internal positions in second-order awareness leads to recognition that the way I see the other is my construction and interpretation of the other. When this recognition emerges, there is space for dialogue, because the dialogical space is enlarged by the recognition of multi-perspectivity and multi-positionality, while the dialogical space is limited or even absent when the recognition is supplanted by the claims to exclusive truth of one of the parties involved.

Full development of the second-order awareness of emotions requires a recognition of the positional history and positional context as discussed at the beginning of this chapter. When an emotion leads to an evaluation of the other (individual, group, or culture), there can be a full awareness of this emotion only when the history of the internal and external positions involved in this evaluation are recognized as factors that co-determine the intensity, duration, and tone of the emotion. The same applies to the positional context: there are always other positions, internal and external, that are co-tuning the emotional experience.

The distinction between the two kinds of emotion experiences, first-order phenomenology and second-order awareness, allows us to distinguish between emotions and feelings in the context of dialogical self theory. Emotion is a broader concept, referring to both kinds of experience. Feeling is the more restrictive concept and can be seen as a subcategory of emotion. It refers to those emotion experiences where there is a reflexive or dialogical awareness of the emotion itself and its place in the organization of the self. That is, there is an awareness of the way the emotion influences one's internal and external positions, including their history and context.

Primary and secondary emotions

Whereas Lambie and Marcel (2002), as emotion theorists, deal with the distinction between awareness and truth claims of emotions, Greenberg (2002) is interested, from a psychotherapeutic perspective, not only in truth claims of emotions but also in different *levels* of emotions. He distinguishes *primary emotions* that he sees as people's gut responses to situations and *secondary emotions* that are emotional reactions to primary emotions (e.g., experiencing anxiety about one's anger). Primary emotions are the first responses to a stimulus situation, such as anger at violation, fear at threat, and sadness at loss and, as such, they are adaptive emotions. They are reactions to something happening here and now and they fade away as soon as the situation that has produced them disappears or has received an adequate response. As contingent on the situation, they come and go and can be seen as adaptive reactions. Primary emotions, however, *can* become maladaptive in the event of the emotional systems malfunctioning as, for example, in the case of traumatic experiences or genetic influences. Primary emotions then disturb the normal ongoing stream of experience and are not adequate in view of the situation in which they occur. Generally, people feel stuck in these emotions and they last long after the situation that caused them. As Greenberg explains, some emotions become maladaptive through traumatic learning. An originally adaptive emotion, such as appropriate fear of gunshots in a battle, become so deeply entrenched in the self that it generalizes to situations that are no longer dangerous. For example, a person ducks for cover and relives horrifying scenes of war every time a car backfires.

Secondary emotions, in Greenberg's view, are responses to or defenses against primary emotions. Often they are troublesome because they obscure what people experience on a deeper affective level. A client may feel depressed but this depression is covering a deeper emotion of anger. Or, a client may feel resentful, but on a lower level she feels hurt and is afraid to admit it. On the basis of their social training in childhood, many men have been told that they have to be strong and, as a result, they have difficulty admitting their primary emotion of fear. Many women, on the other hand, have been told that they should be submissive, and so they may cry when they are actually angry. In our terms, men and women have different position histories and, as a consequence, they are trained to respond with different secondary emotions.

The distinction proposed by Greenberg, from a psychotherapeutic point of view, is very different from the distinction that Lambie and Marcel provided from a theoretical point of view. However, they both emphasize the importance of emotional awareness. Greenberg (2002:60) does so by emphasizing that:

> The first and most general principle of change in emotion coaching is the promotion of increased emotional awareness, which enhances functioning in a variety of ways. Becoming aware of and symbolizing certain types of emotional experience in words provides access both to the information and to the action tendency in the emotion. It also helps people make sense of their experience and promotes the assimilation of this experience into people's ongoing self-narrative. Emotional awareness is not thinking about feeling; it involves experiencing the feeling in awareness.

As this quotation clearly suggests, changing of emotions begins with awareness of emotions. An important part of this awareness is a self-exploration that is profound enough to lead to the discovery of the primary basis of secondary emotions. As long as primary emotions are covered by secondary ones, the person is not able to become fully aware of them, so that their inclusion as part of a developing self is impaired. The lack of accessibility of primary emotions is an obstacle for their inclusion in a meaningful dialogue. The person who communicates her secondary anger but not her primary sadness, keeps the dialogue at a superficial level because it prevents the understanding of the sadness and isolates this emotion from the immediate contact with the other. Moreover, communicating only the secondary emotion prevents the person from receiving support from the other on the level of the primary emotion. Primary emotions can become part of a truly dialogical self when they are taken up in verbal and non-verbal dialogues in which emotions are able to send their messages to the self and the self is able to respond to them in such a way that the emotional part of the self changes and develops in accordance with the rest of the repertoire.

We assume that emotions become feelings when they are lifted up to the level of awareness. As long as primary emotions are covered by secondary ones, they are not accessible to awareness and, therefore, they are emotions but not feelings. They become feelings as soon as they become accessible to self-reflection and dialogue.

Authenticity and the emotion of the other

On the basis of the preceding considerations, it is possible to shed some light on the notion of authenticity. In Lietaer's (1993) and Greenberg's (2002) view, authenticity or "congruence" (between experience and self) can be broken down into two separate components: (i) "the ability to be aware of one's internal experience; and (ii) transparency, that is, "the willingness to communicate to the other person what is going on within oneself"' (Greenberg, 2002: 100). And, in order to understand what is going on in the person, this communication should take into account not only what is taking place on the level of secondary emotions but also, and predominantly, on the level of primary emotions. The advantage of this conception is that authenticity receives a clearly communicative imprint. Authenticity is not only having contact with one's own experiences and emotions, but refers also to communication with the other.

However, a dialogical view of authenticity goes beyond an experiential view. In a dialogical conception of authenticity, dialogue has profound implications for the experience of emotions. First, there is not only a communication from one person to another, but also vice versa. Second, this communicative feedback from an actual or imagined other, organizes it, confirms it, or changes it to some degree. Third, dialogue is more than communication, in that it not only communicates a particular emotion, information, or message, but also adds something to the emotion that was not there at the outset of the communication. New elements are added to the emotion as a result of being embedded in a process of innovative dialogue.

Part of the new elements is the *emotion of the other* with whom the person communicates. When I'm experiencing an emotion in the context of a dialogue, I'm not only experiencing my own emotion but also the actual or imagined emotion of the other. These two emotions are not separate experiential elements that are simply exchanged like bits of information. Instead, they influence and organize each other from the beginning of the dialogical process. Just as two thoughts that are communicated and brought into dialogue may influence and change each other, so two emotions that are communicated influence and change each other. Although to change an emotion, given its nature, needs more energy and time, this does not refute the basic similarity between the communication of emotions and the communication of thoughts.

In order to understand a dialogical view of emotions, a distinction has to be made between communication and dialogue. When people communicate extensively about anything, and do so in an emotional way, this is no guarantee that they are dialogical. Suppose two participants communicate their experiences or points of view, not taking the experiences of the other into account, not listening to the other in an open way, not learning from each other, and not changing their initial experience,[5] emotion, or point of view on the basis of the preceding dialogical interchange. Communication of this kind is more at the monological than at the dialogical end of the continuum. Emotions, particularly negative emotions, such as anger, contempt, sadness, guilt, shame, or sorrow, can become monological when the emotion makes people retreat into themselves. Abraham (1942), for example, compared "melancholic depression" with "normal grief" and discovered that the normal mourner is interested in the "object" of love and occupied with thoughts about the other, while depressed sufferers are thoroughly wrapped up in themselves and beset with self-reproaches that have little or nothing to do with the other. This observation shows that people can report an emotion of love, or any other emotion, towards another person and at the same time be wrapped up in themselves, so that love or any other emotion is suffused with egocentricity.

Generally speaking, we assume that an emotion is dialogical when it meets a real, remembered, imagined, or anticipated position in the other or the self and is renewed, understood, consoled, or, in the broadest sense, influenced by that position in such a way that the emotion, and the self more generally, develops to some higher level of integration. According to the developmental analysis in Chapter 4, promoter positions in particular can function as powerful dialogical agents for the change and development of emotions.

Given the preceding considerations, we propose that authenticity is more than an expression or communication of one's "true," "real," or "primary" emotions towards another. Authenticity emerges at the dialogical interface between two emotions or groups of emotions, that is, between my emotions and the emotions of the actual other or other-in-the-self. When, for example, I am angry with the other, the actual response of the other, including his emotion, organizes and even changes my own emotion, if the emotion of the other is accessible enough during the interchange. The response of the other may evoke in me another emotion (e.g., surprise, sympathy, or compassion) that mitigates or transforms my initial experience of anger. For a dialogical view of authenticity it is essential to note that such a process takes place not only between self and actual other, but also between the self and the imagined other as part of the extended self. In both cases the *alterity of the emotion of the (actual or imagined) other*, including its particular history and context, is taken into account in the transformation of the initial emotion.

In talking about authenticity in terms of including the alterity of the emotions and positions of the other, there is a pitfall that has to be recognized. If the alterity of the other becomes dominant in the exchange, there is a risk that one's own emotions might not receive enough space for expression and development and could be subordinated to the emotions of the other. In our typically Western zeal to "change" and "transform" emotions, we run the risk of changing emotions before they are heard. It has to be remembered that emotions, including negative ones, have their own voice. For many people, it is self-evident to deny negative emotions as phenomena that are unwanted and should be changed as soon as possible into positive emotions, thereby neglecting the possibility that they have an important message to convey (e.g., feeling down can be heard as a message that I have neglected relevant parts of myself). It seems to be better to listen to the voice of the emotion, rather than to prematurely change or transform it.

Dialogical authenticity implies not only listening to the voice of one's own emotions, but also to the voice and messages of the emotion of the other. When these messages are part of a meaningful interchange, then the alterity of the other has a chance to become integrated into one's own emotions, without the risk that their voice is neglected, adapted to the other, or prematurely changed. Dialogical authenticity can be understood by considering it from the perspective of the Buddhist notion of compassion. This tradition has taught for centuries that one is not only concerned with the "suffering" (including emotional reactions) of others but also with the suffering of oneself. This means that when one is emotionally involved in contact with others, dealing with the emotions of the other and incorporating them in one's reaction to the other, implies not only compassion to the emotions and positions of the other but also to those of oneself (Allen and Knight, 2005).

Certainly, authenticity can be seriously reduced when dialogue is simply not possible between two positions or when the dialogue is one-sided, which can be observed when one side is attempting to start a dialogue and the other side is avoiding or rejecting it. It can go so far that one's authenticity even has to be "defended" *against* the other. For example, in a social conflict somebody challenges me by insulting or aggressive remarks, provoking in me the tendency to answer with counter-aggression. However, if I do so, I would feel inauthentic, because I would express from my side the same behavior that I disapprove of in the other *and* myself. Even when the other would like me to be aggressive as an expression of his wish to "fight on the same level," I simply refuse to be so, because I feel that such behavior simply does not fit with my style. In other words, dialogical authenticity is not always possible, particularly when the parties are used to communicating with others in very different styles.

The preceding considerations require a distinction between expressive and dialogical authenticity. In agreement with the modern model of the self, expressive authenticity takes the form of acting on the basis of one's own self-positions and one's emotions in their own specific and personal qualities. This conception is implicit or explicit, based on a restricted view of a self in which the emotions and positions of the other are not constitutive elements. Dialogical authenticity, on the other hand, allows the emotions and positions of the actual other and the other-in-the-self to become involved in an interchange that confirms or transforms the initial emotions or positions. In true dialogical authenticity, emotions and other *I*-positions involved in a dialogical relationship influence each other, while taking each other's alterity into account.

Up to now we have discussed authenticity as a relationship between self and actual other and between the internal and external domain of the extended self. Along similar lines, dialogical authenticity can also be applied to different emotions within the internal domain of the self (e.g., "I expressed my anger towards her, but when I later looked back, I felt regret as I found myself too harsh"). Communication between different emotions within the internal domain is dialogical when the initial emotion is influenced or changed on the basis of its interchange with a counter-emotion in such a way that the two emotions acknowledge each other in their alterity. Apparently, this alterity becomes restricted when a particular emotion is so dominant in the self that it colors the other emotion to such a degree that the other one is not perceived in its own quality. When, for example, pride and strength are pervasive and dominant in the self, emotions of gratitude or compassion are not acknowledged and experienced in their own quality but instead considered as "weakness."[6]

Internal division as a challenge to authenticity: the wolf as part of the self   Through out the history of humankind people have been fascinated by animals and impressed by the great variety of features or capacities that, as humans, they lack (e.g., a body that can fly) or which they have to a lesser degree (e.g., excessive strength and speed or splendid color combinations). Although many cultures have taught that people are "essentially different" and even "higher" than animals, we have never stopped experiencing a strong fascination or attraction to animals and the way they live. Many humans identify with animals and some have gone so far as to make themselves up to look like an animal (e.g., a cat). Writers have vividly described the "animal in themselves" in order to convey something important about the characters in their novels. In his book *Steppenwolf* (1951/1971:52–3), Herman Hesse describes his main character, Harry, as partly human, partly animal, in this way:

And so the Steppenwolf had two natures, a human and a wolfish one. This was his fate, and it may well be that it was not a very exceptional one. There must have been many men who have had a good deal of the dog or the fox, of the fish or the serpent in them without experiencing any extraordinary difficulties on that account. In such cases the man and the fox, the man and the fish lived on together and neither did the other any harm. The one even helped the other. Many a man indeed has carried this condition to such enviable lengths that he has owed his happiness more to the fox or the ape in him than to the man.

So much for common knowledge. In the case of Harry, however, it was different. In him the man and the wolf did not go the same way together, they did not help each other, but were in continual and deadly enmity. The one existed simply and solely to harm the other, and when there are two in one blood and in one soul who are at deadly enmity, then life fares ill. Well, to each his lot and none is light.

Now with our Steppenwolf it was so that in his conscious life he lived now as a wolf, now as a man, as indeed the case is with all mixed beings. But when he was a wolf, the man in him lay in ambush, even on the watch to interfere and condemn, while at those times that he was a man the wolf did just the same. For example, if Harry, as a man, had a beautiful thought, felt a fine and noble emotion, or performed a so-called good act, then the wolf bared his teeth at him and laughed and showed him with bitter scorn how laughable this whole noble show was in the eyes of a beast, of a wolf who knew well enough in his heart what suited him, namely, to trot alone over the steppes and now and then to gorge himself with blood or to pursue a female wolf. Then, wolfishly seen, all human activities became horribly absurd and misplaced, stupid and vain. But it was exactly the same when Harry felt and behaved as a wolf and showed others his teeth and felt hatred and enmity against all human beings and their lying and degenerate manners and customs. For then the human part of him lay in ambush and watched the wolf, called him brute and beast, and spoiled and embittered for him all pleasure in his simple and healthy and wild wolf's being.

This excerpt raises a question about the nature of authenticity in a divided self. When two or more alternating parts of the self are so different, so emotionally conflicting, and so entirely incompatible as the man and the wolf in Hesse's account, we may ask which of the parts serves as a basis for authenticity? When there is so much animosity between two mutually exclusive parts of the self, how do we know which of the two is the most authentic one? This question is difficult, even impossible to answer as long as the self is, at a particular moment, *entirely* located in one position and *not* in the other. Certainly, when Harry is in his wolf-position, he is able to watch, consider, and evaluate himself in his man-position and, in reverse, from his man-position he can appraise his wolf-position. When he finds himself in the man-position, he will claim that this position is the most authentic one. However, when he is in the wolf-position, that position is claimed to be the only "true" source of his authenticity. In other words, as long as the two sides are divided in their views and mutually exclusive in their judgments, each of them claims full authenticity. The question can never be answered as long as the self is subjected to a division of this kind. It could only be answered if Harry were able to leave *both* positions and move to a third one, from which the two conflicting ones could be compared and evaluated on their contributions to Harry's self as a whole and to its relationships with other selves.

A meta-position, with sufficient distance and independence in regard to the emotionally involving conflicting parties would be required to determine which part of the self Harry feels most authentic. He can do so if he undertakes some overview of his different positions and the different situations in which they are actualized.

A similar question can be put about the existence of "shadow positions" or "disowned" parts of the self. If we were to ask Harry in Hesse's story which position was for him a shadow position, he would give different answers depending on the position in which he found himself at that particular moment. From the perspective of the man, the wolf is a shadow, but according to the wolf it is the man who is a shadow. For the man the wolf is an abject, but for the wolf the man is an abject. In other words, in order to answer the question of what is a shadow position, we need to take into account where we find ourselves when answering the question. In their everyday lives, most people live most frequently in the "ordinary positions" that are dominant in their lives and to which they return frequently and regularly. As long as they live in these positions, positively attuned as they mostly are, they will be inclined to refer – if they do – to "deviant" positions as shadows and consider them as "negative" or as "not belonging to myself" or as "inferior." Thanks to the continuity of their ordinary positions, they are able to say that particular positions are shadows more than others. However, in saying that they feel most authentic in their ordinary positions, their judgment is more a matter of habit and continuity than a result of extensive self-reflection. In order to answer the question of which position is a shadow one, it would be necessary to take a meta-position from which the ordinary positions can be evaluated in comparison with positions that are "usually" felt as disowned. As a result of such broadened self-reflection and extended dialogue with oneself and others, some people become aware that their ordinary life is not free from shadow aspects. When people become aware of their rigid life patterns, extended self-reflection or dialogue may lead to a change of habits and ordinary life patterns in the form of the reversal of dominant positions (see also James's, 1902/2004, work on conversions).

As suggested by the preceding considerations, the relationships between emotions are somewhat diverse. Dialogical relationships can take place between emotions of the actual other and those of the self (e.g., between my initial anger and the apparent embarrassment of the other), between internal and external domains of the self (e.g., "I'm very enthusiastic about moving to another city but I imagine my mother would be sad"), within the internal domain of the self (e.g., "I'm ashamed about my anxiety and would be prepared to respond in a different way next time"), or within the external domain (e.g., "I imagine how my family members are involved in a serious conflict and how they find ways to deal with that"). As these examples suggest, a dialogical view necessarily leads to an emphasis on the complexity of emotions. Dialogical relationships bring together emotions originating from different sides and imbued with different histories. Such complex emotions require a tolerance of uncertainty because from the perspective of one emotion the response from the other emotion is unpredictable. Therefore, authenticity, by implication, requires the capacity to cope with emotional uncertainty.

We emphasize the complexity of dialogical authenticity and the corresponding uncertainty in view of some considerations presented in Chapter 1. As we discussed there, the process of globalization creates interfaces where different cultural groups, each with their own traditions, values, and emotion rules, meet. Different cultures meet each other even within the self of one and the same person in the form of a multiplicity of cultural positions. This multiplicity requires a certain degree of dialogical activity in order to deal with cultural positions different in nature and origin. These considerations require a rethinking of the question of what authenticity means in a self that is extended to a globalizing world.

Emotions in different models of the self

For an understanding of emotions in the context of an extended self in space and time, we need to take into account not only the process of globalization but also the historical dimension as expressed in the different models of the self. In the present section we will explore several emotions that have a special affinity with the modern, post-modern, and traditional models. Although we acknowledge that the different models may have some emotions in common, each with their own shadings (e.g., different forms of anxiety),[7] we contend that some emotions are more characteristic of some periods, while other emotions are typical of other periods. Altogether, we want to show that different models of the self, as distinctive of different historical periods, have important implications for the nature of emotions. On the basis of this discussion, we explore what we can learn from this for understanding the emotional implications for a dialogical model of self.

Self-esteem and its costs

As Richardson *et al.* (1998) have noted, the modern sense of the self can be portrayed as a "sovereign self" that has to a large extent shaped the self-image of people living in advanced industrial societies. The modern self assumes an unprecedented autonomy, in the sense of a self having an existence on its own and defining itself increasingly as independent of nature and the social environment. As the main model of the Western self, it can be depicted, as proposed by Sampson (1985), as a "container self" with strict and sharp boundaries between self and non-self, with the other located as purely "outside," and with a strong emphasis on control of the external environment. The modern self has led to an increasing individualism that can take different forms (Bellah *et al.*, 1985). Utilitarian or economical individualism is stimulated by the growth of liberal capitalism which motivates people to maximize their profits and realize their own interests. Expressive individualism is defined by the urge to fully express one's individual experiences and private feelings and has led to an upsurge of movements emphasizing the importance of self-fulfilment, self-growth, and self-expression.

In a climate determined by sovereignty and independence of the individual self, by other-exclusiveness, utilitarianism, and self-fulfilment, it is not surprising that the most central emotions are those that have an affinity with self-esteem (e.g., feeling proud, strong, and self-assertive and, on the negative side, feeling inferior and ashamed). Emotions emphasizing and confirming one's self-esteem are at the heart of the modern model of the self and have led to a dazzling number of training programs (e.g. strength training, achievement motivation training, empowerment training), methods for measuring self-esteem, and educational procedures aimed at the protection and enhancement of self-worth and self-esteem. Books devoted to the study of self-esteem and related concepts number in the thousands.

Despite the enormous attention self-esteem has received both in society and in the social sciences, psychologists are becoming increasingly aware of its costs. In a review article, Crocker and Park (2004) have noted that the pursuit of self-esteem, when it is successful, has emotional and motivational benefits. However, the authors add, it also has both short- and long-term costs, as it diverts people from fulfilling fundamental human needs for competence, relatedness, and autonomy (which the authors see as distinct from independence), and leads to poor self-regulation and poor mental and physical health. Crocker and Park emphasize that, in the pursuit of self-esteem, people often create the opposite of what they need and that this pursuit has high costs not only for themselves but also for others:

Researchers have rarely considered how one person's pursuit of self-esteem affects other people. We suggest that preoccupation with the implications of events and behavior for the self causes people to lose sight of the implications of events and their own actions for others. They have fewer cognitive resources to take the perspective of the other and therefore fail to consider what others need or what is good for others. Consequently, others have reason to mistrust their motives and do not feel safe. The goal of validating self-worth often creates competition or the desire to be superior to others. This, in turn, triggers competition in others, who do not want to be inferior, and can create the desire for revenge or retaliation. These ripple effects rebound to the self, creating a lack of safety for the self, and in the end, create the opposite of what most people really want and need. (Crocker and Park, 2004: 402)

Not only has the pursuit of self-esteem high psychological costs for the individual and the other, Crocker and Park argue, but it has probable long-term costs also for one's physical health. Self-esteem goals may lead to physical health problems through anxiety and stress, in that people with such goals tend to have a high level of anxiety and there is empirical evidence that anxiety has negative effects on health. Stress and anxiety enhance the levels of corticosteroids which, in their turn, increase levels of triglycerides and cholesterol in the blood. Thus, chronic and frequent stress is often associated with heart disease. Corticosteroids, moreover, reduce immune system functioning, resulting in greater susceptibility to some infections.

There is also evidence that the pursuit of self-esteem can lead to poor physical health outcomes as a consequence of health risk behaviors. Crocker and Parks review a series of studies showing that people who are concerned about how they are perceived and evaluated by others tend to consume more alcohol, smoke, sunbathe, and diet excessively, undergo cosmetic surgery, use steroids, drive recklessly, and engage in unsafe sex in order to obtain the approval of peers. The authors add that, although these behaviors may boost self-esteem or diminish anxiety in the short term, they have consequences for health that accumulate over time. The cumulative damage to physical health is often irreparable and puts a burden not only on individuals but also on others and on society.

In the context of a discussion of the implications of the modern model of the self, it is interesting that Crocker and Park refer to the Calvinist doctrine and the Protestant ethic that both link a person's worth to self-discipline, hard work, worldly achievements, and accomplishments. The Protestant ethic is rooted in the Calvinist tenet that only a few people – the "elect" – will go to heaven, as discussed in Weber's well-known thesis on the relationship between the growth of capitalism and Protestant ethic (1958). Although election is predetermined, the way one leads one's life on earth indicates whether one is among the elect or not. Therefore, a belief in one's own worth or value is crucial. Although the religious foundation of the Protestant ethic and Puritan asceticism have largely faded from American culture, most Americans continue to have confidence in the intrinsic value of hard work and self-discipline, and consider economic and societal success as an indicator of one's worth and value as a person (Crocker and Parks, 2004).

Shimcheong: *a Korean form of we-ness*

In a globalizing world it makes sense to learn from other cultural traditions, their values and their practices. In such a world, representatives of a particular cultural group can learn about the assets and shadow sides of the cultural heritage of themselves and of others. Taking into account the local traditions and values of other cultures allows people to broaden and enrich their position repertoire. Therefore, we present a discussion of a particular phenomenon that, in marked contrast to Western individualism and its corresponding pursuit of self-esteem, plays a central role in Korean culture: the experience of *Shimcheong*. Because this phenomenon, and its parts, are not easy for Western readers to understand, we describe it at some length, drawing on a review paper by Choi and Kim (2004).

In Choi and Kim's view, *Shimcheong* is a central phenomenon in communication and interaction in the everyday lives of Korean people. One of the major aims of Koreans is to develop and reinforce "we-ness" achieved through *Shimcheong* communications. Koreans define, understand, and judge relationships in terms of the nature of their *Shimcheong* and, in order to express and share it, they have developed particular sets of communicative grammar and practice. It is also a key term in Korean arts, music, and literature. As the authors explain, the term *Shimcheong* consists of two parts: s*him* meaning mind and *cheong* meaning affection. *Shimcheong* refers to a particular state of mind brought about by situations in which people are engaged in affective forms of we-ness. In order to understand the concept of "mind" in the Korean language it should be noted that its meaning is narrower for Koreans than for Western people. Whereas the English word "mind" implies both cognitive and emotional aspects, the equivalent Korean word *shim* or *maum* concerns emotion rather than cognition. The Korean concept of mind includes interest, motivation, emotion, intention, determination, and mood and is used in phrases like "hurt mind," "mind in pain," "mind not in good mood," "motivated mind," "lenient mind," and "determined mind." The most frequently used expressions of *Shimcheong* are "disappointed *Shimcheong*," "rejected *Shimcheong*," "sad *Shimcheong*," "unfairly treated *Shimcheong*," "depressed *Shimcheong*," and "despairing *Shimcheong*." Typically, *Shimcheong* has negative connotations although it can be a positive emotion when desires are fulfilled. A notable feature of *Shimcheong* is that in these affective connotations the history of the people is involved, that is, the nature of their relationship in the past and the events that occurred. It takes the form of story-telling in which the participants refer to the historical background of their special relationship.

When participants say "*Cheong* has emerged between us," they refer to a kind of relationship that emerged more through non-verbal than verbal communication. Patting a child on the head, firmly grasping the hands of a close friend, and sighing together with a friend in trouble are acts that convey one's own *Shimcheong* to the other. When it is expressed only verbally, it is often considered as a form of cognitive thinking rather than as an expression of an emotional mind, and it may come from a disguised rather than from a "true mind." As far as language is used, the illocutionary function of the spoken words is more important than their lexical meanings. For instance, when Koreans meet a friend and ask, "Where are you going?" or "Did you take a meal?", these questions have a ritualistic function rather than an informational one.

Choi and Kim remind us that people from Confucian cultures, including Koreans, regard as an ideal the exchange of minds based on *we-ness*. Unlike in most Western cultures, this we-ness is not expressed directly but often indirectly. For example, in a Korean TV drama, when a son comes back home from a long leave, mother and son do not display direct expressions of pleasure such as passionate hugging as typical of Western films and TV series. As a special, private and secret emotion, *Shimcheong* has not to be publicly displayed. A exchange between son and mother may illustrate this.

On a rainy day, a mother was waiting for her son to return from school with an umbrella for him at a bus stop. Finally, the bus arrived and the son got angry on seeing his mother and says, "You shouldn't have come out here with the umbrella for me." The mother replied, "My baby, sorry about that." (Choi and Kim, 2004: 9)

A superficial reading of this discourse may suggest a complaint made by the son about his mother and an apology made by the mother. However, at the background of this discourse is a *Shimcheong* of a strong kind. The son is expected to be grateful for the considerate behavior of his mother. However, the son hides his *Shimcheong* of gratitude by getting angry with his mother. The mother also conceals her *Shimcheong* by apologizing to him. Apparently, the strength of *Shimcheong* in close relationships is reinforced by expressing emotions that are *opposite* to the real, hidden emotions (compare playful "insults" that loving people can direct at each other in Western cultures). In Korean culture, parent–child relationships, and mother–son relationships in particular, are based on in-depth

Shimcheong. The expression of opposite emotions is, in the particular cultural context of the Koreans, very different from the "secondary emotions" in Greenberg's sense. Whereas secondary emotions typically suppress primary ones that as a consequence become largely inaccessible, the opposite emotions of *Shimcheong* are of an accessible nature and are signs of a deep and long-lasting relationship.

The exchange of *Shimcheong* in Korea is not limited to the contact among family members and close friends, but also takes place between good colleagues and is even directed at public figures. Although this is not far from what can take place in Western cultures, a difference is that *Shimcheong* is particularly shared on the level of negative figures. While in Western election campaigns, for example, winning stimulates continued future winning, the opposite takes place in Korea, where a sympathy vote expressing compassion with an unlucky candidate is far from negligible. It indicates that a voter gives his vote to a candidate just *because* this candidate is miserable or poor. It is not unusual in Korea for a candidate in prison to win an election. Being locked up in prison often arouses *Shimcheong* of the public, which stimulates citizens to vote for this particular candidate. From a Western perspective, it is surprising to hear that a candidate with a history of several defeats in the past has a higher probability of being elected in the future.

Reading about *Shimcheong* may suggest a comparison with "emotional intelligence," an extremely popular concept in Western countries. There are, however, some notable differences. Emotional intelligence, like other uses of the term "intelligence," is often described as a skill, capacity, or ability to perceive, assess, and cope with emotions. It is, moreover, measured, like other forms of intelligence, in terms of an "emotional intelligence quotient." As such it is conceived as a "trait," indicating that the individual is able to perceive, assess, and manage emotions in a particular way. This conception fits very well with the Western preference for judging others and the self in terms of relatively stable personality traits that show some generalization across a diversity of situations. Emotional intelligence has received immense attention as a welcome complement to cognitive forms of intelligence. However, it has a basic similarity to cognitive intelligence as a trait-like concept. As such it fits very well with the modern model of the self with its celebration of individuality, autonomy, and self-sovereignty.

In marked contrast to the concept of emotional intelligence, *Shimcheong*, in its emphasis on "we-ness," is not so much an individual trait but rather an experience that emerges between people on a level that transcends their individual traits or characteristics. Moreover, *Shimcheong* is, more than emotional intelligence, sensitive to the individual and common *history* of the participants involved in communication. Traits are intrinsically a-historical. They are or may be determined by nature and nurture, but the historical context of the communicating participants is not within their scope. In terms of Pepper's (1942) overview of "world hypotheses" history belongs to "contextualism" in which events and stories are central, whereas personality traits are examples of "formism" in which objects and people are compared, categorized, and classified. These hypotheses represent essentially different forms of analysis and thinking.

Shimcheong is a relevant concept for dialogical self theory because, more than emotional intelligence, it implies *an intrinsic otherness*. Because *Shimcheong* implies (shared) emotions, it takes place in a common space where the other and the self meet and, moreover, where internal and external positions create a platform for the emergence of *we-positions*. Conceived in this way, *Shimcheong* takes into account the position history and context of the parties involved. These possibilities of self and identity pose a challenge to the Western concept of self-esteem. The question is this: is it possible to develop forms of self-esteem that go beyond individualism, as typical of the modern model of the self, and generate we-positions that function in such a way that the costs of the pursuit of individualistic self-esteem are reduced? In our view, this question can be answered only by theories that go beyond the container view of the self and acknowledge the fundamental otherness of self and identity.

Enjoyment and consumerism

As already discussed in Chapter 3, one of the features of the post-modern (or late-modern) society is the mastering of mass production and the movement from production-oriented to consumer-oriented capitalism. This led to an increasing abundance in many Western countries, so that "scarcity psychology" became supplanted by "abundance psychology." In the post-modern society, the over-production resulting from technological advances has led to heightened consumerism and, closely related, to an increase in hedonistic life-styles. This consumerism combined with a hedonistic lifestyle leads people, not only in the West but increasingly in other parts of the world, to purchase and consume goods superfluous to their basic biological needs, on the assumption that purchasing and consuming material goods can be equated with happiness.

In Chapter 3 we explained that, as part of this growing hedonism, the "enjoyer of life" now has a more central position in the repertoire of many people than in earlier historical periods. The coalition-prone tendency of the enjoyer position is further stimulated by an increasing "functional autonomy" of behaviors that were originally engaged in for some other purpose, but later become ends in themselves. For example, food that originally served the function of satisfying a biological need, later took the form of abundant dinners, consumed even when there is not a urgent need for nutrition; or dress as a means of protecting the body was later used to display the body in the form of expensive costumes and lingerie; or fight, as a means of attack or defense, led, among other things, to competition in sport and to an enormous computer game industry. In line with these observations, we argued that as a result of their functional autonomy in an era of growing abundance, many activities become purposes in themselves and produce positions that are prone to be combined with enjoyment in various ways: "I as liking to participate in spiritual courses" or "I as liking to parade myself in the latest fashion," or "I as liking to play violent computer games." With these and other examples, we want to argue that the position as enjoyer is well suited to form coalitions with a great variety of other positions. In the context of the present chapter, we may ask what the emotional implications of the phenomenon of consumerism are.

The limited emotional appeal of consumerism

Mass production in the service of mass consumption is typically oriented to the enhancement of comfort, pleasure, and happiness. The giant machine of mass production and consumption is based on, or at least facilitated by, the formula that any product that makes people feel better, sells better. The advertising industry thrives on the emotions aroused by products. These emotions are typically positive. Negative emotions, however, also play an important role in the advertising industry. Insurance of diverse kinds, for example, provides not only "realistic" protection against particular risks, but also appeals to an explicit or implicit anxiety (e.g., that one's house could burn down, that an accident could happen during travel, or that a family member could suddenly die). Insurance companies survive by selling contracts that serve to reduce anxiety, or even to avoid it, rather than *going into* this anxiety and exploring its potential significance for the further development of the self.

Some products or goods and their consumption may meet a reasonable need in everyday life. However, most advertisements appeal to the enjoyment of possessing and consuming a great variety of materials and goods, with a minimal reference to reason and a maximal appeal to emotion. As a consequence, advertising typically discourages, on the part of the buyer, any dialogue between emotion and reason, with the result that the consumer is invited to buy the product on the spur of the moment without taking into account long-term considerations. Rather than being stimulated by the advertising industry, the emotion–reason dialogue takes place in the private or social domain of the individual, or is addressed to some extent by consumer organizations (e.g., "I feel very attracted to this product, *but* to what extent do I really need it, and what are the consequences of buying it?"). An extreme example of a lack of emotion–reason dialogue is cigarette advertisements (although banned in some countries) depicting an idealized male as an identification object, at the same time avoiding any reference to health risks (unless there is a legal obligation to do so). By presenting an idealized person or an association with sex, people are seduced into buying from impulse or fantasy, instead of engaging first in some process of self-consultation or self-agreement.

Generally, consumerism tends to appeal to immediate emotion, avoids reason–emotion dialogue, stimulates positive emotions only, and avoids or neglects the meaning potential of negative emotions. In this way, consumerism not only makes a very limited appeal to the dialogical self, but creates, at the same time, the illusion of a multiplicity of possibilities by suggesting accessibility to a broad range of positions. Advertising, as the motor of mass consumption, promises a speedy increase of the multiplicity of positions in the self. Typically, advertisements point us to a vast array of positions that are broadly available and easily and quickly accessible and with a minimal investment of effort. Adventure trips take you quickly to very different places in the world, travel companies help you to "do" Europe in one week, or to take part in ten or more kinds of sporting activity within a few days, even without having any prior experience. Playing tennis in the morning, golf in the afternoon, bowls in the evening, and chatting on the internet in between, are only a few in the range of possibilities offered as attractive vacation distractions.

Consumerism and the social meaning of money are closely connected. As Deflem (2003) has explained, following the classic work of the sociologist George Simmel, money in contemporary society becomes more and more functional, that is, it establishes relationships and ties people to one another by the flow of goods and services. In Simmel's view, the price of a product in this exchange is the measure of exchangeability that exists between this product and all other products. Money expresses the *general element* contained in all exchangeable objects but it is *not capable of expressing the individual or unique element of them*. Whereas in earlier times money did have substance-value (e.g., in the form of gold or silver coins), nowadays the substance of money itself no longer plays a role in its exchange function. It has become a pure symbol to *determine qualities quantitatively*. As a general instrument and in its almost unlimited potential as a means, it has entered almost all of people's social inter-actions. The result is a significant increase in economic consciousness, the need to acquire, and monetary greed, not only in the market, but in almost every sphere of social life. Simmel describes this process as the commodification of interactions or the general reduction of quality to quantity.

There seems to be a basic similarity between what is generally under-stood as consumerism and what Simmel described as the commodity of interactions. Consumerism extends beyond a purely *economic* rela-tionship between a supplier and a buyer of a product, whereas com-modification extends beyond the purely *financial* relationship between parties who pay money for products. The similarity is in the change in the nature of relationships between people. In private medicine doctor/patient relationship changes into a party offering a service and another party who buys it and pays for it. The doctor offers a product and the patient places himself in a position to consume it. A priest who pre-pares a ceremony for a funeral may discover, to his dismay, that the family of the deceased want to "order" a ceremony in a way that is not dissimilar from buying a product in a supermarket. A teacher who is motivated to discuss thoroughly a particular topic in her lectures, may discover that the students criticize her presentations as "too slow" and "too difficult." Moreover, they want a summary as an easy take-home message. Common to such examples is that they reflect a basic atti-tude that comes from a particular position that is not often mentioned explicitly by the people involved in the process, but that nevertheless organizes a great variety of social interactions. Rarely do people address themselves in terms of "I as consumer" but, without a doubt, this posi-tion influences and structures many interactions implicitly, below the level of explicit awareness.

Our contention is that this consumer position has important impli-cations for a psychology of emotions. When the consumer position is expanding in the self, then easily accessible and more superficial emo-tions receive more prominence at the cost of less accessible and deeper emotions. This statement is based on the consideration that, when the development of the affective domain of the self is restricted to positive emotions only (as typical of consumerism), with the neglect, suppression, or avoidance of negative emotions, the positive emotions lose depth and become flatter. This conclusion emerged from the application of the Self-Confrontation Method (SCM) (Hermans and Hermans-Jansen, 1995) with a range of people involved in counselling, training, and psychother-apy. The method includes a distinction between positive emotions (e.g., joy, enjoyment, energy, happiness) and negative emotions (e.g., anxiety, disappointment, anger, powerlessness). The procedure invites clients to indicate the extent to which their experiences of their past and present, and possibility for the future imply positive and negative emotions. The case studies are longitudinal, that is, the clients perform the self-investigation a second time, typically after some months, to discover to what extent the experiences and their associated emotions have changed. One of our general findings is that clients want to talk about and express their negative emotions with a consultant, but, in addition, that when their negative emotions are given space for expression and development, the quality and depth of their positive emotions also increase.

With reference to the position of "enjoyer," it makes sense to distinguish between short-term and long-term enjoyment. Short-term enjoyment, characteristic of consumerism, is quick, easy, transient, effortless, and superficial. It can be intense but is rarely deep. It is often expressed in terms of "funny," "nice," "cool," or "amusing." Long-term enjoyment can be intense but is certainly deep. It can be the result of effort and persistence, as in creative work, but it can also come in a flash, like in an unexpected experience of beauty or sudden insight. It is long-term in the sense that it has a more enduring impact on the self. It is typically described as "interesting," "fulfilling," "transforming," or "liberating."

Because "the enjoyer" is prone to create coalitions with a diversity of other positions, consumerism, favoring short-term enjoyment, tends to lead to a "funnification" of the position repertoire. This process reduces the qualitative differences between the different positions and their corresponding spaces, removes their uniqueness and leads to their homogenization and superficialization. The process of funnification taking place at the level of the self can be seen as analogous to the concept of "McDonalization" (Ritzer, 2000) on the societal level.

It should be noted that it is not our intention to restrict a postmodernist view of enjoyment to consumerism. Enjoyment as typical of post-modernism is broader than what we described as "short-term" and "superficial" enjoyment. It also refers to particular forms of artistic enjoyment (see, for example, the work of post-modern painters, architects, composers, and authors). Post-modernism, although often criticized for its pessimism and lack of hope, has contributed to an increased openness to the moment and has liberated the self from the heavy burden of imposed dogma and ideology-based purposes and ideals. It has, moreover, contributed to the significance of discontinuity in the stream of experience that otherwise would be over-stabilized by an emphasis on sameness and continuity. It has also made the world more colourful by its sensitivity to multiplicity and variation.

Despite the various advantages of a post-modern view of the world, we conclude that the homogenizing tendencies of widespread consumerism work as a counter-force to the heterogenizing forces that emanate from the processes of globalization and localization. As we have described in Chapter 1, globalization not only leads to a higher density of positions in the self, but also to an increase in their heterogeneity. We arrived at this conclusion on the basis of the consideration that the process of globalization creates interfaces between different cultures where positions from very different origins meet not only between individuals and groups but also within the multi-voiced self of one and the same person. Indeed, *intercultural* processes of this kind lead to linkages between different localities, including their practices and values, with a heterogenization of the self as a result. On the other hand, the *economically* stimulated process of consumerism, supported by the process of commodification of interactions, counteracts this heterogenization and work in the direction of the homogenization of self and society.

Feeling grateful in a time of consumerism

In the traditional model, as described in Chapter 2, the self is embedded in a cosmic order and participates as a tiny particle in a larger whole. Despite natural disasters and the occurrence of wars, this view of the world is one of totality, connection, and purpose and these characteristics are expressed in myths and celebrated in rituals (Gier, 2000; Richardson, Rogers, and McCarroll, 1998). Part of the traditional worldview is to sacralize the cycles of the seasons and the cyclical procreation of animals and humans. In this model the human self is not so much an autonomous entity but rather a natural part of a sacred whole, which is greater and even more valuable than its parts. In such a worldview, where the individual feels not only embedded in a larger whole but is also highly dependent on the natural and social environment, we believe that the feeling of gratitude or thankfulness is more central than in the other models of the self. When the individual is highly dependent on external contexts and believes in rewards and punishments from natural and supernatural forces, the feeling of gratitude emerges as a response to *receiving* a good harvest, food, nutrition, health, and prosperity, which the individual is only partly in control of. The notion of grace is abundantly present in many religious texts ("We Thank the Lord"), which are distinctive particularly of the historical period in which the traditional model was the predominant one. For a further exploration of the feeling of gratitude, it is relevant to consider an investigation in which it was studied in close relationship with the phenomena of consumerism and individualism.

Gratitude, individualism and consumerism

In a study of ideological changes in society, Nafstadt, Blakar, and Rand-Hendriksen (2008) focused on the phenomena of individualism, consumerism, and gratitude in the light of the consideration that we are living in a time in which individualism and consumerism are increasingly taken for granted as the royal road to happiness (Peterson and Seligman, 2004). As part of their longitudinal study, Nafstadt and her colleagues counted the frequency of articles and words relevant to consumerism, individualism, and gratitude in a widely read Norwegian national newspaper (*Aftenpost*) and monitored changes in these frequencies over more than two decades (1984–2006). From a cultural and political point of view this study is highly relevant because, according to the authors, "the spirit of gratitude" in Norwegian society, traditionally a typical Scandinavian welfare state, is increasingly permeated by the ideology of neoliberalism and consumerism.

The investigators found that from 1984 to 2006 the number of newspaper articles including the words *"kjøpe"* (buy; purchase) and *"selge"* (sell) both increased by 63%. The use of the word *"kunde"* (customer) increased 46%, of *"forbruker"* (consumer) 45%, of *"kjøpepress"* (pressure to buy) 36% and of *"grådig"* (greedy) 86%.

Articles including the words *"jeg"* or *"meg"* (I or me) increased by 44%. On the other hand, usage of words such as *"solidari"* (solidarity) decreased by 60%, *"samhørig"* (belongingness) by 68%, *"velferdssamfunn"* (welfare society) by 60%, and *"felles"* (shared, common, communal, community) by 30%.

Of central interest for the investigators was the use of the word 'takknemlighet' (gratitude, gratefulness, thankfulness). Despite increased usage during the 1980s and early 1990s, it has reduced overall by 27% since 1984.

Of particular significance are the changes in the usage of words 'gi' (give) and 'motta' (receive), because giving and receiving are relevant forms of dialogue (see Chapter 4). The first word decreased by 23%, and the second by 47%, and the number of articles including *both* words decreased by 50% during the last two decades.

Striking differences were found between words referring to "moderation" and "wanting more." Use of the word 'moderasjon' (moderation; temperance) was reduced by 60% during the period of investigation. Likewise, the word 'beskjedenhet' (modesty) decreased by 66%. However, the phrase '*vil ha mer*' (want more), expressing just the opposite of being contented and grateful, increased in frequency by 187 %.

On the basis of their results, the investigators concluded that the current societal ideological spirit, characterized by consumerism, individualism, and the free market ideology, has the effect of marginalizing the virtue of gratitude. In the long run, they expect, these changes will lead to reduced well-being and satisfaction with life because gratitude is not only a virtue but also an important dimension of the "good life."

Some implications for the dialogical self

We discussed three emotions that have an affinity with different models of the self: self-esteem emotions that are central in the modern model, enjoyment as relevant to the post-modern model, and gratitude as having a special significance to the traditional model of the self. Our proposal is that all three feelings have some place in a dialogical model of the self.

Self-esteem and related emotions like pride, strength, and self-confidence are part of a dialogue when a person expresses her own point of view, articulating it in a way that exposes how the person wants to manifest herself and her identity to the outside world. Dialogue gives room for autonomy because it allows one to articulate a particular point of view, experience, or opinion that may deviate from the opinions or experiences of others. Agreement as well as disagreement are main forms of dialogue that give full expression to one's stance towards oneself and the world. Dialogue can lead to the construction of a common space and to commonly felt experiences, but it is also open to deviation, social opposition, and conflict in which different or opposing points of view are expressed, compared, and worked through. Such processes are also at work in the self when a particular position is articulated in its own character and in its relative autonomy. As such it is part of relationships of self-conflict, self-agreement, self-consultation, and self-negotiation.

As part of a dialogical self, enjoyment is long-term rather than short-term. By its speed, transience, and superficial character, short-term enjoyment, typical of consumerism, does not easily allow the development of an initial position on the basis of preceding steps in the dialogical process. In order to develop an initial position over time, some depth, concentration, and elaboration are required. Silence, too, giving space for inner recapitulation, rehearsal, and imagination, is a facilitating factor in dialogical relationships. Indeed, in a dialogue, existing opinions, convictions, and emotions can be questioned and even undermined, leading to a temporary dominance of negative feelings over positive ones. However, the construction and emergence of a common dialogical space, in which the different participants feel that they can contribute to the process and end result, gives profound enjoyment that goes beyond the moment and the situation at hand. It plays a role in one's memory, it stimulates one's imagination and it can add significantly to the quality of future dialogical contacts. Such enjoyment is also typical of the person whose self is involved in a process of creation, particularly when it results in an "*Aha! Moment*" after a process of dialogical scrutiny.

By its nature, dialogue gives room to feelings of gratitude and thankfulness, and there are two reasons why they are intensely connected. First, dialogue profits greatly from the contribution of another person in the outside world or another-in-the-self. When a dialogue with an actual other leads to a valuable insight, understanding, or product, then this result is "something of me," but, at the same time, "something of you," and, finally, "something of us," and this commonality may give rise to feelings of gratitude. These feelings are particularly relevant to the inclusion of the other-in-the-self. Even when the actual other is no longer present or alive, he may be taken up as a valuable position in the self. Such a person can inhabit a deeply entrenched place in the self and one can feel in contact with such a person in verbal or non-verbal dialogues. The "inner presence" of such a person makes one feel grateful, and imagining an encouraging smile is enough to give joy and energy. Second, feelings of gratitude correspond with the receptive function of the *I*. In Chapters 3 and 4 we discussed the phenomenon of self-transcendence and the experience of participating in a broader field of awareness. We emphasized that such experiences cannot be easily understood solely on the basis of the appropriating function of the *I*. In particular, experiences that are beyond one's immediate control evoke feelings of gratitude, often associated with the awareness of "not deserving it."

Dialogical love

An emotion that cannot be missed in an exploration of the dialogical self is love, because love has, as no other emotion, the potential to promote relationships between people and to transform the self. As already said at the beginning of this chapter, emotions, including love, are studied in close relationship with the self. As proposed by Morgan and Averill (1992), the relationship is considered to be bi-directional: emotions, and love in particular, have the capacity to transform the self and, conversely, the self is able to influence and develop feelings of love.

In our study mentioned earlier on the transformative influence of emotions on the self, we invited students to indicate the changes in their selves caused by twelve different (positive and negative) emotions

(Hermans-Konopka and Hermans, 2010). As we described, participants were instructed to select particular verbs in order to indicate what kind of change the behavior, represented by the verbs, produced in the self. A participant could say, for example, "joy is warming me" or "anxiety is imprisoning me." The results showed that of all the emotions included in the investigation, love led to the most positive changes, but, at the same time, to a certain degree of negative changes in the self also. This finding suggests that love has, more than other emotions, a complex and highly transformative influence on the self.

Love as a two-step extension of the self?

In order to explore the specific features of dialogical love, let's take the example of a man who experienced a strong feeling of love for his girl-friend, from whom he was apart for a while, and wrote the following lines in his notebook:

During my bike trip some days ago, I looked with intense interest at the horses, elegantly moving in the meadows near the river. It occurred to me that they aroused more interest in me than ever before. I enjoyed their strength and beauty and I looked at them with love. After a while I became aware that Laura [his girlfriend] was looking at the horses through my eyes ... When I continued my trip, I was conversing with her in my imagination and I expressed my love to her, almost silently speaking sweet words. While I was doing this, I looked at the gently rolling meadows with the majestic mountains at the background. It was as if she was merging with this natural environment and was answering me through its expressive beauty.

  Later, when I was home, I felt a strong urge to know more about her family, her father, mother, brother, and sister. What circumstances do they live in What are their interests? What did they do in the past? How were they connected with her?

It seems that the man did not look at the horses as a self-contained individual but through the eyes of his loved one as a central position in the external domain of his self. However, he looked in a way that suggested that her position (Laura as loving horses) became his own, the internal and external positions in his self fusing together and becoming one and the same. Moreover, he experienced his loved one not just as an individual separated from the environment in which he found himself on his bike trip. Rather, her image tended to fuse with the environment that was felt to radiate the same feelings. His imagined girlfriend was not purely inside, but also not purely outside. Rather, he felt as closely related to the environment (outside) as he felt connected with his loved one in the deeper regions of his self. His love extended his self to the outside world.

The last part of the excerpt, although less poetically described, went one step further. The man was concerned not only about his loved one and the way she looked at the world, but also about her significant others and how they looked at the world. Through her, he became interested in people who were part of *her* environment and he wanted to look at the world from *their* perspective. In other words, his love not only extended his self towards his loved one, but *he extended his self also to the extensions of her self.*

We consider this two-step extension and its corresponding emotional engagement as a distinctive feature of the experience of dialogical love. The loved one opens new doors through which new spaces become accessible, which in turn lead to new experiences that give strong innovative and transformative impulses to the self and its further development. Through this two-step extension, the loved one not only enriches the self with the introduction of new positions, but existing positions are also transformed. During this process, the loved one becomes a central position in the self and is experienced as an important promoter of the lover's development.[8]

When Morgan and Averill (1992: 227) talk about love as "reaching out to another," this insight can be further extended by saying that love has the potential of reaching out to "the other of the other," that is, the loving person can also love significant others who are part of the extended self of the loved one. When Solomon (1993) proposes that a theory of love should be basically a theory of the self and underlines the relevance of a shared self for the experience of love, then one can elaborate on this view by stating that in love one shares one's self not only with the loved one but also with others to whom one extends *through* the loved one. When Person (1988:23) says that love "creates a flexibility in personality that allows a breakthrough of internal psychological barriers and taboos," this insight can be expanded by stating that love also allows a breakthrough of *external* barriers and taboos, referring to spaces that are opened towards the lives and life circumstances of the others beyond the loved one. Put briefly, dialogical love leads to *the co-creation of a common space* that deepens and innovates the lives of loving people and extends beyond their initial selves.

When the relationship between people develops in a dialogical way, the extended contact with the loved one is not limited to positive emotions only. When dialogue between them evolves, there is an acceptance of the emotional domain of the other person as a whole, including both positive and negative emotions. The sharing of positive as well as negative emotions broadens the emotional bandwidth of the relationship. When negative emotions are expressed and shared as part of a loving relationship, they exist on two levels: (i) the level of the original emotion (which is negative); (ii) the level of sharing the emotion with the loved one (who is positive). On the second level, the negative emotions are expressed, ordered, clarified, and, moreover, they *meet the feelings of the other person.* As a result of this sharing and exchange, the initially negative emotions are "dialogised," that is, they are integrated in the domains of the self which is created as a "common dialogical space" (Hermans, 2001a). The reworking of the negative emotions in this space evokes positive feelings that are combined with the negative ones and give them a developmental impetus. As part of this process the negative emotions are developed to a higher level of complexity because they are integrated with other (positive) feelings. As part of a loving relationship, this sharing of negative emotions is more than identifying one's own emotions in the other ("Ah, that's what I also experience!"). It is, rather, a recognition of the emotions of the other in their alterity. Depending on the degree of self-acceptance and acceptance of the other, the partners exchange and share their negative emotions as shadow (or disowned) positions of themselves or the other, as far as they are aware of them.

Love, self-love, and movements in the self-space

In one of his maxims, the Dutch sociologist Johan Goudsblom said, "Love is the cordial treaty of two self-loves." In this expression, the word "treaty" would suggest a kind of diplomatic understanding of two people who, in essence, love themselves but not the other. This way of looking at love brings us back to Fromm's (1956) criticisms of the Freudian libido theory. This theory includes the assumption that, when libido is invested in oneself, the investment of libido in another person is automatically reduced, given the limited amount of available energy. This conception (or reception) of this part of Freud's theory of love has led to various conceptions of "narcissism" originally introduced as a pathological category, but later increasingly used in everyday life to refer to people who "love only themselves, but not another." Fromm strongly criticized Freud's conception, arguing that love for the other person can only develop when it coexists with love for oneself. Later psychoanalyists (e.g., Kohut, 1971) have argued that narcissism is a normal developmental phenomenon. Infants and toddlers feel at the center of the universe and even omnipotent beings, perceiving parents as mythical figures, immortal and powerful. In psychodynamic terms, there is a phase of "primary" narcissism" implying that others and self are immaturely perceived as idealizations.[9] Narcissism, therefore, both as a normal and a dysfunctional phenomenon, can be better analyzed in terms of adaptive or maladaptive forms self-esteem than in terms of love.

The assumption, in the original Freudian theory, that self-love and other-love tend to be mutually exclusive finds its parallel in spatial dynamics in emotions. At first sight, spatial movement in one direction excludes simultaneous movement in the opposite direction. It is self-evident that, when one goes inside a house, one does not, at the same time, go outside the house. Entering the house and leaving the house at the same time is physically impossible. In a similar way one can consider processes in psychological theories. According to psychometric trait theories, extraversion and introversion are considered polar opposites on one psychometric dimension. Seeing polar opposites as mutually exclusive leads to the conclusion that when one is more introverted one is "automatically" less extraverted, and vice versa.

The experience of dialogical love, however, does not comply with the idea of mutual exclusion of opposite directions. In deep love one makes a movement towards the other person. Indeed, one is "reaching out" to the other. However, at the same time one goes "deeper inside" than one usually does in more superficial kinds of relationships. The person is reaching out to the other, that is, he opens himself and goes "toward" the other. At the same time, however, the person goes into the deeper regions of the self. Love is spatially bi-directional. When a person moves out to the other, it may seem "illogical" to say that, if he is doing this, he is closing his eyes. However, closing the eyes at a moment of intense meeting may be precisely the moment that the loving person is going to the intimate and most inner regions of the self, at the same time feeling intensely connected with the other and making a movement towards the other, on a deeper level of experience.

Closing one's eyes may be a sign of intense engagement in an activity. When Herbert von Karajan is conducting his *Wiener Philarmoniker* with closed eyes, this does not at all mean that he is moving away from the orchestra or from his audience, but that he is going inside, in a moment of intense concentration, so that he can tune in with the music, the orchestra, and the audience. The same happens with some professional singers. Some address themselves directly to the audience. They send their sounds into the outside space, from here to there. Other singers, however, sing "to the inside" and address themselves or the others-in-the-self in a way that they feel not only "close to themselves" but also, and at the same time, in immediate contact with their audience. A similar process can take place when a teacher feels inspired and can communicate with her class in a way that she is, at the same time, closely with herself, and with the class. It is at these moments that the teacher feels safe and inspired enough to leave her careful preparations aside and allow improvisation, as being fully in the present moment. In activities and experiences of this kind, the conductor, performer, or teacher does not feel a separation between sympathy or love for the other (including the music or subject matter) and sympathy and love for the self. Instead, they coincide.

Dialogue in the form of giving and taking, in its early manifestation already present in the first year of life, is another example of love as a coincidence of movements in opposite directions. Take the example of a woman who is wondering if she will marry a certain man or not. She asks herself: what has he to offer me and what can I offer him? She is concerned about losing much of her present freedom, which is very precious to her. On the other hand, she gains safety and protection and expects that her partner will bring into her life the stability that she so much desires. When she adopts the position of her partner, she estimates that he may have similar considerations, although she is not sure. Taking everything together, she hopes that there can be a good balance between what they can offer to each other and what they receive from each other, on the condition that they give each other sufficient freedom. This thinking in terms of giving and taking and the balance between them, can be usually studied on the basis of an economic model of demand and supply. A good relationship can be defined in terms of an optimal balance of demand and supply at both sides of the relationship. The model is based on the idea that when you give goods or money to the other party, you should receive an equivalent of goods or money back in order for the exchange to be satisfactory. Giving and receiving are mutually exclusive in the sense that at the moment that I give something, I do not receive something. Certainly, I can receive the equivalent later, but the act of giving is not identical to the act of receiving. They are sharply distinguished as separate actions. This is essentially different in a relationship that is governed by dialogical love. In a relationship of this kind, giving and receiving coincide. The person who is giving, at the moment of giving himself, experiences receiving, because he is giving something to a loved extension of himself.

In what sense is a relationship of deep love dialogical? It is not dialogical according to the usual definition in terms of turn-taking. When participants are involved in an explicit dialogical process, they speak and listen alternately. That is, when one person speaks, the other listens. This alternation of turns is needed to realize a well-ordered, explicit dialogue. The distinctive feature of love is that the turns coincide. Giving love is at the same time receiving love. This coincidence of question and answer and of giving and taking occurs, for example, when two people embrace each other, exchange a gaze of understanding, or when they are making love. This can also take place in one's memory, dream, imagination, and anticipation.

Love as a dialogue with coinciding turns creates a particular experience of time. In turn-taking a person who listens has to wait for his turn in order to speak, and the person who speaks has to wait until he knows the answer of the other. From a purely formal point of view, turn-taking can be described as a series of future-oriented moments. Although the content can refer to the past or present, the process is driven by a future orientation and, at the same time, to a future openness. In contrast, love, by its coincidence of turns, slows down the experiential process and finds the rest and peace to be fully in the present. The present contact has intrinsic value and the present is not subordinated to any future goal or orientation. Paradoxically, love, because of its transformative potentials, has a greater influence on the future of the self than other emotions. Deep love may lead to dramatic changes in one's life. Love, experienced in the present and directed to the other as a promoter position, can change the future.

Summary

Love is one of the most significant human emotions. It is special in the sense that it has, more than other emotions, an impact on the self. More than other emotions and feelings, it extends the self. This extension takes place both in space and time. From a spatial perspective, it extends the self to the other and even to the extensions of the other's self. From a temporal perspective, it functions as a promoter position that has the potential to generate and integrate a broader range of future positions. As a dialogical phenomenon love is not a separate emotion, but part of a relationship. Given the bi-directional relationship, love not only transforms the self, but is also transformed by the self. Love is not just a separate emotion, but part of a dialogical relationship. In fact, love *is* a dialogical relationship with long-term implications. Love as a central and influential position in the self shows a sharp contrast to the position that we have described as the "consumer position." While consumerism is driven by the need for possessions, comfort and fun ("want more") and, as a consequence, is quickly driven out of the present, love is a form of being *in* the present that opens new "doors of perception" as Huxley (1957) would have it. While consumerism gives short-term enjoyment, love gives long-term enjoyment. While consumerism keeps the self at a superficial level of experience, love goes deep. While consumerism tends to subordinate the other as a commodity in the interest of the self, love recognizes and values the alterity of the other. While consumerism is based on an economical model of giving and taking, love blossoms on a basis where giving and receiving coincide. In other words, consumerism stimulates monological relationships, while love engenders dialogical relationships. While consumerism by its individualistic nature does not give rise to we-positions, love, in this respect not very different from the Korean experience of *Shimcheong*, is able to create them. Finally, while consumerism avoids the experience of negative emotions, dialogical love helps to accept them and is open to the exploration of their potential meaning. Together, these differences suggest that love, in the extended sense of the term, could be a proper answer to consumerism.

A stage model for changing emotions

In the beginning of this chapter, we proposed that a most fertile way to understand emotions is to consider them in close relationship to the self. We elaborated on this view by seeing emotions and self as bi-directional: emotions have an impact on the self and organize the self in significant ways, and, in reverse, the self has the capacity to confirm, allow, and change emotions. We also proposed understanding emotions as movements in a metaphorical space in which one places oneself or is placed in relation to somebody or something. In the final part of this chapter, we will present a stage model for changing emotions conceived of as dialogical movements in a metaphorical space. This model is based on the idea that the person is able to go into an emotion, to leave the emotion, to go to another emotion (counter-emotion), and to develop dialogical relationships between them. The model is aimed at stimulating the dialogical movements between emotions in such a way that they stimulate the self to higher levels of development. The model consists of seven stages: (1) identifying and entering an emotion (2) leaving the emotion; (3) identifying and entering a counter-emotion; (4) leaving the counter-emotion; (5) developing dialogical relations between emotion and counter-emotion; (6) creating a composition of emotions; and (7) introducing a promoter position.

Before exposing the model, we want to emphasize that the model is not strictly prescriptive. The different stages can be modified and the order can be changed depending on the needs of coach and client. Moreover, it is not necessary to go through all the stages. Depending on the emotional capacities of the client and the purposes of the application, the exercise of some stages can be selected while other ones are omitted or presented at some later point in time.

Stage 1: Identifying and entering an emotion

For identifying an emotion that is, in a particular period of one's life, significant to the self, a certain degree of emotional awareness is required.

As defined by Lane and Schwartz (1987) emotional awareness is the individual's ability to recognize and describe emotions in oneself and others, with special attention to their complexity. Emotional awareness helps to make sense of emotional experience and to overcome avoidance. It stimulates processing this experience and assimilating it into one's personal narrative (Greenberg, 2002). For an awareness of emotions it is required that the person is not stuck at what Lambie and Marcel (2002) have described as the level of first-order phenomenology. On this level the person considers his way of experiencing the other or oneself as "the truth" ("He is a bastard" or "I'm a total failure"), not being able or willing to become reflexively aware of the emotion ("I know that I am angry") underlying this statement. Some degree of awareness of an emotion is required in order to *identify* it as an emotion and to process it in dialogical ways.

Going into an emotion is required for getting acquainted with its experiential quality and getting in touch with its message. When entering the emotion is avoided, the person cannot know the emotion "from the inside." People may have different reasons for not entering an emotion. A person who is used to responding to emotions in a rational way may feel safe using intellectual "arguments" as an answer to emotional situations, and is neither able nor willing to recognize the underlying emotional process (e.g., the change from anxiety to safety). In order to understand what we mean by the rationalization of emotions, a distinction between reacting to emotions in a *rational* and in a *reasonable* way is required. When a person responds to emotions continually on the level of *rational* thinking, the awareness and accessibility of the emotion is often blocked and a dialogical relationship with the emotion does not take place. In contrast, responding to emotions in a *reasonable* way requires the person to first acknowledge the emotion and to enter it before answering with a reasonable response. Entering an emotion leads the person to become immersed in it, to identify with it temporarily, and to speak through the emotion rather than about it. After entering the emotion, the person is able to leave it in order to move to a more reasonable position from which the emotion and its action tendencies are evaluated. In this way, a dialogical relationship may develop between "I as emotional" and "I as reasonable," and this dialogue is supposed to allow, confirm, or change the emotion, that is, articulate it, calm it down, stop its generalization and enable the person to see its relationship with other emotions or positions.

The striving to have emotions under control may be another stumbling block for entering an emotion. Emotions as "passions" may totally occupy the space of the self so that, for a certain time, the person does not see anything other than the prevailing emotion, which colors the whole experiential world of the person. Emotions, certainly intense ones, cannot be fully controlled over a long period without significant repercussions to the self. A person who, for one reason or another, feels a strong need to be in control of his emotions, may become distrustful of them because, unlike well-organized thinking, emotions typically come over a person and can even be overwhelming.

There are two responses to emotions that we often observe in our clinical practice and that we see as inadequate reactions. Some people want ongoing control of their emotions, not allowing themselves to be subjected to them and not willing to listen to their specific messages. Other people follow them almost blindly, often believing that the expression of emotions makes them "sincere" and even "authentic." As an answer to these extremes, we advocate a reaction to emotions that is guided by an emotion–reason dialogue. The advantage of this reaction is that emotions are recognized for their own qualities and appreciated as relevant sources of evaluation of self and environment, whereas reason allows us to distance ourselves somewhat from the emotions and is willing to listen to them before giving a response in which they are compatible.

Stage 2: Leaving the emotion

A dialogical view of emotions implies that a person is able not only to enter an emotion and identify with it but also to leave it or disidentify from it. For the process of identification and dis-identification, the dimension flexibility–rigidity is crucial. As Hermans and Hermans-Janssen (1995) have argued, flexibility of the self involves the person being able to move from one position to another in a differentiated position repertoire. For example, in a flexible self there is movement to and between positions involving self-assertion and positions involving contact and union, and, moreover, between negative emotions and positive emotions. The authors argue that for psychological health what is not so important is whether a specific position is included in the self or not, but rather the way in which positions are organized (e.g., in opposition, in coalitions, around promoter positions). This organization allows or does not allow people to move flexibly from one to another position, in agreement with the requirements and possibilities of the situation. For the flexibility of the self, emotional flexibility is crucial because *I*-positions have their affective components, and emotions function as temporary *I*-positions.

Stage 3: Identifying and entering a counter-emotion

In this step another emotion, clearly different from the initial emotion, and seen by the participant as a "helpful response" to the initial emotion, is identified. We call this emotion a "counter-emotion." The idea behind this choice of term is that the counter-emotion is able to change an emotion that needs to be changed. In including this step, we refer to an insight of Greenberg (2002) that an emotion can be changed by another emotion. It is not our intention to claim that changing an emotion necessarily and exclusively requires the influence of another emotion, because this would overlook the fact that reason also is able to confirm, inhibit, or change existing emotions. However, we believe that introducing a counter-emotion can be very useful as a means of influencing and transforming an emotion that is maladaptive in a particular period of life. In fact, we assume that an emotional counter-position, in combination with a meta-position (closely related to taking a "reasonable" position), will be an especially powerful tool for changing dominant emotions.

Our experience as trainers shows that participants, when doing an exercise relating to the stage model, typically select a negative emotion (e.g., anxiety, anger, guilt, shame) as the first step, and a positive one as a counter-emotion. Their intention is to change or develop a negative emotion into a more positive one. However, in their zeal to replace negative emotions by positive ones, many people seem to forget that negative emotions are potentially adaptive (e.g., anger in case of injustice or guilt in case of anti-social behavior). Therefore, a well-balanced application of the stage model requires a distinction between negative emotions that are considered maladaptive and negative emotions that have to be acknowledged as potentially important messages or signals for changing the self.

Stage 4: Leaving the counter-emotion

This stage is similar to the second one and the process is analogous. However, it is connected with an emotion that is very different from the first one. In most cases, the participants select a dominant negative emotion as the initial one and a positive, less dominant but valuable emotion as a counter-emotion. Usually it is easy to leave an emotion that is not very often experienced and not deeply rooted in the repertoire. However, when the counter-emotion is used as an escape from another emotion, leaving the counter-emotion is not easy at all. We should take into account that in some situations in everyday life people rush into a counter-emotion as a flight from a dominant negative emotion.

A counter-emotion as a flight reaction can even become addictive. An example is the emotion of hubris, a form of exaggerated pride or grandiosity which can become addictive as a means of escaping inferiority or personal insignificance (Lewis, 1995). Initially it is a transient experience but later the person focuses her actions on regaining it. Such emotional reactions have some similarities with addictive behaviors in which actions are focused on experiencing the object of addiction over and over again.

Addictive emotions as counter-actions of problematic emotions (e.g., anxiety, powerlessness) can be described, in Schwartz's term (1995), as "firefighters." These firefighters are to be understood in relation to another group of positions, called "managers" (e.g., hyperactive ones), that have the job of keeping unacceptable parts of the self under control or exiled. However, when the managers are not successful, a different kind of agent is needed, and these are called "firefighters." These emotions function as counter-emotions with the task of getting "exiles" (e.g., unwanted positions or emotions) under control in an emergency, and they do so in an exaggerated way. For example, when a person experiences maladaptive shame, a manager in the self becomes active (e.g., the perfectionist) who wants to get rid of it and dissociates from it so that it becomes an exile. However, when this does not suffice, compensating forces in the form of alcohol or drugs are often evoked and function as firefighters. This experience can become addictive, because it can gain control of a person's life when he searches for it in a compulsive way.

In light of the distinction made above, we should distinguish between a healthy and an addictive counter-emotion. An addictive counter-emotion suppresses the exiled emotion and, as a result of over-control, adds to the inflexibility of the position-repertoire, which is stuck in a pattern of fighting against an undesirable emotion and becoming addicted to a counter-emotion at the same time. When this counter-emotion has the quality of a firefighter, it becomes addictive and rigid, with the consequence that it is very difficult or even impossible for the person to leave this emotion.

Stage 5: Developing dialogical relations between emotion and counter-emotion

An argument for the changing of an emotion by an opposite emotion is provided by Greenberg (2004:10) when he proposes that emotional change takes place when the person succeeds in synthesizing opposite emotions, described as the "dialectical synthesis of opposite schemas". Moreover, an emotion can be changed by the introduction of innovative elements. Change in psychotherapy is stimulated by providing new information to an activated emotional structure. Elaborating on these views, we propose that an emotion can be changed when it receives an innovative dialogical impulse from a counter-emotion.

A basic assumption of dialogical self theory is that the self consists of a multiplicity of positions. However, when the person is immersed in one position or when she is not able to leave it, this position can be experienced as an "*I*-prison." The person can be so identified with a position that he has no access to any different position. Take the example of a person who describes himself as "depressed." Suppose that, at the same time, other people and even professionals see this person as depressed. Depression then becomes his identity, a way of functioning in society. It becomes a basic story in his life and there are no other stories or themes available. The sense of the self is fused with the experience of depression. This happens when emotions are so overwhelming that the person is stuck in them and no movement in the direction of another position is possible.

When the person feels imprisoned in one emotion only, the notion of space becomes particularly important. This space is necessary for exploring what is going on between the emotion and other parts of the self. When there is no experiential space or distance between an emotion and the rest of the self, the emotion is all that is experienced and, as long as the self is locked up in the emotion, the possibilities of emotion work are very limited. In this light, White and Epston (1990:40) proposed the concept of "externalization," which shows that the distance between the self and the problem can be increased so that the client does not entirely coincide with his problem. According to the authors, externalization "frees people to take a lighter, more effective, and less stressed approach to 'deadly serious' problems." What the authors call "externalization" can be translated in our terms as an increase of the self-space beyond the emotion that has hitherto functioned as an *I*-prison.

A precondition for a dialogical relationship between emotions is that the self is able to dis-identify from a space-absorbing position. For the process of dis-identification, space beyond a dominant emotion is necessary. When the person does not experience any space beyond the limiting emotion, leaving the emotion is not possible and, consequently, a dialogue between the emotions cannot evolve. Certainly, as we have already argued, an open and innovative dialogue between participants creates a dialogical space. But it is also valid to say that, in order to start a dialogue between emotions, there should be a space in the self beyond the (dominating) emotion. This implies that other positions are needed as accessible parts of the self in order to enlarge its space. The proposed stage model can be effective only if other emotions are available and accessible so that that a dialogue between emotions becomes possible.

Some emotions are more space-giving than other emotions. For example, love is a space-providing emotion *par excellence*. On the contrary, anxiety is typically space-limiting and space-reducing (although as adaptive anxiety it is able to give important information about the environment or about the self). Between these extremes a great variety of emotions provides more or less space in the self. For the stage model it is relevant to know which emotions are giving space and to what extent they are able to do so.

As we said earlier, emotions are not purely internal processes but *I*-positions in a socially extended self. Having a place in the self, each *I*-position offers a particular view of the world and a particular horizon that limits this view. When there are different positions, there are different views of the world. This implies that, when the dominating emotion has a particular perspective, the counter-emotion has a *different perspective*. When we succeed in creating a movement from one emotional position to another, a different view of the world and oneself results. In this sense, the stage model offers an extension of perspectives and contributes to the flexibility of the self.

A dialogical relationship between emotions also implies that the different emotions have something to tell and are able to send out *different messages* to the self and to each other. What has emotion A to tell to emotion B and what is emotion B's answer? In reverse, what is the answer of emotion A to the message produced by emotion B? The advantage of this procedure is that emotions can learn from each other so that one emotion sends messages to the other (advice, experiences, questions, etc.) that may contribute to its innovation and further development. Such dialogical relationships can emerge between two emotions within the internal domain of the self (e.g., "I disagree with my irritation because I want to be more compassionate"); between the internal and external domain (e.g., "my father was enjoying his family life and I'm grateful that I could learn this from him"); and even within the external domain (e.g., "When my friend was depressed, his wife took care of him so that eventually he could resume his normal life again").

Magda, one of the participants in our workshops, complained about problems in her decision making process. She was increasingly dissatisfied with her job and was losing all enthusiasm and interest in her further development as a professional. She did not know what she wanted and what would be a good alternative for her. In an emotional coaching trajectory we discovered that anxiety and anger played an important role when she was thinking about herself. She discovered that the message of her anxiety was that it was dangerous for her to make "big steps" in her career, while her anger caused her to defend herself against her "competitive" colleagues. We also discovered that both emotions were connected with the voices of two significant others, her mother and father, who used to respond with the same emotions when confronted with problematic situations. This finding was a basis for searching for an emotional voice that was very different from anger and anxiety. She referred to joy as a counter-emotion and discovered that she experienced this emotion as her "own voice" that told her she could be a creative person able to enjoy variation and change in her life. She realised that this emotion was a better basis for taking decisions than being focused on what she was afraid of or what she angrily disliked. When she looked at her anger from the perspective of her joy, she became aware that she had learned to respond with anxiety and anger as a result of her upbringing, but that this way of coping with difficult situations was not "really her own." After the exercise she clearly felt that there was more space in her than just anger and anxiety and that other ways of responding to problematic situations were at least *possible*. By including the voice of joy, she felt that she could make more balanced decisions and be more sensitive to her own wishes, which were often in conflict with the expectations of her parents.

In performing emotional coaching trajectories with a diversity of clients, we discovered that dialogue between an emotion and a counter-emotion is not always easy and self-evident. It often has to be stimulated in the direct contact between client and coach because most clients are not used to such a procedure in their everyday lives. Moreover, when somebody is strongly immersed in a particular emotion, the transition to another emotion is impeded because the client is fully embodied in this position for some time before she can gradually leave it. In our applications of the model presented here, we also discovered that sometimes clients find it easier to engage in a dialogue between an emotion and the self as an unspecified whole, than to entertain a dialogue in which two emotions directly address each other. In such a case, clients explore the dialogical relationship between the emotion and the self (as undefined) and between the counter-emotion and the self (as undefined). In general, the dialogue between two emotions, conceived of as two *I*-positions, requires a developed dialogical capacity or some emotional training.

Stage 6: Creating a composition of emotions

In the next phase emotions are considered as parts of a composition and the participant is invited to focus on the meaning of the composition and its specific parts. The notion of composition reflects the conceptualization of the self as an organized position repertoire and, at the same time, allows us to consider this organization from an artistic perspective. The essential quality of a composition is its *pattern* and, as parts of this pattern, positions and emotions can be viewed as taking their place in a larger whole.

In its original formulation, the dialogical self is described as a dynamic multiplicity of *I*-positions in the *landscape* of the mind, with the possibility of an emergence of dialogical relationships between the several positions (Hermans, Kempen, and Van Loon, 1992). In this description the concept of "landscape" refers to the spatial basis of the dialogical self, in which different positions (internal and external) are involved in processes of positioning and counter-positioning. The notion of composition is an expression of the spatial nature of the dialogical self, with the connotation that the emphasis is not on the specific places of positions but on their patterning. As we have argued in Chapter 3, the patterning of positions opens the door to the "aesthetization" of the position repertoire.

The composition of the repertoire goes beyond the consideration of one or a few positions only. A composition, as a pattern in which a greater number of positions are brought together, enables the person to take a meta-position. A meta-view allows an *overview* of different positions and their pattern, so that the person considers the patterned positions from some distance, having at the same time an affective, and even an artistic, relation with them. Therefore, viewing the repertoire as a composition avoids its splitting up in the form of dichotomies. Viewing and experiencing the repertoire as a composition functions as a counter-force to the good versus bad, winner versus loser, pleasant versus unpleasant or in-group versus out-group dichotomies, so that it prevents the exclusion or devaluation of important parts of the position repertoire. The notion of composition is introduced in dialogical self theory as an antidote to the phenomenon of splitting identities.

Stage 7: Introducing promoter positions in the context of emotions

In the final stage of the model, we introduce the notion of promoter positions already introduced in Chapter 4. In the application of the stage model, there are two main possibilities. First, emotions are changed by a particular promoter position that plays a significant role in the person's life (e.g., "I as a fighter," or "the wise part of myself" in the internal domain; or "my inspiring teacher," "my quiet friend," or "Buddha" in the external domain of the self). Second, particular emotions function as promoter positions themselves. When emotions are defined as temporary positions, this does not exclude the possibility that particular emotions (e.g., dialogical love) have an important and long-lasting effect on the future development of the position repertoire. On the assumption that some emotions, more than others, can function as promoter positions, the same principles apply to promoter emotions as to promoter positions: (a) they imply a considerable openness towards the future and have the potential to produce a diverse range of more specialized but qualitatively different emotions in the future of the self (e.g., love leads not only to compassion but also to the sharing of joy, enjoyment and pain); (b) by their openness and broad bandwidth they integrate a variety of new and already existing emotions in the self (e.g., love mitigates anger and anxiety and stimulates the development of trust); (c) by their central place in the position repertoire, they have the potential to reorganize the self towards a higher level of development. For example, falling in love with somebody may initially disorganize the self and involve a preponderance of decentering movements. However, when the relationship develops further, centering movements become stronger than the decentering ones. As a result of these movements, love stimulates the self to reach a higher level of integration; and (d) they function as "guards" of the continuity of the self but, at the same time, they give room for discontinuity (e.g., whereas love as an integrative part of a relationship gives a significant continuity and even deep certainty in the self, this relationship leads to the experience of a variety of other emotions that create a certain amount of discontinuity). Promoter emotions provide continuity in the future development and function at the same time as being important innovators of the self.

Different people will refer to different emotions that have a promoter function for them. In our view, dialogical love is one of the most significant promoter emotions. It is certainly possible that different people have different emotions in their repertoire that have similar functions to what we have described as dialogical love. A useful model is to conceive of emotions as representing a continuum ranging from emotions that fulfil all the "promoter criteria" (see the above points a–d) to emotions to which none of the criteria apply. Moreover, different people will point to different emotions that have a promoter function for them in a particular time and situation.

In the presentation of the stage model we have focused on the dialogical change of an emotion by a counter-emotion. It should be noted that this is only one application of the model. A wider use is realized when the model is applied to the relationship between an emotion and the self in a broader sense. In that case the question arises whether a particular emotion is relevant to the further development of the self as a whole. What is the message of a particular emotion for the self? How does the self respond to this message? How can the energy emerging from the emotion be utilized for the realization of particular goals in which the self is involved? Such questions can be addressed by engaging not in dialogues between two specific emotions but between a particular emotion on the one hand and the self as a whole or significant parts of it (e.g., a promoter position or a meta-position) on the other hand.

Case example

In order to illustrate the stage model for a dialogical change of emotions, we present the case of a 44-year-old woman, Irene, who took part in the exercise at the time when she was plagued by anxiety in numerous contacts with other people, but also, and in particular, when she was alone.

1. Identifying and entering an emotion   When applied in practice, the model is most useful when in the first phase the client selects and identifies an emotion that she experiences as *maladaptive*. The selection requires some questioning from the coach in order to ensure that the starting emotion is one that needs change in order to become a more adaptive emotion. The psychologist did this by asking and discussing with Irene which emotion she experienced as a "burden" and made her feel "blocked" in her daily life. When she was invited to give a name to this emotion, she referred to it as "anxiety."

Then, she was asked to refer to a situation in her life in which this anxiety most typically occurred. She described this situation as follows: "Morning coffee and thinking about the day." Then the psychologist asked her to describe the part of her body where she felt this anxiety. She answered: "Anxiety in my belly, like a rope, makes me feel tense, I lose contact with my breath, I lose myself in anxiety, I am frozen, I am dead. It makes me small."

2. Leaving the emotion   When Irene was invited to leave this emotion, she made it clear that she found this very difficult: "It is like a glue, always with me, always there, more or less, more prominent or more in the background." After saying that, she walked around and felt that the emotion became less intense, although it was still there.

3. Identifying and entering a counter-emotion   From a practical point of view, the best way to select a counter-emotion is to ask the client if she knows a emotion which is *very different* from the first one and which could be *helpful* to cope with it. As an answer to this question, Irene referred to "freedom" as a counter-emotion. When asked about a situation, in which she experienced this emotion, she said, "When I'm with my friends, there I can just talk about anything or be silent, just be as I am, not thinking about how I should behave." After talking about this situation, she felt "lighter" than before.

4. Leaving the counter-emotion   It was clearly easier for Irene to leave her feeling of freedom than her anxiety. After leaving her feeling of freedom, she came back to the situation in the here and now and returned to her ordinary posture and bodily feelings.

5. Developing dialogical relations between emotions.   As part of the dialogue between the emotion and the counter-emotion, Irene was asked to enter her anxiety again. Her bodily posture changed: she did not move and was bending as if she had a burden on her shoulders. When asked if she had any images in her mind, she said, "I see a dark space, like a prison. I do not have my face any more. I do not have my body. Where am I? I am not existing."

When asked what her anxiety had to tell her, she said, "Stay there in your cellar, in its coldness, don't move because there is a danger outside. There is always a hidden danger. Life is not worth living."

Then she was invited to go into her emotion of freedom and to report which images occurred to her. She said, "There is more space, a window is open, there is a field, I want to walk, I want to move, I want to breathe. It is green outside." While saying this, her bodily posture and movement changed. She walked around and looked through the window. When she walked, she moved her arms up, as if she had become lighter.

When asked what freedom had to tell her, she said: "You can move, you can walk around, look at people, make contact. Let your self be, let your self live." Apparently, the emotion of freedom permitted her to move not only more freely in physical space but also to enter an enlarged metaphorical space in her self.

A significant dialogical moment was introduced when the coach asked Irene what response she would give to the message of freedom. She said: "I don't want to be in this terrible place any more! Let me go, let me leave! I want to move. Let me move I want to do it!" Apparently, anger joined and supported freedom for a moment, expressed by her statement, "I will not let you imprison me! I will fight with you!"

The coach finished this phase by inviting Irene to take a *meta-position* from which she could view, from some distance, the several emotions and their interconnection. From this position Irene said, "Try to leave your prison, try it, open the window, open the door." At this point in the exercise she indicated that she felt warmth in her belly and a desire to move and to walk. Her breath was deep and open.

6. Creating a composition of emotions   After the quite powerful dialogical movements between the emotion and the counter-emotion, Irene was invited to place the two emotions as part of a broader composition of emotions and positions, so that she could gain an impression of how her emotions were organized as parts of a pattern. This was done by allowing Irene to make a composition of emotions and positions in the form of a pattern of stones (different in size, color, and texture), in which each stone represented a particular emotion or position. For this purpose, she selected – apart from anxiety and freedom – some additional emotions and positions as represented by the stones: "I as lonely," "I as feminine," "I as artistic," "I as spiritual," "I as relaxed," "I as resting in my body," "I as depressed," "I as a girl," and, in addition to these, a stone for which she had initially no name (unknown position).

In organizing the stones as part of a pattern, something peculiar happened. Irene placed the stone referring to the unknown position near the stones referring to "anxiety" and "depressed." After some reflection, she gave a name to this stone, which she had initially selected on purely emotional grounds. She called it "grief" and found it so important that she moved this stone to the centre of her composition. Despite the negative tone of this position, she felt very good about finding out how important it was for her, "That's OK, it's true, I feel it, it's deep, it flows. I am afraid of this terrible pain, this grief, but it feels good now, it does not kill me."

Concentrating on her grief, she felt that it changed her anxiety. Therefore, she decided to replace the large anxiety stone for a smaller one, indicating that anxiety was less dominant in her repertoire than before. Irene's most important finding in the composition stage was that there was grief under her anxiety. By recognizing grief as a primary emotion underlying the secondary one of anxiety, she could enter it and open herself for its place as a central emotion, with the result that her fear decreased.

7. Developing a promoter position.   As a promoter position Irene referred to herself as an artist, a position that was for her connected with joy and creativity on a long-term basis. It also gave her lightness and freedom. When asked what message this position had to tell her, she said, "You can have it all [all her emotions and positions], that's all okay, just follow yourself. Be an artist in the project, be an artist in planning the next steps. Take your time for it, enjoy it! Life is not so heavy." As this statement suggests, Irene experienced this position as a source of other positions that had the potential to enrich her future life.

It became clear that Irene's artistic position had a strong accepting quality. It stimulated her to be like she actually was without avoiding problematic emotions. She felt able to consider and accept all her positions as belonging to the same overarching pattern. In general, "I as accepting", "I as artistic," "I as loving," and "I as spiritual" are promoter positions for many people. They have in common that they do not lead to a dualistic organization of the self, that is, they do not split up the emotional domain, and the position repertoire as a whole, into mutually exclusive opposites. Rather, they approach the repertoire as it is. They contribute to the experience of "suchness" that is also typical of a broader field of awareness, as discussed in Chapter 3. Like the creation of a composition, these specific positions contribute to the integration of the repertoire and its expansion as part of a larger whole.

Features and applications of the stage model

One of the special features of the stage model is that it brings together very different and even opposite emotions. It draws on the range of the emotional repertoire and has the potential to bring background emotions into the foreground so that a broader range of emotions is available for emotion work. Moreover, the different or opposite emotions are not only acknowledged in their separate value and existence, but also brought in contact with each other. They are not considered as things in themselves or as isolated processes, but as voiced *I*-positions. As such the person is *in* the emotion and is able to leave it and move to another one, with the *I*-ness of the different emotions as a guarantee of their continuity. As metaphorical movements in the self, the emotions are placed as *I*-positions in front of each other so that the *I* can move from the one emotion to the other, feeling their specific intensities, depths, tones, and action tendencies. As voiced positions, they can tell their messages so that their specific meaning becomes articulated. Dialogical relationships between the different emotional voices can be stimulated, so that the different emotions have the opportunity to convey messages, each from its own perspective, to each other so that they are no longer limited or even imprisoned in one perspective only. Such positioning exercises and dialogical movements can add new elements to the existing emotions so that they are subjected to a process of innovation. This innovation is particularly relevant to some negative emotions (e.g., anger, anxiety, guilt, and shame) that, certainly when they are intense and dominate other emotions, make the self conservative and monological. The stage model provides a procedure for the transformation of monological emotions into dialogical ones, with an enrichment of the emotional domain of the self as a result.

In the broader context of this book, the stage model makes it possible to address not only emotions in the internal domain of the self but also emotions in the external domain. As part of an extended self, both the positions and the emotions of the other-in-the-self are subjected to monological or dialogical relationships or some mixture of them. The emotion of the person herself can be compared, contrasted, and subjected to dialogue with the emotions of the other-in-the-self or even with the actual other.

A particular challenge to the stage model is its cultural potential. As we have argued in Chapter 1, the self is involved in processes of globalization and localization, with the consequence that the self finds itself at the interface of different local situations, resulting in friendships and love relationships across the borders of cultures, in international contacts, travelling, and exposure to narratives, myths, and religious traditions from different cultures. At this cultural interface, different emotions meet each other and are able to engage in dialogical relationships with each other. Such processes not only lead to more complex emotions, but may also broaden the range of existing emotions. The advantage of an enlargement of the range of emotions is that people from different cultural origins have more emphatic possibilities of understanding each other and more emotional resources to interact with each other as citizens of a world community.

Summary

In this chapter we started from the assumption that emotions can only properly be understood and investigated when they are considered in their immediate relationship with the self. More specifically, the relationship between self and emotion is conceived of as bi-directional: emotions have an impact on the self and, in reverse, the self has the potential to influence and change emotions.

As self-inclusive phenomena, emotions were treated as temporary self-positions. Considering emotions as forms of positioning has the apparent advantage that emotions are studied in their social context, that is, as interactional and dialogical phenomena they are influenced by counter-emotions, originating from the internal or external domains of the self.

Because emotions are seen as metaphorical movements in the spatial organization of the self, it is possible to create spatial procedures for studying the ways in which emotions are part of the spatial organization of the self. We devised a procedure in which emotions in the context of the broader position repertoire were represented as stones organized as parts of an artistic composition. A dialogical element was added to this procedure by considering emotions as voiced positions that can give a message to the self so that emotions are approached as providers of "emotional information."

Two developments in the literature of emotions are particularly important for our conception of a well-functioning emotional self. One is the distinction between "first-order phenomenology," in which emotional experiences have a "truth pretension" (e.g., "he *is* a bastard"), and "second-order awareness" that involves a reflexive awareness of the emotion ("I'm aware that I'm angry"). We argued that second-order awareness is a necessity for the dialogical processing of emotions. Another distinction is between "primary" and "secondary" emotions. Primary emotions are first responses to a stimulus situation (e.g., anger at violation, fear at threat) and they fade away as soon as the situation that has produced them disappears or has received an adequate answer. Secondary emotions are responses to or defenses against primary emotions and often obscure what people experience at a deeper affective level. We argued that primary emotions are accessible to dialogical processing if they are freed from secondary emotions that may obscure them.

The concept of emotional authenticity was analyzed and described as a process that emerges at the dialogical interface between two emotions or groups of emotions, that is, between my emotions and the emotions of the actual other or other-in-the-self. Authenticity implies that the person is willing and able to listen to his own emotions and act on the basis of them. However, authentic emotions also take into account the emotions of the other-in-the-self and the actual other and are susceptible to their influences and innovative elements, so that one's own emotions are allowed, confirmed, or developed as a response to the emotions and positions of the other. In dialogical authenticity, the alterity of the other receives an answer from one's own emotions and positions.

We addressed three emotions that we consider particularly significant to different models of the self: (i) self-esteem emotions as relevant to the modern model; (ii) enjoyment as a typical emotion of the post-modern model; and (iii) gratitude as characteristic of the traditional model. In the discussion of self-esteem emotions, we gave attention to the costs of a persistent pursuit of self-esteem as typical of the modern model with its bias of self-sovereignty and independence. By way of contrast, we discussed the Korean phenomenon of *Shimcheong*, in which we-ness is celebrated. The difference between *Shimcheong* and the Western concept of emotional intelligence was highlighted. In the discussion of enjoyment we referred to increasing consumerism and its implications for the emotional domain of the self in contemporary society. This discussion led to the distinction between short-term enjoyment (typical of consumerism) and long-term enjoyment (typical of experiences that reach the deeper regions of the self). Referring to the relevance of the emotion of gratitude for the self, we summarized the result of an investigation which showed that words relevant to individualism and consumerism (e.g., "purchase" or "want more") have increased in recent decades, while words referring to solidarity or gratitude have decreased in the same period.

A central emotion for the dialogical self is love. We considered this emotion in the sense of "deep love" or "dialogical love" and argued that this emotion can be understood when one realizes that love is not oriented to the other as a separate person but also to the extensions of the self of the other. Conceived in this way, deep love is an "extension of an extension." In spatial terms, love was described as a movement in two directions at the same time: to the inner parts of the self and to the other as having an existence in the world. In this context, the difference between self-love and love for the other was discussed.

Finally, a stage model was described for the articulation, clarification, and change of emotions according to a dialogical procedure. The model consists of seven phases: (1) identifying and entering an emotion; (2) leaving the emotion; (3) identifying and entering a counter-emotion; (4) leaving the counter-emotion; (5) developing dialogical relations between emotion and counter-emotion; (6) creating a composition of emotions; and (7) introducing a promoter position in the context of emotions. In order to illustrate the use of the stage model in practice, an actual case was presented. Finally, in order to place the model in the broader context of the present book, the interpersonal and cultural implications of the model were highlighted in the context of the process of globalization.

NOTES

1 The notions of consonance and dissonance can also be applied to the communication *between* different people. Emotions are consonant when person A defines the emotion of person B in agreement with the experience of person B. There is dissonance when person A defines the emotion of person B in a way that is different from the experience of person B. For example, a mother may say to her child: "You are not sad, because *we* are positive people who always see the sunshine of life."

2 Emotions as organismic positions can become involved in the processes of self-conflict, self-criticism, self-agreement, and self-consultancy described in Chapter 3 as examples of the functioning of the self as a society of mind. Self-conflict: "I want her, but I cannot do this because she is married." Self-criticism: "As a father I criticize myself because I was too inconsiderate to my son." Self-agreement: "I make an agreement with myself to be strong next time and not permit him to intimidate me again." Self-consultancy: "I want

to consult myself so that I know what I have to do next time when I'm again in a situation of unsafe sex."

3 Whereas emotions are considered to be temporary ways of positioning that come and go according to the events that are taking place and to one's reactions to events, social positions or roles (e.g., father, psychologist, participant of a course) and personal positions (e.g., lover of classical music or interested in football) are considered to be of a more stable nature. Only when particular emotions become persistent across situations are they considered to be stable positions (e.g., "I'm depressed," or "He is hostile.")

4 Dialogical relationships lend themselves to be studied in terms of traits and individual differences. Puchalska-Wasyl, Chmielnicka-Kuter, and Oles (2008) devised a questionnaire method, called the Initial Questionnaire, for the assessment of three types of "internal activity" (i) change of perspective, (ii) monologue and (iii) dialogue. The purpose of this questionnaire is to determine which *I*-positions are reflected by the participant's imagined interlocutors and which of them provide new and different points of view. The participants receive a list of potential positions and select those that apply to them. They are permitted, moreover, to add positions phrased in their own terms. The selected and added positions, both internal and external ones, are then assessed as belonging to the dialogue, monologue, or perspective categories. In order to investigate the relationship between internal activity and traits, the researchers calculated the correlations between the Initial Questionnaire and the Revised NEO Personality Inventory (NEO PI-R) for several groups of Polish students. They found that persons with many inner dialogues scored significantly lower on assertiveness and higher on self-consciousness, fantasy, aesthetics, feelings and openness than people having internal monologues. They concluded that:

people entering into imaginary dialogues in comparison with ones having mainly monologues are characterized by a more vivid and creative imagination (Fantasy), a deep appreciation of art and beauty (Aesthetics) and receptivity to inner feelings and emotions (Feelings). They are curious about both inner and outer worlds and their lives are experientially richer. They are willing to entertain novel ideas and unconventional values and they experience positive as well as negative emotions more keenly (Openness). At the same time these persons are more disturbed by awkward social situations, uncomfortable around others, sensitive to ridicule, and prone to feelings of inferiority (Self-Consciousness). They prefer to stay in the background and let others do the talking (Assertiveness). (Puchalska-Wasyl et al., 2008: 257–8)

5 Changing the initial emotion as part of dialogue is a delicate issue. In some circumstances people feel a strong need to protect their emotion, and corresponding views and convictions, against the influence of others, particularly in circumstances in which innovative dialogue is experienced as implying costs to one's identity, affiliated as it is with such views and convictions. In such cases, dialogue may be experienced as making the person overly vulnerable to the influences of others. For example, Hubert Hermans remembers vividly the time he was invited to spend a year at the Netherlands Institute for Advanced Study in the Humanities and Social Sciences (NIAS) (1976–77), just after the first publication of his *Self-Confrontation Method* (1974). In the beginning of his stay at the Institute, he abstained from giving a presentation

about this work, because he felt it was highly "vulnerable" to potential criticism from his new colleagues. He experienced his recent work as a "small plant in the stage of its first growth" that was in need of protection until it was strong enough to be brought it into the arena of critical discussion.

6 Hesse (1951/1971) metaphorically described an impoverished position repertoire in this way: "Imagine a garden with a hundred kinds of trees, a thousand kinds of flowers, a hundred kinds of fruits and vegetables. Suppose, then, that the gardener of this garden knew no other distinction than between edible and inedible. Nine-tenths of this garden would be useless to him. He would pull up the most enchanting flowers and hew down the noblest trees."

7 In its connectedness with a broader animistic world, the traditional self experiences anxiety in the form of fear of ghosts, supernatural powers, devils, and demons. The modern self with its characteristic individualism, experiences anxiety in the form of fear of loneliness, while one of the characteristic emotions of the post-modern self is anxiety in the form of loss of hope, as a loss of belief in meaningful progress.

8 Although dialogical love as described in this section may sound an "ideal," it is not free from implicit or explicit tensions between positions. This tension was discussed at the world's first conference on intimate relationships with love robots, where participants discussed the personal relationships that will develop between humans and robots in future decades. Given the revolutionary developments in robotics, some participants thought that the construction of robots in the future would be so sophisticated that people would have sex with them, fall in love with them, and even marry them. Two types of robots were compared: "reliabots" who are unconditionally reliable and faithful and would never leave the owner in spite of possible aggressive or neglectful behavior; and "freebots" who put themselves in a "permanent non-responding mode" when seriously abused or maltreated. Which robot would you prefer, if you were to prefer any? In order to answer this question, the participants compared the intimate relationships with a robot with intimate relationships between living humans. It was concluded that people typically prefer a partner who is *faithful*, but who, at the same time, feels *free* to become engaged in a relationship or not. Apparently, most people prefer a relationship in which the loving partner is placed in two positions, faithful *and* free, namely, love as a multi-voiced process. This implies a tension in the sense that an increasing dominance of one position as part of an intimate relationship restricts the development of the other one, particularly in societies that put a high premium on independence. See www.unimaas.nl/humanrobot.

9 For a review see Vaknin, 2006. www.globalpolitician.com/21571-narcissism.

6   Practical implications for organizations, motivation, and conflict-resolution

*All married couples should learn the art of battle as they should learn
the art of making love. Good battle is objective and honest – never
vicious or cruel. Good battle is healthy and constructive, and brings to
a marriage the principle of equal partnership.*

Ann Landers

In this final chapter, we explore some practical implications of dialogical
self theory for the functioning of individuals, groups, and organizations.
The guiding idea is that dialogue and the dialogical self are not only theoretical developments but also basic principles that have the potential to
give form to the interaction within and between individuals and groups.
Dialogue needs not only study but also practice and has the potential to
enrich this practice. With this idea in mind, we will discuss some topics
where the practical implications of the dialogical self seem to be most
productive. We ask the following questions: How can organizations function in a more dialogical way? How can motivation profit from insights
into the functioning of the dialogical self? Is it possible to develop forms
of conflict resolution that take some basic insight in the dialogical nature
of the self into account? How can dialogue be stimulated and used to
solve social problems in emotional situations? It is not our intention to
give any final answers to these challenging questions or to restrict practical implication to the three topics mentioned above. It is our goal to
stimulate further thinking and exploration in such a way that readers find
their own ways of coping with similar questions and problems in their
own situations.

Organizations and the dialogical self

Usually, organizations are seen as social arrangements which are devised
to pursue collective goals, which control their own performance and
which have boundaries that separate them from their environment.[1]
Accordingly, there have been many attempts to define the culture of an
organization in terms of a set of features or characteristics. For example,

Handy (1985) distinguishes four types of culture: a "power culture" in which power is concentrated among a few people; a "role culture" where participants have clearly delegated authority (e.g., hierarchical bureaucracy) derived from a person's institutional position; a "task culture" where teams have the task of solving particular problems and power depends on the expertise of the team members; and a "person culture" where individuals believe that they are superior to the organization and the emphasis is not on the goals of the organization but on the purposes of individual people.

Handy's theory is only one example of prevailing theories on organizational culture. Other well-known theories are from Deal and Kennedy (1982), Schein (1985) and Hofstede (1980). Although these theories and implied categorizations have been very influential in the social sciences and beyond, they have also come in for criticism. There are scholars who have expressed skepticism about the unitary view of culture proposed by mainstream organizational theories. They have emphasized that cultural assumptions entail the risk of suppressing dissent and reproducing existing management propaganda and ideology, in this way blocking the necessary innovation of the organization. Indeed, in an increasingly interconnected world, it would be naive to believe that an organization as a whole can be characterized by one culture only or that one type of cultural engineering would reflect the interests of all stakeholders within a particular organization. Parker (2000), for example, has suggested that complex organizations might have many cultures, and that subcultures might overlap and contradict each other. The neat typologies of cultural forms published in textbooks, he argues, rarely acknowledge such complexities.

From the perspective of dialogical self theory, the objection to the unitary bias of mainstream theories of organizational culture is particularly relevant. This objection refers to the more general problem of how to define culture. Many definitions of culture are proposed and developed on the often implicit assumption of a homogeneous society metaphor. Such a metaphor results in overly unitary views of cultures in which cultures are seen as internally homogeneous and externally distinctive. For example, considering countries or regions as representing cultures in themselves, as exemplified by mainstream cultural theories, reflects a homogeneous society metaphor. Such a view is guided by the assumption that a culture can be characterized in terms of a pattern of dimensional traits that is used to characterize a culture as an undifferentiated whole. Other cultures are then described in terms of another pattern that also qualifies the culture as a whole. However, any approach based on a homogeneous society becomes increasingly obsolete as a result of the increasing process of globalization.[2] As discussed in Chapter 1, individuals and groups living in a globalizing world society are no longer located in one particular culture, homogeneous in itself and differentiated from other cultures, but are increasingly living at the interfaces of cultures (Appadurai, 1990; Arnett, 2001; Bhatia, 2007; Hermans and Kempen, 1998; Raggatt, 2000; Spiro, 1993; Wolf, 1982). The increasing interconnectedness of nations and cultures is not only reflected in an increasing contact between different cultural groups but also in increasing contact between cultures within the individual person. This process may result in multiple and multi-voiced identities – as a business representative educated in a French school system but working for a Chinese company; English-speaking employees living in India but giving technical training courses via the internet to adolescents in the United States; and a scientist with university training in Zimbabwe working as an immigrant in the UK. As parts of a heterogeneous and even contradictory self, such positions or voices may become engaged in mutual negotiations, agreements, disagreements, tensions, and conflicts. As different cultural voices, they are involved in various kinds of interchanges that are taking place on a continuum between monologue and dialogue, producing positive or negative meanings in fields of uncertainty. The global–local nexus is not just a reality outside the individual but is rather incorporated as a constituent of a dialogical self in action.

Dialogical self theory resists not only any container view of culture but also of organizations. A container view of organizations would suggest that it is possible to define an organization as an essence in itself and as having an existence that can be described as separate from its environment. However, organizations that are part of a globalizing world cannot be sufficiently described in terms of the specific region or nation to which they belong, because they are part of processes that transcend any localized group, region or culture. When organizations are becoming increasingly international, intercultural, and inter-local and, correspondingly, populated by people with multi-voiced selves and identities, then the objections that can be raised against any container view of culture in general applies also, more specifically, to any container view of the culture of organizations (Sillince, 2006).

Extended organizations

Not only is the self extended, but organizations are also increasingly extended towards their local and global environment. This is clearly reflected by the increasing popularity of the term "stakeholder" that has been commonly used to refer to a person, group, or organization that has a legitimate interest in a project or entity. It includes everyone who has an interest (or "stake") in what the entity is doing. It refers not only to individuals and groups who have direct interest in what is going on in the organization (e.g., employees, salespeople, shareholders, investors, and customers) but also to the members of the broader community who are affected, in one way or another, by the functioning of the organization (e.g., labor unions, professional associations, prospective employees and customers, ecological movements, schools, local communities, and even the global community). This extension of the organization to the broader environment has led to a major debate in the field of corporate responsibility about whether a company or firm should be managed for shareholders only or for the broader group of stakeholders.[3]

One of the implications of an extended view of self and organization is that a *broader range of roles* ("social positions" in the present theory) is involved when corporate responsibility is extended to a heterogeneous group of stakeholders of an organization involved in the processes of globalization and localization. Given its specific mission and goals, an organization requires a certain amount of coordination of its parts, even when these parts are globally distributed. Moreover, the extension of the organization from shareholder to stakeholder requires a certain amount of communication between all the different parties involved. Given the need for coordination and communication, dialogical relationships are becoming increasingly important in the everyday activities of organizations, certainly when innovation is a high priority issue.

Many organizations in the world find themselves involved in a process of change from a hierarchically structured authoritarian organization, typical of the traditional period in collective history, towards a more democratic organization, stimulated by the Enlightenment project of the modern period that favored equality above authoritarianism. This trend is further stimulated by the decentralizing tendencies typical of the postmodern period in history (see Chapter 2). One consequence of the process of democratization is that social power is no longer located in one or a few positions in the organization, but spread over a larger and more heterogeneous range of stakeholders who can no longer be "directed" by any superordinate institutional position. That does not mean that institutional power is disappearing. It means, rather that it is distributed among a broader range of roles or positions that have, in one way or another, interest in the functioning, profit, risks, and failures of the organization. This distribution of power has the consequence that the self is no longer governed by one or a few dominating positions in the internal or external domain, but that different positions or coalitions of positions in the self are involved in relationships of relative dominance.

In our view, the process of democratization in extending organizations requires stakeholders with an extended dialogical self. Such a self has a broadened range of external positions, that is, positions that refer to other parties having an interest in the functioning of the organization and its implications for the broader society. Corresponding to the diverse range of stakeholders, a diverse range of values is involved. While shareholders are exclusively or primarily interested in financial and economical values, ecological movements are concerned with the quality of the environment. Whereas the labor unions are involved in the wages, benefits, and working conditions of their members, universities are interested in the education and training of their students and in performing scientific research. When all those parties are involved as stakeholders of extended organizations and when these stakeholders have different value systems, they can only interact in productive ways when the extended selves of their members take into account the alterity of the other parties involved in the organization (for the notion of alterity as part of dialogical processes, see Chapter 3).

Organizations, like selves, are continually involved in processes of decentralization and centralization. The process of globalization mainly has a decentralizing influence on the self. When a firm is populated by different cultural voices, each with their own values, practices, and traditions, decentralizing processes may result in disorganization and fragmentation. At the same time, diversity is a challenge to the organization because it entails the possibility of innovation. However, innovation, although initially a decentralizing force, requires a certain amount of centralization in a later stage in order to ensure a minimal integration of the apparent diversity. Apparently, organizations find themselves located in a field of tension between, on the one hand, decentralizing movements that result from their increasing multiplicity, and, on the other, centralizing movements that are needed to ensure a minimal amount of coordination and integration of positions and associated activities in the service of their mission. We hypothesize that the best condition for the development of an organization is when it is able to make decentralizing movements in response to the variety of needs and purposes of its different stakeholders, and to make centralizing movements in the service of the coordination, integration, stability, and the survival of its parts. Like a self, an organization has parts (e.g., leaders), that are more central to the mission of the organization than other parts. These parts are particularly relevant in times of dramatic change, because, more than other parts, they have the potential to create the necessary centralizing movements. What applies to the self (Chapter 4), also applies to organizations: they can reach a higher level of development when they find ways to combine the innovative potentials of decentralizing movements and the integrating potentials of centralizing movements.

The dialogical leader

For the combination of centralizing and decentralizing movements in an organization a particular kind of leadership is required. In the context of a discussion of effective organizations, Van Loon (2003) proposed the notion of "dialogical leadership," that he described in terms of a flexible movement between a diversity of *I*-positions that are relevant to the functioning of the organization as a whole. Examples of important leadership positions are "I as entrepreneur," "I as manager," "I as coach," and "I as professional." From the perspective of different positions the leader pursues different goals. For example, as an entrepreneur she is concerned about developing a vision for the future of the organization, as a manager to plan and organize, as a coach to stimulate colleagues to develop themselves in the light of the mission, and as a professional to contribute to the organization from the perspective of a particular discipline. Depending on the prevailing needs of the organization, the leader actualizes a particular position in a particular situation. Moreover, dialogical relationships between the different positions are needed so that the positions can negotiate with and learn from each other. The vision the leader develops about the future of the organization as an entrepreneur has consequences for the way she plans and organizes activities as a manager and for the ways her personnel are coached. This does not mean that the leader has to perform all these activities herself. Indeed, other people are involved in the realization of the purposes emanating from the different *I*-positions. The kernel is that the different positions are part of the repertoire of the leader so that she knows when and where these positions can be actualized and what she can learn from these positions in their interconnection.

It is not only internal positions that are involved in dialogical leadership, but external positions are also of central concern. The people with whom the leader discusses entrepreneurial strategies are often people other than those with whom she engages in the position of manager or coach. Or, as entrepreneur, she talks with the same person in a way different from that as manager or coach. That is, she evokes in the participant another position from the one she evokes as manager. For example, some leaders run the risk of focusing on short-term tasks and the solution of immediate problems, and in doing so they are narrowing their attention to tasks of immediate urgency, not feeling able to work actively on long-term entrepreneurial purposes. In an extreme case they become "firefighters" and neglect tasks and purposes that are relevant to the long-term future of the organization. A dialogical leader is able not only to differentiate between relevant positions in her self, but also to differentiate between corresponding positions in other participants of the organization and to invite them to make a "position-shift" so that the same problem can be seen from a different perspective.

Authentic leadership It is a generally accepted view that good leadership is authentic leadership. As Shamir and Eilam (2005) observe, a review of the literature shows that there is no single accepted definition of authentic leadership. However, the authors note that certain elements are shared by all contributors on the topic. Authentic leaders are portrayed as being engaged in self-reflection and self-knowledge, and as having a personal point of view, giving them a certain degree of clarity about their selves. They are also described as identifying strongly with their leadership role and as acting on the basis of their personal values and convictions. In terms of dialogical self theory, authentic leadership is rooted in the self, that is, the person functions according to his personal and social positions and their affective properties. However, in addition to existing conceptions of authentic leadership, we emphasize – in line with the discussion of this topic in Chapter 5 – that authenticity is based on communication not only on the part of the person to the other (e.g., acting on the basis of one's self-concept), but also vice versa. In that context, we emphasize that authentic leadership takes the communicative feedback from an actual or imagined other into account, so that the positions both of the leader and his colleagues become part of dialogical relationships. We propose that dialogue is more than communication, in that it does not simply communicate a particular emotion, reasonable argument, or message, but also *confirms* it or *adds* something to it that was not there at the onset of the communication. Such new elements (e.g, insights, common feelings, or compassion) are added to the emotion as a result of being part of a process of innovative dialogue.

We propose that authentic leadership takes into account their own emotion, the emotion of the other, and the distinction between the two. When I'm experiencing an emotion in the context of a dialogue, I'm experiencing not only my own emotion but also the actual, imagined, or anticipated emotion of the other. These two emotions are more than separate experiential elements simply exchanged like bits of information. Rather, they take each other into account from the beginning of the dialogical process. Such a dialogue can have different forms. When I can easily identify with the emotion of the other, my own emotion does not just stay the same but receives *confirmation* by the emotion of the other. When, as a result of an interchange, I discover that my emotion is different from the emotion of the other, then I'm aware of my emotion as "different from yours" and I can take these difference into account in future communications. It is also possible that, as a result of a co-constructive interchange, we develop a common emotion in which I find myself together with you.

A dialogical leader contributes to the realization of collective goals as formulated in the mission statement of the organization. He does so not on the basis of a separation between the collective goals of the organization and his personal goals. Rather, he is attuned to his personal aims and to the collective aims of the organization, feeding them and innovating them on the basis of his personal and social positions and those of his colleagues. When the organization does not allow the leader to coordinate and integrate his own positions in accordance with those of his social environment, then this leader is not able or allowed to function as an authentic leader in the organization. The leader can only be authentic when he manages to coordinate his own positions and those of his coworkers in such a way that they are arranged as *coalitions in the service of the realization of the mission of the organization*. These coalitions are not developed like "homogeneous packages" that require blind conformation to the purposes of the organization. Instead, they are heterogeneous enough to allow participants to contribute to the common activities each from their own point of view. Productive coalitions allow non-conformity and unorthodox points of view (Zomer, 2006).[4]

It is essential for dialogical leadership that the leader himself is introduced into the position repertoire of his colleagues as a promoter position. In this sense, the leader is not purely outside the self of the participants of the organization but included as a common part of their external positions. As an inspiring leader, he receives a place in the self of the participants, who take him as a model for the realization of the mission of the organization. One of the central features of a promoter position is that it has the potential to generate and integrate a broader range of future positions. As a promoter position in the selves of the participants, the leader has access to their selves so that his inspiration leads to the coordination and integration of their positions in productive coalitions.

The leader can only function as a promoter in the self of his colleagues when he has affectively rooted positions available and accessible in his own self that are able to create inspiration and commonality in the selves of his colleagues. Although the actualization of positions is contingent on the needs and circumstances of the organization, some positions seem to be of more importance than others. A position that is particularly relevant as a promoter is "I as acceptant." By this position we do not mean that the leader has to agree with everything that happens in the organization. Rather, we have in mind a leader who is able to listen patiently and profoundly to the voices of his co-workers and to those of himself. Acceptance means that things happen as they happen and the leader sees things as they are, without denying their existence or avoiding confrontation with problems or conflicts. Another position that has a promoter function is "I as artistic." This position has the advantage that a larger variety of other positions can be seen as parts of an overarching artistic pattern. Positions are not seen in their isolation but as belonging to a larger composition so that they become meaningful as part of that encompassing pattern. Such a pattern gives rise to an atmosphere that makes people feel part of something that transcends their purely practical concerns and daily worries. A third position that has a promoter spirit for many leaders is "I as spiritual." Although this term has many meanings, this position has for many people the special feature that it can open the door to participation in a broader field of awareness, as discussed in Chapter 3. In any organization in which the participants are driven by the persistent pursuit of self-esteem or are under the spell of enhancing their ego, the risk is that they follow aims that are not in tune with the mission of the organization. In such cases energy is invested in purely personal positions that may deviate from or even work against relevant collective goals. Positions, such as acceptant, artistic, and spiritual, as promoters in the self of the leader, can only become productive if the leader succeeds in inspiring his colleagues to develop similar positions in their own selves. Along these lines they can grow into the selves of all participants so that they become collective positions or voices in the service of the mission of the organization.

Promoter positions are not restricted to the internal domain of the leader only. External ones are also relevant to dialogical leadership. For example, important figures in the history of the organization, such as the founder or any other iconic figure who has contributed in exceptional ways to the development of the firm or company, function as sources of inspiration and as models to the leader and, facilitated by him, to all participants of the organization. Shared narratives around such figures are often the cement of the organization and contribute significantly to the fostering of a heterogeneous, yet integrative organizational culture.

In sum, on the basis of the material presented in earlier chapters of this book, we outline a model of a "dialogical leader" that has several defining features. A dialogical leader is able to move in flexible ways between different *I*-positions, such as entrepreneur, manager, coach, and professional, and to establish dialogical relationships between such positions so that they can learn from each other in the service of the mission of the organization. Moreover, a dialogical leader is authentic in the sense that she acts on the basis of her emotions and reason and, moreover, takes into account the emotions and reason of the other with whom she is involved in interaction. Further, the leader is allowed to be introduced as part of the external domain of the participants of the organization. As a promoter position in the selves of the participants, she coordinates and integrates the positions of the participants in coalitions in the service of the mission of the organization. Such coalitions are not homogeneous and do not lead to a suffocating conformity but give room for divergent and dissident voices. Three positions in particular serve as promoters: the acceptant, the artistic, and the spiritual. Finally, relevant figures in the history of the organization function as promoter positions in the external domains of the leader and the participants. The model of the dialogical leader transcends not only the notion of the container self, so typical of the modern model of the self, but also the notion of the container organization. In principle, all stakeholders who are part of an extended organization are dependent on the actuality and needs of the parties involved, and these parties are potential positions in the external domain of the self of the dialogical leader.

The need for a heterogeneous position repertoire of the self in organizations: two examples

During the preparation of this book, I (Hubert Hermans) have given several lectures about the dialogical self in the context of organizations. Two discussions will be briefly presented here, one that took place in a group that was interested in exploring and introducing innovations in school organizations (high schools) and another that was organized by a group that served as a "think tank" of a police organization. Although the nature and mission statements of the two organizations were very different, the discussions of both groups resulted in conclusions that were strikingly similar.

Competence-oriented education   The school innovation group was primarily concerned about the development of competence-oriented education. The core of this education is that students acquire competences – knowledge, skills, and attitudes – that are relevant to the corresponding professional practice (e.g., learning to cooperate in a team). As part of this program, students learn to communicate and cooperate with other students and their teachers in a variety of tasks. Teachers and students all have access to relevant information such as schedules, course material, and obtained marks. The learning process evolves on the basis of a personal development plan which students draw up under the supervision of their teachers. In this plan students are required to reflect on their own educational development.[5]

It appears that competence-oriented education is not self-evident for many teachers, trained as they are to function as experts in a conventional school system. They are used to transfer knowledge to their students, explaining the subject matter and giving tasks of an increasing complexity. The students acquire the relevant knowledge and receive marks for their achievements. This all takes place in an educational process that is to a high degree controlled by the teacher.

During our discussion in the innovation group, we observed that in the conventional school system the teacher was mainly in one position, that of the knowledgeable expert who transfers his know-how to the students. However, in the new system, he has to act from another position, that of a coach. Whereas the expert position allows him to teach, the coach position requires him to coach and supervise. We concluded that in the new learning process both positions are needed. When students, as organizers of their own learning process, need support and advice, they approach the teacher as coach, but when they are in need of information or expert knowledge (not easily accessible via the internet), they address the teacher as an expert. That is, teachers are required to expand their repertoire beyond existing conventions and to move flexibly from one position to another and back. Each of the positions is in need of specific skills, attitudes, and knowledge and implies a different relationship with the student.

On the part of the students a similar process can be observed. When they are learning from the teacher as an expert, they are required to be in a receptive position. However, when they are coached by the teacher as part of their personal educational development, they are addressed in self-reflexive and self-responsible positions. The relationships between an expert teacher and a receptive student and between a coaching teacher and a self-responsible student open dialogical possibilities between them so that positions learn from each other both within and between selves.

Towards a serviceable police organization   A similar line emerged in a discussion with a group of police commissioners who regularly came together as a think-tank for the innovation of the police organization in the Netherlands. In this group there was extensive discussion of the specific culture of the police organization. The organization was described as a hierarchical one with a strong command structure. Like police organizations in many other countries, its paramilitary nature is emphasized by uniform dress, classroom order, and by stress on correct behavior (see also Harrison, 1998). Its culture is strongly determined by the authority police officers have as "guardians of the law." They represent a puritanical morality by which they think in terms of right *or* wrong, good *or* bad, in this way judging in terms of mutually exclusive opposites.[6] This or–or thinking leads often to the claim that there is only one truth so that alternative explanations of events are often not taken into account. This results in a monological way of thinking because assumptions of truth are typically associated with a lack of openness towards another person who gives another meaning to a particular event or situation. In combination with the strong command structure, assumptions of truth often lead to misunderstandings that are not sufficiently dialogically processed. As Harrison (1998), in agreement with Drummond (1976), notes, the hierarchical structure of the larger police departments shows the problem of distance in command which can result in considerable message distortion, both from the top down and the bottom up.

The participants in our discussion agreed that not only was the police organization traditionally hierarchical but also that its organizational culture was dominated by a right versus wrong dichotomy. Things are good *or* bad. However, they added that the police organization was making an important transition from a "guardians of the law" orientation to a service orientation. An example of this change is the introduction of "district cops" who are closer to the people living in a particular area of the city and have more opportunity to establish a closer relationship with them, with the advantage that they not only give support where necessary but also receive support when they need it. The introduction of a more service-oriented police is not without problems because, in the experience of many officers, a service orientation often conflicts with the conventional belief that their task is to act in order to maintain the law. It is not only in the Netherlands, but in the USA too, that this resistance is noticed. As Harrison (1998) observes, the move toward a "community-oriented police" meets with substantial resistance from the rank and file. Cries like "we are cops, not social workers" are voiced frequently.

Despite the resistance of the traditional police culture toward a more community-oriented performance, the members of our group saw this model as the most desirable for future police organization: a culture in which not one position ("I as maintaining the law") but at least two positions ("I as maintaining the law" and "I as service-oriented") were part of the repertoire of police officers. In spite of the resistance of hardliners, the commissioners proposed that a "multi-positional" or "multi-voiced" self should be a central ingredient in future training programs for police officers. They added that such a training program could only be successful when part of an organizational culture that becomes more communicative and dialogical. Such programs, introduced at the bottom of the organization, could only be successful if actively supported at the top.

There were three apparent points in common between the discussions in the education group and the police group. They both emphasized the importance of developing a broader position repertoire for the members of their organizations. Moreover, they agreed on the necessity of flexible movement between the different positions, as compatible elements in the repertoire of the participants of the organization. Finally, they made a plea for a more open organizational culture in which different, seemingly contradictory, roles should be trained for and developed. The two groups also found it desirable that conventional roles should not be abandoned in favor of new ones, but rather combined with them. In terms of dialogical self theory, the old positions are included as parts of a coalition with the new ones in order to meet the needs of a contemporary society challenged by the growing need for multiplicity and diversity in the culture of organizations.

Motivation: beyond individual traits

From a dialogical point of view, motivation finds its basis not in an individual trait but in social relationships. Traditionally, psychologists create tests for several forms of motivation starting from the assumption that they can be understood in terms of relatively stable personality dispositions. For example, McClelland *et al.* (1953) developed a Thematic Apperception Test (TAT) scoring procedure for the assessment of the achievement motive. In his earlier work, Hermans (1970) constructed a personality questionnaire for the assessment of the same motive in an attempt to find an alternative to the complex TAT procedure. However, what the two procedures have in common is that they are both based on the individual difference paradigm (Lamiell, 1987). In the course of time, we became aware that motivation has social aspects that cannot be explained by this paradigm in any satisfactory way, based as it is on a conception of "personality" as having an existence separate from the environment. Therefore, we explored a dialogical approach to motivation that goes far beyond any trait approach in its basic assumption of a spatially and temporally extended self.

A dialogical theory of motivation takes into account the spatial nature of the self. On a most basic level this means that *motivation is creating space*: when one wants to motivate another person or oneself to invest energy in achieving a particular goal, the primary activity is to provide experiential space for the parties who work on this goal. To illustrate the importance of space: remember a talk or conversation with somebody in which you felt constricted by a "lack of space." You want to convey a particular experience, plan, or proposal but the other person begins to say that he has some "objections." You try again, explaining more of your thoughts, trying to express what you have experienced or what you want. However, your respondent seems to stick to his initial point of view and repeat what he has already said. Gradually, you begin to become aware that, whatever you say or propose, it doesn't seem to make any difference. You feel that the other is responding to your remarks from his own frame of reference only and that this frame is entirely closed to any argument or experience you bring in. Rather than tuning in to your experiences or arguments, your respondent seems to rely on generalizing statements or even on stereotypical opinions rather than on what you have said or argued during the discussion. You have the feeling of "not coming across" and dialogue seems to be impossible. Even when you try to be dialogical, you feel that it "does not work" because you do not find an "entrance" to the self of the other. Typical of this monological communication, is the feeling of lack of space and lack of openness, expressed not only verbally but also in body language.

The reverse experience can be found when you are part of a relationship that you experience as "motivating" or "inspiring." Some people give you the feeling that they are open to what you have to tell. You notice that they listen quietly and do not interrupt; they ask open questions that may give you new perspectives, and sometimes reveal something about themselves that invites you to think more creatively about yourself; they do not judge, do not give unsolicited advice, do not provide quick interpretations and do not force you to fit with their system of reference. Such a dialogical exchange takes place not only at the verbal but also at the non-verbal level. Some people are able to listen in such a way that, when you tell them something, your words "come back" as different from the way you sent them out, even when the other person doesn't say a word. The intensity and concentration of listening, and the corresponding openness of the embodied selves of the conversational partners can be, in some cases, enough to facilitate a dialogical process.

What is the difference between motivating and de-motivating communication? The main feature of de-motivating communication is that the selves of both partners, or of one of them, are governed by particular positions that overly restrict and close the repertoire. Typically, the participants, or one of them, are talking from a defensive position which, on emotional grounds, receives top priority in the self and makes the participants respond from this position only (e.g., when defining one's point of view as the only "right" one so that the possible "right" of the participant is felt as a threat). Sometimes this position goes together with a critical one which means that any suggestion or proposal on the part of the other is answered from these positions only. Together the defensive and critical positions close off the self and, as a result, strongly restrict the space between and within the selves of the participants. They do not allow themselves to take any risk and reduce their tolerance for uncertainty as much as possible. Moreover, the restriction and closure of their selves prevents the emergence of a common space, with the result that the motivation to cooperate on a common task is considerably reduced.

In contrast, a motivating communication emerges when the participants allow each other to express not only the positions from which they enter into communication, but also experience the freedom to move to other positions as they are felt relevant by the participants to the realization of their goals. They feel free to move to and fro between different positions so that the topic of discussion can be viewed from different angles. The free movement among positions and openness to new inputs allows a common space to emerge that enables the participants to develop a shared perspective that was simply not there at the beginning of their communication. In this dialogical space they allow themselves to take risks and enjoy the positive aspects of exploration and uncertainty.

Basic self-conflict and the possibility of integrative motivation

The notion of space is only one factor that is necessary for understanding the process of motivation. In order to explore this process at a deeper level, we should pay attention to what can be described as the "basic conflict" of the self. This conflict drives the self into two directions: the tendency to become involved in one position only and to develop this position to the fullest on the one hand, and the tendency to develop the self as a whole, with its rich variety of parts, on the other. These two aims can never go perfectly together as long as the realization of one position necessarily implies that the development of other positions receive a lower priority in the development of the self as a whole.

As a preliminary to a discussion of basic self-conflict, we cite this well-known passage from James (1890: 309–10):

I'm often confronted by the necessity of standing by one of my empirical selves and relinquishing the rest. Not that I would not, if I could, be both handsome and fat and well-dressed, and a great athlete, and make a million a year, be a wit, a *bon-vivant*, and a lady-killer, as well as a philosopher; a philanthropist, statesman, warrior, and African explorer, as well as a 'tone-poet" and saint.

But the thing is simply impossible. The millionaire's work would run counter to the saint's; the *bon-vivant* and the philanthropist would trip each other up; the philosopher and the lady-killer could not well keep house in the same tenement of clay. Such different characters may conceivably at the outset of life be alike *possible* to a man. But to make any of them actual, the rest must more or less be suppressed. So the seeker of his truest, strongest, deepest self must review the list carefully, and pick out the one on which to stake his salvation.

As this quotation suggests, a great variety of positions is possible to an individual, but in order to make any of them actual the rest have to be more or less suppressed. One of the interesting aspects of the quotation is that James seems to think of the relationship between the different positions in terms of their mutual competition or conflict. The actualization of one position "runs counter" to the realization of another one, so that the person is, more or less, forced to choose and to focus on one or a few of them. The existence of such conflicts impedes the development of the self as a whole, as this whole is closely connected with the development of a variety of other positions that are desirable, yet not realizable at the same time.

It can be asked to what extent the developmental paths of the different positions are mutually exclusive. In an exploration of this question, Schachter (2002) criticized some basic assumptions in Marcia's (1966) Ego Identity Status Theory. In this theory the notion of "identity achievement" implies that the adolescent has made a *commitment* to a sense of identity that he has *chosen* among a variety of alternatives. In agreement with James's view on the "suppression of the rest," Marcia's theory is focused on sameness and continuity as basic elements of a mature identity, an identity that is constrained by structural elements such as closure, consistency, and commitment. As Schachter argues, this identity theory is challenged by post-modern conceptions that portray a relatively unconstrained, mutable, multiple, Protean, changing self that is inconsistent across situations.

In his own research with a group of Jewish orthodox young adults, Schachter (2002) found empirical evidence for his objections to the notion of "identity achievement." On the basis of his interviews, he found that in the view of his respondents a "good identity" implied not only a certain degree of consistency, sameness and continuity, but also what he called "the inclusion of all significant identifications." His respondents did not restrict themselves to one commitment but instead tried to develop different contradictory or seemingly contradictory identifications. For example, they were not only committed to particular religious views, but also found the enjoyment of sex an important part of their lives. The realization of a certain degree of continuity in their experiential process did not exclude the development of different identifications in a diversity of areas of life.

We consider the simultaneity of identifications, or, in our terms, of *I*-positions, as crucial to a profound understanding of motivation. As argued in the previous chapters, we acknowledge the existence of conflicts, contradictions, and oppositions in the self, but, at the same time, propose that many conflicts, contradictions, and oppositions can be reconciled or mitigated by the development of coalitions of positions as an expression of centering movements in the self. In this light, we propose the thesis that *strong coalitions create strong motivation.*[7] As argued in Chapter 1, we live in a era in which the self is "visited" by an increasing number and heterogeneity of positions or voices, leading to an increase of possible conflicts and contradictions in the self. However, when these become frequent and intense, the development of the self as a whole becomes problematic, because, if we would follow James's insight, in the case of conflicting positions the development of one position would run counter to the development of another. However, the possibility of developing coalitions, even of conflicting positions, creates a condition for combining them in such a way that their energy is used in the service of a common purpose. Coalitions have the advantage of creating cross-fertilizations between otherwise conflicting positions. When it is possible to transform win–lose relationships between positions into win–win relationships, the motivation for a particular task or purpose profits from the energy of both positions. However, when win–lose relationships continue to prevail, the development of one position is thwarted by a conflicting position (Nir and Kluger, 2006).

Nir (2008) suggests a negotiational view of the self and explains that transforming a win–lose relationship into a win–win relationship is possible by creating a *space* within the self where the conflicting positions are allowed to express themselves fully so that new forms of cooperation can be explored. The process, termed the Negotiational Self Method, takes place in four stages. In the first stage, a conflict is identified and defined in "for" and "against" terms (e.g., "for getting close to a new person" and "against getting close to a new person"). In the second stage, positions that are relevant to the conflict are encouraged to voice themselves and are mapped under the two poles of the conflict. For example, "I as fearful" would be placed under the "against getting close to a new person" pole, and "I as trustful" under the "for getting close to a new person" pole. Thus, an array of positions is elicited, and each position is placed at one of the two poles. In the third stage, self-knowledge is expanded by inquiring into the needs, interests, and motives that each position represents, creating space to express themselves from their own point of view. For example, to inquire into the underlying needs of "I as fearful" different questions can be used, such as "What specifically are you afraid of?", "Why are you afraid of this?" and "What do you achieve by being afraid?" The answers to these questions may reveal that all "I as fearful" really wants is to make sure that the self is safe and secure, and that nothing bad will happen to it. This understanding helps re-establish "I as fearful" not as a position that is working *against* the self, but rather as an *I*-position that is trying to work *for* the self (although sometimes with high win–lose costs to the self). Finally, drawing on the preceding stages, the fourth stage leads to the formulation of a win–win solution, which aims to incorporate the needs of different and opposing *I*-positions into a single integrative solution (e.g., learning to approach new people in a way that guarantees some safety, rather than avoiding them on the basis of anxiety).

As this example shows, the transformation of a conflicting position (e.g, "I as fearful") is possible by going through a process in which the different needs, expectations and affective properties of the conflicting relationship are explored in a dialogical space. This process has several features: (a) the position ("I as fearful") is fully heard, acknowledged, and validated as important and valuable to the self; (b) a deeper understanding of the fearful position may be achieved so that the self becomes aware of the underlying security and safety needs it represents for the self; and finally (c) in the integrative solution that is reached, "I as fearful" experiences that its needs for security can be satisfied without having to suppress the needs of other positions, and without at the same time giving up its safety needs. Therefore, reaching integrative solutions over time may transform "I as fearful," or for that matter any other conflicting position that is experienced as disturbing the self. The result of this transformation is that "I as fearful" is less in need of dominating the self in order to make sure its security needs are met, and becomes more open to collaborating with other *I*-positions (Nir, 2008).

As the negotiational approach of Nir and Kluger (2006) shows, dialogue in the self, supported by dialogue with the facilitator, makes an integrative solution to a conflict possible. Thanks to a thorough dialogical exchange, conflicting positions can be explored and transformed in a dialogical space. Without a profound dialogue, any attempt to form a coalition between conflicting positions would most likely result in a jungle in which each position tries to overpower the other and neither takes the perspectives and needs of the other position into account. Dialogue is the basis for a process that leads to fertile coalitions and win–win relationships within the self so that the best forces in each of the conflicting parties are combined to maximize the profit for the self as a whole.

A negotiational approach to positions and emotions is also significant
in the context of a globalizing society. As we have argued in Chapter 1,
external conflicts (e.g., with other cultural groups) and internal conflicts
(with shadow positions in the self) are not to be viewed separately from
each other. Confronting oneself – and coming to terms – with the stranger
in the self, is a precondition for coming to terms with the stranger in
a multi-cultural environment. In a globalizing society, individuals and
groups of very different origin meet each other in a compressed world.
Such a world is full of interfaces where individuals, groups, and cultures,
new to each other, meet, while having little knowledge about each other's
origin, traditions, and value systems. The chance of inter-group conflict,
fueled by intra-individual conflicts, is high and, therefore, requires effective internal and external negotiational procedures that are useful for the
co-construction of common spaces.

The reconciliation of conflicting positions was also found in Branco
et al.'s (2008) study of a lesbian woman, Rosanne, raised in a conservative Catholic environment. As a response to her conflicting positions "I
as lesbian" and "I as Catholic," she developed a third position, in the
form of "I as a missionary" that was able to combine the energies generated by the two original positions. The third position enabled her not
only to participate *in* but also to work *for* the lesbian community, particularly for members with a marginalized position in society. A reconciliation of positions was also found in the case of a man who lived for a long
time with an unproductive coalition between the perfectionist and the
doubter, with the enjoyer being in conflict with both of them (Hermans,
2001a). In the course of counselling, he developed a new coalition in
which the perfectionist was trained to delegate tasks at the right time,
so that he gradually learned to combine his striving for perfection with
enjoyment of the result. As part of the new, more productive, coalition
between the perfectionist and the enjoyer, the original conflict between
the perfectionist and the enjoyer was reduced. This new coalition contributed significantly to his work motivation because both the perfectionist and the enjoyer invested their energy in their mutual cooperation.

We can see, also on the collective level, instances of reconciliation of
conflicting positions. Sports events, for example, have the potential to
create productive coalitions. In the final of the UEFA European football competition in 2008 in Vienna, the irresistible attacking football of
the Spanish team of coach Luis Aragonés led them to a first major tro-
phy success in forty-four years. Football was able to create what politics
could not achieve: to unite strongly opposed geographical regions. The
winning team brought together players from three areas – Catalonia, the
Community of Madrid and the Basque country – in a successful coalition

that was able to transcend, at least for some time, any political controversy. The event highlighted central elements of the Olympic ideal: the combination of excellence, knowledge, and a peaceful world.

For the development and creation of motivation, strong coalitions are necessary, in both the internal and the external domains of the self. Motivation is the result not only of positions and their motivating impulses but also of external positions and their motivating impulses. Sometimes, motivation is fueled by the energy to go from an internal position *against* an external position in the self. We can observe this motivation wherever a person fights for the just recognition he never received in his past, and, in order to redress this injustice, wants to show to himself and others that he is able to do it in his own and independent way (e.g., "I'm a fighter and will show my father that I'm able to make this career in which he never believed"). Even when the actual other (the father in this example) is no longer alive, such a position as part of the extended domain of the self may continue to function as a motivating source during a lifetime, evoking and energizing a strong anti-position in the internal domain of the self. More frequently, however, strong motivation results when internal and external positions form *coalitions*. When people talk about their lives and job histories, one often hears them mentioning how their fathers, mothers, and teachers played a significant role in their job history and in their motivation to become involved in particular activities and occupations. Some people may say, "In developing these skills in myself, I was inspired by my teacher," or "I see this project as a tribute to my friend who died too early." Motivation results from internal–external coalitions with mutually complementary positions. For example, the Iranian-Dutch novelist Kader Abdolah revealed in an autobiographical speech[8] that his work was strongly influenced by his father, who was mute and deaf and with whom he used to communicate by means of a language of private gestures. In the contact with his father he became vividly aware of the role of limitations in a person's life. As a reaction to this awareness, he developed several "dreams" in which he imagined himself to be without the limitations of his father. One of them was to become the president of his country, another to become a famous writer. Later in his life, he fled to the Netherlands. In a moment of "illumination" he decided to write in Dutch. He went to a library and asked for a book in Dutch but explained that he could not understand the language. The librarian then gave him a very simple but popular booklet particularly loved by children. On the basis of this book he learned the language and finally became a first-rank author. Reflecting on his experiences, he became aware that the limitations of his father had had a long-lasting influence on his motivation. He considered that his choice to become a novelist in a strange language was a powerful response to the handicaps of his father, motivating him to explore the ultimate boundaries of learning and development. In terms of dialogical self theory, he developed a coalition of positions in which "my father as handicapped" and "I as a dreamer" were central parts in a coalition with strong motivating energies. As the example suggests, motivation is particularly strong when it has a broad basis in the repertoire, that is, in a diversity of internal and external positions. Motivation profits from a large number of heterogeneous positions that form together a coalition and are oriented in the same direction. As part of a coalition, positions are organized in such a way that they cooperate in order to achieve complex aims or tasks.

Integrative motivation is also a necessary ingredient in the personnel policy of organizations. Personnel policy is located in a field of tension between two needs. "Good policy" is in need of individuals and teams who fit sufficiently well with each other to realize the mission(s) of the organization. This "fitting" refers to a centralizing movement in the organization that keeps expertise and talents together in integrative ways. At the same time organizations are in need of an innovation policy that challenges the organization with the introduction of new expertise, talents, and tasks so that they break existing structures, habits, and rituals. Moreover, as part of the process of globalization, the extended environment in which organizations are located is frequently changing. These two factors together, the introduction of new talents and tasks and a changing environment, produce de-centering movements in the organization. Good policy takes into account both centering and de-centering movements in the service of the development of the organization and its mission. Such a policy requires the stimulation of a broad bandwidth of positions in the selves of the members of the organization. The bandwidth is sufficiently broad when participants have the opportunity to introduce a variety of new positions into their work, while at the same time being able to integrate these positions into coalitions that are organized in the light of the mission. The mission should be formulated and reformulated in a way that permits the emergence of productive coalitions of positions both within individuals (cooperation between positions in the self) and between individuals (cooperation between the positions of different individuals).

To summarize: in his work, James (1890) describes a basic self-conflict that is reflected in some modern theories of self and identity. This conflict emerges from the tension between the development of a specific position and the development of the self as a whole (in the sense of a large variety of positions). Although the basic self-conflict can never be fully resolved, it leaves room for the reconciliation of conflicts and for bringing together opposites that seem to be mutually exclusive at first glance. Our main argument is that coalitions of conflicting or opposing positions have the potential of creating a strong motivation that surpasses the interests of positions in their isolation. As in a society, different positions in the self form a productive group when they combine their specific kinds of expertise in order to realize complex goals. Such a group creates a form of "integrative motivation." Such motivation emerges in a field of tension between centering and de-centering movements in the self. This motivation is relevant to the development not only of individuals but also of teams and organizations.

Making the role of the other

Motivation as a social process implies the construction of coalitions of internal and external positions. We can ask what the nature of external positions is as part of cooperation with other positions. In order to answer this question we must bear in mind that a dialogue with an actual other is only possible when this other as an external position in the self is sufficiently congruent with the intentions, experiences, and expectations of the actual other. When my construction of the other as part of my self is very different from, or even in contradiction with, the actual other, then misunderstandings in the interaction are probable, unless I'm able to adapt the image I have about the other under the influence of my dialogue with the actual other. However, from a motivational point of view, it is worthwhile to pose the question of whether the other as external position should be in *perfect* agreement with the actual other. The answer to this question is, in our view, that a perfect agreement is not only impossible (see Barresi, 2002, for arguments), but even undesirable. An accepted psychological insight is that the expression of positive expectations about the achievements of the other is more motivating than negative expectations. Believing in the capacities of others, trusting them, and having confidence in their qualities and capacities, are more motivating than negative expectations about the others' achievements and resources. When we combine the preceding considerations, it can be concluded that motivational processes are facilitated when external positions in the self are constructed in such a way that they are somewhat *above* the talents and qualities of the other, yet, at the same time, being in sufficient correspondence with them. A "positive construction" of the other on a realistic basis provides a stimulating condition for a dialogical relationship that motivates the other to develop his capacities and talents in optimal ways. With a variation on Mead's (1934) well-known concept of "taking the role of the other," we would suggest that the facilitation of motivation requires "making the role of the other" part of a dialogical communication that strengthens belief in the potentials of the other.

In educational situations, educators and teachers, on the one hand, and children and pupils on the other, can increase their motivation via positive constructions of each other. As an example, we quote a 10-year-old Italian girl, reflecting about herself and her teachers at school (Ligorio, forthcoming):

> The first day when I got here I didn't know anyone, but in my mind, I told myself that the teachers were good and nice and now we have a very strong relationship. If we have trouble doing things, they are always ready to help us go through our uncertainties. Teachers are now a part of me as if they were half of my body; they know so many details about me. They helped me to find the other side of me that was obscure, that I didn't know, they made me feel confident about talking and doing things, they gave me a "treasure" that I will keep with me for ever.

As this quotation shows, the girl has included the teachers as external positions in her dialogical self and, moreover, has constructed them on the basis of positive expectations ("in my mind, I told myself that the teachers were good and nice") from the day she arrived. As the text suggests, her positive expectations were confirmed by reality at school. The positive construction of the other in the self has, under optimal conditions, realistic motivational consequences.

There is another striking element in this quotation. The girl is not only motivated from her side towards the teachers and the school, but she also experiences the teachers as motivating towards her ("They helped me to find the other side of me ... they made me feel confident about talking and doing things, they gave me a 'treasure'... "). Her motivation is not a purely individualized orientation. Rather, the imagining and perceiving the teachers as motivating is part of her own motivation. This observation reflects a more general characteristic of dialogical motivation: the motivation of the self is other-inclusive, that is, the imagined or perceived motivation of the other is part of the motivation of an extended self.[9]

The difference between motivation and emotion

What is the difference between emotion and motivation? One of the core elements of mainstream emotion theories (e.g. Arnold and Gasson, 1954; Frijda, 1986; Lazarus, 1991) is the *action tendency* (or action readiness) of an emotion which can be understood in terms of readiness to act towards the environment in a specific way. There is, for example, an urge to attack, run, or embrace, which includes a sense of urgency or impulse to behave in a particular way. Emotion can be the beginning of a motivational process and even a continuing driving force, but motivation is more than emotion. When somebody is motivated to perform well in a job or to contribute to the development of a loving relationship with somebody or to create an artistic composition, these are only possible when there is a well-organized complex of activities that are coordinated towards a particular goal. An action tendency or urge as emotional component can certainly contribute to a motivational activity but only if it is part of a broader, differentiated complexity of goal-oriented action.

From the perspective of the present theory, we have described emotions as ways of positioning, that is, as ways of placing oneself in relation to others or to oneself or being placed in relation to others or oneself. When I position myself as angry towards another person, I not only experience anger but, moreover, orient myself as opposed to him, in my memory, imagination, anticipation, or expectation. Placing myself in an emotion (e.g., "I'm so angry at him") or being placed by an emotion (e.g., "I was overwhelmed by grief"), there is always a movement involved that "takes place" in the metaphorical space of the self. In the case of positioning myself in an emotion, I allow the emotion, I identify with it, and I *go into it*. In the case of being positioned by an emotion, I'm subjected to a force coming from the emotion that *goes into me* even when the *I* is not ready or willing to identify with it.

In addition, motivation takes place as a movement in a metaphorical space of the self ("I see myself going step by step in my career"), but there is an important difference with emotions. Motivation typically develops on the basis not only of one position but also of a complexity of positions organized by an explicit goal orientation. For example, when a person is motivated to become a physician, she can only do so when her internal and external positions are organized over time in the service of a particular purpose. For example, the person may position herself as an expert, as ambitious, as concerned to assist people who are in need of help, as fellow-student, and later as a colleague (internal positions). Moreover, she can become emotionally involved in working towards her goal (e.g. as enjoyer, as passionate, or as loving). At the same time, the person is oriented to and dependent on other people or groups of people. For example, her father and mother support her in becoming a physician, she works together with sympathetic co-students, and she imagines becoming part of a professional association (external positions). And her external position can become loaded with emotions (e.g., her father as enthusiastically encouraging). All such internal and external positions become involved as a web of positions or coalitions that are needed to make the necessary steps toward a complex goal. Motivation implies emotions but transcends them in organized ways of goal orientation.

Emotions, however, are not always in the service of goal-oriented motivation and can even thwart it. The motivation-reducing role of strong emotions can be observed, for example, when a person is motivated to attain a desired goal but is so disappointed by a failure that the motivation is seriously reduced or when a person is motivated to achieve an important goal but is paralyzed by anxiety about or fear of success. Apparently, emotion functions in some situations as a driving force in motivational processes but in other situations as an obstacle.

Conflict-resolution

Conflict is a normal phenomenon both between and within selves. In their simple forms, conflicts are frequent and transient and can easily be solved. Two people may disagree about which restaurant to choose but they may easily agree after a brief discussion (although some can't stop quarrelling even during the meal). However, in the case of complex problems, it is more difficult to find adequate answers and conflicts tend to become more profound. On the basis of extensive experience of solving complex problems, Kahane (2004) observes that tough problems usually don't get solved peacefully. They often fail to get resolved at all as people get stuck in their attempts to give an adequate answer, or they are decided by force. Family members involved in a conflict may replay the same argument over and over, when a parent lays down the law and a son or daughter ignores the rules of the house. Members of a company may become involved in a conflict when a boss decrees a new strategy, thereby arousing resistance in his co-workers. Or communities are split over a controversial issue and a long series of fruitless debates follows. In many cases people involved in a problem cannot find a solution that is satisfying to all parties involved, or one of the parties imposes a solution on everybody else (Kahane, 2004).

In Kahane's view, tough problems are complex in three ways. First, cause and effect are often separated in space and time so that the different aspects of the problem are difficult to grasp at one glance. Second, they are generatively complex, that is, they unfold in unpredictable and unfamiliar ways, creating a high degree of uncertainty. Third, they are complex from a social point of view, because the parties involved have very different opinions and their points of view may become polarized and loaded with strong negative emotions. Parties often stop listening to each other and learning from each other and the interchange becomes stuck.

What can a dialogical approach contribute to managing conflicts where there are complex problems? How can people involved in a conflict deal with differences? Under what conditions are people able to listen to each other and learn from each other in proposing and developing solutions to the problems at hand? How do we deal with emotions in conflicts? In addressing such questions, we take as a starting point the view that conflict and dialogue are not mutually exclusive categories but that conflict can, under specific conditions, stimulate and even deepen the dialogue both between and within the selves of different people.

The awareness of difference and its reduction by emotions

The primary and most prominent principle that should be taken into account when one wants to work on conflict resolution is the awareness, recognition, and acceptance of difference. Difference is all-pervasive: in nature, nurture, individual history, collective history, and in the globalizing world with its diverse localities. In our contemporary world with mass media that have a potential reach to all corners of the planet, differences become visible in the living rooms of people all over the world. Given the widespread visibility of differences between individuals, groups, and cultures, one would expect that people get used to difference and are able to integrate it in their views and daily lives. One would also expect that the increasing visibility of differences would facilitate the recognition and acceptance of difference in case of conflicts. This expectation, however, is not confirmed when we observe how most people deal with tough problems and conflicts. What is the reason?

One of the main reasons for our inadequate ways of coping with social conflicts is that they imply strong negative emotions. The most prominent negative emotions in conflicts are anger and anxiety. As we have seen in Chapter 5, emotions are given, at least temporarily, top priority in the self and, as a consequence, push other positions to the background for a while or subordinate them to the impulses emanating from the dominant emotion. As long as emotion governs the self, it is difficult or even impossible to take a meta-position that, in less emotional circumstances, enables the person to take into account positions that will be relevant tomorrow and those that were relevant some days before.

The emotional nature of social conflicts not only restricts the self and its view on the world, but is also often accompanied by exclusive truth claims. On this we refer to Lambie and Marcel's (2002) distinction between "first-order phenomenology" and "second-order awareness." In the former case the emotion experience has phenomenological "truth," while in the latter case there is a reflexive awareness of the emotional experience. When the experience of anger takes the form of "he *is* a bastard" there is first-order phenomenology, while in the phrase "I'm furious with him" anger takes the form of second-order awareness. Or in the case of anxiety, there is first-order phenomenology when one says "he is dangerous" (or "strange" or "alien" or a "monster"), but there is second-order awareness when one says, "I feel anxiety" (or "threatened" or "uneasy"). In the first case, the emotion experience refers to "how the world is" or "how the self is" while in the second case, there is a recognition and awareness that one *experiences* or *thinks* about the world or oneself in a particular way.

Emotion experience as first-order phenomenology leads, moreover, to a blurring of the distinction between the other-in-the-self and the actual other. It implies the conviction that the way I see the other is not a matter of "my definition" but a truth about the other as he really is (e.g., the other as enemy). Awareness that the other-in-the-self is an imagined other who can never fully coincide with the "real other" is absent as long as the self sticks to this phenomenology. It is not taken into account that the actual other has his own perspective that never fully coincides with the way he is imagined. In this way, emotions as first-order phenomena raise the problem of *exclusive truth claims* about the other. This claim does not leave room for the awareness that the other may be different from the way I'm seeing him and, moreover, it is blinding me to the existence of *other perspectives* from which I may view the other person and his concerns, intentions, and expectations. As a consequence, productive and creative dialogue is impeded or even becomes impossible when emotion experiences are expressed in the claim that one's "truth" matches so-called objective reality. Emotions in the form of truth claims are an even more serious obstacle for dialogue when, under the expressed (secondary) emotion (e.g., anger), there is another (primary) emotion (e.g., anxiety) that is not accessible and exerts its influence on the secondary one below the level of awareness (see Chapter 5). This problem can be observed not only on the individual level but also on the collective level, particularly in situations of globalization where a heightened level of uncertainty leads to defense and confirmation of local identities and even to aggression, with anxiety or xenophobia as the underlying primary emotion (see Chapter 1).

Cultural differences and the problem of the claim to truth

One of the prominent features of a globalizing world is that the differences between localities and cultures are becoming more visible, subjected as they are to media scrutiny. This does not mean, however, that traditions, practices, values, and the meaning of events are considered from the *perspective* of the other culture. As Avruch and Black (1993) observe, it is not just the general public but conflict resolution scholars, too, who tend to ignore cultural differences in their pretension to develop universally applicable models of conflict resolution. However, as the authors point out, people from different cultures have different perceptions of what causes conflict, and of which responses are appropriate. In order to be effective in conflict resolution, one should start with a cultural analysis that focuses on the differences between cultures. The main problem in intercultural contacts is that one sees one's own culture as the norm. It is experienced not as *a* way of understanding the world, but as *the* way of understanding the world. Moreover, one's own culture is not seen as a subjective interpretation of the world but rather as "objective reality." When confronted with others who deviate from our cultural assumptions, we tend to view them as abnormal, strange, aberrant, or at least "peculiar." On the basis of these considerations, Avruch and Black propose engaging in a cultural analysis that attempts to understand the meaning of an event within its own cultural context. In order to achieve this perspective, one has to suspend one's evaluative reflex and, instead, constantly shift back and forth between different cultural perspectives.

There is a striking parallel between the field of emotions and the field of culture. Emotional experience can be distinguished in first-order phenomenology and second-order awareness, whereas on the level of cultural experience a distinction can be made between culture as representing "objective reality" and culture as a subjective perspective. Both distinctions have a deeper commonality that is essential to any form of social conflict resolution: the distinction between a claim to objective truth and subjective awareness. For people or groups involved in a conflict, it seems of crucial importance that they are aware of their thinking, feeling, talking, and experiencing from a particular position. When the principle of multi-positionality is recognized and accepted, an important condition is fulfilled for acknowledging and accepting that *another perspective is possible.* Awareness and acceptance of this possibility serves as the great door to dialogue. Dialogue can only develop when conflicting parties see their own perspective or position as not being the only one. This awareness moves the communication from the polarizing right–wrong or good–bad dichotomies to considerations in terms of positional differences. Along these lines, the acceptance of differences invites the *exchange* of positions so that their dialogical processing can start. In this exchange the different positions are perceived not as mutually exclusive but as mutually complementary. In the context of conflict resolution, this means that the different partners are invited to move back and forth between the two conflicting positions in dialogical ways.

The dialogical movement between positions can take place between individuals, between groups, and between representatives of different (sub)cultures. It can also take place between different cultural positions in the self of one and the same individual. Conflicts are rarely purely external, that is *between* different people. They are also remembered, rehearsed, anticipated, and even developed *within* the self. That is, they bring about intensive communication in the internal domain of the self (from which internal position do I look at myself?), between external positions (how do other people position themselves toward my opponent?) and between internal and external positions (how do I position myself towards my opponent?). Between-conflicts coexist with within-conflicts and can influence each other. A clarifying example is Clarke's (2004) description of the case of Hawa, a woman who emigrated from Turkey to the Netherlands. She developed two main cultural positions in her self, "I as Turkish" and "I as Dutch," which were involved in an intense conflict. During counseling, however, the relationship between the two positions changed significantly. While initially they were experienced as mutually exclusive, they became mutually complementary at a later point in time.[10]

Narratives and storytelling

For conflict resolution a mutual understanding of the histories of the parties involved in a conflict is paramount. What preceded the conflict? What was the beginning of it? What were the relevant circumstances that led to the conflict? Answers to those questions help the parties to understand not only the positions in which they find themselves but also their historical context. Addressing such questions is relevant to conflict resolution not only at the individual but also at the collective level.

In different contexts around the world, the recounting of personal and collective stories has been used as a means of reducing inter-group conflict and encouraging reconciliation between adversaries. The most prominent example is the Truth and Reconciliation Commission (TRC) which was established in South Africa in 1995 in order to "promote national unity and reconciliation in a spirit of understanding which transcends the conflicts ... of the past by ... establishing as complete a picture as possible of the causes, nature and extent of the gross violations of human rights which were committed during the period ... including ... the perspectives of the victims and the motives and perspectives of the persons responsible for the commission of the violations... [11]

Inspired by the TRC, institutions in several countries have established committees and started projects to promote reconciliation in cases of inter-group conflict. One example is the activities of PRIME, the Peace Research Institute in the Middle East, a jointly run Palestinian/Israeli non-governmental research organization that undertakes cooperative social investigations with the aim of exploring crucial psycho-social and educational aspects of the Palestinian–Israeli conflict (Adwan and Bar-On, 2006). One of the objectives is to design educational projects for young people and organize peace-building encounters between the two parties. As part of the project, Palestinians visit places where their homes once were and Israelis go to see refugee camps where the Palestinians now live. Visiting each other's places not only contributes to the knowledge of each other's history but also helps people to imagine the circumstances in which others live. Moreover, the project allows the participants to share their life stories with one another and explore ways of decreasing hatred and violence between the two groups.[12]

Another project of PRIME involves Palestinian and Jewish Israeli high-school teachers who come together to jointly prepare a textbook, in both Hebrew and Arabic, that includes the narratives of both sides on a number of key historical events (e.g. the 1948 war, the first Intifada). The narratives from each side are translated into the other's language, with blank pages left for the students to write down their own thoughts and feelings evoked by the texts. The plan is to use the textbooks in conjunction with class discussions and activities in the hope of reducing mutual animosity and hatred of the other.[13]

The project leaders' idea for this joint textbook emerged from the awareness that, in periods of conflict, nations tend to teach their children their own narratives as the only correct one, thereby ignoring the narratives of their adversaries. Such texts tend to convince children that they must dehumanize the enemy, leading to the development of negative attitudes toward the other, a state of affairs that characterizes the Palestinian–Israeli situation.[14]

In this example of Palestinian–Israeli cooperation there are two elements that are relevant to conflict resolution from a dialogical point of view. The first is the importance of place. Visiting the places that are important in the history or life circumstances of the adversary creates an enduring impression in one's memory, and helps to create a "space of imagination" in the self that refers to the past, present, or future situation of the adversary. As we have emphasized in Chapter 5, movements are central aspects of emotions: emotions are expressed in physical and metaphorical movements and, conversely, such movements can arouse the corresponding emotions. Visiting a place that is significant in the life of the other is an emotional experience that stimulates identification with the other and with the emotions of the other as somebody who is living *there*, a place located both in a physical and metaphorical space. The second element is the common construction of an educational text-book. When representatives of two groups involved in conflict succeed in finding a common activity to which they both contribute from their own specific point of view, such activity creates a common position. As we have seen in Chapter 3, conflicting positions can meet each other in the construction of a "third position" as a way of transcending social dichotomies and reconciling divisions and oppositions. The common construction of a third position and the corresponding involvement in common activities create centralizing and integrative movements in the self that have the potential of lifting the parties up to a higher level of integration.[15]

The difference between content and style

People may strongly disagree with each other, or even be involved in conflict, but at the same time like each other's style. Conversely, people may strongly agree in their common purposes but differ so much in their styles that this leads them into conflict. Take two colleagues who work together on a common industrial project – an older one with much professional experience and a younger one with strong ambitions. They both present themselves as advocates of high-quality service and agree on the necessity of continual improvement of their product. On this overt level they experience much commonality and there is no sign of conflict. However, after a period of cooperation, they become involved in an intense dispute that they cannot resolve. They decide to talk about their problem in an evaluation session, together with a third colleague. In this session the younger man objects to the older colleague's authoritarian style as creating an unequal relationship. The older man, in his turn, accuses his colleague of being overly ambitious, because all his advice and suggestions are not accepted and may even be ignored. Exchanging their experiences during the evaluation session they discover that they were used to having discussions at the content level, that is, on plans and purposes on which they explicitly agreed, and, therefore, they expected that they would be able to work well together without any trouble. However, to their surprise, the clashes and strong negative emotions were intense. Reflecting on this, they realized that they had never discussed the style aspects of their cooperation: they agreed on their explicit and jointly supported positions (e.g., "we as aiming at high quality products") but not on the more implicit ways these positions were expressed in their behavior. Finally, a profound discussion of the style aspects of their interaction led to the inclusion of new positions in their repertoire. The older colleague admitted that he was "maybe too authoritarian" in his approach, founded as it was on his implicit expectation that the younger colleague should have respect for his rich experience. On the other hand, the younger colleague became aware that he was "maybe overly ambitious" in his aims, leading him to do things "in his own way." As part of the session, the colleagues explored the personal history of their positions ("too authoritarian" and "overly ambitious") and discussed how their respective sensitivities to the behavior of the other as deriving from these positions could be taken into account.

The example above illustrates two aspects that are relevant to the understanding of conflict and conflict resolution. First, there is a distinction between content and style. From the perspective of *content*, people may be aware of their behavior and the positions that underlie this behavior (e.g., devising procedures for quality control on the basis of a common position "we as striving for high quality"). However, they are less aware of the *stylistic* aspects of their behavior, that is the *way* they are realizing their purposes and the corresponding *implicit* positions that are expressed by this behavior. They agree on content but clash on style. Typically, people cooperate on the basis of explicit (common) positions and on the purposeful actions that follow from them, but not about the stylistic form of this behavior, a difference which may then result in conflict. Second, for conflict resolution it makes sense to translate the stylistic aspects of their behavior in terms of *explicit* positions, in this way expanding their position repertoire. The inclusion of such positions expands the bandwidth of the repertoire, with the result that people are better able to position and reposition themselves according to the needs, wishes, and sensitivities of the other party.

Shadow (disowned) positions are often expressed in the style of one's behavior and by their nature people are not always aware of them. This creates a situation in which one party acts in the expectation that he is behaving toward the other party on the basis of explicit and acceptable positions, and even on common positions, whereas the other party is emotionally reacting, and often increasingly so, to the stylistic aspects of the behavior of the other. This results in misunderstandings that are based on content-style discrepancies. Becoming aware of such a misunderstanding and making it explicit is often the beginning of a dialogue in which misunderstandings and conflicts are explored and investigated in terms of their origin and possible consequences. Rather than considering misunderstandings and conflicts as in opposition to dialogue, it is more productive to see them as a challenge to and even as a starting point for dialogue.

Although social conflicts are challenges to dialogue, they often get stuck in monological relationships, loaded as they are with intense negative emotions. Parties take a position, firmly fix it, and tend to close themselves off from the other. As a result, they stick to that position, confirming it and repeating the same point of view over and over. In this way they get entangled in a monological relationship with each other. Yet it is possible that people stuck in a monological relationship with an actual other are nevertheless more dialogical about the conflict *within* themselves. The reason is that conflicts are often confrontations with new or unexpected positions in the internal domain of the self, shocked as it is by the emotional conflict with the opponent. As a result of this shock, more happens in the self than becomes apparent in the actual contact with the other. Being alone with themselves, the participants tend to take a broader range of considerations into account than when they are directly involved in the hot fight with the actual other. People involved in a serious conflict have a chance to self-reflect and self-dialogue in ways that are different from before, even when their opponent does not notice this.

Role confusion

Conflicts may also emerge from role confusion. There is role confusion in a social relationship when there is a lack of common awareness of the differences in roles (social positions) on which the communication or cooperation is based. More specifically, role confusion emerges when one party behaves on the basis of one particular social position, while the other party expects the person to behave from another, different, social position. Suppose a teacher and student meet in order to discuss a thesis that the student proposes at the end of her study. In the course of the talk, a topic is addressed that stimulates the interest of the teacher and they engage in a vivid and stimulating exchange. Some time after the talk the student receives a mark that is lower than she expected on the basis of the exchange that she experienced as interesting and rewarding, and, at the next meeting, she expresses her disappointment to the teacher. When they reflect about what had happened, they discover that the student was perceiving the teacher, in the course of their vivid exchange, more as an enthusiastic colleague than as a judging teacher, and therefore expected a high mark. The teacher, however, sharing the enthusiasm of the student during the talk, later returned to her position as a critical teacher, giving the student a mark that, in her view, she deserved on the basis of the quality of the thesis. In their evaluation session, they became aware of the existence of role confusion, which made it easier for the student to accept the mark.

More generally, when the position repertoire of people involved in communication becomes more heterogeneous, there is a higher chance of role confusion. Take the example of what we have earlier described as a "dialogical leader." One of the characteristics of such a leader is that his repertoire, including such varied positions as entrepreneur, professional, manager, and coach, is significantly broadened in comparison with the leadership in the hierarchical structure of traditional organizations. This extension of the range of positions on the part of leaders in contemporary organizations and the corresponding extension of the repertoire of their co-workers, increases the chance of role confusion. Therefore, dialogical clarity about positions and the transition from one position towards another one is required in order to avoid unnecessary confusion.

Inter-group dialogues and its obstacles

For a proper understanding of the nature of social conflicts, it should be noted that conflicts between groups cannot be solved on a purely individual level, because they involve not only the individual, but also the local and even the global levels. The Israeli–Palestinian conflict not only provides an arena for studying the far-reaching implications of inter-group conflicts but has also resulted in thorough and continuing discussions and thoughts about the possibilities and impossibilities of inter-group dialogue. A useful example that fits very well with dialogical self theory is the work on inter-group dialogue between Palestinians and Israelis, and between Israelis and Germans, as presented by Chaitin (2008). We include some of the views of this author because she emphasizes not only the potentials of dialogue but also the obstacles that prevent it taking place.

In order to give an impression of Chaitin's and her colleagues' views on inter-group dialogue, we summarize some of the main principles that they mention as underlying their work. First, they see dialogue, on the group level, as a *learning process* in agreement with Bohm, Factor and Garret (1991), who state that

Dialogue is a way of observing, collectively, how hidden values and intentions can control our behavior, and how unnoticed cultural differences can clash without our realizing what is occurring. ... [It is] an arena in which collective learning takes place and out of which a sense of increased harmony, fellowship and creativity can arise... (1991, paragraphs 1–3)

In this sense, inter-group dialogue is an innovative enterprise. As soon as parties involved in conflict decide to enter into dialogue, Chaitin notes, they are not only initiating a conversation, but they cross a threshold into a new relationship with one another. This is possible because dialogue enables participants to say and hear statements they have never said or heard before, and these statements have the potential for thorough change. The innovative quality of dialogue is not always easy, Chaitin adds, as the learning process may lead to the discovery of uncomfortable or unpleasant things about one's own attitudes and behaviors. Although dialogue has great potential for connecting conflicting parties, it is, at the same time, a risky enterprise because it makes the participants vulnerable and undermines the established beliefs that gave them a sense of security.

Second, the goal of inter-group dialogue is not necessarily conflict resolution. Certainly, conflict resolution is a valuable goal when both parties are explicitly motivated to find a common solution to a pressing conflict, if the range of possible options permits it. Within the range of the possible, one can explore the construction of third positions and coalitions of positions. However, it should be acknowledged that conflict resolution is not the main or sole purpose of inter-group dialogue. As Chaitin emphasizes, the foremost goal of inter-group dialogue is not the solution to a conflict, but rather an increase in *mutual understanding*. Parties who enter into dialogue do this out of a true concern not only for themselves but also for their "adversary." The focus is on strengthening and improving the relationship, even when the conflict is not resolved. In an inter-group dialogue, the communicating partners allow each other space to tell their stories from their own point of view and, as a result, they feel an increasing respect for each other, even when they disagree on central issues or continue to be involved in the conflict. This view resonates well with the emphasis on the co-construction of a dialogical space as one of the recurrent themes in the present book.

Third, Chaitin emphasizes the constructive role of *silence* in inter-group dialogue. Although it may seem paradoxical and counter-intuitive, silence is a central part of dialogue and shapes it to a significant degree. As a constitutive part of dialogue, silence is not to be understood simply as the absence of words because such an absence is often heavy with tension and is even confusing. Silence is truly dialogical when the participant is fully attentive to self and other. In order to reach this state, it is necessary that the person "silences" inner arguments and stories and places the other and the self in the light of the present moment. Thus, rather than a passive state, silence is a responsive state that influences both the style and content of the dialogue. Dialogue involves both speech and silence.

Obstacles to dialogue between groups

In order to achieve a proper understanding of the possibilities of dialogue it is necessary to have an insight into its obstacles. Taking into account her experiences with inter-group dialogue between Jewish Israelis and Germans and Palestinians, Chaitin (2008) discusses six obstacles that hamper dialogue between them: a collective identity rooted in victimhood; problems in being empathetic to the suffering of the other; strong emotions and over-use of defense mechanisms; blame and scapegoating; recurrent family patterns; and group-think. On the basis of the author's considerations, we summarize each of them.

The development of an identity rooted in *victimhood* is a serious obstacle to dialogue between individuals and between groups. Particularly in violent and long conflicts, at least one party, and sometimes both, reconstruct their identity around its victimization by the other side. In such situations, it is very difficult for parties to look beyond their own suffering and to develop a more complex identity. When an individual or group identity is tightly bound up in victimhood, there is a negative dependence on one's enemy as an external (alienated) position in the self. At the same time, one's definition of self is determined by the identification of the enemy as the embodiment of evil. Victimhood tends to reduce the multiplicity and multi-voicedness of the self to such a degree that it functions as an *I*-prison that seriously reduces the range of possible actions. In the case of enduring and escalating conflicts, this may lead to the over-use of military action or to violence.

The *loss of empathy* for the suffering of others is a second obstacle to open and connecting dialogue. Empathy is characterized by non-judgmental responses that express acceptance and understanding of the other and his situation. Empathy as a central ingredient of dialogue requires an openness not only to the experiences and stories of the other, but also to the emotions that are expressed between the words. When empathy is reduced, it is difficult or even impossible for the parties to see reality from the other's point of view and to understand how they view the situation or the conflict from their specific angle. It is even difficult to have access to the emotions of the other as involved in the conflict. In fact, these emotions are often very similar on both sides (e.g., powerlessness and anger).

Strong emotions and the over-use of *ego defense mechanisms* create another obstacle for developing an open and innovative dialogue between conflicting parties. In this context, Chaitin refers to literatures that show that victims of humiliation and violence often displace their anger toward the aggressor on others. As a psychological defense mechanism, displacement is used to distort one's perception of reality in order to ward off anxiety. Anger and aggression towards third parties, even weaker ones, is then evoked in order to protect the individual from expressing risky hostility toward the original, more powerful target. Anger and aggression displaced to third parties may lead people to see threat everywhere and all of the time, so that it becomes increasingly difficult for them to distinguish peaceful periods from non-peaceful ones or opportunities for dialogue from non-opportunities. People who have been deeply harmed or humiliated by others often use additional defenses such as projection and rationalization. When people see themselves as victims and project their own feelings of aggression and hatred on their enemies, it is easier for them to rationalize that their lack of empathy toward the other party is justified. As part of this justification, they refer to the harm they have suffered in the past, at the same time denying or ignoring the harm that is suffered on the other side of the conflict. Due to the massive use of defenses, it is difficult or impossible for victims of social trauma to understand the other's perspective and to be empathetic toward them. In this way, the overuse of defenses functions as an emotionally based obstacle to dialogical change and development. In terms of the developmental model, discussed in Chapter 4, the overuse of defences leads to a regression to lower levels of integration.

An additional obstacle to dialogue is found in *recurring family patterns*. Family members tell each other myths and themes that often revolve around issues connected to important past events, such as the Palestinian–Israeli conflict or the Holocaust. Such myths and themes often receive a ritualistic character. This leads to the repeated telling of stories about extreme persecution or heroism, with the use of conspicuous reminders of past events or losses, in the form of photo albums, videos and yearly memorials. Chaitin expects that in situations of extreme fear, evoked by present-day and past events connected with the Palestinian-Israeli conflict, family myths and rituals centered around suffering and victimhood may become re-inscribed in different generations. If these myths and rituals are connected with an ideology that couples militarism and sacrifice with patriotism, such family patterns reinforce the perception that the war between the conflicting parties is "natural," "inevitable," and even "heroic." Apparently, repeating family stories and patterns tend to reinforce particular positions that become more and more dominant in the self, associated as they are with a closed and biased *position history* (see Chapter 3). As a result conflicting parties become locked up in themselves with the consequence that recurrent and over-stabilized positions are no longer accessible for dialogical change and development.

Other obstacles to dialogue are *blame and scapegoating*. According to Chaitin, they can be seen as two sides of the same coin. Blame can be turned inward, as exemplified by Holocaust survivors who are wondering why they survived while others did not. It can also be turned outward to a scapegoat in the external environment, as exemplified by the familiar phenomenon of blaming the enemy. When people search for scapegoats, they tend to deny their own contribution to the conflict and project the full responsibility on others. From the perspective of a perpetrator, scapegoating has two "positive" effects: it removes negative feelings about the self that is defined as not responsible for the problems around the conflict and, at the same time, it provides a sense of gratification by feeling able to identify the "guilty." This, in turn, can lead to the justification of aggression toward the scapegoat and to a strict and rigid separation between "good" and "bad." Seeing oneself as blameless and the other as responsible for the conflict and associated problems, fuels the conviction that the other deserves punishment. Placing the other exclusively at the "wrong side" of the good–bad dichotomy, in combination with the desire to punish the other party, makes any dialogue out of the question.

Finally, Chaitin refers to *group-think* as an obstacle that hampers dialogue. As Janis (1982) observed, groups may make faulty decisions because group pressures lead members to think into one direction only, failing to take different possibilities into account and adopting a biased view of reality. Groups which are affected by group-think tend not only to ignore alternative ways of dealing with the conflict, but also to neglect the perspective of the adversary. Especially when the other is categorized as an enemy, the people belonging to this category are "deindividuated" and "dehumanized" and seen as objects or "abjects" rather than as fellow human beings. Group-think encourages the members of a particular group to reinforce each other's views, while at the same time warding off the views of deviant group members, critics, or members of the conflicting party. The result is that dialogue, leading to views that deviate from the group norm, is systematically avoided or ignored so that any attempt at dialogue is doomed to fail.

The various obstacles to dialogue remind us that dialogue is not self-evident. It is not something that is "always there" or easily accessible. Maybe dialogue is the most precious "instrument" that humans have *in* and *between* themselves and that they can, under facilitating circumstances, learn to use (see Chapter 3 for the notion of "good dialogue"). At the same time, this instrument can be neglected, silenced or even damaged. The described obstacles, as presented in the context of serious and long-lasting conflict, demonstrate that dialogue is faced with serious challenges that have to be met in order to make it work.

It is our conviction that dialogue can only become fertile, effective and innovative when we are aware of its constraints and obstacles. Seen in this way, dialogue requires a form of self-confrontation that has realistic consequences if we admit that the obstacles are not only outside, in society, but also deeply entrenched in our selves. Therefore, it is our view that dialogue *between* individuals and groups can be successful only when it goes together with dialogue *within* individuals and groups.

The dialogical paradox

Unfortunately, many people, both individuals and groups, eschew social conflicts and react to them with avoiding or ignoring behavior. As a result, conflicting parties become separated from each other so that exchange stops and dialogue has no chance to develop. Instead of entering a dialogue, parties employ forms of "othering." When engaged in this process, people, groups, or organizations attempt to maintain their apparent internal unity through an active process of opposition (e.g., "We are against them"), hierarchization (e.g., "We are better"), or exclusion (e.g., "We do not want any contact"). In those cases, the other individuals or groups are classified as foreign or "other" through realizing a hierarchical dualism in which one unit, typically the one to which one belongs, is privileged or favored, whereas the other is devalued in one way or another (Cahoone, 1996).

One of the main challenges to dialogue is dealing with difference. As already said, conflict resolution begins with the awareness, recognition, and acceptance of differences between individuals and between groups. At the same time, the perception of difference entails the risk that people, in their tendency to eschew conflict, resort to forms of othering. This reaction leads us to draw attention to a "dialogical paradox": *there where dialogue is most needed, it does not take place.* Apparently, dialogue is particularly useful and even necessary when very different people are living closely together. Differences are increasingly present and visible in a globalizing world. Being part of an intensely interconnected world, populated by very different individuals and groups, creates the unavoidable necessity of dialogue. At the same time, some individuals or groups react to these differences by taking the "easiest solution": retreating to their own ground and confirming their internal unity in opposition to and separation from the other. Indeed, dialogue costs more energy, but, once developed, it is more rewarding not only to the self of the individual but also to the selves of other individuals, with their different social, cultural and historical backgrounds.

Some guidelines for conflict resolution

On the basis of the preceding considerations and taking into account insights described in the previous chapters, we summarize some guidelines that may be useful for social conflict resolution: (a) be aware of the existence of differences between people; recognize and accept them as natural parts of human relationships; (b) make a distinction between subjective awarenes and "truth claims"; (c) acknowledge the existence of a multiplicity of positions from which a particular problem and its solution can be viewed; (d) do not reduce the self of the other to one position only, and recognize that the self of the other is or can be as multi-voiced as your own self; (e) take into account that every opinion is determined and constrained by the (sub)culture in which one is raised. This culture does not imply any objective truth but rather a cultural position that can be dialogically related to any other cultural position; (f) give the participants of a conflict the opportunity to tell their individual or collective narratives and to clarify their associated positions; give particular attention to the history and context of positions that are relevant to the emergence and development of the conflict; (g) because in a social conflict often strong negative emotions are involved, it is recommended to allow the participants the opportunity to identify these emotions; explore if these emotions are surface expressions of primary emotions that are hidden at a deeper level and create an opportunity to express them; then move to a different emotion (counter-emotion) that is relevant to the conflict; ask the participants to formulate the messages that are generated by the emotion and the counter-emotion; (h) make a distinction between content and style of the interactions and try to formulate the often implicit aspects of one's behavior in terms of explicit positions so that the repertoire of the participants receives a broader bandwidth; (i) be aware of role confusions, particularly in situations in which there is a multiplicity of heterogeneous positions in one and the same person or group; (j) stimulate the reconciliation of conflicts by the creation of a third position that transcends the interests, emotions, and expectations that are associated with the conflicting ones. A third position can also be created by inviting a facilitator who transforms the dialogue between the conflicting parties into a trialogue that includes the facilitator. The facilitator represents a meta-position and may even stimulate the development of a common position. The facilitator invites the parties to engage in self-reflection and dialogue and stimulates the emergence of new perspectives from which the conflict can be clarified and solutions explored; (k) transform emotions into motivation or, more specifically, combine emotions and positions in such a way that the energy of emotions is used in the service of realizing common goals in which the interests of different individuals go well together; (l) make a productive use of the potentials of self-dialogues, including self-conflicts, as providing innovative impulses to the development of solutions to the conflict with the actual other; (m) create a dialogical space in which silence receives a chance to enhance the quality of the dialogue. Silence becomes dialogical when there is full attention to the other and the self in the present moment; (n) accept the view that conflict resolution cannot be achieved under all circumstances. In the event that a solution cannot be achieved, there is at least the possibility of mutual understanding.

As a general perspective, we want to emphasize that conflicts place the participants at a crossroads where, forced by the pressing elements of the situation, they move in a monological or dialogical direction. In which direction the process will evolve depends on the resources available in the selves of both parties and their facilitators.

Summary

In this final chapter we elaborated on some practical implications of dialogical self theory. The focus was on three topics: the culture of organizations, the issue of motivation, and the relevance of conflict resolution.

When organizations become increasingly international, intercultural, and inter-local, they become increasingly populated by people with multi-voiced selves and identities. Objections that can arise against any container view of self and culture also apply to any container view of the culture of organizations. Organizations are becoming increasingly complex and *extended*, particularly when one takes the notion of "stakeholders" into account. Stakeholders are not only individuals and groups that have a direct interest in what is going on in the organization, such as its employees, salespeople, customers, and shareholders, but also members of the broader community who are affected by the local economy or environment of the organization, such as the labor unions, professional associations, ecological movements, universities, and other groups in a globalizing society. We argued that the distribution of power over a larger variety of stakeholders has the consequence that the self of participants of an organization is no longer governed by one or a few dominating positions in the internal or external domain of the self. Instead, different positions or coalitions of positions in the self are involved in relationships of relative dominance. We described contemporary organizations as located in a field of tension between centralizing movements necessary for the coordination and integration of activities, and decentralizing movements necessary for the adaptation and innovation of the organization to changing circumstances with implications for the development of the self.

For the culture of an organization dialogical leadership is indispensable. A dialogical leader is able to make flexible movements between a variety of *I*-positions, such as entrepreneur, manager, coach, and professional. The different positions are part of the repertoire of a leader who knows when and where these positions could be taken. Moreover, as a result of their dialogical relationships, the different *I*-positions learn from each other in the service of their further development. Moreover, a dialogical leader is authentic in the sense that she acts on the basis of emotions and positions that are other-inclusive, that is, these emotions and positions take into account the communicative feedback from the part of the others with whom she cooperates. We also analyzed the capacity of a dialogical leader to create coalitions between people in realizing the mission of the organization. We argued that dialogical leadership is developed in an optimal way when the leader is included as a promoter position in the selves of her colleagues.

The increasing complexity of the tasks of organizations requires a broadening of the range of positions in the self and, moreover, flexible and dialogical movements from the one to the other position. We illustrated this thesis by discussing changes in two types of organizations: the expansion of the repertoire of teachers in school organizations (including not only the position of expert but also of coach) and the expansion of the repertoire of members of police organizations (including not only the traditional position of guardian of the law but also of service-oriented member of a community).

Furthermore, we presented a discussion in depth of the process of motivation as relevant both to individual selves and to the development of organizations. First, we emphasized the importance of "creating space" for the motivation of the other and the self. Starting with an insight from James (1890), a *basic self-conflict* was described that emerges from the tension between the development of a specific position and the development of the self as a whole, that is, of a large variety of possible positions. Although the basic self-conflict can never be fully resolved, it leaves room for the reconciliation of conflicts and for bringing together opposites that seem to be mutually exclusive. Our main argument is that coalitions of conflicting or opposing positions have the potential of creating strong motivation that surpasses the interests of positions in their isolation. Such coalitions create forms of "integrative motivation" emerging in a field of tension between centering and de-centering movements in the self. We emphasized that such motivation is relevant to the development not only of individuals but also of teams and organizations.

Finally, we discussed the process of social conflict resolution on the basis of the view that conflict and dialogue are not mutually exclusive categories, but that conflict is a challenge to dialogue and can function as its starting point. Because conflicts are typically associated with strong negative emotions, the repertoire of the conflicting parties is generally restricted to one or a few positions and it is difficult or almost impossible to take a meta-position from which a larger variety of possibilities can be taken into account. A particular problem for conflict resolution is the phenomenon of an "exclusive truth claim" that tends to reduce the multi-positionality of the self so that only one view of the conflict and its solution is allowed. For the solution of conflicts it is necessary that both parties arrive at the awareness that their view is not truth but perspective, and that more perspectives are possible. Further, we emphasized the relevance of narratives and storytelling to conflict resolution. For example, visiting places that are significant to the lives of the adversary and becoming engaged in common activities, to which the participants contribute each from their own point of view, may contribute to conflict resolution and mutual understanding.

The difference between content and style was also discussed as an issue relevant to conflict resolution, because often parties agree on the content of (common) goals and purposes but clash on differences in style, that is, the way in which purposes and goals are expressed in behavior. Attention was also given to the phenomenon of role confusion, implying that one party expects the other party to respond from a particular position, unaware that the other party is actually responding from another position. A special discussion was devoted to the Israeli–Palestinian conflict with attention to some of the main psychological obstacles to dialogue between these groups.

Essential for the understanding of the way many people deal with conflicts, is what we call the "dialogical paradox": there where dialogue is most needed, it does not take place. This paradox becomes visible in all those cases where people avoid, ignore, or withdraw from conflicts or fight with each other in ways dominated by monological power. Elaborating on the preceding analysis, we presented some specific guidelines for the solution of social conflicts.

NOTES

1 www.en.wikipedia.org/wiki/Organization.
2 One might object against this thesis, referring to the importance of localization as the other side of globalization: local cultures become even more relevant as a counter-force to the increasing processes of globalization. However, describing cultures in terms of sets of stable traits or characteristics

would refute the fact that cultures and sub-cultures *react and respond* to each other when they meet at cultural and sub-cultural interfaces. Such highly dynamic phenomena can only poorly be described in terms of traits that are intrinsically static and socially not responsive.

3 www.en.wikipedia.org/wiki/Stakeholder_%28corporate%29.

4 In a research project in different organizations in the Netherlands, Zomer (2006) devised a "Team Confrontation Method" (TCM) based on a Self-Confrontation Method (SCM) originally developed by Hermans and Hermans-Jansen (1995). The TCM is constructed in such a way that it allows for the assessment and development of individual and collective voices and, moreover, for the assessment and development of individual and collective affective experiences. In the application of this method in a series of longitudinal case studies, Zomer emphasized the importance of deviant voices for the realization of the purposes of the teams and their functioning as part of the organization.

5 www.winvision.nl/Winvision/EN/Case+Studies/Digital+Portfolio.http.

6 The establishment of mutually exclusive opposites is not only a feature of some organizations, but world ideologies are also used to divide selves into parts that are incompatible with each other. Traditionally, Christianity positions people as "pure" versus "sinful," communism as a political system splits people into "conforming" versus "deviant," and liberal capitalism tends to categorize people as "winners" versus "losers." Such mutually exclusive opposites create rather rigid hierarchical structures in the self with one part defined as "good" and the other as "bad." Generally, such dichotomies create not only a structural tension in the self but also tend to separate people from each other so that dialogue both between and within selves is hampered. Therefore, it makes sense to give special attention to shadow positions as representing the "bad" side of the self and to subject them to dialogical processing.

7 We make a distinction between "strong" and "weak" coalitions. In the case of a strong coalition two positions are combined in a way that the coalition is more that the sum of its parts. The strength of the one position increases the strength of the other position with a simultaneous profit of the coalition. Two or more specialists working together on a common project, each from their own expertise and each contributing to the realization of a common goal, is an example of a strong coalition. Typically, strong coalitions emerge when two or more positions are *mutually complementary*, stimulating each other, as part of a coalition, to some higher level of development. In the case of a weak coalition, the strength of one position is used by the other position in order to maintain or defend itself. When a dependent person cooperates with a dominant one, there is the risk that the dominant one becomes more dominant and the dependent more dependent over time. In that case the two positions do not stimulate each others' strengths, and together form a weak coalition. Typically, weak coalitions emerge when one position is functioning as a *compensation* for the other one. Strong and weak coalitions can also be part of the self. When I talk with a hard and assertive voice in order to compensate for my shyness, the two positions are part of a weak coalition. However, when I combine my technical skills with my artistic interest in

order to create an artistic product, the two positions create a strong combination and are mutually *complementing*.

8 Presented at the opening of the academic year at Radboud University, Nijmegen, the Netherlands, September 2007.

9 In our work on self-narratives (Hermans and Hermans-Jansen, 1995) we have developed a Self-Confrontation Method that recognizes two basic motives, the striving for self-assertion (S-motive) and the longing for contact and union with something or somebody else (motive). A central part of this model is that these motives are expressed in the affective component of "valuations" (personal meaning units that refer to important events in the past, present, and future). The method is devised to assess the affective organization of the valuation system and to facilitate its further development. Although the method and the underlying theory have clearly dialogical elements (e.g., Hermans, 2006), it should be noted that the theory underlying the Self-Confrontation Method can be further elaborated in a dialogical direction. This can be done by locating basic motives not only in the internal but also in the external domain of the self. For example, my motivation to assert myself is an *answer* to your motivation to assert yourself (S-motive), and my longing for contact and union is answered by your longing for contact and union (O-motive). When the motivational part of valuation theory is developed in this way, basic motives are not simply individual properties but part of dialogical relationships between and within selves. Along these lines basic motives of any kind can be integrated into dialogical self theory.

10 For more details of this case, see Chapter 1.

11 Julia Chaitin (2010).

12 ibid.

13 ibid.

14 ibid.

15 For levels of integration see Chapter 4.

References

Abbey, E., and Falmagne, R. J. (2008). Modes of tension work within the complex self. *Theory and Psychology*, 14: 95–113.

Abraham, K. (1942). *Selected papers on psychoanalysis*. London: Hogarth Press.

Adams, M. (2004). Whatever will be, will be: Trust, fate and the reflexive self. *Culture and Psychology*, 10: 387–408.

Adwan, S., and Bar-On, D. (2006). Sharing history: Palestinian and Israeli teachers and pupils learning each other's narrative. In S. Mcoy-Levy (ed.), *Troublemakers or peacemakers? Youth and post-accord in peace building* (pp. 217–34). University of Notre Dame Press.

Akkerman, S., Admiraal, W., Simons, R.-J., and Niessen, T. (2006). Considering diversity: Multivoicedness in international academic collaboration. *Culture and Psychology*, 12: 461–85.

Allen, N. B., and Knight, W. E. J. (2005). Mindfulness, compassion for self, and compassion for others: Implications for understanding the psychopathology and treatment of depression. In P. Gilbert (ed.), *Compassion: Conceptualizations, research and use in psychotherapy* (pp. 239–62). London: Routledge.

Allport, G. W. (1961). *Pattern and growth in personality*. New York: Holt, Rinehart & Winston.

American Psychiatric Association (2000). *Diagnostic and statistical manual of mental disorders* (4th edn., text rev.). Washington, DC: APA.

Anderson, W. T. (1997). *The future of the self: Exploring the post-identity society*. New York: Tarcher/Putnam.

Angyal, A. (1965). *Neurosis and treatment: A holistic theory*. New York: Wiley.

Annese, S. (2004). Mediated identity in the parasocial interaction of TV. *Identity: An International Journal of Theory and Research*, 4: 371–88.

Appadurai, A. (1990). Disjuncture and difference in the global cultural economy. In M. Featherstone (ed.), *Global culture: Nationalism, globalization and modernity* (pp. 295–310). London: Sage.

    (1996). *Modernity at large: Cultural dimensions of globalization*. Minneapolis: University of Minnesota Press.

    (1999). Dead certainty: Ethnic violence in the era of globalization. In B. Meyer and P. Geschiere (eds.), *Globalization and identity: Dialectics of flow and closure* (pp. 305–24). Oxford, UK: Blackwell.

Aristotle (1954). *Ethica Nicomachea* [Nicomachean ethics] (trans. R. W. Thuijs). Antwerp: De Nederlandse Boekhandel.

Arnett, J. (2002). The psychology of globalization. *American Psychologist*, 57: 774–83.

Arnold, M. B., and Gasson, S. J. (1954). Feelings and emotions as dynamic factors in personality integration. In M. B. Arnold and S. J. Gasson (eds.), *The human person* (pp. 294–313). New York: Ronald.

Aron, A., Mashek, D., McLaughlin-Volpe, T., Wright, S., Lewandowski, G., and Aron, E. (2005). Including close others in the cognitive structure of the self. In M. Baldwin (ed.), *Interpersonal cognition* (pp. 206–32). New York: Guilford Press.

Aveling, E. L., and Gillespie, A. (2008). Negotiating multiplicity: Adaptive asymmetries within second generation Turks' "society of mind." *Journal of Constructivist Psychology*, 21: 200–222.

Averill, J. R. (1997). The emotions: An integrative approach. In R. Hogan and J. A. Johnson (eds.), *Handbook of personality psychology* (pp. 513–41). San Diego, CA: Academic Press.

(2004). A tale of two snarks: Emotional intelligence and emotional creativity compared. *Psychological Inquiry*, 15: 228–33.

Avruch, K., and Black, P. W. (1993). Conflict resolution in intercultural settings. In D. J. D. Sandole and H. van der Merwe (eds.), *Conflict resolution theory and practice* (pp. 131–45). Manchester University Press.

Ayubi, N. (1999). The politics of Islam in the Middle East with special reference to Egypt, Iran and Saudi Arabia. In J. Haynes (ed.), *Religion, globalization and political culture in the Third World* (pp. 71–92). Basingstoke: Macmillan.

Bakhtin, M. (1973). *Problems of Dostoevsky's poetics* (2nd edn.; trans. R. W. Rotsel). Ann Arbor, MI: Ardis. (Original work published 1929 as *Problemy tvorchestva Dostoevskogo* [Problems of Dostoevsky's Art]).

Bakhtin, M. M. (1981). *The dialogic imagination*. Austin, TX: University of Texas Press.

(1986). *Speech genres and other late essays* (trans. V. W. McGee; ed. C. Emerson and M. Holquist). Austin, TX: University of Texas Press.

Baldwin, M. W., and Holmes, J. G. (1987). Salient private audiences and awareness of the self. *Journal of Personality and Social Psychology*, 53: 1087–98.

Baldwin, M. W., Carrell, S. E., and Lopez, D. F. (1990). Priming relationship schemas: My advisor and the pope are watching me from the back of my mind. *Journal of Experimental Social Psychology*, 26: 435–54.

Barber, B. R. (2004). *Strong democracy: Participatory politics for a new age*. Berkeley, CA: University of California Press.

Barresi, J. (1994). Morton Prince and B.C.A.: A historical footnote on the confrontation between dissociation theory and Freudian psychology in a case of multiple personality. In R. Klein and B. Doane (eds.), *Psychological concepts and dissociative disorders* (pp. 85–129). Hillsdale, NJ: Lawrence Erlbaum Associates.

(2002). From "the thought is the thinker" to "the voice is the speaker": William James and the dialogical self. *Theory and Psychology*, 12: 237–50.

(2008). Black and white like me. *Studia Psychologica*, 8: 11–22.

Beebe, J. (2002). An archetypical model of the self in dialogue. *Theory and Psychology*, 12: 267–80.

Bellah, R. N., Madson, K., Sullivan, W. M., Sandler, A., and Tipton, S. M. (1985). *Habits of the heart: Individualism and commitment in American life*. Berkeley: University of California Press.

Belzen, J. (2006) Culture and the 'dialogical self': Toward a secular cultural psychology of religion. In J. Straube, D. Weideman, C. Kolbl, and B. Kielke (eds.), *Pursuit of meaning: Advances in cultural and cross-cultural psychology* (pp. 129–52). London: Transaction Publishers.

Benedict, R. (1934). *Patterns of culture*. Boston, MA: Houghton Mifflin.

Bertau, M.-C. (2004). Developmental origins of the dialogical self: Some significant moments. In H. J. M. Hermans and G. Dimaggio (eds.), *The dialogical self in psychotherapy* (pp. 29–42). London: Brunner-Routledge.

(2008). Voice: A pathway to consciousness as "social contact to oneself." *Integrative Psychological and Behavioral Sciences*, 42: 92–113.

Betz, H.-G., Brzustowski, G., and Perrineau, P. (2004). *La droite populiste en Europe. Extrême et démocrate?* [The populist right in Europe. Extreme and democratic?] Paris: Autrement.

Bhabha, J. (1999). Enforcing the human rights of citizens in the era of Maastricht: Some reflections on the importance of states. In B. Meyer and P. Geschiere (eds.), *Globalization and identity: Dialectics of flow and closure* (pp. 97–124). Oxford, UK: Blackwell.

Bhatia, S. (2002). Acculturation, dialogical voices and the construction of the diasporic self. *Theory and Psychology*, 12: 55–77.

(2007). *American karma: Race, culture, and identity in the Indian diaspora*. New York: New York University Press.

Bhatia, S., and Ram, A. (2001). Locating the dialogical self in the age of transnational migrations, border crossings and diasporas. *Culture and Psychology*, 7: 297–309.

Binmore, K. G. (2005). *Natural justice*. Oxford University Press.

Blachowicz, J. (1999). The dialogue of the soul with itself. In S. Gallagher and J. Shear (eds.), *Models of the self* (pp. 177–200). Thorverton, UK: Imprint Academic.

Blackman, L. (2005). The dialogical self, flexibility and the cultural production of psychopathology. *Theory and Psychology*, 15: 183–206.

Blossfeld, H.-P. (2007). Globalization, rising uncertainty and the transition from youth to adulthood in modern societies. *Paper presented at the workshop Global versus Local Dynamics on Networks*. Dresden, 4–5 October.

Bohm, D., Factor, D., and Garrett, P. (1991). *Dialogue – a proposal*. www.davidbohm.net/dialogue/dialogue_proposal.html

Boor, M. (1982). The multiple personality epidemic: Additional cases and inferences regarding diagnosis, dynamics and cure. *Journal of Nervous and Mental Disease*, 170: 302–4.

Borsch, A., Cremers, S., De Groot, M., and Veen, C. (2006). Dialogische vaardigheden in ontwikkeling bij kinderen van 4–12 jaar [Developing dialogical capacities of children of 4–12 years old]. Masters thesis, University of Nijmgen, The Netherlands.

Bragg, E. A. (1996). Towards ecological self: Deep ecology meets constructionist self-theory. *Journal of Environmental Psychology*, 16: 93–108.

Branco, A. U., Branco, A. L. and Madureira, A. F. (2008). Self-development and the emergence of new *I*-positions: Emotions and self-dynamics. *Studia Psychologica*, 6: 23–39.

Braude, S. E. (1991). *First person plural: Multiple personality and the philosophy of the mind*. London: Routledge.

Brewer, M. B. (1991). The social self: On being the same and different at the same time. *Personality and Social Psychology Bulletin*, 17: 475–82.

Bromberg, P. (2004). Standing in the spaces: The multiplicity of self and the psychoanalytic relationship. In H. J. M. Hermans and G. Dimaggio (eds.), *The dialogical self in psychotherapy* (pp. 138–51). London: Brunner-Routledge.

Bronson, G. W. (1972). *Infants' reactions to unfamiliar persons and novel objects*. University of Chicago Press.

(1978). Aversive reactions to strangers: A dual process interpretation. *Child Development*, 49: 495–9.

Bruner, J. (1983). *Child's talk: Learning to use language*. New York: Norton.

Buber, M. (1970). *I and Thou: A new translation with a prologue "I and You" and notes by Walter Kaufmann*. Edinburgh: T. & T. Clark.

Burgoon, J. K., and Jones, S. B. (1976). Toward a theory of personal space expectations and their violations. *Human Communication Research*, 2: 131–46.

Burns, R. B. (1979). *The self concept: In theory, measurement, development, and behaviour*. London: Longman.

Buss, D. M. (1995). Evolutionary psychology: A new paradigm for psychological science. *Psychological Inquiry*, 6: 1–30.

Butler, R. N. (1975). *Why survive? Being old in America*. New York: Harper & Row.

Cahoone, L. (1996). *From modernism to postmodernism: An anthology*. Cambridge, MA: Blackwell.

Callero, P. L. (2003). The sociology of the self. *Annual Review of Sociology*, 29: 115–33.

Carson, R. C., Butcher, J. N., and Mineka, S. (1996). *Abnormal psychology and modern life* (10th edition). New York: HarperCollins.

Cascio, J. (2005). The Democratization of History. worldchanging.com/archives/003073.html

Castells, M. (1997). *The information age: Economy, society and culture. Vol. II: The power of identity*. Oxford, UK: Blackwell.

Chaitin, J. L. (2010). Narratives and Storytelling in conflicts and conflict resolution: Ben-Gurion University of the Negev, www.narrative-mediation.crinfo.org/documents/mini-grants/narrative-mediation/Narratives_and_Storytelling.pdf.

Chaitin, J. (2008). Bridging the impossible? Confronting barriers to dialogue between Israelis and Germans and Israelis and Palestinians. *International Journal of Peace Studies*, 13: 33–58.

Chandler, M. J., Lalonde, C. E., Sokol, B. W., and Hallett, D. (2003). Personal persistence, identity development, and suicide: A study of native and non-native North-American adolescents. *Monographs of the Society for Research in Child Development*, 68: 1–128.

Chaudhary, N. (2008). Persistent patterns in cultural negotiations of the self: Using Dialogical Self Theory to understand self–other dynamics within culture. *International Journal for Dialogical Science*, 3: 9–30.

Chen, H.-R. (2006).The interpenetration between globalization and localization: Continuity and dialogical hybridity in global and local commercials in contemporary Taiwan. Paper presented at the annual meeting of the International Communication Association. New York, 5 October.

Choi, S.-C. and Han, G. (2008). Shimcheong psychology: A case of an emotional state for cultural psychology. *International Journal for Dialogical Science*, 3: 205–24.

Choi, S.-C., and Kim, K. (2004). Monological and dialogical nature of intersubjective emotion of Shimcheong. Paper presented at the Third International Conference on the Dialogical Self. Warsaw, 26–29 August.

Clarke, K. (2003). Met jezelf in gesprek gaan: De Zelfkonfrontatiemethode en burn-out [Talking with yourself: The self-confrontation method and burn-out]. In R. van Loon and J. Wijsbeck (eds.), *De organisatie als verhaal* [The organization as a narrative] (pp. 176–95). Assen, The Netherlands: Van Gorcum.

Clarke-Stewart, A., Perlmutter, M., and Friedman, S. (1988). *Lifelong human development*. New York: Wiley.

Clifford, J. (1988). *The predicament of culture: Twentieth-century ethnography, literature, and art*. Cambridge, MA: Harvard University Press.

Cohen, R. A. (2002). Maternal psyche. In E. E. Gantt and R. N. Williams (eds.), *Psychology for the other: Levinas, ethics and the practice of psychology* (pp. 32–64). Pittsburgh, PA: Duquesne University Press.

Colapietro, V. (2006). Practice, agency, and sociality: An orthogonal reading of classical pragmatism (commentary on Wiley). *International Journal for Dialogical Science*, 1: 23–32.

Collins, P. H. (2000). *Black feminist thought: Knowledge, consciousness, and the politics of empowerment*. London: Routledge.

Cooper, M. (1999). If you can't be Jekyll be Hyde: An existential-phenomenological exploration on lived-plurality. In J. Rowan and M. Cooper (eds.), *The plural self: multiplicty in everyday life* (pp. 51–70). London: Sage.

   (2003). "I–I" and "I–Me": Transposing Buber's interpersonal attitudes to the intrapersonal plane. *Journal of Constructivist Psychology*, 16: 131–53.

Cooper, M., and Hermans, H. J. M. (2007). Honoring self-otherness: Alterity and the intrapersonal. In L. Simão and J. Valsiner (eds.), *Otherness in question: Labyrinths of the self* (pp. 305–15). Greenwich, CT: Information Age.

Cortini, M., Mininni, G., and Manuti, A. (2004). The diatextual construction of the self in short message systems. *Identity: An International Journal of Theory and Research*, 4: 355–70.

Cote, J. (1996). Sociological perspectives on identity formation: the culture–identity link and identity capital. *Journal of Adolescence*, 19: 417–28.

Crocker, J., and Park, L.E. (2004). The costly pursuit of self-esteem. *Psychological Bulletin*, 130: 392–414.

Dabrowski, K. (1964). *Positive disintegration*. Boston: Little Brown and Co.

Damon, W., and Hart, D. (1982). The development of self-understanding from infancy through adolescence. *Child Development*, 4: 841–64.

Deal T. E. and Kennedy, A. A. (1982). *Corporate cultures: The rites and rituals of corporate life*. Harmondsworth: Penguin Books.

Deflem, M. (2003). The sociology of the sociology of money: Simmel and the contemporary battle of the classics. *Journal of Classical Sociology*, 3: 67–96.

Deikman, A. J. (1999). 'I'- awareness. In S. Gallagher and J. Shear (eds.), *Models of the self* (pp. 421–7). Thorverton, UK: Imprint Academic.

Derryberry, D., and Tucker, D. M. (1994). Motivating the focus of attention. In P. M. Niedenthal and S. Kitayama (eds.), *The heart's eye: Emotional influences in perception and attention* (pp. 167–96). San Diego; CA: Academic Press.

Dewey, J. (1929), *The quest for certainty: A study of the relation between knowledge and action*. New York: Minton, Balch & Co.

Diehl, G. (1977). *Picasso*. Naefels, Switzerland: Bonfini Press.

Dimaggio, G., Salvatore, G., and Catania, D. (2004). Strategies for the treatment of dialogical dysfunctions. In H. J. M. Hermans and G. Dimaggio (eds.), *The dialogical self in psychotherapy* (pp. 190–204). New York: Brunner-Routledge.

Dimaggio, G., Salvatore, G., Azzara, C., and Catania, D. (2003). Rewriting self-narratives: The therapeutic process. *Journal of Constructivist Psychology*, 16: 155–81.

Drummond, D. S. (1976). *Police culture*. Newbury Park, CA: Sage.

Ehrsson, H. H., Charles Spence, C., and Passingham, R. E. (2004). That's my hand! Activity in premotor cortex reflects feeling of ownership of a limb. *Science*, 305: 875–7.

Erikson, E. H. (1968). Identity, psychosocial. In *International encyclopedia of social sciences* (rev. edn), 7: 61–5.

Ewing, K. P. (1990). The illusion of wholeness: Culture, self, and the experience of inconsistency. *Ethos*, 18: 251–78.

Eysenck, H. J., and Eysenck, M. W. (1985). *Personality and individual differences: A natural science approach*. New York: Plenum.

Falmagne, R. J. (2004). On the constitution of "self" and "mind": The dialectic of the system and the person. *Theory and Psychology*, 14: 822–45.

Featherstone, M. (1995). *Undoing culture: Globalization, postmodernism and identity*. London: Sage.

Felling, A. J. A. (2004). *Het process van individualisering in Nederland: een kwarteeuw sociaal-culturele ontwikkeling* [The process of individualization in The Netherlands: A quarter of a century of social-cultural development]. Lecture, Radboud University Nijmegen, The Netherlands.

Field, T. M., Woodson, R., Greenberg, R., and Cohen, D. (1982). Discrimination and imitation of facial expressions by neonates. *Science*, 218: 179–81.

Fisher, S., and Cleveland, S. E. (1968). *Body image and personality*. New York: D. Van Nostrand.

Fogel, A. (1993). *Developing through relationships: Origins of communication, self, and culture*. University of Chicago Press.

Fogel, A., De Koeyer, I., Bellagamba, F., and Bell, H. (2002). The dialogical self in the first two years of life: Embarking on a journey of discovery. *Theory and Psychology*, 12: 191–205.

Forman, R. K. C. (1999). What does mysticism have to teach us about consciousness? In S. Gallagher and J. Shear (eds.), *Models of the self* (pp. 361–77). Thorverton, UK: Imprint Academic.

Foucault, M. (1980). *Power/knowledge: Selected interviews and other writings.* New York: Pantheon.

Frijda, N. H. (1986). *The emotions.* Cambridge University Press.

Fromm. E. (1956). *The art of loving.* New York: Harper and Row.

Gadamer, H.-G. (1989). *Truth and method* (2nd rev. ed; trans. rev. by J. Weinsheimer and D. G. Marshall) . New York: Continuum.

Garvey, C. (1984). *Children's talk.* Cambridge, MA: Harvard University Press.

Gazzaniga, M. (1985). *The social brain.* New York: Basic Books.

Georgaca, E. (2001). Voices of the self in psychotherapy: A qualitative analysis. *British Journal of Medical Psychology*, 74: 223–36.

Gergen, K. J. (1991). *The saturated self: Dilemmas of identity in contemporary life.* London: Sage.

Geschiere, P. (1999). Globalization and the power of indeterminate meaning: Witchcraft and spirit cults in Africa and East Asia. In B. Meyer and P. Geschiere (eds.), *Globalization and identity: Dialectics of flow and closure* (pp. 211–37). Oxford, UK: Blackwell.

Giddens, A. (1991). Modernity and self-identity: Self and society in the late modern age. Cambridge, UK: Polity Press.

(1992). *The transformation of intimacy.* Cambridge, UK: Polity.

Gier, N. F. (2000). *Spiritual titanism: Indian, Chinese, and Western perspectives.* New York: SUNY Press

Gieser, T. (2006). How to transform into goddesses and elephants: Exploring the potentiality of the dialogical self. *Culture and Psychology*, 12: 443–59.

Gilbert, P. (1989). *Human nature and suffering.* New York: Guilford Press.

Gillespie, A. (2005). Malcolm X and his autobiography: Identity development and self-narration. *Culture and Psychology*, 11: 77–88.

Gilroy, P. (1993). *The black Atlantic.* London: Verso.

Girard, G. (1979). *Violence and the sacred.* Baltimore, MD: Johns Hopkins University Press.

Goffman, E. (1959). *The presentation of self in everyday life.* London: Penguin Books.

Gonçalves, M. M., Matos, M., and Santos, A. (2009). Narrative therapy and the nature of "innovative moments" in the construction of change. *Journal of Constructivist Psychology*, 22: 1–23.

Goolishian, H. A., and Anderson, H. (1992). Strategy and intervention versus nonintervention. A matter of theory? *Journal of Marital and Family Therapy*, 18: 5–15.

Greenberg, L. S. (2002). *Emotion-focused therapy: Coaching clients to work through their feelings.* New York: American Psychological Association.

(2004). Introduction. Emotion: Special Issue. *Clinical Psychology and Psychotherapy*, 11: 1–2.

Greene, J. R., Alpert, G. P. and Styles, P. (1992). Values and culture in two American police departments: Lessons from King Arthur. *Journal of Contemporary Criminal Justice*, 8: 183–207.

Gregg, G. S. (1991). *Self-representation: Life narrative in identity and ideology.* New York: Greenwood Press.

Griffin, J. H. (1960/1996) *Black like me.* New York: Signet.

(1979/2006). Beyond otherness. In J. H. Griffin, *Black like me: The definitive Griffin estate edition* (pp. 209–12). San Antonio, TX: Wing Press.

Guilfoyle, M. (2003). Dialogue and power: A critical analysis of power. *Family Process*, 42: 331–43.

Guntrip, H. (1971). *Psychoanalytic theory, therapy, and the self.* New York: Basic Books.

Habermas, J. (1987). *The philosophical discourse of modernity* (trans. Frederick Lawrence). Cambridge University Press.

Hacking, I. (1995). *Rewriting the soul: Multiple personality and the science of memory.* Princeton University Press.

Haddad, Y. Y., and Esposito, J. L. (1998). *Islam, gender and social change.* Oxford University Press.

Hall, S. (1991). The local and the global: Globalization and ethnicity. In A. D. King (ed.), *Culture, globalization and the world system: Contemporary conditions for the representation of identity* (pp. 19–39). London: Macmillan.

(1992). The question of cultural identity. In S. Hall, D. Held, & T. McGrew (eds.), *Modernity and its futures* (pp. 273–316). Cambridge, England: Polity Press.

(1996). Who needs "identity"? In S. Hall and P. du Gay (eds.), *Questions of cultural identity* (pp. 1–17). London: Sage.

Handy, C. B. (1985) *Understanding organizations* (3rd edn). Harmondsworth: Penguin Books.

Harré, R. (2004). Positioning theory. www.massey.ac.nz/~alock/virtual/positioning.doc.

Harré, R., and Van Langenhove, L. (1991). Varieties of positioning. *Journal for the Theory of Social Behaviour*, 21: 393–407.

Harrison, S. J. (1998). Police organizational culture: Using ingrained values to build positive organizational improvement. *Public Administration and Management: An Interactive Journal.* www.pamij.com/harrison.html.

Hayward, J. (1999). A rDzogs-chen Buddhist interpretation of the sense of self. In S. Gallagher and J. Shear (eds.), *Models of the self* (pp. 379–94). Thorverton, UK: Imprint Academic.

Heidegger, M. (1962). *Being and time* (trans. J. Macquarrie and E. Robinson). Oxford: Blackwell.

Hermans, H. J. M. (1970). A questionnaire measure of achievement motivation. *Journal of Applied Psychology*, 54: 353–63.

(1974). Waardegebjeden en hun ontwikkeling [Value areas and their development]. Amsterdam: Swets & Zeitlinger.

(1994). Buber on mysticism, May on creativity and the dialogical nature of the self. *Studies in Spirituality*, 4: 279–305.

(1996a). Voicing the self: From information processing to dialogical interchange. *Psychological Bulletin*, 119: 31–50.

(1996b). Opposites in a dialogical self: Constructs as characters. *Journal of Constructivist Psychology*, 9: 1–26.

(2000). Valuation, innovation and critical personalism. In J. Lamiell & W. Deutsch (eds.), *Theory and Psychology: Special Issue on William Stern*, 10: 801–14.

(2001a). The dialogical self: Toward a theory of personal and cultural positioning. *Culture and Psychology*, 7: 243–81.

(2001b). The construction of a personal position repertoire: Method and practice. *Culture and Psychology*, 7: 323–65.

(2002). The dialogical self as a society of mind: Introduction. *Theory and Psychology*, 12: 147–60.

(2003). The construction and reconstruction of a dialogical self. *Journal of Constructivist Psychology*, 16: 89–130.

(2004a). The dialogical self: Between exchange and power. In H. J. M. Hermans and G. Dimaggio (eds.), *The dialogical self in psychotherapy* (pp. 13–28). New York: Brunner-Routledge.

(2004b). Introduction: The dialogical self in a global and digital age. *Identity: An International Journal of Theory and Research*, 4: 297–320.

(2006). Moving through three paradigms, yet remaining the same thinker. *Counselling Psychology Quarterly*, 19: 5–25.

Hermans, H. J. M., and Dimaggio, G. (eds.) (2004). *The dialogical self in psychotherapy*. New York: Brunner-Routledge.

Hermans, H. J. M., and Dimaggio (2007). Self, identity, and globalization in times of uncertainty: A dialogical analysis. *Review of General Psychology*, 11: 31–61.

Hermans, H. J. M., and Hermans-Jansen, E. (1995). *Self-narratives: The construction of meaning in psychotherapy*. New York: Guilford Press.

(2004). The dialogical construction of coalitions in a personal position repertoire. In H. J. M. Hermans and G. Dimaggio (eds.), *The dialogical self in psychotherapy* (pp. 124–37). New York: Brunner-Routledge.

Hermans, H. J. M., and Kempen, H. J. G. (1993). *The dialogical self: Meaning as movement*. San Diego, CA: Academic Press.

(1998). Moving cultures: The perilous problems of cultural dichotomies in a globalizing world. *American Psychologist*, 53: 1111–20.

Hermans, H. J. M., Kempen, H. J. G., and Van Loon, R. J. P. (1992). The dialogical self: Beyond individualism and rationalism. *American Psychologist*, 47: 23–33.

Hermans, H. J. M., Rijks, T. I., and Kempen, H. J. G. (1993). Imaginal dialogues in the self: Theory and method. *Journal of Personality*, 61: 207–36.

Hermans-Konopka, A., and Hermans, H. J. M. (2010). The dynamic features of love: Changes in self and motivation. In J. D. Raskin, S. K. Bridges, and R. A. Neimeyer (eds.), *Studies in meaning 4: Constructivist perspectives on theory, practice, and social justice*. New York: Pace University Press.

Hesse, H. (1951/1971). *Steppenwolf*. Harmondsworth: Penguin Books.

Hevern, V. (2004). Threaded identity in cyberspace: Weblogs and positioning in the dialogical self. *Identity: An International Journal of Theory and Research*, 4: 321–35.

Hewitt, J. P. (1984). *Self and society* (3rd edn). Boston, MA: Allyn & Bacon.

Hilgard, E. (1977). *Divided consciousness*. London: John Wiley.

Hochschild, A. R. (1983). *The managed heart: Commercialization of human feelings*. Berkeley, CA: University of California Press.

Hofstede, G. (1980). *Culture's consequences: International differences in work-related values*. Beverly Hills, CA, Sage .

Hogg, M. A., and Vaughan, G. M. (2002). *Social psychology* (3rd edn). London: Prentice-Hall.

Holquist, M. (1990). *Dialogism: Bakhtin and his world*. London: Routledge.

Holzman, M. (1972). The use of interrogative forms in the verbal interaction of three mothers and their children. *Journal of Psycholinguistic Research*, 1: 311–36.

Hong, Y., and Chiu, C. (2001). Toward a paradigm shift: From cross-cultural differences in social cognition to social-cognitive mediation of cultural differences. *Social Cognition*, 19: 181–96.

Honos-Web, L., Surko, M., Stiles, W. B., and Greenberg, L. (1999). Assimilation of voices in psychotherapy: The case of Jan, *Journal of Counseling Psychology*, 46: 448–60.

Horner, Th. M. (1983). On the formation of personal space and self-boundary structures in early human development: The case of infant–stranger reactivity. *Developmental Review*, 3: 148–77.

Huxley, A. (1957). *The doors of perception*. London: Chatto and Windus.

Hviid, P. (2007). A review of "I am I: Sudden flashes of self-awareness in childhood." *International Journal for Dialogical Science*, 2: 361–4.

Ignazi, P. (2003). *Extreme right parties in Western Europe*. Oxford University Press.

Ingraham, B. D. (2007). *A pragmaticist glance at the post-modern*. www-jime.open.ac.uk/00/ingraham/ingraham-13.html.

Izard, C. E. (1990). Facial expressions and the regulation of emotions. *Journal of Personality and Social Psychology*, 58: 487–98.

James, W. (1890). *The principles of psychology* (vol. 1). London: Macmillan.

(1902/2004). *The varieties of religious experience: A study in human nature* (Gifford lectures on natural religion delivered at Edinburgh, 1901–1902). New York: Barnes & Noble.

Janis, I. L. (1977). *Decision making: A psychological analysis of conflict, choice, and commitment*. New York: Free Press.

(1982). *Groupthink: Psychological studies of policy decisions and fiascoes* (2nd edn). New York: Houghton Mifflin.

Jaynes, J. (1976). *The origin of consciousness in the breakdown of the bicameral mind*. Boston: Houghton Mifflin.

Johnson, M. (1987). *The body in the mind: The bodily basis of meaning, imagination, and reason*. University of Chicago Press.

Jones, R. H. (2004). *Mysticism and morality: A new look at old questions*. Lanham, MD: Lexington Books.

Josephs, I. E. (2002). "The hopi in me": The construction of a voice in the dialogical self from a cultural psychological perspective. *Theory and Psychology* 12: 161–73.

Journal of Constructivist Psychology (2008). Special issue: *Performing research on the dialogical self*, 21: 185–269.

Jung, C. G. (1959). Mandalas. In *Collected works* (vol. 9, part 1). Princeton University Press (first German edition, 1955).

Jurgens, F. (2005). Het onsterfelijke ik [The immortal I]. *HP/De Tijd*, 7 October.

Kahane, A. (2004). *Solving tough problems: An open way of talking, listening, and creating new realities*. San Francisco, CA: Berrett-Koehler Publishers.

Kahn, J. S. (1995). *Culture, multiculture, postculture*. London: Sage.

Kaufman, D. (1991). *Rachel's daughters: Newly orthodox Jewish women*. New Brunswick, NJ: Rutgers University Press.

Kaye, K. (1977). Toward the origin of dialogue. In H. R. Schaffer (ed.), *Studies in mother–infant interaction* (pp. 89–117). London: Academic Press.

Kelly, G. A. (1955). *The psychology of personal constructs*. New York: Norton.

Kemper, T. D. (1978). *A social interactional theory of emotions*. New York: Wiley.

Kenen, R. H. (1984). Making agreements with oneself: prelude to social behavior. *Sociological Forum*, 1: 362–77.

Kinnvall, C. (2004). Globalization and religious nationalism: Self, identity, and the search for ontological security. *Political Psychology*, 25: 741–67.

Kluger, A., Nir, D., and Kluger, Y. (2008). Personal position repertoire (PPR) from a bird's eye view. *Journal of Constructivist Psychology*, 21: 223–38.

Kohnstamm, P. (2007). *I am I – sudden flashes of self-awareness in childhood*. London: Athena Press.

Kohut, H. (1971). *The analysis of the self*. New York: International Universities Press.

König, J. (2009). Moving experience: Dialogues between personal cultural positions. *Culture and Psychology*, 15: 97–119.

Konrath, S. H., and Ross, M. (2003). Our glories, our shames: Expanding the self in temporal self appraisal theory. Paper presented at the American Psychological Society conference, Atlanta, Georgia, May.

Kraut, R. E., and Johnson, R. E. (1979). Social and emotional messages of smiling: An ethological approach. *Journal of Personality and Social Psychology*, 42: 853–63.

Kristeva, J. (1982). *Powers of horror: An essay of abjection*. New York: Columbia University Press.

(1991). *Strangers to ourselves*. New York: Columbia University Press.

Kronsell, A. (2002). Homeless in academia: Homesteading as a strategy for change. In M. McKoy and J. Di Georgio-Lutz (eds.), *A world of hegemonic masculinity. Women in higher education: Empowering change* (pp. 37–56). Westport, CT: Greenwood.

Lacan, J. (1977). *Ecrits: A selection* (trans. A. Sheridan). London: Tavistock.

LaFromboise, T., Coleman, H.L.K., and Gerton, J. (1993). Psychological impact of biculturalism: Evidence and theory. *Psychological Bulletin*, 114: 395–412.

Lambie, J. A., and Marcel, A. J. (2002). Consciousness and the varieties of emotion experience: A theoretical framework. *Psychological Review*, 109: 219–59.

Lamiell, J. T. (1987). *The psychology of personality: An epistemological inquiry.* Columbia University Press.

Lane, R., and Schwartz, G. (1987). Levels of emotional awareness: A cognitive–developmental theory and its application to psychopathology. *American Journal of Psychiatry,* 54: 309–13.

Lazarus, R. S. (1991). *Emotion and adaptation.* New York/Oxford: Oxford University Press.

Leary, D. E. (2006). The missing person in the conversation: Oliver Wendell Holmes, Sr., and the dialogical self (commentary on Wiley). *International Journal for Dialogical Science,* 1: 33–40.

LeDoux, J. E. (1996). *The emotional brain: The mysterious underpinnings of emotional life.* New York: Simon & Schuster.

LeDoux, J. (2002) *Synaptic self: How our brains become who we are.* New York: Penguin Viking.

Lee, D., and Lishman, J. R. (1975). Visual proprioceptive control of stance. *Journal of Human Movement Studies,* 1: 87–95.

Leiman, M. (2004). Dialogical sequence analysis. In H. J. M. Hermans and G. Dimaggio (eds.), *The dialogical self in psychotherapy* (pp. 255–69). London: Brunner-Routledge.

Lengelle, R., and Meijers, F. (2004). Mystery to mastery: An exploration of what happens in the black box of writing and healing. *Journal of Poetry Therapy,* 22: 59–77.

Lester, D. (1992). The disunity of self. *Personality and Individual Differences,* 13: 947–8.

Levin, D. M. (1988). *The opening of vision. Nihilism and the postmodern situation.* New York: Routledge.

Levinas, E. (1967). Martin Buber and the theory of knowledge. In P. A. Schlipp and M. Friedman (eds.), *The philosophy of Martin Buber* (pp. 133–50). London: Cambridge University Press.

(1969). *Totality and infinity: An essay on exteriority* (trans. A. Lingis). Pittsburgh, PA: Duquesne University Press.

Lewis, M. (1995). *Shame: The exposed self.* New York: Free Press.

Lewis, M. D. (2002). The dialogical brain: Contributions of emotional neurobiology to understanding the dialogical self. *Theory and Psychology,* 12: 175–90.

Lichtenberg, J., Lachmann, F. M., and Fosshage, J. (1992). *Self and motivational systems: Toward a theory of psychoanalytic technique.* Hillsdale, NJ: Analytic Press.

Lietaer, G. (1993). Authenticity, congruence and transparency. In D. Brazier (ed.), *Beyond Carl Rogers* (pp. 17–46). London: Constable.

Lifton, R. J. (1993). *The Protean self: Human resilience in an age of fragmentation.* New York: Basic Books.

Ligorio, M. B. (forthcoming). Dialogical relationship between identity and learning. *Culture and Psychology.*

Ligorio, M. B., and Pugliese, A. C. (2004). Self-positioning in a text-based virtual environment. *Identity: An International Journal of Theory and Research,* 4: 337–53.

Lindegger, G. (forthcoming). *Psychotherapy and Culture.*

Linell, P. (1990). The power of dialogue dynamics. In I. Markovà and K. Foppa (eds.), *The dynamics of dialogue* (pp. 147–77). New York: Harvester Wheatsheaf.

Loehlin, J. C., McCrae, R. R., and Costa, P. T. Jr. (1998). Heritabilities of common and measure-specific components of the Big Five personality factors. *Journal of Research in Personality,* 32: 431–53.

Lovell, G. (2000). *Consultancy, ministry and mission: A handbook for practitioners and work consultants in Christian organizations.* Warsaw: Burns and Oates.

Lupton, D. (1998). *The emotional self: A sociocultural exploration.* Thousand Oaks, CA: Sage.

Lyra, M. C. D. P. (1999). An excursion into the dynamics of dialogue: Elaborations upon the dialogical self. *Culture and Psychology,* 4: 477–89.

Lysaker, J. (2006). "I am not what I seem to be" (commentary on Wiley). *International Journal for Dialogical Science,* 1: 41–6.

Lysaker, P. H., and Lysaker, J. T. (2002). Narrative structure in psychosis: Schizophrenia and disruptions in the dialogical self. *Theory and Psychology,* 12: 207–20.

(2008). *Schizophrenia and the fate of the self.* Oxford University Press.

Mancuso, J. C., and Sarbin, Th. R. (1983). The self-narrative in the enactment of roles. In Th. R. Sarbin and K. Scheibe (eds.), *Studies in social identity* (pp. 254–73). New York: Praeger.

Maratos, O. (1973). *The origin and development of imitation in the first six months of life.* Ph.D. thesis, University of Geneva.

Marcia, J. E. (1966). Development and validation of ego identity status, *Journal of Personality and Social Psychology,* 3: 551–8.

Markovà, I. (1987). On the interaction of opposites in psychological processes. *Journal for the Theory of Social Behaviour,* 17: 279–99.

(2006). On "the inner alter" in dialogue. *International Journal for Dialogical Science,* 1: 125–48.

Marsella, A. J. (1998). Toward a "global-community psychology": Meeting the demands of a changing world. *American Psychologist,* 53: 1282–91.

Marty, M. E., and Appleby, R. S. (1993). *Fundamentalisms and the state.* University of Chicago Press.

Masuda, T., Gonzalez, R., Kwan, L., and Nisbett, R. E. (2008). Culture and aesthetic preference: Comparing the attention to context of East Asians and Americans. *Personality and Social Psychology Bulletin,* 34: 1260–75.

May, R. (1975). *The courage to create.* New York: Norton.

McAdams, D. P. (1985). *Power, intimacy, and the life story: Personological inquiries into identity.* Chicago: Dorsey Press. (Reprinted by Guilford Press, 1988.)

(1988). Biography, narrative, and lives: An introduction. *Journal of Personality,* 56: 1–18.

(2006). The problem of narrative coherence. *Journal of Constructivist Psychology,* 19: 109–26.

McClelland, D., Atkinson, J., Clark, R., and Lowell, E. (1953). *The achievement motive.* New York: Appleton.

McIlveen, P., and Patton, W. (2007) Dialogical self: author and narrator of career life themes. *International Journal for Educational and Vocational Guidance*, 7: 67–80.

Mead, G. H. (1934). *Mind, self, and society*. University of Chicago Press.

Meltzoff, A. N., and Moore, M. K. (1994). Imitation, memory, and the representation of persons. *Infant Behavior and Development*, 17: 83–99.

Meyer, B., Geschiere, P. (eds.) (1999). *Globalization and identity: Dialectics of flow and closure*. Oxford, UK, Blackwell.

Mills, M., and Blossfeld, H.-P. (2003). Globalisierung, Ungewissheit und Wandel in Lebensläufen Jugendlicher und junger Erwachsener [Globalization, uncertainty and changes in early life courses]. *Zeitschrift für Erziehungswissenschaft*, 6: 188–218.

Minsky, M. (1985). *The society of mind*. New York: Simon & Schuster.

Moghaddam, A. (2005). The staircase to terrorism: A psychological exploration. *American Psychologist*, 60: 161–9.

Montaigne, M. de (1603). *The essayes: Or morall, politike and millitarie discourses* (trans. J. Florio). London: Blount. (Original work published 1580.)

Morgan, C., and Averill, J. R. (1992). True feelings, the self, and authenticity: A psychosocial perspective. In D. D. Franks and V. Gecas (eds.), *Social perspectives on emotion* (vol. 1, pp. 95–124). Greenwich, CT: JAI Press.

Morin, A. (2005). Possible links between self-awareness and inner speech. Theoretical background, underlying mechanisms, and empirical evidence. *Journal of Consciousness Studies*, 12: 115–34.

Morioka, M. (2008). Voices of self in the therapeutic chronotope: "Utushi" and "Ma." *International Journal for Dialogical Science*, 3: 93–108.

Murray, H. A. (1962). The personality and career of Satan. *Journal of Social Issues*, 28: 36–54.

Nafstad, H. E., Blakar R. M. and Rand Hendriksen, K. (2008). The spirit of society and the virtue of gratitude: Shifting societal ideologies of gratitude. In T. Freire (ed.), *Understanding positive life. Research and practice on positive psychology* (pp. 291–312). Lisbon: Climepsi Editores.

Nagy, E., and Molnar, P. (2004). Homo imitans or homo provocans? Human imprinting model of neonatal imitation. *Infant Behavior and Development*, 27: 54–63.

Nandy, A. (1997). The twilight of certitudes: Secularism, Hindu nationalism, and other masks of deculturation. *Alternatives*, 22: 157–76.

Neimeyer, R. A., and Buchanan-Arvay, M. (2004). Performing the self: Therapeutic enactment and the narrative integration of traumatic loss. In H. J. M. Hermans & G. Dimaggio (eds.), *The dialogical self in psychotherapy* (pp. 173–89). New York: Brunner-Routledge.

Neisser, U. (1988). Five kinds of self-knowledge. *Philosophical Psychology*, 1: 35–59.

Neugarten, B. L. (1970). Adaptation and the life cycle. *Journal of Geriatric Psychiatry*, 4: 71–87.

Newberg, A. B., Eugene, G.D.A., and Rause, V. (2001) *Why God won't go away: Brain science and the biology of belief*. New York: Ballantine Books.

Newson, J. (1977). An intersubjective approach to the systematic description of mother–infant interaction. In H. R. Schaffer (ed.), *Studies in mother–infant interaction* (pp. 47–61). London: Academic Press.

Nienkamp, J. (2001). *Internal rhetorics: Toward a history and theory of self-persuasion*. Carbondale and Edwardsville, IL.: Southern Illinois University Press.

Niessen, T., Abma, T., Widdershoven, G., and Van der Vleuten, C. (2008). Contemporary epistemological research in education. *Theory and Psychology*, 18: 27–45.

Nir, D. (2008). The negotiational self: Identifying and transforming negotiation outcomes within the self. Unpublished dissertation, School of Business, Mount Scopus, Hebrew University of Jerusalem.

Nir, D., and Kluger, A. N. (2006). Resolving inner conflict, building inner harmony – the negotiational self. Workshop given at the Fourth International Conference on the Dialogical Self. Braga, Portugal, June 1–3.

Nouwen, H. (1994). *Here and now: Living in the spirit*. New York: Crossroad.

Obeysekere, G. (1977). Social change and the deities: Rise of Kataragama cult in modern Sri Lanka. *Man*, 12: 377–96.

Osatuke, K. et al. (2004). Hearing voices: Methodological issues in measuring internal multiplicity. In H. J. M. Hermans and G. Dimaggio (eds.) *The dialogical self in psychotherapy* (pp. 237–54). London: Brunner-Routledge.

Padel, R. (1992). *In and out of the mind: Greek images of the tragic self*. Princeton University Press.

Parker, M. (2000). *Organizational culture and identity*. London: Sage.

Parkinson, B. (1996). Emotions are social. *British Journal of Psychology*, 87: 663–83.

Pearson, D. et al. (2001). Prevalence of imaginary companions in a normal child population. *Child: Care, Health and Development*, 27: 13–22.

Pepper, S. (1942). *World hypotheses*. Berkeley, CA: University of California Press.

Pereira Reis, E.M., and Schwartzman, S. (1977). The process of spatial dislocation and social identity building: Brazil. *International Social Sciences Journal*, 30: 98–115.

Persinger, M. A. (1987). *Neuropsychological bases of God beliefs*. New York: Praeger.

Person, E. S. (1988). *Dreams of love and fateful encounters: The power of romantic passion*. New York: Norton.

Peterson, C., and Seligman, M. E. P. (2004). *Character strengths and virtues. A handbook and classification*. New York: Oxford University Press.

Piaget, J. (1978). *The development of thought: Equilibration of cognitive structures*. London: Blackwell.

Pieterse, J. N. (1995). Globalization as hybridization. In M. Featherstone, S. Lash, and R. Robertson (eds.), *Global modernities* (pp. 45–68). London: Sage.

Puchalska-Wasyl, M., Chmielnicka-Kuter, E., and Oles, P. (2008). From internal interlocutors to psychological functions of dialogical activity. *Journal of Constructivist Psychology*, 21: 239–69.

Putnam, F. W. (1989). *Diagnosis and treatment of multiple personality disorder.* New York: Guilford Press.

(1993). Dissociative disorders in children: Behavioral profiles and problems. *Child Abuse and Neglect,* 17: 39–45.

Quinn, N. (2006). The self. *Anthropological Theory,* 6: 362–84.

Radden, J. (1999). Pathologically divided minds, synchronic unity and models of self. In S. Gallagher and J. Shear (eds.), *Models of the self* (pp. 343–58). Thorverton, UK: Imprint Academic.

Raggatt, P. T. F. (2000). Mapping the dialogical self: Towards a rationale and method of assessment. *European Journal of Personality,* 14: 65–90.

(2007). Forms of positioning in the dialogical self: A system of classification and the strange case of Dame Edna Everage. *Theory and Psychology,* 17: 355–82.

Redfield, J. (1994). *The Celestine prophecy.* London: Bantam.

Reichelt, S., and Sveaas, N. (1994). Therapy with refugee families: What is a "good" conversation? *Family Process,* 33: 247–62.

Richardson, F. C., Rogers, A., and McCarroll, J. (1998). Toward a dialogical self. *American Behavioral Scientist,* 41: 496–515.

Richers, N. (1998). "How did they do it? Language learning in Bruner and Wittgenstein." www.bu.edu/wcp/Papers/Lang/LangRich.htm

Riesman, D., Denney, R., and Glazer, N. (1950). *The lonely crowd.* New Haven: Yale University Press.

Rinpoche, R.T., and Mullen, K. (2005). The Buddhist use of compassionate imagery in mind healing. In P. Gilbert (ed.), *Compassion: Conceptualizations, research and use in psychotherapy* (pp. 239–62). London: Routledge.

Ritzer, G. (1992). *Sociological theory* (3rd edn). New York: McGraw-Hill.

(2000). *The McDonaldization of society: An investigation into the changing character of contemporary social life* (3rd edn). New York: Pine Forge Press.

Robertson, R. (1995). *Globalization: Social theory and global culture.* London: Sage.

Rochat, P. (2000). Emerging co-awareness. Paper presented at the First International Conference on the Dialogical Self, Nijmegen, The Netherlands, June 23–26

Rochat, P., Querido, J. G., and Striano, T. (1999). Emerging sensitivity to the timing and structure of protoconversation in early infancy. *Developmental Psychology,* 35: 950–57.

Rojek, B. (2009). In quest of identity: Reading Tabucchi in the light of Hermans' concept of the dialogical self. *Psychology of Language and Communications,* 13: 89–97.

Roland, A. (1996). *Cultural pluralism and psychoanalysis.* New York: Routledge.

Rose, A. J. (2002). Co-rumination in the friendships of girls and boys. *Child Development,* 73: 1830–43.

Rosenberg, M. (1979). *Conceiving the self.* New York: Basic Books.

Rosenberg, S. S., and Gara, M. A. (1985). The multiplicity of personal identity. In P. Shaver (ed.), *Self, situations and social behaviour: Review of personality and social psychology* (vol. 6). Beverly Hills, CA: Sage.

Rothenberg, A. (1990). Creativity in adolescence. *Adolescence: Psychopathology, Normality, and Creativity*, 13: 415–34.

Rowan, J. (1990). *Subpersonalities: The people inside us*. London: Routledge.

(2010). *Personification: Using the dialogical self in psychotherapy and counselling*. London: Routledge.

Rowan, J., and Cooper, M. (eds.), (1999). *The plural self: Multiplicity in everyday life*. London: Sage.

Rowiński, T. (2008). Virtual self in dysfunctional internet use. *Studia Psychologica*, 8: 107–27.

Said, E. (1978). *Orientalism*. London: Routledge & Kegan Paul.

(1999). *Out of place: A memoir*. New York: Knopf.

Sakellaropoulo, M., and Baldwin, M. W. (2006). Interpersonal cognition and the relational self: Paving the empirical road for dialogical science. *International Journal for Dialogical Science*, 1: 47–66.

Salgado, J., and Hermans, H. J. M. (2005). The return of subjectivity: From a multiplicity of selves to the dialogical self. *E-Journal of Applied Psychology*, 1: 3–13.

Salvatore, G., Dimaggio, G., and Semerari, A. (2004). A model of narrative development: Implications for understanding psychopathology and guiding therapy. *Psychology and Psychotherapy*, 77: 231–54.

Sampson, E. (1985). The decentralization of identity: Toward a revised concept of personal and social order. *American Psychologist*, 11: 1203–11.

(1993). *Celebrating the other: A dialogic account of human nature*. San Francisco, CA: Westview Press.

Sarbin, Th. R. (1986). The narrative as a root metaphor for psychology. In Th. R. Sarbin (ed.), *Narrative psychology: The storied nature of human conduct* (pp. 3–21). New York: Praeger.

Sarbin, T. R. (1989). Emotions as narrative emplotments. In M. J. Packer and R. B. Addison (eds.), *Entering the circle: Hermeneutic investigation in psychology* (pp. 185–201). Albany, NY: SUNY Press.

Savin-Williams, R. C., and Demo, D. H. (1984). Developmental change and stability in adolescent self-concept. *Developmental Psychology*, 20: 1100–10.

Schachter, E. (2002). Identity constraints: The perceived structural requirement of a 'good' identity. *Human Development*, 45: 416–33.

Schein, E. H. (1985). *Organizational culture and leadership*. San Francisco, CA: Jossey-Bass.

Schore, A. N. (1994). *Affect regulation and the origin of the self: The neurobiology of emotional development*. Hillsdale, NJ: Erlbaum.

Schore, A. (2004). Dialogue between neurobiological research on the development of the self and theory of the dialogical self. Paper presented at the Third International Conference on the Dialogical Self, Warsaw, Poland: Warsaw School of Social Psychology, August 26–29.

Schwartz, R. (1995). *Internal family systems therapy*. New York: Guilford Press.

Semerari, A., Carcione, A., Dimaggio, G., Nicolo, G., and Procacci, M. (2004). A dialogical approach to patients with personality disorders. In

H. J. M. Hermans and G. Dimaggio (eds.), *The dialogical self in psychotherapy* (pp. 220–34). London: Brunner-Routledge.

Shamir, B., and Eilan, G. (2005). "What's your story?" A life-stories approach to authentic leadership development. *Leadership Quarterly*, 16: 395–417.

Shaver, P. R., Wu, S., and Schwartz, J. C. (1992). Cross-cultural similarities and differences in emotion and its representation: A prototype approach. In M. S. Clark (ed.), *Review of personality and social psychology* (vol. 13, pp. 175–212). Newbury Park, CA: Sage.

Sillince, J. A. A. (2006). The effect of rhetoric on competitive advantage: Knowledge, rhetoric and resource-based theory. In: S. R. Clegg, C. Hardy, T. B. Lawrence, and W. R. Nord (eds.), *The Sage handbook of organization studies* (2nd edn) (pp. 800–813). London: Sage.

Simão, L. M., and Valsiner, J. (eds.) (2007). *Otherness in question: Labyrinths of the self*. Charlotte, NC: Information Age Publishing.

Simmel, G. (1990). *The philosophy of money* (ed. by D. P. Frisby). London: Routledge.

Skinner, D., Valsiner, J., and Holland, D. (2001). Discerning the dialogical self: A theoretical and methodological examination of a Nepali adolescent's narrative. *Forum: Qualitative Social Research*, 2: 1–18.

Solomon, R. C. (1993). *The passions: Emotions and the meaning of life*. Indiana: Hackett Publishing Company.

Spinelli, E. (1994). *Demystifying therapy*. London: Constable.

Spiro, M. E. (1993). Is the western conception of the self "peculiar" within the context of the world cultures? *Ethos*, 21: 107–53.

Stein, G. (1933). *The autobiography of Alice Toklas*. New York: Random House.

Stemplewska-Zakowicz, K., Walecka, J., and Gabinska, A. (2006). As many selves as interpersonal relations (or maybe even more). *International Journal for Dialogical Science*, 1: 71–94.

Stemplewska-Zakowicz, K., Walecka, J., Gabinska, A., Zalewski, B., and Zuszek, H. (2005). Experiments on positioning, positioning the experiments. In P. Oles and H. J. M. Hermans (eds.), *The dialogical self: Theory and research* (pp. 183–99). Lublin, Poland: Wydawnictwo KUL.

Stern, D. (2004). *The present moment in psychotherapy and everyday life*. New York: Norton.

Stern, D. N. (1977). *The first relationship: Infant and mother*. Cambridge, MA: Harvard University Press.

Stern, W. (1924). *Wertphilosophie* [Philosophy of values]. Leipzig, Barth.

Stiglitz, J. E. (2002). *Globalization and its discontents*. New York: Norton.

Stiles, W. B. (1999). Signs and voices in psychotherapy. *Psychotherapy Research*, 9: 1–21.

Stone, H., and Winkelman, S. (1989). *Embracing our selves: The voice dialogue manual*. Mill Valley, CA: Nataraj Publishing.

Straus, E. W. (1958). Aesthesiology and hallucinations. In R. May, E. Angel, and H. F. Ellenberger (eds.), *Existence. A new dimension in psychiatry and psychology* (pp. 139–69). New York: Basic Books.

Stuart Mill, J. (2004). *Utilitarianism* (originally published in 1863). Adelaide, Australia: eBooks.

Sylvester, C. (1994). *Feminist theory and international relations in a postmodern era.* Cambridge, MA: Cambridge University Press.

Tappan, M. B. (2005). Domination, subordination and the dialogical self: Identity development and the politics of "ideological becoming." *Culture and Psychology*, 11: 47–75.

Taylor, C. (1989). *Sources of the self: The making of the modern identity.* Cambridge, MA: Harvard University Press.

Thomae, H. (1968). *Das Individuum und Seine Welt* [The individual and his world]. (2nd edn, 1988). Göttingen Hogrefe.

Tomasello, M. (1993). On the interpersonal origins of self-concept. In U. Neisser (ed.), *The perceived self: Ecological and interpersonal sources of self-knowledge* (pp. 174–84). Cambridge University Press.

Vaknin, S. (2006). Narcissism at a glance. *Global Politician Newsletter.* www.globalpolitician.com/21571-narcissism.

Valsiner, J. (2002). Forms of dialogical relations and semiotic autoregulation within the self. *Theory and Psychology*, 12: 251–65.

(2004). *The promoter sign: Developmental transformation within the structure of the dialogical self.* XVIII Biennial Meeting of the International Society for the Study of Behavioral Development, Ghent, July 11–15.

Valsiner, J., and Han, G. (2008). Where is culture within the dialogical perspectives on the self? *International Journal for Dialogical Science*, 3: 1–8.

Van Halen, C., and Janssen, J. (2004). The usage of space in dialogical self-construction: From Dante to cyberspace. *Identity: An International Journal of Theory and Research*, 4: 389–405.

Van Loon, R. (2003). De "dialogical leader." In: R. van Loon and J. Wijsbek (eds.), *De organisatie als verhaal* [The organization as a narrative] (pp. 109–34). Assen, The Netherlands: Van Gorcum.

Van Meijl, T. (2006). Multiple identifications and the dialogical self: Maori youngsters and the cultural renaissance. *Journal of the Royal Anthropological Institute*, 12: 917–33.

(2008). Culture and identity in social anthropology: Reflections on 'unity' and 'uncertainty' in the dialogical self. *International Journal for Dialogical Science*, 3: 165–90.

(2009, in press). Anthropological perspectives on identity: From sameness to difference. In M. Wetherell and C. T. Mohanty (eds.), *The Sage handbook of identities.* London: Sage.

Van Nijnatten, C. (2007). The discourse of empowerment: A dialogical self theoretical perspective on the interface of person and institution in social service settings. *International Journal for Dialogical Science*, 2: 337–59.

Van Spengler, L. (2008). *De kunst van het kiezen* [The art of choosing]. Utrecht: PS Items.

Vasil'eva, I. I. (1988). The importance of M. M. Bakhtin's idea of dialogue and dialogic relations for the psychology of communication. *Soviet Psychology*, 26: 17–31.

Verhofstadt-Deneve, L., Dillen, L., Helskens, D., and Siongers, M. (2006). The psychodramatic 'social atom method' with children: A developmental dialogical self in action. In H. J. M. Hermans and G. Dimaggio (eds.), *The dialogical self in psychotherapy* (pp. 152–70). London: Brunner-Routledge.

Vygotsky, L. S. (1929). The problem of the cultural development of the child. *Journal of Genetic Psychology*, 36: 415–34.

(1962). *Thought and language*. Cambridge, MA: MIT Press.

(1987). *Thinking and speech* (ed. R. W. Rieber and A. S. Carton; trans. N. Minick). New York and London: Plenum Press.

(1999). Consciousness as a problem in the psychology of behavior. In N. Veresov (ed.), *Undiscovered Vygotsky* (pp. 256–81). Frankfurt am Main: Peter Lang. (Originally published in 1925.)

Wade, R. (2007). *Where did "I" go? The loss of the self in postmodern times.* www.probe.org/theology-and-philosophy/worldview – philosophy/where-did-i-go-the-loss-of-self-in-postmodern-times.html.

Wallerstein, I. (1991). The national and the universal: Can there be such a thing as world culture? In A. D. King (ed.), *Culture, globalization and the world system: Contemporary conditions for the representation of identity* (pp. 91–105). London: Macmillan.

Watkins, M. (1986). *Invisible guests: The development of imaginal dialogues.* Hillsdale, NJ: Erlbaum.

(2003). Dialogue, development, and liberation. In I. Josephs (ed.), *Dialogicality in development* (pp. 87–109). Westport, CT: Praeger.

Weber, M. (1958). *The Protestant ethic and the spirit of capitalism.* New York: Scribner. (Original work published 1904–5).

Weiss, S., and Wesley, K. (2007). Postmodernism and its critics. www.as.ua.edu/ant/Faculty/murphy/436/pomo.html.

Weller, R. P. (1994). *Resistance, chaos and control in China.* London: Macmillan.

Wertsch, J. V. (1991). *Voices of the mind: A sociocultural approach to mediated action.* London: Harvester Wheatsheaf.

Whelton, W. J. (2001). *Emotion in self-criticism.* Unpublished doctoral dissertation. York University, Toronto, Canada.

Whelton, W. J., and Greenberg, L. S. (2004). From discord to dialogue: Internal voices and the reorganization of the self in process-experiential therapy. In H. J. M. Hermans and G. Dimaggio (eds.), *The dialogical self in psychotherapy* (pp. 108–23). New York: Brunner-Routledge.

White, M., and Epston, D. (1990). *Narrative means to therapeutic ends.* New York: Norton.

Wilber, K. (1997). *The eye of spirit: An integral vision for a world gone slightly mad.* Boston, MA: Shambhala.

Wiley, N. (2006). Pragmatism and the dialogical self. *International Journal for Dialogical Science*, 1: 5–22.

Winnicott, D. W. (1964). *The child, the family and the outside world.* Harmondsworth Penguin.

Winnicot, D. W. (1971). *Playing and reality.* London: Tavistock.

Wittel, A. (2001). Toward a network sociality. *Theory, Culture and Society*, 18: 51–76.

Wolf, E. R. (1982). *Europe and the people without history.* Berkeley, CA: University of California Press.

Zomer, P. (2006). The Team Confrontation Method: Design, grounding and testing. Unpublished dissertation, Radboud University, Nijmegen, The Netherlands.

Index

absurdity, 79 n. 3
acceptance, 228–32
agency, *see* self
aging, 252 n. 19
agreement, 52–3
alterity, 10, 108, 183–5, 184, 325
  of the emotion of the other, 276
Americanization, 22
amygdala, 14, 51, 255
animals, 278
anxiety, 79 n. 3
  toward strangers, 213
applications of dialogical self theory, 19–20
Aristotle, 31, 52, 90
art, 72, 91, 159, 164–8, 291, 310, 329–30,
  344
atmosphere, 182, 186, 198 n. 32
attention, joint, 12, 205–7, 210
  affective aspects of, 206
  self-reflexive, 206
audience, 34
  private, 67–8
authenticity,
  emotional, 15, 274–81, 304
autobiography, 151
autonomy, 286
  functional, 155
  personal, 5
  striving for, 106
Avila, Teresa of, 170, 171
awareness
  field of, 11, 167, 172, 189–90, 220, 295
  of differences, 346–7
  unifying, 10

Bakhtin, Mikhail, 2, 34, 36, 52, 53, 74,
  142, 187
bandwidth,
  and conflict resolution, 360
  emotional, 297
  of dialogue, 177–9
biology,

and self, 44–7
and the social, 48–52
body, *see* position
brain,
  dialogical, 51–2
  split, 131
Broca's area, 256
Buber, Martin, 164–7

cacophony, 1, 32
Calvinism, 283
capacity, dialogical, 30, 137
Cartesian, *see* Descartes René
causation,
  downward, 102
  upward, 102
centralization, 325, *see also* movements
civilization, 24–6
class, 48–91, 60, 65, 75
coalition, of positions, *see* position
colonialism, 90
comfort zone, 185
commodification, of interactions, 290
communication
  dialogical, 7
  monological, 6
community, linguistic, 11
compassion, 277
composition, 9, 10, 162–8, 167,
  see also emotions
conflict
  multi-level, 13, 244–7
  Palestinian–Israeli, 19, 350, 354
  resolution of social, 18, 345–61
  uni-level, 13, 244
confusion, 79 n. 3
  role, 353–4
consumerism, 15, 155, 287–92
continuum, between dialogue and
  monologue, 53, 62
contradiction, of cultural positions, 34
conventions, social, 11

CPSIA information can be obtained at www.ICGtesting.com
Printed in the USA
LVOW122317060113

314576LV00011B/264/P